Anything

Edited by Cynthia C. Davidson

Anyone Corporation
New York, New York

The MIT Press
Cambridge, Massachusetts
London, England

Anything

Editor
Cynthia C. Davidson

Senior Editor
Thomas Weaver

Design
2x4
Alice Chung
Michael Rock

Any designers, 1994–2001:
Katie Andresen
Jenny Chan
Chin-Lien Chen
Alex Ching
Alice Chung
Penny Hardy
Ebon Heath
Karen Hsu
David Israel
Michael Rock
Susan Sellers
Georgie Stout
Henk van Assen

Anything is the tenth and last book in a series of volumes documenting the annual international, cross-disciplinary conferences sponsored by the Anyone Corporation from 1991–2000 to investigate the condition of architecture at the end of the millennium.

Printed and bound in the United States of America.

Library of Congress Cataloging-in-Publication Data

Anything / edited by Cynthia C. Davidson
  p. cm.
  "Anything is the tenth in a series of ten planned volumes documenting the annual international, cross-disciplinary conferences being sponsored by the Anyone Corporation to investigate the condition of architecture at the end of the millennium"—T.p. verso.
  Includes bibliographical references.
  ISBN 0-262-54130-0 (pb : alk. paper)
  1. Architecture—Philosophy—Congresses. 2. Architecture, Postmodern—Congresses.
  I. Davidson, Cynthia C.
  II. Anyone Corporation.
NA2500 .A633 2001
724'.6—dc21

2001030467

Anyone Corporation is a not-for-profit corporation in the State of New York with editorial and business offices at 41 West 25th Street, 11th floor, New York, New York 10010. Email: anyone@anycorp.com

Board of Directors
Peter Eisenman, President
Cynthia C. Davidson
Arata Isozaki
Philip Johnson
Rem Koolhaas
Phyllis Lambert
Ignasi de Solà-Morales

The Anything conference was supported in part by the Austrian Cultural Institute, New York; the Cultural Services of the French Embassy; the Consulate General of the Netherlands, New York; and the Consulate General of Spain, New York.

The Anything conference and this book were supported in part by an award from the National Endowment for the Arts.

NATIONAL
ENDOWMENT
FOR THE ARTS

TABLE OF CONTENTS

For Ignasi de Solà-Morales.
Architect, teacher, critic, friend.
1942-2001

ACKNOWLEDGMENTS

Anything is the final book in a series of ten that began with an idea in 1990 to establish architecture as the host of a cross-cultural and multidisciplinary discussion on architecture and contemporary culture, and to do so at the symbolic time of the end of the second millennium. To sustain such a project over ten years – producing ten conferences and then ten documentary books – required the participation of a multitude of sponsors and hosts, who made it financially feasible, and then of architects, theorists, historians, artists, philosophers, sociologists, economists, and many others, who shared their work and ideas in discussions and books like this one, giving content and meaning to the exercise. This book documents the final conference, Anything, which took place on June 1, 2, 3, 2000, at the Solomon R. Guggenheim Museum in New York City. To end the series it seemed fitting to bring the transient event home, to try to settle in with the experiment and all of its data, perhaps even to identify directions that may be emerging in architecture. The indomitable and indefatigable Thomas Krens, director of the Guggenheim and a former cosponsor of **ANY** magazine seminars, assumed the fiscal responsibilities of the host. The extraordinarily efficient and empathic Julian Zugazagoitia took on the task of accommodating the conference in Frank Lloyd Wright's bowl-shaped auditorium, now called the Peter B. Lewis Theater. International consulates based in New York stepped forward to help underwrite the cost of the meeting: The Austrian Cultural Institute; The Cultural Services of the French Embassy; the Consulate General of the Netherlands; and The Consulate General of Spain; and then the National Endowment for the Arts awarded the Anyone Corporation a grant to help support the conference and preparation of this book.

Having been held in ten different cities, each Any conference and thus each Any book has had its own special character; its own unique atmosphere and expectations. In New York, as in all previous venues, this meant showing the town off a little during the evenings. On Thursday, the contemporary art and architecture dealer Frederieke Taylor kindly opened her home with its spectacular view of downtown Manhattan for cocktails and dinner on the terrace, hosted by several of the infamous Century Club Roundtable architects: Richard Meier, Charles Gwathmey, David Childs, Robert A.M. Stern, Cesar Pelli, Henry N. Cobb, Philip Johnson, and Peter Eisenman. On Friday evening, Phyllis Lambert generously picked up the tab for dinner at the Brasserie, a hot restaurant redo by New York architects Diller+Scofidio in the basement of the Seagram Building. On Saturday night, the Municipal Art Society threw a cocktail party organized by Nicolas Rojas at the opening of "Eavesdropping on Architecture," an exhibition on the first nine years of the Anyone project, designed and installed by former Any staffer Matthew Berman and his partner in workshop/apd, Andrew Kotchen, in the Urban Center Gallery.

And on Sunday, for those who chose to stay the whole weekend, Philip Johnson and David Whitney graciously received a busload of participants at the Glass House in New Canaan, Connecticut, where the grounds and all of the buildings were open for a couple of hours of strolling under a beneficent spring sunshine. And then it was over, except, of course, for the enormous work to be done to prepare this volume. Edwin Gunn, as he has for ten years, transcribed the tapes of presentations and discussions with care and intelligence. Thomas Weaver, working on his second Any book, combed through pages and pages of material and organized images and schedules to help us meet deadlines; Sabu Kohso appeared once again to translate from the Japanese; and 2x4, Inc., for the seventh time, applied their graphic skills to produce the final object. Together they formed a wonderful team, and I am grateful to each of them for their contributions, and also to Roger Conover of MIT Press, who for the past seven years has published the Any volumes, each of which has sold out.

For all of the weeks and months and people that the Anything conference and this book required to produce, they were in the beginning made possible by one considerable factor: in the summer of 1990, the Shimizu Corporation in Tokyo agreed to an immensely generous ten years of support to sustain the conference series. Without Shimizu and its president, Harusuke Imamura, there would not have been an Any project. I cannot thank them enough for standing by the project for the entire decade.

Finally, in this last acknowledgments for the Any books, I want especially to thank four singularly important people: Arata Isozaki, Phyllis Lambert, and Ignasi de Solà-Morales for their ongoing concern and guidance and for entrusting me with this work; and Peter Eisenman, who suggested I take it on in the first place, and who has never wavered in his support. Three weeks before the first conference in Los Angeles, I gave birth to my son Sam; he slept in a bassinet on the floor at the Anyone meeting, making Jacques Derrida perceptibly nervous. Now Sam is turning ten and is studying French himself. He is another measure of a decade spent with Any, and perhaps why, in the end, I wanted to bring Anything home to New York.

For all of the networks and exchanges that the itinerant Any engendered, there is one final resting place for the project: I am deeply gratified that the Canadian Centre for Architecture in Montreal is acquiring the entire Any archive this year — records of conferences, books, **ANY** magazine, and the Writing Architecture series; in essence, the documentation of a dense and experimental activity in architecture at the end of the 20th century. This acquisition gives added importance to the work so many individuals undertook for Any; I trust that they too will be pleased that it is seen to mean so much.

— C.C.D., New York City

ANYBODIES

1 AKIRA ASADA
TEACHES AT THE INSTITUTE OF ECONOMIC RESEARCH IN KYOTO AND IS EDITOR OF THE JOURNAL **CRITICAL SPACE.**

2 BEN VAN BERKEL AND
3 CAROLINE BOS ARE FOUNDING PARTNERS IN THE AMSTERDAM FIRM UN STUDIO VAN BERKEL & BOS. THEY ARE CURRENTLY WORKING ON AN ADDITION TO THE WADSWORTH ATHENEUM IN HARTFORD, CONNECTICUT.

4 GIULIANA BRUNO
IS PROFESSOR OF VISUAL AND ENVIRONMENTAL STUDIES AT HARVARD UNIVERSITY AND AUTHOR OF **ATLAS OF EMOTION: JOURNEYS IN ART, ARCHITECTURE, AND FILM** AND **STREETWALKING ON A RUINED MAP.**

5 DANIEL BUREN
WAS BORN IN 1938 IN BOULOGNE-BILLANCOURT, FRANCE. HE LIVES AND WORKS IN SITU.

6 GERMANO CELANT
IS A CONTEMPORARY ART CURATOR BASED IN GENOA AND NEW YORK. HE RECENTLY CURATED THE GIORGIO ARMANI EXHIBITION AT THE SOLO-MON R. GUGGENHEIM MUSEUM, NEW YORK.

7 DAVID CHILDS
IS CHAIRMAN OF SKIDMORE, OWINGS, & MERRILL, AND PRINCIPAL ARCHITECT OF THE NEW PENNSYLVANIA STATION IN NEW YORK.

8 JEAN-LOUIS COHEN
IS DIRECTOR OF THE INSTITUT FRANÇAIS D'ARCHITECTURE IN PARIS AND THE SHELDON H. SOLOW PROFESSOR IN THE HISTORY OF ARCHITECTURE, INSTITUTE OF FINE ARTS, NEW YORK UNIVERSITY.

9 BEATRIZ COLOMINA
IS PROFESSOR OF ARCHI-TECTURAL HISTORY AND THEORY AT PRINCETON UNIVERSITY AND AUTHOR OF **PRIVACY AND PUBLICITY.**

10 HUBERT DAMISCH
IS A HISTORIAN OF ART AND PHILOSOPHY AND THE DIRECTOR OF STUDIES AT L'ÉCOLE DES HAUTES ÉTUDES EN SCIENCES SOCIALES IN PARIS. HIS MANY BOOKS INCLUDE **ORIGIN OF PERSPECTIVE.**

11 CYNTHIA DAVIDSON
IS DIRECTOR OF THE ANYONE CORPORATION AND FOUNDING EDITOR OF **ANY** MAGAZINE AND THE WRITING ARCHITEC-TURE BOOK SERIES.

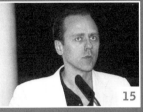

12 ELIZABETH DILLER
IS ASSOCIATE PROFESSOR OF ARCHITECTURE AT PRINCETON UNIVERSITY AND FOUNDING MEMBER OF DILLER+SCOFIDIO, NEW YORK. CURRENT D+S PROJECTS INCLUDE **FACSIMILE,** A PERMANENT MEDIA INSTALLATION FOR THE MOSCONE CONVENTION CENTER IN SAN FRANCISCO, AND **TRAVELOGUES,** AN INSTALLATION AT THE NEW JFK INTERNATIONAL AIR TERMINAL IN NEW YORK.

13 PETER EISENMAN
IS THE IRWIN S. CHANIN PROFESSOR OF ARCHITECTURE AT THE COOPER UNION IN NEW YORK. HE IS CURRENTLY WORKING ON THE CITY OF CULTURE OF GALICIA IN SANTIAGO DE COMPOSTELA AND THE MEMORIAL TO THE MURDERED JEWS OF EUROPE IN BERLIN.

14 ELIZABETH GROSZ
TEACHES PHILOSOPHY AT THE STATE UNIVERSITY OF NEW YORK IN BUFFALO. SHE IS THE AUTHOR OF **JACQUES LACAN: A FEMINIST INTRODUCTION** AND **VOLATILE BODIES: TOWARD A CORPO REAL FEMINISM.** HER **ARCHITECTURE FROM THE OUTSIDE** WAS PUBLISHED IN THE WRITING ARCHITECTURE SERIES THIS YEAR.

15 INGO GÜNTHER
IS A NEW YORK-BASED ARTIST WHOSE WORK, TYPICALLY FEATURING GLOBES, HAS BEEN EXHIBITED EXTENSIVELY IN EUROPE AND JAPAN. HE IS CURRENTLY WORKING ON THE HISTORY OF THE AESTHETICS OF DIPLOMACY.

16 ZAHA HADID
IS AN ARCHITECT BASED IN LONDON. HER OFFICE IS CURRENTLY WORKING ON A SKI JUMP IN INNSBRUCK, A BRIDGE IN ABU DHABI, A SCIENCE CENTER IN WOLFSBURG, GERMANY, AND A FERRY TERMINAL IN SALERNO, ITALY.

17 JACQUES HERZOG
IS AN ARCHITECT AND FOUNDING PRINCIPAL OF HERZOG & DE MEURON IN BASEL. CURRENT WORKS INCLUDE AN ADDITION TO THE DE YOUNG MUSEUM IN SAN FRANCISCO AND A HOTEL PROJECT, IN COLLABORATION WITH THE OFFICE FOR METROPOLITAN ARCHITECTURE, FOR ASTOR PLACE, NEW YORK CITY.

18 GARY HILL
IS A SEATTLE-BASED ARTIST WHOSE WORK HAS BEEN EXHIBITED EXTENSIVELY IN AMERICA, EUROPE, AND JAPAN. AMONG HIS MANY AWARDS ARE THE KURT SCHWITTERS AWARD AND A JOHN D. AND CATHERINE T. MACARTHUR FOUNDATION GRANT.

19 STEVEN HOLL
IS AN ARCHITECT AND PRINCIPAL OF STEVEN HOLL ARCHITECTS, NEW YORK. HIS WRITINGS ON ARCHITECTURE AND LIGHT WERE RECENTLY PUBLISHED IN **PARALLAX.**

20 CATHERINE INGRAHAM
IS CHAIR OF GRADUATE ARCHITECTURE AT PRATT INSTITUTE, BROOKLYN, AND AUTHOR OF **ARCHITECTURE AND THE BURDENS OF LINEARITY.**

21 OSAMU ISHIYAMA
IS PROFESSOR OF ARCHITECTURE AT WASEDA UNIVERSITY, TOKYO, AND DESIGNER OF THE JAPANESE PAVILION AT THE 1996 VENICE BIENNALE.

22 ARATA ISOZAKI
IS AN ARCHITECT IN TOKYO. HIS REALIZED PROJECTS INCLUDE THE TEAM DISNEY BUILDING IN ORLANDO, THE INTERNATIONAL VILLAGE OF THE ARTS IN AKIYOSHIDAI, AND THE ADDITION TO MIAMI'S BASS MUSEUM OF ART.

23 FREDRIC JAMESON
IS DIRECTOR OF THE GRADUATE PROGRAM IN LITERATURE AT DUKE UNIVERSITY. HIS BOOKS INCLUDE **POSTMODERNISM, OR, THE CULTURAL LOGIC OF LATE CAPITALISM** AND **THE SEEDS OF TIME**. A **JAMESON READER** EDITED BY MICHAEL HARDT AND KATHI WEEKS WAS PUBLISHED IN 2000.

24 KOJIN KARATANI
IS A LITERARY CRITIC AND PROFESSOR OF LITERATURE AT HOSEI UNIVERSITY, TOKYO. HE IS THE AUTHOR OF **ORIGINS OF MODERN JAPANESE LITERATURE** AND **ARCHITECTURE AS METAPHOR**.

25 ROMI KHOSLA
IS AN ARCHITECT AND ECONOMIST BASED IN NEW DELHI AND AN ECONOMIC CONSULTANT FOR UNESCO IN EASTERN EUROPE.

26 JEFFREY KIPNIS
IS PROFESSOR OF ARCHITECTURE AT OHIO STATE UNIVERSITY AND ARCHITECTURAL CURATOR AT THE WEXNER CENTER FOR THE ARTS, COLUMBUS, OHIO.

27 REM KOOLHAAS
IS THE PRINCIPAL OFFICER OF THE OFFICE FOR METROPOLITAN ARCHITECTURE (OMA) AND TEACHES AT HARVARD UNIVERSITY'S GRADUATE SCHOOL OF DESIGN. HE IS THE AUTHOR OF **DELIRIOUS NEW YORK** AND **S,M,L,XL**

28 THOMAS KRENS
IS DIRECTOR OF THE SOLOMON R. GUGGENHEIM FOUNDATION, NEW YORK.

29 SANFORD KWINTER
TEACHES ARCHITECTURE AT RICE UNIVERSITY AND IS A FOUNDING EDITOR OF ZONE BOOKS. AT ANYTHING HE PRESENTED ON BEHALF OF BRUCE MAU.

30 PHYLLIS LAMBERT
IS FOUNDING DIRECTOR AND CHAIR OF THE CANADIAN CENTRE FOR ARCHITECTURE, MONTREAL. SHE IS PRESENTLY CURATING "MIES IN AMERICA," A MAJOR TOURING EXHIBITION THAT WILL OPEN IN JUNE 2001 AT THE WHITNEY MUSEUM OF AMERICAN ART, NEW YORK.

31 RALPH LERNER
IS DEAN OF THE SCHOOL OF ARCHITECTURE AT PRINCETON UNIVERSITY AND PRINCIPAL OF RALPH LERNER ARCHITECT.

32 GREG LYNN
IS FOUNDER OF GREG LYNN FORM IN LOS ANGELES. HE TEACHES AT THE SCHOOL OF ARCHITECTURE AT THE UNIVERSITY OF CALIFORNIA IN LOS ANGELES AND IS THE AUTHOR OF **ANIMATE FORM**.

33 BRUCE MAU
IS A GRAPHIC DESIGNER BASED IN TORONTO AND HEAD DESIGNER OF BRUCE MAU DESIGN. HE IS DESIGN DIRECTOR OF ZONE BOOKS AND AUTHOR OF **LIFE STYLE**.

34 RAFAEL MONEO
IS JOSEP LLUIS SERT
PROFESSOR OF ARCHITEC-
TURE AT HARVARD UNIVER-
SITY'S GRADUATE SCHOOL
OF DESIGN AND PRINCIPAL
OF HIS OWN FIRM IN MADRID.
HIS CURRENT PROJECTS
INCLUDE THE CATHEDRAL
FOR THE ARCHDIOCESE OF
LOS ANGELES.

35 JEAN NOUVEL
IS AN ARCHITECT BASED IN
PARIS AND PRINCIPAL OF HIS
OWN PRACTICE. RECENTLY
COMPLETED WORKS INCLUDE
A COURTHOUSE IN NANTES,
A HOTEL IN LUCERNE, AND A
HOTEL AND PIER STUDY FOR
THE EAST RIVER, BROOKLYN,
NEW YORK.

36 WOLF PRIX
IS AN ARCHITECT AND
CO-FOUNDER WITH HELMUT
SWICZINSKY OF COOP
HIMMELB(L)AU, VIENNA.
HE IS CURRENTLY WORKING
ON AN URBAN ENTERTAIN-
MENT CENTER IN GUADALA-
JARA, MEXICO.

37 HANI RASHID
IS PARTNER IN THE FIRM
ASYMPTOTE AND PROFESSOR
OF ARCHITECTURE AT COLUM-
BIA UNIVERSITY'S GRADUATE
SCHOOL OF ARCHITECTURE,
WHERE HE DEVELOPED THE
SCHOOL'S ADVANCED DIGITAL
DESIGN PROGRAM.

38 SASKIA SASSEN
IS PROFESSOR OF SOCIOLOGY
AT THE UNIVERSITY OF
CHICAGO AND AUTHOR
OF **GUESTS AND ALIENS**
AND **GLOBALIZATION AND
ITS DISCONTENTS.**

39 IGNASI DE SOLÀ-MORALES
IS AN ARCHITECT AND PRO-
FESSOR OF ARCHITECTURAL
THEORY AND HISTORY
AT THE BARCELONA SCHOOL
OF ARCHITECTURE. HIS
**DIFFERENCES: TOPOGRAPHIES
OF CONTEMPORARY
ARCHITECTURE** WAS PUB-
LISHED IN THE WRITING
ARCHITECTURE SERIES.

40 MARK C. TAYLOR
IS THE CLUETT PROFESSOR
OF HUMANITIES AT WILLIAMS
COLLEGE AND AUTHOR OF
**DISFIGURING: ART, ARCHI-
TECTURE, AND RELIGION**
AND **HIDING.**

41 BERNARD TSCHUMI IS
DEAN OF THE GRADUATE
SCHOOL OF ARCHITECTURE,
PLANNING, AND PRESERVATION
AT COLUMBIA UNIVERSITY
AND PRACTICES ARCHITEC-
TURE IN BOTH NEW YORK
AND PARIS.

42 ANTHONY VIDLER
IS CHAIR OF ART HISTORY
AT THE UNIVERSITY OF
CALIFORNIA IN LOS ANGELES.
HIS BOOKS INCLUDE **WARPED
SPACE** AND **THE ARCHITEC-
TURAL UNCANNY.**

**43 PAULINA
WALLENBERG-OLSSON**
IS A SWEDISH-BORN ARTIST
WHO HAS TOURED WITH
GARY HILL PERFORMING
A SERIES OF WORKS DIS-
TILLED THROUGH SOUND,
TEXT, AND VOCALS.

"look at this
in another way"

"s are
improving"

ON PASSING TIME IN SPACE, AIRPORTS, AND URBAN PHENOMENA

BERNARD TSCHUMI

I generally avoid academic symposia that last more than one day, and perfectly understand Paul Virilio, who placed a sign over his phone that said, "No travel. No lectures. No conferences." It is hard to pass time in space, especially with others. (As Sartre said, "L'enfer, c'est les autres," before he began to feel the need to be politically responsible.) In this age of digitalization and in this space, this city of congestion, New York, what is it that makes us deal with others in a place over-populated by others? I would argue that it is abstraction — after all, abstract art was invented in New York (those who say it originated with the Russians or Dutch are wrong; abstraction was really theorized in

Kansai International Airport competition entry.

this city) — and that it developed as a way to deal with others, to maintain a necessary distance from people. In architecture, modern abstraction provided a means to exclude all the messiness of subjective relations — people's emotions and their embarrassing lives. The 1950s, the height of modernism, was also a time when a developing new artifact began to offer significant change in the shape of a way to generalize distance. Flying. Flying away. When I first arrived in New York, Anthony Vidler told me that Peter Eisenman saw two psychoanalysts at the same time, and he asked, "What about you? What do you do when you can't cope with the parts of you?" I remember my response: "I take an airplane." That was over twenty years ago, but I still felt that the way to abstract oneself was in the real place of no place. No genius loci there. Have you ever seen a genius loci in an airport?

In 1988 I accepted an invitation to participate in a limited architectural competition that I did not want to win. I tried very hard to lose it and ultimately succeeded, though only just — we got second prize. The project was for an airport on an artificial island in Osaka Bay in Japan, a competition for the Kansai International Airport that ultimately was won, and built, by Renzo Piano. My project was probably the first of a number of proposals for airport cities, and I took the luxury of not wanting to win the competition because it allowed me to pursue a specific concept: the abstraction of architectural experiences. My Kansai Airport was a linear city, one mile long, that took the multiplicity of events of airport life and turned them into a concentration of metropolitan activity, a new and unprecedented form of international life. "Such a project," I wrote in my proposal, "could make Osaka and Japan forerunners of the most intense mode of city life, in which people would fly to Kansai International because it would be the place to be." This fantastic capacity was possible because airports no longer serve isolated functions. They are not unitary buildings; they extend and redefine the metropolis; they explode boundaries and limits. They are also one of the fastest growing industries today, attracting entrepreneurs of all kinds. Kansai was designed as an event, a spectacle, a new city of exchange and interchange, of commerce and culture, of 24-hours-a-day, continuous invention. "It would have two hotels with a thousand rooms," I wrote, "office space, mile-long entertainment, culture, and a sports center with cinemas, exhibition spaces, swimming pools, golf courses, shooting galleries, and so forth, all serviced by travelators and conveniences of different kinds." Shopping was the least of it; travel only part of it. This disjunction of experience provided the opposite of the seeming continuum of mall culture. It was an abstracted city, a city of abstraction.

The important part of this project was not only the abstraction but also the attraction it offered. The airport project attempted to do what major and minor cities throughout

Urban home of the future proposal for **Time** magazine.

the 1990s have tried to do with architecture: to use it as a magnet for the flow of bodies and capital. But the very nature of the airport also concentrated an intensely architectural experience, showing that architecture is about passing time, a "thing" for passing time in space. After all, everybody except for architects has to arrive at airports two or three hours before takeoff, and despite the billions that Mr. Miller has made in duty-free shopping and the projections for future retailing in airports, shopping is only one component. The vast opportunities opened up by passing time in space permit recreational and cultural activities of all kinds, from movies to exhibitions to spontaneous performances of street theater. The airport provides a captive audience ready to be edified, illuminated, or exploited. And one of the interesting things about the recent focus on shopping – a phenomena that has proliferated in an era of expanding disposable income – is that "consumer culture" has become an oxymoron. Those sectors of the world where shopping has become a national pastime (and here, developing Asian cities are exemplary) are also those areas that offer the least attention to contemporary art and culture, when measured in production or subsidies for the arts. Indeed, an era that has produced a fantastic display of surfaces and visually seductive environments has had little effect on the expansion of the forms and definitions of culture.

This focus threatens to confuse "the public" with "consumers" in a sublation of terms that is rapidly becoming a contemporary commonplace. But to answer the question of whether things are improving, my response is that little is being done today to expand our definitions of the passing of time in space by and through architecture. Our definitions of culture do little to embrace new and interactive ways of passing time; the ways in which we use space and the questions we ask of it have hardly changed.

In 1999 **Time** magazine asked several architects to speculate on the urban home of the future. I suggested that we think of those "lost" spaces on the rooftops of Manhattan as the remains of urban space. The private house that developed out of these studies is at once an exercise in exhibitionism and voyeurism, and a speculation on the particularities, and social possibilities, of passing time in space. The fluidity of the walls supports an infinite range of mobile, electronically generated images. In the same way, the spaces of this private domain unfold with a broad range of cultural forms – from a couple embracing to performances to idiosyncratic dances, along with other art forms – all of which are displayed publicly to the urban streetgoers below. The house is at once a mingled form of private and public spectacle and an inquiry into the ways of passing time. As a speculation on some of the roles that culture might inhabit in everyday life, it proposes a means to invent new and interactive ways of relating to others while maintaining the abstraction we all require to exist today.

FROM METAPHOR TO ALLEGORY

FREDRIC JAMESON

In a famous passage from *The Anatomy of Criticism*, Northrop Frye affirms that all interpretation is allegorical, insofar as it substitutes for the text something else which purports to be the meaning of that text:

> It is not often realized that all commentary is allegorical interpretation, an attaching of ideas to the structure of poetic imagery. The instant that any critic permits himself to make a genuine comment about a poem (e.g., "in *Hamlet* Shakespeare appears to be portraying the tragedy of irresolution") he has begun to allegorize. Commentary thus looks at literature as, in its formal phase, a potential allegory of events and ideas.[1] Northrop Frye, *Anatomy of Criticism* (Princeton: Princeton University Press, 1957), 89.

This presupposes the meaning or interpretation to be another text (*allos*), and in this way operates to severely limit the general validity of that meaning (and also to add to it the "bad infinite" of other endless interpretations on its basis, since each new text of meaning must now be interpreted in its turn). In any case, we probably all feel today that although Frye strikes a powerful blow here for allegory, in a period in which it was still much despised and maligned, his argument makes it so unlimited a matter that if he wins, he loses, and the word ceases to mean very much because it now means everything.

One would want indeed to start out from these limits and boundaries in order to find something both universal and particular that allegory might usefully be. Principal among these boundaries must necessarily be the nonallegorical: unless there are texts that cannot under any circumstances be considered to be unallegorical (by which I do not necessarily mean "literal" in the traditional sense), no theory of allegory will amount to very much, nothing much will be achieved in the way of separating allegory off, both as a specific kind of textual structure and a specific kind of interpretive process. On the other hand, it does not seem very hopeful to ask for some general theory of the nonallegorical in order to construct a theory of allegory itself.

But then there are specific kinds of texts which are so closely related to allegories that one feels it might be useful to begin by saying why they are not then simply allegorical: for example, parables or fables. This kind of clarification would provide a much more productive gloss on Frye's claim by foregrounding precisely those texts in which meaning or interpretation is very precisely another text, the moral of the first one. It would then offer the example of a specific textual structure of a binary type – narrative plus moral or commentary – which is so strong that it can continue to exist in the absence of one of its components: the parable is thus presumably a fable whose commentary or moral has been omitted, or can be omitted; while the maxim or proverb gives us the example of a moral or commentary that can go on existing in the absence of its narrative exemplum.

The fable is therefore essentially a binary structure: picture and caption, narrative and moral. I want to distinguish it from allegory by positing the latter as a ternary structure: there is still the narrative on the one hand, and its meaning, interpretation, or reading on the other. But now the movement from the first to the second is mediated by some third component, which I will call Peirce's interpretant, or the allegorical code or system; this can be embedded in the text somehow, or can be found to float outside it in the form of cultural knowledge or ideas and ideologies in the public sphere. But it is always a kind of system in terms of which the text or the narrative demands to be translated. To this, I also want to add the allegorical instrument of coding, which is the ethical opposition between good and evil, between the valorized or idealized and the tabooed – a fundamental mechanism in the very construction of subjectivity itself.

But now I also need to delimit allegory in two other directions, and to oppose it to two other phenomena: first of all, to the symbol, whose valorization in the Romantic period was historically very much at one with the degradation of allegory and its repudiation as a structure. We then also need to differentiate allegory from that other related trope with which it is so often associated, namely, the metaphor, with which traditionally and classically Quintilian identified it, defining allegory as an extended metaphor: "Allegory, which is translated in Latin by inversion, either presents one thing in words and another in meaning, or else something absolutely opposed to the meaning of the words. The first type is generally produced by a series of metaphors."[2] Quintilian, *Institutio Oratoria*, trans. H. E. Butler (Cambridge, Massachusetts: Harvard University Press, 1970), vol. VIII, 6.44. His observation is useful, insofar as it makes us aware of what changes when you "extend" a metaphor into the allegorical: the metaphorical starting point becomes narrativized, and so we have some first feature, namely that allegories are somehow always matters of narrative. As for the difference with the symbol, here one would rather want to speak of unification and division, whether in the psyche, the world, or anything else. The symbol is a centered, unified phenomenon whose meaning is intrinsic and immanent. If the allegorical is attractive for the present day and age it is because it models a relationship of breaks, gaps, discontinuities, and inner distances and incommensurabilities of all kinds. It can therefore better serve as a figure for the incommensurabilities of the world today than the ideal of the symbol, which seems to designate some impossible unity. Thus, these first two opposites of the allegorical circumscribe the latter as narrative and as discontinuous.

At this point, I want to turn to some recent work on painting, where I think the problem of the metaphorical is rather dramatically set forth. T. J. Clark's recent (and monumental) *Farewell to an Idea: Episodes from a History of Modernism* offers seven remarkable probes of modern painting, from David's *Death of Marat* (1793) to Jackson Pollock, touching in passing on Pissarro and Cézanne, on El Lissitzky and Picasso. It does not offer any monolithic definition, let alone explanations, of modernism, although it carefully limits its work to painting, as though the experiments in that medium offered a kind of sealed laboratory of the most specialized kind. Indeed, painting already confronts us with that kind of inexplicability: people tell stories in language, sing songs, build dwellings to live in; why they should learn to stare at various pieces of painted canvas is perhaps less obvious or less natural. Is it an activity that is fully satisfying in itself? Many people say so; but perhaps the Pierre Bourdieu-style inversion of the question is the better place to begin – namely, how they justify to themselves this satisfying activity, how they make it have a meaning. Theodor Adorno once said that in order for the experience of an art object to be fully aesthetic, it has to be more than aesthetic, it has also to be trans- or extra-aesthetic; in order to be art, then, art must be something more than art. Something like this seems also to be Clark's position: "In order to represent at all, as I see it, marks in pictures have to be understood as standing for something besides themselves; they have to be construed metaphorically. . . . Metaphor is inescapable in the case of markmaking, and what at any rate would an escape from it be like?" [3] T. J. Clark, *Farewell to an Idea: Episodes from a History of Modernism* (New Haven:Yale University Press, 1999), 336.

What, then, would the nonmetaphorical in art be like? Housepainting, perhaps? The colors of a house or wall generally respond to some conventional color scheme that is culturally meaningful even if it does not exactly mean something. Would it be like random marks on a surface? But we are talking about a "picture," that is, art, and we will therefore not be able to avoid trying to make the marks mean something, even if that something is "sheer randomness," the aleatory, or chaos, or meaninglessness itself. Perhaps we need to inflect the question somewhat: maybe the escape from metaphor can take place, not in the painting but in the viewer. In that case, we have to imagine the ascetic reductions of empiricism if not of positivism as such: the reduction not even to pure perception but to the atomic constituents of pure perception itself, namely, sense-data. Can we have an experience of the marks which are that of an as yet nonconceptual, nonmeaningful sense-datum? The idea of sense-data is a positivist myth (passionately adopted, to be sure, by a certain number of late-19th-century painters). There can be no "pure" or meaningless experience of sense-data. Does

this not condemn us forever to be metaphoric, in Clark's sense? Of course one understands that he has rigged the whole discussion in advance by calling brushstrokes "marks" (*Zeichen*), which is to say one version of the more general notion of the sign. But the sign always means something else by definition: and so must marks. So why call that operation metaphorical?

Clark's comments on the mark and metaphor come from the Pollock chapter, in which he goes on to identify the "two broad metaphorical poles" of Pollock's work in the period from 1948 to 1950: they are "figures of totality" on the one hand, and "figures of dissonance" on the other. Clark has, in other words, ranged a certain number of visual experiences on both sides under larger formal categories which in fact correspond to conceptual abstractions or universals: totality then corresponds to the one, while what he ("a bit warily") calls dissonance no doubt corresponds generally to what is today called heterogeneity or the absolutely specific. Perhaps this philosophical identification of the more properly visual poles is already itself metaphorical; and perhaps we also need to ask, what becomes of that more formal philosophical category that is the tension or contradiction between the two poles? To see a picture as staging this particular philosophical content is surely already to translate it into something else, something else which can then itself receive further metaphorical content. My quarrel, however, is not with that discussion or with the new levels of meaning found in Pollock's work, but rather with the terms *metaphor* and *metaphorical*, which one finds used equally significantly throughout Clark's other writings.

Let me offer another, perhaps fundamental, example for modern painting: it is the discussion of flatness in Clark's earlier book on impressionism, *The Painting of Modern Life* (1985). The rising to the surface of painting is, of course, one of the basic features of the latter's modernism, and this is how Clark sets about dealing with it:

> I think that the question we should be asking . . . is why that literal presence of surface went on being interesting for art. How could a matter of effect or procedure seemingly stand in for value in this way? What was it that made it vivid? . . . The answer must take approximately this form. If the fact of flatness was compelling for art . . . that must have been because it was made to stand for something: some particular and substantial set of qualities which took their place in a picture of the world. So that the richness of the avant-garde . . . might best be described in terms of its ability to give flatness such complex and compatible values – values which necessarily derived from elsewhere than art. [4] T. J. Clark, *The Painting of Modern Life: Paris in the Art of Manet and his Followers* (NewYork: Knopf, 1985), 12–13.

Clark then specifies some of these values, along with their

elsewheres, in four different ways. In other words, flatness can mean at least one of the following: the popular, "le peuple," as in workmanlike surfaces and manual labor. Or it can mean modernity and the media – posters, prints, photographs, and the like. Or it can mean Art itself as an autonomous quasi-sacred activity. Or it can mean, as for Cézanne, "the evenness of seeing itself, the actual form of our knowledge of things." Presumably it could also mean several of these things at once, or several in tension with one another. Following Kenneth Burke, painterly flatness is therefore understood here as a "symbolic act": it is a meaningful procedure whose ordinary meaning is then augmented by several others, which find symbolic expression through it and in addition to it. However, are these additional meanings metaphors?

What I want to argue here has to do with the relative merits of the terms *metaphor* and *allegory*. As I have said, classically allegory was often described as little more than an extended metaphor. 5 Quintilian, op. cit., 44–58. Meanwhile, in the more modern literary tradition, allegory has typically been opposed to the symbol in an opposition openly articulated in the Romantic period; and the concept of the symbol has remained the dominant one throughout what we call modernism. At the waning of high modernism, the repressed and stigmatized notion of allegory began to reappear in all kinds of unrelated places, most obviously in the reappearance of Walter Benjamin's works in Germany in the 1950s, and in the United States with a famous early essay of Paul de Man. This is the context which perhaps authorizes us to reinterrogate the pages we have quoted from Clark in order to see where they stand with respect to the symbol. Are we to understand, for example, that the immense and nonrepresentational wall of paint above David's corpse of Marat is a *symbol of le peuple?* Surely not; and we could think of any number of personified characters and emblems which, in contrast, do offer just such symbols. Clark's point was that "the people" is no doubt real enough, since the revolution somehow took place; but that this word is incoherent sociologically and politically and is also profoundly ideological – which is to say that "the people" as a concept can have no stable meaning, and that therefore you can have no symbol of it, a symbol being constituted by a fullness of meaning. David's wall background rather expresses a crisis of meaning and thereby a crisis of representation, and it is through this crisis that the wall becomes a metaphor. A crisis of this kind cannot be symbolized but it can be designated.

This is where the notion of allegory comes in, for in my view, allegory always arises from a crisis in representation (a historical and specific crisis, it should be understood, and not some timeless and eternal one). Allegory is a structure that designates difficulties, if not outright impossibilities, in meaning and representation, and also designates its own peculiar structure as a failure to mean and to represent in the conventional way. You will now more readily understand why I would have preferred to call David's wall an allegory rather than a metaphor (to do Clark justice, he does say that the wall is "metaphorical" of the crisis in representing the people, which is an altogether more prudent and satisfactory way of putting it). I believe that in his discussion of flatness and the predominance of the surface in modernist painting, the meanings he attributes to that crucial feature are also in one way or another allegorical of their objects, for those objects are all more or less unrepresentable ideas: work, modernity, art, perception.

I want now to complicate matters a little by adding a new problem and a new concern not yet registered in the notions of meaning or representation, and this is narrative. What Quintilian calls an "extension" of metaphor is in fact a narrativization of it, and I would argue that the whole nature and implications of the figure are utterly transformed in the process. The same holds for the symbol, which like metaphor is an essentially nonnarrative matter (and by the same token, although one might imagine a construction of a symbol by way of narrative – as in Emile Zola, for example, or in Albert Camus's *The Plague* – surely any undue "extension" of it, causing one to search for point-by-point parallels and allusions, is bound to also transform the former symbol into a structure more likely to be described as allegorical by its readers).

Now apparently we have two distinct characterizations of allegory (as opposed to symbol or metaphor): it is the expression and the result of a crisis in representation on the one hand, and of narrative on the other. (By the same token, in presupposing a stable meaning that can be conveyed, a symbol is essentially nonnarrative.) What then is the relationship between these two constitutive features, each of which could presumably exist without the other? We are, I assume, willing to admit the existence of nonallegorical narratives; while problems or difficulties in representation and meaning can no doubt be conveyed in ways that are not allegorical, for example, as in philosophical discourse.

I want to suggest that in fact these two features of allegory are one and the same. Allegory is a narrative process precisely because it needs to tell the narrative of the solution to its representational dilemma. Or, if you prefer, in allegory the crisis of representation and of meaning is conceived precisely as a dramatic situation that the allegorist is called upon to resolve in some way. The narrative here is thus very often a dialectical one: the crisis embodies a contradiction, which is articulated as a binary opposition, and the allegorical narrative will consist in the attempt to overcome this opposition in one way or another, which obviously does not always have to involve a synthesis between the two allegedly irreconcilable terms. (I do, however, want to strengthen this constitutive or structural relationship between allegory and opposition by quoting, in passing, from Jean de Meun: "Thus things go by contraries: one is the gloss of the other. If one wants to define one of the pair, he must remember the other, or he will never, by any intention, assign a definition to it; for he who has no understanding of the two will never understand the difference between them, and without this difference no definition that one can make can come to anything.")[6] De Lorris Guillaume and Jean de Meun, *The Romance of the Rose*, trans. Charles Dahlberg (Princeton: Princeton University Press, 1971), 351.

Rather than continue in this abstract vein, I think we need to see the process in action concretely. And while I think one could very well rewrite Clark's interpretations in terms of allegorical narratives, I would like now to turn to architectural materials, and in particular to the great history of modern architecture, *Architettura contemporanea*, written in 1976 by Manfredo Tafuri and Francesco Dal Co, where the term *allegory* is used openly and explicitly (or may I even say, shamelessly). This is all the more arresting, since the term *metaphor* has also scarcely been absent from architectural theory. Although Charles Jencks's pathbreaking introduction of "semiotics" (rhetoric, really) into architectural discourse with *The Language of Post-modern Architecture* in 1977 obviously made for an enlarged use of the term *metaphor*, the practice of metaphor largely antedates his examples. For instance, "concrete grills, now the sign of the parking garage," are no doubt derived from the metaphor of grills on the hood of the car; or Kisho Kurokawa's Nagakin Capsule Tower, in which the "stacking" of the rooms or hotel compartments evokes a variety of speaker systems, tape decks, and the like (which the rooms in fact contain). These are, then, already metonymies which have been metaphorized.[7] Charles Jencks, *The Language of Post-modern Architecture* (New York: Rizzoli, 1977), 40–41.

Before that, Le Corbusier's dramatic inflection of his building shapes in the direction of those modern machines he admired, such as the ocean liner and the airplane, are clearly enough metaphors (a word perhaps too weak to designate Ledoux's notorious Enlightenment brothel project). But here too there are complications, for Le Corbusier's metaphors also operate on a second level of connotation as *allegories* of modernity itself, and of the intention of the building to be "absolument moderne." The building is then the metaphor of an ocean liner, which is itself an allegory of modernity in general.

There does seem to be some point in retaining the term *metaphor* for certain local, one-to-one, meanings. Thus, in Daniel Libeskind's Jewish Museum in Berlin, a number of irregular and often broken slits and openings are revealed, seemingly at random, in the walls, from floor level up to heights through which no viewer could be expected to see. We are told that the invisible relationships between these slits (as those that traverse the void inside the building, crisscrossing space like the grid of an infrared alarm system) model a map of Berlin on which lines have been drawn to connect the historic dwellings of the most important Jewish writers, composers, artists, and poets of the city. Like the twelve-tone system itself (Arnold Schoenberg, with his stay in Berlin, was also an interest for the architect), it cannot be supposed that the casual viewer perceives the detail and content of this scheme, although he may intuit it allegorically as a sheer network of relationships. But it certainly overflows the architectural form and function itself, as a figure overflows the literal meaning of its support term.

Clearly enough, as the previous paragraph suggests, a mode of speech in which a metaphor is characterized as being "allegorical" of something will not be terribly helpful in the clarification process we are undertaking here. Thus, for example, "Glass, extolled by Scheerbart and Taut, is in itself highly symbolic: transparent, it is the allegory of a new collective purity, produced by the rarefaction of its material, it symbolizes the passage from the real to the unreal, from weight to weightlessness; in that sense, it is also allegorical of cosmic liberation."[8] Manfredo Tafuri and Francesco Dal Co, *Modern Architecture*, trans. Robert Erich Wolf (New York: Abrams, 1979), 129. This passage, from the Tafuri and Dal Co history, and taken as exemplary of the rigorous application of the term *allegory*, does seem to offer an excessive, aberrant use. The fact that an element or material (think of Gaston Bachelard's "psychoanalysis" of the various elements) is in question, rather than the specific placement of that material within a construction, may suffice to explain the lapse, and in this case the term *metaphorical* certainly seems preferable.

Tafuri and Dal Co's *Modern Architecture* in fact presents a twofold interest: it is an allegorical structure, but it also has the generic interest of offering a successful history of one of the arts that is not a mere handbook or manual, a list of dates or a reference work, but a narrative in its own right. In this sense, there are very few works which invent distinctive solutions to the form problems inherent in writing a history of literature or of painting or of architecture. The writing of such histories, indeed, intensifies the dialectic between continuity and discontinuity present in all historiography to the point where it is well-nigh insuperable. For the works themselves (literary, musical, pictorial, architectural) are radically individualized – they have their closure; they are neither events that take their place in a meaningful series nor are they organic or natural phenomena that fold into each other and evolve. How, then, do we tell a story about such discontinuous artifacts? The recourse to styles and movements on the one hand (impressionism, expressionism, realism, surrealism), and to genres on the other (the introspective novel, the epic, the confessional lyric), are both spurious solutions insofar as they presume a solution in advance of the fundamental philosophical problem of style or genre – namely, the relationship of the individual text to the universal classifying system it is supposed to participate in. Thus the Tafuri and Dal Co volume has a supplementary interest insofar as it offers a unique solution to this dilemma: a solution, however, that I suspect unfortunately cannot be exemplary, since in this area of a history of artistic works, the only real successes are ad hoc constructions that are not repeatable. Still, they all articulate and dramatize the problem, which is the essential thing.

The narrative has two beginnings: a false start and a seemingly extraneous digression. The false start is given with art nouveau, judged to be a regressive style and ideology which is class-bound and solves none of the architectural dilemmas of modernity. I take this opening salvo to be part and parcel of the authors' generalized attack on style as such. (We may recall Le Corbusier's similar position: "The styles are a lie"; "architecture has nothing to do with the various 'styles'"; etc.)[9] Le Corbusier, *Towards a New Architecture*, trans. Frederick Etchells (New York: Dover Publications, 1986), 87, 37. What is meant by this, I think, is the purely aesthetic solution: that the concept of style is seen as a reduction of the complex problems an individual building tries to resolve to a matter of purely artistic or aesthetic invention – one which could be undertaken, in other words, by the various avant-gardes. The attack on the avant-garde is then another basic leitmotiv of the "narrative" and suggests that the category of style need not be limited to criterias of beauty, as in the historical case of art nouveau.

After this opening gambit, however, we suddenly pass to a discussion of the emergence of city planning in the United States in the late-19th century, and in particular to the work of the great landscape artists such as Frederick Law Olmsted. This would not seem to be an auspicious beginning for a study of an essentially European modernist architecture, and we need to grasp the logic of the new departure. The point is that it is around issues of parks and open spaces that the struggle for political power in the North American cities crystallizes:

> Within a few decades the battle for parks became synonymous with an overall process of urban reform that had a great deal to do with the problem of political and institutional reforms in an era dominated by political bosses and by the most unbridled competitive free market. Similarly, the battle for the defense of

nature ended up in a project aiming to ensure to the state and collectivity the control over the exploitation of natural resources on the territorial level. By the end of the century a reform of the institutional apparatus of the American system became the key to all progress.[10] Tafuri and Dal Co, op. cit., 25.

The Progressive movement emerges from this struggle and produces the reality of city planning, dramatizing its necessary relationship to political power as well as the limitations imposed on it by social class. Nothing of the sort can happen with the already ancient and fully formed European city, which can at best – and this is no mean achievement – produce the utopian visions of the garden city and the like. Thus this American chapter allows Tafuri and Dal Co to lay in place the city as one pole of the examination of architectural history, whose other pole is clearly that of the individual buildings themselves. Theirs must therefore be what they call "a binocular vision of history: seeing the great change in the approach to planning and also the response of architecture as such. Particular attention must be devoted to where those separate spheres have interlocked (if they have) and where they have gone their separate ways."[11] Ibid., 305.

Perhaps this is to put the matter somewhat too statically: for we do not simply confront here two parallel themes and traditions, which sometimes intersect and sometimes do not. On the contrary, the two poles of the city and the building form an inescapable binary opposition that is a contradiction in its own right. The history of architecture is then the story of successive attempts to resolve this fundamental contradiction; its telos will be not exactly the place of the solution but the search for the right way to grasp its inevitable failure. This at once gives the book its narrative form: once the reader knows what to look for, this immense compendium reads like an exciting novel (and in the process, as I suggested above, also offers a remarkable, distinctive, and no doubt unrepeatable solution to the permanent problem of artistic historiography).

From the outset, we must be careful to see the flexibility of the scheme, for any proper contradiction can be articulated in a variety of ways. This means that the content of each pole is variable, and the new stage sets the fundamental contradiction (of capitalist modernity) in a variety of ways, each of which permits the individuality of a distinct new attempt at solution or synthesis. We have defined the contradiction at its outset as the opposition between the city and the building; but we have also already said enough to indicate that the city can mean planning, so that its more purely architectural opposite would then be the anarchy of the individual commission, or even the fluctuations in the value of land or site. At the same time, the city sets in place the question of political power, in which case its opposite is surely the pure aestheticism of architecture as style, or paper architecture. In the light of other canonical descriptions — for Tafuri and Dal Co, as for many of us, the central text is still Georg Simmel's *Die Großstadt und das Geistesleben* — the city is also chaos and anxiety, in which case its aesthetic opposite is one or another form of order, or at least of allaying or coming to terms with that anxiety. Yet if the new industrial city is a more standardized form of chaos or alienation, its opposite number might just as plausibly be the regional or the national, as in Holland, Scandinavia, and Catalonia. But if the city is degeneracy and a flood of degraded messages and images, including now dead architectural styles — remember that for Adolf Loos, the riot of ornament and ornamentation in Vienna made it a "tattooed city" — then its opposite could be the purism and the purity of a Loos or even of Le Corbusier. But perhaps the city is also sheerly industry and engineering, and in that case — as for the very history of the emergent Bauhaus itself — its opposite can be not only mysticism but also other forms of a mystique of the art. For Tafuri and Dal Co the contradiction is concretized in social life and even more specifically in the role of intellectuals: so we have engineers versus artists, and eventually, as the artistic pole gathers momentum and begins to fight back, we have the emergence of avant-gardes, as opposed to politicians and planners, or to engineers. This is properly the place of architectural and urban utopias, and it is fair to say that not the least of the originalities of Tafuri and Dal Co is to have taken familiar and stereotypical Marxian positions — Marx's and Engels' dismissal of utopias, the later Stalinist dismissal of the avant-garde or the experimental in art — and to have transformed both into vital and contemporarily meaningful stances, implacably negative judgments which are not demoralizing or paralyzing but rather energizing and productive of future praxis.

The variety of solutions to the multiple articulations of this contradiction (totality versus the individual work) also allows them inventively to transform the fundamental and even dogmatic value of high modernist theory — the valorization of innovation or the new, the *Novum* in Ernst Bloch's sense. Here the Novum is not the more conventional stylistic innovation, although I dare say that stylistic invention is always its by-product and its aftereffect. Rather, it is simply a creative response to the contradiction itself, a more thoroughgoing attempt to resolve it, even as the contradiction becomes more thoroughgoing throughout historical time, and deepens and reveals itself more and more as a desperate crisis. So as architectural innovation grows ever more desperate, its attempts become grander and more impressive, its failures become more conclusive. These attempts must always fail, but now we will be able to see the reasons.

After significant sections on Frank Lloyd Wright and Louis Sullivan — the skyscraper as an isolated event within the city, and which cannot be integrated into it (unless, as at present, the city simply becomes a forest of skyscrapers and the originality of the form is lost); Wright's construction of his own alternative utopian terms in the building, in nature and the transfigured and democratic American countryside — the authors turn to regionalist architecture and significantly conclude their discussion as follows:

> After [Gaudí], the utopia that looked to a return to origins, national or otherwise, was burned out, reduced to ashes. In any event, a romantic fable has chiefly one task: to organize the dream, to define it as a metaphorical model of archetypal verity. The Neo-Romanesque of Berlage, Saarinen, or Moser, like the obsessive eclecticism of Catalan Modernism, aspired to organize what can be called a collective dream, to give substance to a symbolic code capable of welding the solidarity — urban or national — of communities fragmented by inner conflicts. Here the private and crepuscular dream of Art Nouveau ceded its place to the image of an arduous process of constructing a new world. But image it was and image it remained, nostalgically suspended between past and present: the real innovatory processes were scarcely touching European architectural thinking.[12 Ibid., 92]

I do not want to exaggerate the importance of the word *metaphorical* in this summation, nevertheless, I think it is significant. To call these wonderful buildings in their ensemble "a metaphorical model of archetypal verity" is not only to deny them the narrative dynamism of the allegorical: it is also to suggest that the attempt is focused uniquely on the single pole of the building and its plan and shape, and not on the tension between that pole and the city. To address that tension would be to transform this metaphorical model into an allegorical act. We begin to see this in the next chapters, where the Werkbund begins to address problems of the city and its realities, as do, in different ways, Tony Garnier and his successors in France. Meanwhile, Loos and theorists like Karl Krauss and the young Ludwig Wittgenstein begin to give a name to this crisis, while the new avant-gardes greet their dilemma with an immense yet doomed explosion of creativity. Not surprisingly, this section returns us to painting, which becomes something like the abstract thought of which architecture should be the act and realization, always assuming that such an act is possible in the first place (remember that Le Corbusier always spent an hour or so painting in the early morning, before turning to his architectural work). Along with painting, the avant-garde raises once again the question of the intellectual:

> Between intellectuals and metropolis yawned a gulf that could be bridged only by accepting dissent. The intellectual, in substance, discovered that his own singularity no longer had its

place in the massified metropolis dominated by a technical capacity for infinite duplication . . . the metropolis became the very sickness to which the intellectual felt himself condemned. . . . Faced with the "disease" represented by the metropolis, the intellectuals have attempted to define a new role for themselves by appealing to original purity, to the infancy of humanity, the mythical season in which man and nature were not yet enemies, to, in short, the mythical moment in which the communion of man with cosmos was permitted by the precapitalist relationships of production. . . . [Yet] every project of conciliation was constrained to reveal itself as merely utopian. Anxiety as the condition of metropolitan existence was to become the guiding idea for the Expressionist poets and painters.[13 Ibid., 98–99.]

It is not merely shadows of the artistic avant-garde that hover across these passages but also those of the intellectual and philosophical avant-garde: Friedrich Nietzsche and Charles Baudelaire, Benjamin and the Viennese. Perhaps we need to reinforce these anti-avant-garde positions by recalling Tafuri's similar pessimism about the great negative, critical, or deconstructive intellectual forces of modernity. They level everything, he argues, thinking of Sigmund Freud, Nietzsche, and other critics of modernity, in order to liquidate the vestiges of the past: "All the work of demolition served to prepare a clean-swept platform from which to depart in discovery of the new 'historic tasks' of intellectual work."[14 Manfredo Tafuri, *Architecture and Utopia*, trans. Barbara L. Lapenta (Cambridge, Massachusetts: MIT Press, 1979), 70.] The result is a situation in which a completely fungible reality is made available for late capitalism to use and manipulate for its own ends.

We are not quite as far as that, however, in our reading of the history, where we have indeed arrived at the moment of the masters – the moment of Le Corbusier, whose greatness is to have omitted the anxiety of the avant-garde: "In the face of the machine, Le Corbusier experienced the same intoxication as the avant-garde, but without the bewilderment and disorientation."[15 Tafuri and Dal Co, op. cit., 136.] (In fact, according to this account, all of the modern "masters" are as hostile to the avant-gardes as their interpreter Tafuri, or indeed, to Tafuri's philosophical master, Adorno.)

Le Corbusier does not, of course, resolve our basic contradiction either, but he invents a new way of dealing with it:

[In the idea of the *Ville Radieuse*] the dialectic between norm and exception explicit in the *grands travaux* remained unresolved. Unlike the projects of the 1920s, those for community buildings in the next decade used allegory in a new way. Where the earlier ones alluded to the completeness of a compositional system based on syntheses imposing a different category of order on the fragmented objects, the later one made clear just how ineffectual that aim was if confined to the scale of the single architectural object. If the former are composition, the latter are montage, and the Palace of the Soviets is eloquent evidence for this point. But the technique of montage was deduced directly from the city read as a coacervation of fragments. . . .[16 Ibid., 143.]

The earlier work, the individual buildings, attempted a resolution of the crisis; the new and immense structures look to allegorically keep faith with that crisis by incorporating its logic of multiplicity. (We will see in a moment why these efforts too must be failures – already the Soviet allusion suggests that without state power the projects remain purely utopian.) Walter Gropius and the Bauhaus offered another direction, while giving rise to a tension between expressionism and engineering on the one hand, and between modular or prefabricated architecture and individual artistic creativity on the other.

It is worth anticipating the evolution of these stories, whose denouements certainly provide a kind of judgment on the achievements themselves. The professionalism of Gropius after his departure from Germany is well-known, and constitutes an abandonment of the architectural struggle itself (at least as it is conceived by Tafuri and Dal Co). The case of Le Corbusier, though, is more interesting. In this later period, Le Corbusier's work becomes Corbusian – the famous "International Style" – which is to say that his creative practices harden over into a kind of ideology (just as, alternatively, the experiments of the various avant-gardes also congeal into a kind of international avant-garde ideology in their own right).[17 Ibid., 250.] This is the work of the codification of Le Corbusier's lesson to CIAM, and indeed, in a kind of conceptual climax, CIAM will be characterized as *ideological*: given the relatively early use of the word *modern* in its title ("Congrès Internationaux d'Architecture Moderne," founded in 1928), it can be credited as one of the most influential sources for the ideology of "modernism" in general. "To it probably belongs the credit for having founded a large measure of the predominant ideology of modern architecture, endowing architects with a model of action as flexible as it was already out of date."[18 Ibid., 247.] (Nor should the relationship with such ideology-producing texts as Henry-Russell Hitchcock and Philip Johnson's *International Style* be overlooked.)

It is the reason for this characterization that interests us for the moment:

The approach of the CIAM reflects all the limits of radical architectural thought: the absolute continuity postulated between production in series and construction of the city expressed a utopian conviction. In flatly mechanistic fashion it applied to the entire urban scale the system of design and production applicable to the small scale of the private dwelling. . . . The CIAM discussions made it seem almost as if the nature of the city was thought to be identical with that of the architecture it contained, so that once control over the modes of formation and production of the buildings that made up the city was assured, one would also have the key to planning its entire development.[19] Ibid., 246.

This is to say that in order for a "solution" to qualify from the outset on either the level of urban planning or on that of the individual building, the incompatibility of the two levels must be registered from the outset, and acknowledged and even lived with the appropriate degree of anxiety (still a basic experience for Tafuri and Dal Co and a kind of test of authenticity).

We must now set in place one of the two narrative climaxes of this long story in the work of Ludwig Mies van der Rohe. Following the logic implicit in the discussion of Le Corbusier, we can suggest that the extraordinary valorization of Mies in this book is a tribute to the way in which, according to its authors, he more than any other modern architect kept faith with the contradiction itself. His resolution of it was to embrace it, to manifest and articulate it at its most unresolvable, to practice "composition as the expression of insoluble dichotomies."[20] Ibid., 152. It is the apotheosis of failure, and the very essence of that icy nihilism of glass that we earlier heard celebrated in different ways. "Where the Neue Sachlichkeit ended by codifying the style of the new 'tattooed city,' Mies built silence."[21] Ibid., 153. The glass surfaces of his buildings are analogous to Kurt Schwitters' *Merzbau* in that they accumulate the reflections of all the junk and detritus of the city, but "in the neutral mirror that breaks the city's web. In this, architecture arrives at the ultimate limits of its own possibilities. Like the last notes sounded by the *Doctor Faustus* of Thomas Mann, alienation, having become absolute, testifies uniquely to its own presence, separating itself from the world to declare the world's incurable malady."[22] Ibid., 342. Despite the allusions to Stéphane Mallarmé, the evocation of this particular negative aesthetic utopia resembles nothing quite so much as Roland Barthes's "écriture blanche," white, or bleached, writing.

But this is only one of the book's climaxes: in fact, it has two, just as the fundamental contradiction it explores has two poles. If Mies dramatizes the kind of negative solution available in the pole of the individual building, we have yet to see what is possible at its other pole, that of the city itself. Here, it would seem, a different combination of success and failure is available. In the first place, from the Werkbund on, the utopian speculations about essentially middle-class garden cities and satellite cities gets inflected in the direction of industrial building on the one hand, and housing for factory workers on the other. It is not until the postwar period that the ideal of the Siedlung – a worker's housing block within the city itself – becomes an active preoccupation of architects and planners in both Austria and Weimer Germany. The result – what can be called enclave architecture – is, in the second place, made possible only because leftist, mostly social democratic parties are in power in the cities and provinces in question and support the new projects.

Although Frankfurt is a crucial site for such experiments (under the leadership of Ernst May), the authors reserve their most enthusiastic encomia for developments in Vienna, where "the new projects rose like pugnacious islands proclaiming themselves proletarian monuments of very different dimensions and form from the architecture of 19th-century Vienna surrounding them."[23] Ibid., 192. They continue:

The Red strongholds had their peak in the Karl-Marx-Hof, designed in 1927 by Karl Ehn, author of other significant working-class projects such as the Bebelhof. Stretching more than five-eighths of a mile and covering just under 190,000 square yards, for 1,382 habitations plus nurseries, collective laundries, a library, offices, shops, an out-patients' clinic, and green areas, the Karl-Marx-Hof is the most "epical" of the Viennese superblocks. The huge arches opening in its massive buildings, the articulation of its masses, and the emphasis on simple volumes, make it, as it were, an individual, a symbolic unity pridefully counterposed to the urban context. One cannot help thinking that the essence of the great bourgeois novel is the drama that counterposes the positive hero to society. What Ehn created can be thought of as the greatest novel-in-architecture of European urbanistic culture between the two wars. . . . In the work of Ehn lives the ultimate "utopia of the semantic," lost in the tragic affirmation of the socialist humanity that opposes the annulment of *Kultur* and its traditions. Here we truly have Socialist Realism, here the myth of the totality of the new man promulgated by Lukács is completely accepted. The myths of the bourgeoisie shaped the most complete "Magic Mountain" of Austrian Marxism.[24] Ibid., 192–93.

Great realism, socialist realism, versus Mallarmé: the semantic fullness of content as opposed to the nihilistic void of all meaning. The twin climaxes of *Modern Architecture* thus stand in complementarity to each other as positive to negative, the concrete realization of the urban as opposed to the radical empty cipher at its center. Mies fulfills the destiny of the individual building, the Karl-Marx-Hof signifies that of the modern industrial city. Being versus nothingness: the allegory of the fulfilled totality, the allegory of its absolute negation.

However, it is important to understand that the Siedlungen are not more successful – I am tempted to say, in an ontological sense – than Mies's glassy voids. It is a failure that goes well beyond the empirical destiny of these projects. First, the Great Depression suddenly deprives the municipalities of the finances with which they could be funded; and second, and not unrelated, the coming of power of Nazism in Germany and later on the Anschluss spell more than an end to such workers' "monuments."

The deeper, and as it were, ontological contradiction lies elsewhere. To the degree to which the Siedlungen are successful as projects; in other words, to that very degree to which they afford housing of real architectural quality, along with the whole panoply of urban services (including proximity to the work place) – to that very degree they become attractive to middle-class dwellers. Their prices then go up along with the value of the land and its rate of taxation, and the Siedlung in question ceases, owing not to its failure but to its very success, to be a solution to the problem of workers' or low-cost housing. The Sartrean paradoxes seem relevant here: if Mies's void can strike one as a kind of exemplification of the slogan "loser wins," then the Siedlungen dramatically articulate the meaning of "winner loses."

There is another way of describing all this, and it is, in keeping with our topic, an allegorical one. The Siedlungen attempted to create the conditions of a revolutionary transformation of society within the carefully controlled limits of a closed enclave. That is to say, the enclave stood as an allegory of revolutionary society as a whole, just as socialism in one country offered the allegory of a socialist construction on a world scale. But in the long run, the enclave purporting to represent a radically different mode of production cannot be tolerated within a given system, whose laws and dynamic seep through the barriers and gradually assimilate it back into the larger context. Here, then, the allegory ends up undoing itself, and from an act that symbolically resolves the fundamental contradiction between the building and the city, it turns back into an act that offers a merely symbolic resolution, leaving the contradiction itself intact and indeed more virulent in its operation and effects than it was before.

These two points, at which we end the narrative of the Tafuri and Dal Co history, are narrative endings which fail to bring closure either to the architectural and urban dilemmas they grapple with or to history itself. Can one say, in that sense, that they constitute elements of a kind of reflexive narrative that foregrounds the very category of the ending itself, as well as the very possibility of the resolution of a contradiction? I have hoped here to argue something more modest: not merely the usefulness of the conceptual structure of allegory for architectural criticism, but also the way in which the very appeal to that structure forces the critic out beyond the static bounds of metaphor and symbol and into a process whereby it becomes necessary to construct a whole history in order for the allegory to become operative. And also to reconstruct a fundamental contradiction in terms of which building, style, structure, plan, project, acquire their meaning and are able to be read, in Clark's words, "as standing for something besides themselves."

Now it is time to turn from the modern to the postmodern period. I hope it is clear that the contradiction around which Tafuri and Dal Co organize their history – between the individual building as an aesthetic creation and the city as an anarchy of forces and styles – was an intractable one. None of their architects or planners were able to solve it; nor, in a certain sense, could it ever be solved, for all kinds of very different philosophical, empirical, and political reasons. I now want to suggest that in the postmodern period, a time of nascent globalization, this contradiction no longer exists as such: not because in the intervening break it has somehow miraculously been resolved, but rather because the two terms have been modified beyond recognition. In other words, the city in the form it took in the modernist period, with all its impending crises of various kinds, no longer exists; and the building as a locus of artistic and functional possibilities no longer exists either. This does not mean that the "crisis" no longer exists. (I am sure that everybody will agree that things are far worse today than in the period in which Le Corbusier reflected on the future and the destiny of the city; only it may not be right to use the word *crisis* for this new state of things.) Perhaps I can put this in a different way by suggesting that the logic of the crisis presupposes an order that has been thrown into instability for a longer or shorter period of time, if not indefinitely. But supposing one confronts a permanent instability, a permanent chaos, from which a kind of order briefly emerges, only to vanish again. Can that still be called a crisis?

The notion of a contradiction presupposes that you can articulate a troubled or conflictual situation; that you can posit oppositions and force fields within it such that it becomes unthinkable, even if you are unable to resolve it. I am suggesting that today we are closer to an antinomy than a contradiction, since within it even those conflictual oppositions our historians posited for the modern period are no longer detectable in that form. I want to argue that the notion of the contradiction offered the hope of a solution, even when it might have seemed utopian or fantastic; and that this was owing to the very structure of the contradiction itself, for when you have two opposing terms, it becomes irresistible to speculate on possible mediations or syntheses between them. (On some level, of course, I am repeating current doxa about the disappearance of utopias and the waning of the political in our time.) Still, the narrative of Tafuri and Dal Co reminds us that the modernist situation not only provided the space for the elaboration of utopias alongside this or that pragmatic, yet nondialectical program, but that it also suggested that another ultimate form of dialectical authenticity lay, as in the case of Mies, with a lucid and implacable commitment to the contradiction itself, beyond any hope of solution or resolution. "Like its object, thought remains shackled to the determinate contradiction," said Adorno.[25] Theodor Adorno, *Philosophy of Modern Music*, trans. Anne G. Mitchell and Wesley V. Blomster (New York: Seabury Press, 1973), [28]. This possibility, I believe, has also disappeared from the scene in this age of postmodernity.

Let me now, though, outline the reasons for the disappearance both of the classical building and the classical city. These reasons lie deeply embedded in the logic of globalization itself. In the third world, one of the poisoned gifts of the new late stage of capitalism has been the Green Revolution, which destroyed the older peasant mode of agriculture with hybrids and chemical fertilizers (not to mention current genetic experimentation), and set those peasant countries on the path to the ratios of the advanced countries, in which on the whole no more than seven percent of the population is still engaged in agricultural pursuits. The mass of unemployed peasants then moved, in desperation, to the cities, where staggering demographies now defy every political solution or form of urban planning. Oddly, there is a structural resemblance of these enormous agglomerations with the equally desperate structures of the first world, whose problems are in effect caused from the other end of the social spectrum, and in particular by the upper-class strategies of gentrification and land speculation, which have driven the poor and the unemployed out of the cities into peripheral areas. The fiscal crisis of the Western cities (as it is so often described) merely underscores the fundamental point I want to make here: namely, that in our time the city's problems cannot be solved by any properly urban mechanisms, and that therefore older modernist visions of planning, zoning, immanent urban solutions of all kinds, are no longer thinkable. This does not mean that the dilemmas of the postmodern city can be solved by extra-urban means or by the state itself: probably they cannot be solved at all. But the older modernist urbanisms are no longer on the cards, which is to say that even the concept and image of the city that used to be available in the modernist period is no longer present. There is no such thing now as what used to be designated by that word city; true postmodernity would probably mean being able to invent a new one. In any case, I trust that the relationship between globalization and this dissolution of the urban has also become clear: the Green Revolution as a worldwide capitalist development on the one hand, and the land spec-

ulation that has accompanied the new global finance industry on the other.

I also want to dispel certain thoughts of celebrating globalization under the rubric of some new contradiction of the local and the global, or through some conflict between the old-fashioned state and decentralization on a political, as well as social, basis. Saskia Sassen has pointed out in *Globalization and its Discontents* that the finance industry must very definitely occupy crucial centers, even if the relationship of those world centers to the individual cities in which they are housed is problematic, at least for the categories of the modern. Once upon a time the local and the regional had to do with nature, that is to say, with older agricultural modes: the local in the older sense has disappeared along with them, leaving in its place so many tourist images for the delectation of a now worldwide society of the spectacle. To oppose non-Western to Western values is to be taken in by old culturalist ideologies and the propaganda of contemporary religious (which is to say, fundamentalist) movements. The world today is standardized and at least tendentially postmodernized. What were formerly "non-Western cultures" are merely the ingredients of an immense image hybridity, it being understood that there is no "Western" culture either, and that global modernity is neither Western nor non-Western.

In terms of the state today, and of the other pole of the former contradiction – the individual building – I want for the moment only to quote a remark made in conversation by Peter Eisenman: "You could build the most remarkable building in the middle of Tokyo and no one would pay any attention." I do not know whether architects build private homes any longer today (they would need, like Rem Koolhaas's villa in Bordeaux, to have unique specifications in order to generate some kind of symbolic value), but one has the impression that innovation in office buildings – if any are still needed – is today simply a matter of greater and greater height. So only museums are left, which already have some purely lateral or marginal relationship to the city fabric: black holes of the past into which the new urban crowds eagerly implode, as Jean Baudrillard remarked a number of years ago.

But first, I want to see whether we can find any equivalent today for the purity of the Miesian contradiction. Such an equivalent would then necessarily have to be radically impure and welcoming of chaos as enthusiastically as Mies's glass repels it. I believe that, alone among the architects who have come after modernism, Koolhaas has succeeded in providing a program for what Robert Venturi and Denise Scott Brown only described as a situation. I should also add that at this point Koolhaas offers the image of the first truly global architect, the first true architect of globalization: not because he builds buildings all over the world (lots of great architects do that) but because, as in his Pearl River Delta project, he eagerly seeks out urban and architectural difference, not for culturalist or pluralist-humanist reasons, but because such fresh collisions "cause epidemics. . . . Globalization destabilizes and redefines both the way architecture is produced and that which architecture produces."[26] Rem Koolhaas, *S,M,L,XL* (New York: Monacelli Press, 1995), 367. For Koolhaas, whose experience thus ranges from Japan to Los Angeles, from China to the former Berlin Wall, from Singapore to Atlanta, globalization brings "the return of Babel," whose exhilarating program establishes "an infrastructural project to *change the world*, its aim montage of *maximum possibility* collected from any point, lifted from any context, pilfered from any ideology. It promises the final installment of the Promethean soap opera."[27] Ibid., 367–68.

Koolhaas's culture of congestion, to return to that as illustrated in *Delirious New York*, marks a first articulation of a new, postmodern, truly globalized approach to chaos and demography. It asks us to revel in the new situation and to affirm it in such a way as to derive enthusiasm and energy from it. From the labyrinth that is *S,M,L,XL* (an extraordinary, spatial book that could have gone a long way toward helping print culture overcome the CD-ROM had it not compromised itself by agreeing to number its pages) I want to quote a characteristic passage, about the Forum des Halles in Paris:

> Here an entire urban region is now a seamless, almost Babylonian amalgam of destruction, kitsch resurrection, authentic historical particles, a delirium of infrastructures, a mass grave of both good and bad intentions that crawl out of the pit like the rejected species of an alternative evolution. . . .
>
> What about the culmination of La Défense, where all the geometric rigor of a city collapses in a maelstrom of randomness and incoherence, made more pathetic by the profusion of roads, ramps and other "connections" that resemble a wind-tunnel test accidentally executed in concrete? Yet it mysteriously works or, at least, is *full of people*.[28] Ibid., 205.

"Full of people." This is the crux of the Koolhaas aesthetic. His immense megastructures are planned not to channel or organize city crowds but to augment and magnify them, to increase the chaos: to let it happen, if one can imagine reading this expression as the sign of an active rather than a passive operation. So it is clear that what used to be negative in the older modernist era has now become positive in the era of globalization, and marks the place of the first affirmation of Koolhaas's part. Yet so far, there does not seem to be any opposition at work here; even allowing for the obsolescence of contradiction, an antinomy also demands some kind of

binary tension: with what kind of term does congestion seem incompatible and somehow irreconcilable?

I believe that it is to be found in the image of the act of leveling, bulldozing, clearing away, flattening out: the true gestural equivalent of the end of nature in which the tabula rasa of late capitalism, and its speculators and developers, finds its active embodiment. The razing of all the qualities of the former "site" offers all the exhilaration of a new kind of reduction: something one senses in Koolhaas's celebration of the American "typical plan," and in his manifesto for an abstract "generic city" as the emergent form of the new globalized world. For the logic of the tabula rasa was already evident in Koolhaas's seemingly perverse celebration of the so-called "Typical Plan," by which he means the standard engineering layout reproduced throughout "nonsignature" engineering – constructed office buildings across the United States.

> It is zero-degree architecture, architecture stripped of all traces of uniqueness and specificity. It belongs to the New World. The notion of the typical plan is therapeutic; it is the End of Architectural History, which is nothing but the hysterical fetishization of the atypical plan. Typical Plan is a segment of an unacknowledged utopia, the promise of a post-architectural future. Just as *The Man Without Qualities* haunts European literature, "the plan without qualities" is the great quest of American building.[29] Ibid., 335–36.

His evocation of Singapore, however, is even more vivid. Singapore is unique in being a one-time-only combination of late-capitalist anarchy and communist planning and regimentation. As Koolhaas puts it, it "installs a condition of permanent instability, not unlike the 'permanent revolution' proclaimed by the students of May '68":

> The new republic's blueprint, its dystopian program [becomes]: *displace, destroy, replace*. In a delirium of transformation the island is turned into a petri dish: gigantic clearances, levelings, extensions, expropriations create laboratory conditions for the importation of social and architectural cultures that can be grown under experimental protocols, without the presence of anterior substance. Singapore is turned into a test bed of tabula rasa. The transformation of the *entire* island in the name of an apocalyptic demographic hypothesis is in apparent contrast to its smallness and its permanent land shortage. . . . A regime like the one in power in Singapore is a radical movement: it has transformed the term *urban renewal* into the moral equivalent of war.[30] Ibid., 1035.

I want now to turn to the status of the individual building in our newly globalized and modernized era, and for this I want to examine the work of Peter Eisenman, and in particular his Aronoff Center at the University of Cincinnati, surely one of the most extraordinary buildings of the last decade. I see it in terms of a phenomenon that has lately been a matter of fascination for me: namely, the way in which a building that does not and cannot fit into the city fabric is capable not merely of separating itself out and turning away from that fabric altogether, but at one and the same time of replicating that entire city fabric within itself, becoming itself a miniature city and a microcosm of its external context. Remember that Mies's buildings remained events within the city: even if they constituted black holes or an icy void at its center. Nonetheless, they did something to it. For Tafuri, in much the same fashion, the skyscraper is considered a kind of unique event within the metropolis: a strike, an interruption, a sudden touch-down, which is necessarily made to comment on the city and to emit a message about it.

The kind of building I am thinking of will no longer be an event inside the city, it will no longer comment, its exterior will neither allude nor repel. This will be something paradoxical enough to say about a very large form disposed across a hill on the order of Marcel Duchamp's *Nude Descending a Staircase*, or better still (Eisenman's own image, and the alleged inspiration of Aronoff in the first place), the interlocking of those conveyor-belt plates that move your baggage out along the airport display ramp. But perhaps Aronoff's parasitic relationship to the remnants of the two already existing structures it so unexpectedly "completes" and incorporates can be thought to be some kind of protective concealment from the logic of the urban fabric outside it.

What I want to stress here, however, is the way in which the interior of the building, through which hundreds of students stream every day, offers a unique and somehow self-contained experience: the way in which it substitutes for the city, which in its disaggregation today can no longer offer the classical spatial-urban pleasures. It is useful to contrast this temporal experience with the one Le Corbusier so carefully planned out in advance for his visitors at the Villa La Roche:

> This house . . . will be rather like an architectural promenade. One enters, and the architectural vista presents itself immediately to view; one follows a set route, and a great variety of perspectives present themselves: there is a play of light, highlighting the walls or casting shadows. Bays open onto perspectives of the exterior, and one rediscovers architectural unity.
> 31 Le Corbusier, *Oeuvres Complètes*, vol. 1, 1910–1929, ed. Willy Boesiger (Zurich: Editions Girsberger, 1929), 60.

"One follows a set route": what intervenes between this dictate of the modernist demiurgic act and the aleatory pathways of the Eisenman center is not only an aesthetic of chance but, above all, the computer. Eisenman delights in those computer-generated variants of space in his building, which he himself could not consciously have planned or predicted. Far from a new or neoclassical sense of order, it is a chaos, indeed a Koolhaasian "culture of congestion," that is simulated within this miniature city – this mimesis not of a traditional city center but of an underground post-world war III warren of corridors and ancillary spaces of all shapes and kinds. Pedestrian bridges and misplaced monumental staircases trace out a kind of miniature indoor Venice, whose *campos* surge without warning out of artificial alleyways and stairwells, down upon which the windows of offices gaze. The equally aleatory multiplication of vistas and points of view, perspectives and gazes, projects some new role for sight in these spaces of urban futurity, a free-floating sight and visibility abstracted from the familiar humanist supports. If the skyscraper remains the emblem of a heroic modernism, perhaps just such underground cities can lend their image and their concept to the styles and production of a globalized future.

But the two "poles" of our present opposition – congestion on the tabula rasa of a bulldozed surface, congestion in movement underground – do not seem to add up to a contradiction in the modernist sense. So their problem, whatever it is, cannot yet be solved. Perhaps the utopian approach today is not the older modernist one of projecting a possible solution to an impossible contradiction but rather one of reconstructing the problem and the contradiction itself in the first place.

THE LONE-
LINESS OF
THE LONG
DISTANT
FUTURE

ROMI
KHOSLA

I want to address two areas from "the rest of the world" through the design of two pro-posals, both of which form spaces and situations that perhaps are a little difficult to understand from our position here in the West. By the rest of the world, I mean, of course, those parts of the globe which cannot reach that plateau where the passing of history has ended and a sense of prosperity, peace, and superiority seems to exist as the norm.

The impact of the global free-market economy and the terrible threat of modern war technologies have recently destroyed futures in both Kosovo and Jerusalem. Both are places from the rest of the world, where 100 million people have been thrown into poverty over the last ten years. Under economic, social, and political conditions far worse than in the 1930s, both places have sought shelter in a past that is simultaneously being quickly reinvented. Both the Kosovars and the Palestinians feel that they have lost their identity and freedom, and hence are suspicious of exponents of the modern world.

At the Anytime conference in Ankara, I spoke about abstract and ancient futures and the extent to which this polarization was beginning to influence architectural ideas across those parts of the globe where ancient futures are being offered as the only viable alternative to the modern world. I argued that in many parts of the world, to be modern is increasingly regarded as synonymous with a transatlantic corporate culture – in terms of dress, music, food, and language – and something to be avoided and fought against at all costs. I have continued to work on this idea, more or less on my own, par-ticularly while spending time in Jerusalem and Kosovo. Until recently, land in both places has been appropriated or destroyed by modern weapons originating in the arse-nals of the West, as well as in the garage sales that the erstwhile Soviet republics have been holding to bolster state finances. In Kosovo and in Israel the joysticks of destruc-tion are modern, while the rhetoric of reconstruction is traditional, ancient, and often religious. With every calamitous outbreak, it is always architecture that is destroyed, and the search for solutions is inevitably monopolized by the military.

My proposals, then, are part of an effort to argue that solutions for reconstruction can be articulated through an architecture that is contemporary and modern; that new civic and secular spaces need not be contested in the same way that religious space is inevitably fought over; that new spaces can be created that are contemporary and relate to futures beyond the ancient; that new types of housing can be built on the foundations of those traditional houses that the bombs and bulldozers have flattened.

My own perceptions of the new millennium are based on certain assumptions about the emergence of a new global society, or world order, or whatever else one may like to call it. This new order is demolishing the institutions of previous international struc-tures, which were formed in the last century to regulate political and financial affairs,

and replacing them with alternative constructs that seem to advocate pressurized reconciliation backed by the threat of force. If we assume that the need to demolish those institutions is because they now appear outdated and irrelevant and did not deliver a promised utopia, then let us agree that the constructs that are being offered as replacements look to create a global society full of new humanism, freedom, and democracy. The old, now discarded idea of utopia was critical to the formation of new architectural ideas in the early part of the 20th century. Indeed, utopia was to a certain extent given form by that new architecture. My proposals, then, are a sort of heroic attempt at exploring some ideas about how architecture could respond to the newly emerging reality in the absence of a utopian agenda.

Beginning on March 21, 1999, the United States-led NATO forces launched cruise missile and bomb attacks at targets across the Federal Republic of Yugoslavia. Within 78 days, as a consequence of the retaliations to this attack, large parts of Kosovo were bombed and bulldozed into rubble. Half of the housing stock was destroyed, the electrical infrastructure was devastated, and the agricultural system seriously damaged. I was sent to Kosovo by the United Nations to propose a national housing reconstruction strategy. The architectural proposal focuses on a site in the village of Chabra, where not a single house was left standing. The only affordable and available building material was the rubble of former structures, so for the reconstruction project, this rubble was packed into metal gabions to form the walls of the new houses, emblematically combining the reality and metaphors of the crisis there. In addition to the walls, the only other elements of the new houses in Chabra are a series of solar panels donated to provide electricity, and a green house for growing essential foods during the snows of winter.

At the site of my second proposal, Jerusalem, it became clear to me that there are, in many ways, two cities. The old city, enclosed within ancient walls, belongs to the Arabs, while the new Jerusalem belongs to the Israelis. Between the two cities lies a blurred space – a buffer zone – in which both communities hesitate to implement radical change. If either of them actually initiated anything, a riot would ensue, because such movement would cause a shift in the imagined lines of control, with one of the two contenders emerging as victorious claimant to the whole of Jerusalem. The Ottoman walls neatly define the boundaries of old Jerusalem. The new Jerusalem is well-settled around a new city center full of boutiques and extending into endless suburbs that are constantly expanding as the Jewish population grows larger than the Arab one within the city limits.

The site for the proposal is in the "fuzzy" zone. Within the buffer between the two cities lies a square-shaped site that separates the tense outer edges of the old and the new cities and is currently used as a car park. New Jerusalem is a macro city of literati where

Rubble in Kosovo (above); metal gabions in Chabra, Kosovo.

the civic order of Zion has been codified into a series of written rules and regulations. Inevitably, as in all macro urban cultures, these rules resist the pressures of emergent, ever-changing relationships and initiatives arising from the collaborations and negotiations of citizens interacting and adjusting to each other. These actively enforced municipal regulations resist the dynamics that convert folk cultures into urban civilizations. The Arab city, on the other hand, is the Meso city of intellectuals, of spoken cultures – a city that is reluctant to codify its civic order into written rules and regulations.[1] **Meso** is derived from the Greek word **mesos**, meaning "middle." I have coined the term **Meso city** to signify a city of temporary stability, mediating its spaces and forms between the pressures of the micro world of citizens and the macro city world of civic order, written rules and regulations, and the imposition of state law on the city's regulatory orders. Here the community meshes its activities not along functional regulations but on the basis of a permissiveness bordering on the turbulence of a moving stream; where tolerance and acceptability of the ensuing chaos is almost an asset to use and exploit in new ways. As the unfortunate jewel that has to be shared between Muslims, Jews, and Christians, the old city becomes the battleground where the orthodox in each community fight for it to become their own.

The project proposes Jerusalem as one of ten stations strung along a new rail link, stretching from Haifa to Nazareth, Jenin, Nablus, Ramallah, Jerusalem, Bethlehem, Beersheba, and Gaza. The train moves across the physical and ideological barriers that both sides have imposed. It is about connectivity of the economy and its people, and about new markets and choices. It is a train for commuters and for goods and services. Equally significantly, the railbed forms a new nationwide water carrier that will be able to bring water from the desalination plants of Haifa, the Sea of Galilee, and the aquifers under the West Bank in Palestine to be distributed to the dry agricultural terraces of the West Bank and the deserts of the Negev in Israel. Both the track and the water carrier are integrated. The train rides, so to speak, on the tube carrying the water. Each of the ten stations on the route provides a civic concourse for economic and social exchange.

The Jerusalem station represents a kind of celebratory architecture that could provide alternative humane solutions to the hastily sketched military response to a divided city. The conditions leading up to the proposals for this Jerusalem station are described in my new book, which explains more fully the context of the proposal.[2] Romi Khosla, **The Loneliness of the Long Distant Future** (New Delhi: Tulika Press, 2000). This content is based on my own refusal to accept the viability of a separate Palestine and Israel. Instead, my proposal assumes the gradual integration of both these parts as the only viable alternative to the disastrous consequence of setting up two conflicting lilliputian nations.

Given conditions today, however, one may understand why I call this paper "The Loneliness of the Long Distant Future."

Temporary tents in Chabra, Kosovo.

New Jerusalem and old Jerusalem (below).

SCALE AND SPAN IN A GLOBAL DIGITAL WORLD

SASKIA SASSEN

I want to discuss the questions of scale and span under conditions of digitalization and globalization. In her introduction to the Anything conference, Cynthia Davidson cited William Gibson's comment that the impact of the digital might well be to eliminate and neutralize everything that architecture has historically represented.[1] In parallel to what Gibson anticipated in 1991, today we read and hear a lot of comment and analyses arguing that the impact of the digital on cities will be to neutralize what cities have traditionally represented. In abstract terms, one could see this representation as centrality — a centrality dependent upon and influenced by different cultures, different places, different times, and different articulations of urban space.[2]

My effort here is to examine the impact of digitalization and globalization on the architectural, the urban, and the city in a way that resists the dominant interpretations, which posit that digitalization (and to a large extent, globalization, as in electronic markets) entails an absolute disembedding from the material world. With this type of interpretation comes, then, the neutralization of such conditions as the architectural and the urban — not in general terms, however, but as conditions that are produced, articulated, and inflected by crucial instantiations of the embeddedness of the digital. Mine is a particular kind of reading of digitalization: it seeks to detect the imbrications of the digital and nondigital domains and thereby to insert the condition of the architectural and urban in mappings, both actual and rhetorical, from which this digitalization can be easily excluded.[3] I use notions of *scale* and *span* (or *scope*) to capture the precise locations of this insertion. The risk in this type of effort, it seems to me, lies in generalizing, in using metaphors and figurative language — in brief, to hover above it all. Rather, we need to go digging.

The difficulty that analysts and commentators have had in understanding the impact of digitalization on cities and architecture — indeed, on multiple configurations — essentially is the result of two analytic flaws. The first (and this is especially evident in the United States) restricts interpretation to a technological reading of the capacities of digital technology. This would be the required and proper reading for engineers, but if one is trying to understand the impact of a technology, such a reading becomes problematic. The difficulty is that a purely technological reading inevitably leads one to a place that is a nonplace, where one announces with absolute certainty the neutralization of many of those configurations marked by physicality and place-boundedness, including architecture and the urban.[4] The second flaw, I would argue, is a continuing reliance on analytical categorizations that were developed under other spatial and historical conditions — that is, conditions preceding the current digital era. Thus the tendency is to conceive of the digital as simply and exclusively digital, and the nondigital, whether represented in terms of the material or the actual (both conceptions are equally problematic), as simply and exclusively that, nondigital. These either/or categorizations filter out alternative conceptualizations, thereby precluding a more complex reading of the impact of digitalization on material and placebound conditions.

One such alternative categorization captures these imbrications. Let me illustrate this through the case of finance. This is certainly a highly digitalized activity, yet it cannot simply be considered exclusively digital. To have electronic financial markets and digitalized financial instruments requires enormous amounts of matériel, not to mention human talent (which has its own type of physicality). This matériel includes conventional infrastructure, buildings, airports, and so on. Much of this matériel is, then, inflected by the digital. Conversely, much of what takes place in cyberspace is deeply inflected by the cultures, material practices, and imaginations that take place outside cyberspace. Much, though not all, of what we think of as cyberspace would lack any meaning or referents if we were to exclude the world outside cyberspace. In brief, therefore, digital space and digitalization are not exclusive conditions that stand beyond the nondigital. Digital space is embedded in the larger societal, cultural,

1 "While the advent of nanotechnology promises to render architecture a dead technology, something akin to its traditional practice already flourishes in the virtual landscape of the computer. Our century's only crucial architectures are structures of information. The microchip is a cathedral. A library is something on the other end of a modem. The Postmodern, in retrospect, will seem a breathing space prior to the advent of the Posthuman." William Gibson, "Letter to Anyone," in *Anyone*, ed. Cynthia C. Davidson (New York: Rizzoli, 1991), 264.

2 The variety of dynamics that I am describing are all located on edges, borders, and frontier zones. As a researcher, I find these thresholds particularly interesting because it is precisely at the points of transaction between new and old spatial modes that all kinds of things appear to happen. This has a whole series of implications for very specialized research agendas in several fields, as well as for the city itself.

3 For a development of some of these ideas see "Digital Networks and Power" in ed. M. Featherstone and S. Lash, *Spaces of Culture: City, Nation, World* (London: Sage, 1999); and *ANY* 19/20: "The Virtual House," 1997.

4 Another consequence of this type of reading is to assume that a new technology will inevitably replace all older technologies that are less efficient, or slower, at executing those tasks that the new technology is best at. We know that inevitable replacement is historically not the case.

subjective, economic, and imaginary structurations of lived experience and the systems within which we exist and operate.

So in terms of the impact of the digital on architecture, on urbanism, and on the city, yes, there has been a profound transformation, but it is one not necessarily marked by the neutralization of capital fixity or of the built environment or, in the end, of the city. Rather than being neutralized, these emerge with renewed and strategic importance in some of their features, that is to say, not as a generalized condition but as a very specific condition. A first impact, then, is a particular type of built environment – a conventional communication system, a city, in essence, a particular type of spatiality – that accommodates and furthers the new digital dynamics.

A second impact is the complex overlapping of the digital (as well as the global) and the nondigital, which brings with it a destabilizing of older hierarchies of scale and often dramatic rescalings. As the national scale loses significance, along with the loss of key components of the nation-state's formal authority over that scale, other measures gain strategic importance. Most especially among these are subnational scales, such as the global city, and supranational scales, such as global markets or regional trading zones. Older hierarchies of scale (emerging in the context of the ascendance of the nation-state) continue to operate, and are typically organized in terms of institutional scope: from the international, down to the national, the regional, the urban, and the local. Today's rescaling cuts across institutional scope and, through policies such as deregulation and privatization, negates the encasements of territory produced by the formation of national states. This does not mean that the old hierarchies disappear, but rather that rescalings emerge alongside the old ones, and that they can often trump the latter.[5]

5 I develop some of these issues in *Losing Control? Sovereignty in an Age of Globalization* (New York: Columbia University Press, 1996) and in the book I am currently working on, *De-Nationalization*.

These transformations, although resulting from digitalization and globalization, and continuing to entail complex imbrications of the digital and nondigital and between the global and the nonglobal, can be captured in a variety of instances. For example, much of what we might still experience as the "local" (an office building or a house or an institution right there in our neighborhood or downtown) is actually something I would rather think of as a "microenvironment with global span"

6 See Saskia Sassen, "Geographies and Countergeographies of Globalization" in *Anymore*, ed. Cynthia C. Davidson (Cambridge, Massachusetts: MIT Press, 2000), 110–19.

insofar as it is deeply internet-worked.[6] Such a microenvironment is in many senses a localized entity – something that can be experienced as local, immediate, proximate. It is a sited materiality. But it is also part of global digital networks, which lend it immediate far-flung span. To continue to think of this simply as local is not especially useful or adequate. More importantly, the juxtaposition between the condition of being a sited materiality and having global span captures the enfolding of the digital and nondigital and illustrates the inadequacy of a purely technological reading of the capacities of digitalization. This would lead us to posit the neutralization of the place-boundedness of that which precisely makes possible the condition of being an entity with global span.

A second example is the bundle of conditions and dynamics that marks the model of the global city. To single out one key dynamic: the more globalized and digitalized the operations of firms and markets, the more their central management and coordination functions (and the requisite material structures) become strategic. It is precisely because of digitalization that simultaneous worldwide dispersal of operations (whether factories, offices, or service outlets) and system integration can be achieved. And it is precisely this combination that raises the importance of central functions. Global cities are strategic sites for the combination of resources necessary for the production of these central functions.[7]

Conceptualizing digitalization and globalization along these lines creates operational and rhetorical openings for recognizing the ongoing importance of the material world, even in the case of some of the most dematerialized activities.

7 There are other dimensions that specify the global city; see the fully updated edition of my book *The Global City* (Princeton: Princeton University Press, 2001).

One could examine, for example, the digital through one of its most powerful capabilities: the dematerializing and liquefying of that which was material and/or hardly mobile. (I would also argue that this capability still contains a complex imbrication with the nondigital.) Digitalization brings with it an amplification of those capacities that make possible the liquefying of that which is not liquid. Thereby, digitalization raises the mobility of what we have customarily thought of as immobile, or barely mobile. At its most extreme, this liquefying dematerializes its object. Once dematerialized, it becomes hypermobile – instantaneous circulation through digital networks with global span. It is important to underline that the hypermobility gained by an object through dematerialization is but one moment of a more complex condition. Representing such an object as simply hypermobile is, then, a partial representation since it includes only some of the components of that object, i.e., those that can be dematerialized but achieve that condition as a function of what we could describe as highly specialized materialities. Much of what is liquefied and circulates in digital networks and is marked by hypermobility remains physical in some of its components.

Take, for example, the case of real estate. Financial services firms have developed instruments that liquefy real estate, thereby facilitating investment and circulation of these instruments in global markets. Yet, part of what constitutes real estate remains very physical. At the same time, however, that which remains physical has been transformed by the fact that it is represented by highly liquid instruments that can circulate in global markets. It may look the same, it may involve the same bricks and mortar, it may be new or old, but it is a transformed entity. We have difficulty capturing this multivalence through our conventional categories: if it is physical, it is physical; and if it is liquid, it is liquid. In fact, the partial representation of real estate through liquid financial instruments produces a complex intertwining of the material and the dematerialized moments of that which we continue to call real estate.

Hypermobility, or dematerialization, is usually seen as a mere function of the new technologies. This understanding obscures the fact that it takes multiple material conditions to achieve this outcome. Once we recognize that the hypermobility of the instrument, or the dematerialization of the actual piece of real estate, had to be *produced*, we introduce the overlapping of the material and the nonmaterial. It takes capital fixity to produce capital mobility, that is to say, state of the art built environments, conventional infrastructure – from highways to airports and railways – and well-housed talent. These are all at least partly place-bound conditions, even though the nature of their place-boundedness is going to be different from what it was 100 years ago, when it might

have been marked by immobility. Today it is a place-boundedness that is inflected and inscribed by the hypermobility of its components. Both capital fixity and mobility are located in a temporal frame where speed is ascendant and consequential. At the level of the material, speed alters such dynamics as obsolescence and the value of investment.[8]

For example, the new transnational professional class is hypermobile. We conduct ourselves as if we could download our bodies, but at any given moment, part of the task and part of what takes us around the globe have to do with things that are place-bound, and our interventions – which justify what we are, who we are, and why we are here or there – are also place-bound. So again, we are confronted with conventional categories that polarize: Is it hypermobile? Is it fixed? Is it place-bound? Is it mobile? All of these questions typically miss much of what is happening. One example that captures the essence of this polarization is the private digital network that MCI Worldcom has created, connecting 4,000 buildings in Europe with 27,000 buildings in the United States. By connecting these buildings – which are not just any buildings – this digital network creates a spatiality that in some ways is a local event. It is a microenvironment; it connects across the Atlantic a set of buildings that are scattered over two continental territories where the space itself becomes a kind of space for mobility that might as well be a microspace or a local space. The firms that are locating to those buildings are also paying premium rates. We have, then, a digitally connected space among select, very fixed entities.

A corollary to these microenvironments is the redefinition and reconfiguration of ideas of the center. The MCI Worldcom network spans a huge geographic distance, yet it is constructed as a space of centrality. The enormous agglomeration of

8 Much of my work on global cities has looked to conceptualize and document the fact that the global digital economy requires massive concentrations of material conditions in order to be what it is. Finance is an important intermediary in this regard; it represents a capability for liquefying various forms of nonliquid wealth and for raising the mobility (i.e., hypermobility) of that which is already liquid, a subject I developed in "Juxtaposed Temporalities: Producing a New Zone" in *Anytime*, ed. Cynthia C. Davidson (Cambridge, Massachusetts: MIT Press, 1999), 114–21.

buildings that physically characterizes this digital network, despite being manifest in all our major cities, cannot be read in the same ways that we looked at urban centers 20 or even ten years ago. A new urban history is being constructed, even though it is deeply embedded and almost camouflaged by the older social spatial historics within which it is taking place. For us to more fully understand the impact of the digital and of globalization, we need, therefore, to suspend the category "city." Rather, we need to construct a more abstract category of centrality and of spaces of centrality, that, ironically, could allow us to recover the city, albeit a recovery as just one instantiation within a much broader set of issues.[9]

If we begin to unpack the impact of the digital and of globalization through these kinds of questions, and not simply confine our analysis to the technical capacities of technologies, we can chart an enormously interesting conceptual map with which we can explore these issues. Through this mapping of globalization and digitalization, one can also see the extent to which we have existed in a consciousness deeply embedded in the idea of the national: territories, administration, identities, citizenship — all formed in national terms. One of the impacts of the rescaling described earlier is the removal of layers of institutional encasing "constructing" the national, and the freeing up subnational systems of circulation.

9 See Saskia Sassen, "Reconfiguring Centrality" in *Anywise*, ed. Cynthia C. Davidson (Cambridge, Massachusetts: MIT Press, 1996), 126–32.

The global city is precisely the synthesis of these two scales — the old and the new. It overrides and neutralizes older hierarchies of scale and functions as an enormously complex sited materiality with global span. In the era of globalization, the state also participates in the neutralization of these national encasings. The state, therefore, is not just a victim of globalization. It actively participates in producing laws that facilitate the partial denationalization of the global city, creating opportunities for foreign actors, foreign markets, foreign firms, and foreign cultural institutions to be operative in what was once constructed as the national. In this combination of elements, I would argue, lies a very different reading of the impact of the digital on architecture and the city. The direction in which it takes us could lead to a rich and complex agenda for research, theorization, and argument.

ARCHI-TECTURE AS INT-ERFACE

HANI RASHID

Today the art and science of architecture are being radically influenced and inflected by the advent of digital interfaces and the new spatial models they are spawning. The intersection of first reality (physical space) and virtual reality (digitally produced environments) has afforded our studio, Asymptote, the opportunity to operate in areas that have traditionally excluded architects and in situations that have not previously engaged the discipline of architecture. These new areas include information-data environments, Web-based spatial experiences, and "real-time" technologically enriched environments.

DATA, INFORMATION, AND PIXEL REAL ESTATE

In 1998 the New York Stock Exchange (NYSE) approached Asymptote with an intriguing project. As the NYSE had been developing a strategy for dealing with the ever-increasing complexity of managing their data, they wanted to develop a virtual environment that would facilitate the reading, correlating, and navigating of massive amounts of information. The NYSE determined that the complexity of the real-time information to be contended with on a daily basis required an innovative solution reliant on three-dimensional "visualization." As our design for the computer-simulated environment proceeded, it became apparent that there were indeed a number of architectural issues to deal with. Primarily one had to consider how to navigate through a realm comprised of data, which in turn instigated an approach where information would be fused with a virtual terrain or landscape through composition, form (tectonics), and movement.

The design of the Virtual Trading Floor began as a reinterpretation and transformation of the existing physical trading environment, in which the NYSE floor was idealized and refined for eventual virtual deployment. This was accomplished by developing a wireframe model that corresponded to the real trading floor layout and its constituent elements, along with their relative placement and physical location. The architectural idealization needed to provide absolute flexibility, particularly to accommodate the data feeds that would eventually be programmed into it. The modeling also had to provide for constant shifts in scale, enhanced levels of detail, and the insertion of numerous other kinetic virtual objects. This reconfiguration of the actual trading floor was necessary because of the technological demands placed on the model to function in real time, and the economy of form necessary to process and animate extremely large quantities of data. The project itself also posed an interesting opportunity to reconsider the trading floor's "reality," where our version of the trading floor, although virtual and not intended to be constructed outside of a computer environment, is effectively a direction for possible future trading environments. The Virtual Trading Floor is both a reflection of the existing environment as well as a provocation for a new physically augmented architecture. The objects and assemblies that constitute the Virtual Trading Floor include two facilities of computer servers and networks, news and data feeds, and almost limitless data mining capabilities. All of the information relevant to the NYSE and its daily activity of trades and transactions is mapped into this fully navigable, multidimensional world. Although the virtual reality environment was initially designed for the operation needs of the NYSE, the project has recently evolved to cater to other uses, including a large-scale Internet initiative and a television broadcasting environment. These mutations and elaborations of the project have further architectural implications as the virtual realm slowly usurps the real trading floor as a "place." The fact that the general public will soon be able to navigate a virtual trading floor, check stock news and valuations, make trades, and meander about at will, is unprecedented and begs the question, what actually constitutes architectural experience and presence? And for those who do inhabit and are familiar with the real trading floor, what new insights into their environment will be attained, and how might these alter one's understanding of what constitutes architecture?

New York Stock Exchange Virtual Trading Floor.

AN INTERNET MUSEUM

In 1999 Asymptote was commissioned, as part of the Solomon R. Guggenheim Foundation's architectural initiatives, to design a new museum. One unprecedented aspect of the prestigious commission was that the site for this new museum was to be located not in a city but rather within the Internet. The program brief itself was also innovative in that it described a museum dedicated to art that is digitally produced, displayed, and archived. Designing such a "structure" raised a number of intriguing issues, such as what constitutes an event in cyberspace, and what the opportunities and criteria are for such new architectural experiences. The visual language, for example, although borrowing from architecture in terms of tectonics and form, needed to respond to time-based experiences and the prospects of mutation and transformation. Although theoretically possible in actual building, the notion of mutability and flux had far more potential in a terrain constituted of pixels and binary code. The requisite that this museum could be visited by anyone, anywhere, and at any time was exciting and provocative. It presented an interesting opportunity not only to develop a new type of interface and event-space for the Internet but also for architectural possibility and exploration.

The Guggenheim Virtual Museum (GVM) is designed as an architectural entity to be delivered primarily to users over the Internet. The "museum body" itself is thought of as a mnemonic vessel, a catalogue that contains and provides access to the information stored within it. Moving, or more appropriately, navigating, through this museum was conceived more in terms of a meander through or across a territory than as a sequential experience of space by a prescribed path or any sort of click-through model. In opposition to such "page-based" environments, this architectural experience is predicated on the notion that, although a logical infrastructure is embedded in the site, the possibility for arbitrary discovery and association of content is important. Moving about these "spaces" involves certain architectural conventions while also drawing on filmic devices for transition, such as jump cuts, fades, morphs, and so on. The fusion of these "spatial" paradigms allowed the GVM to evolve as something closer to a landscape than an object, where apparent limits between interiority and exteriority are thrown into question. This rethinking of movement and time, which transforms the museum into an evolving and fluid entity, also enables an unconventional approach to the programming of such an entity. The galleries, archives, public areas, and even "external landmarks" are all derived from readings of "first reality" situations and artifacts, however, their use and occupancy is unlike that of any building experience. It is possible, for instance, to simultaneously visit a gallery and watch a media event at the Mediasphere, or "switch" instantaneously from one experience to another. The "circulation spaces," for example, are fluid and changing as their morphology and spatial characteristics are based upon the visitor's decisions with respect to certain preferences and choices. The exhibition spaces are not rooms per se but evolving entities that continually reconfigure according to certain criteria attributed to the selected artist's works. The Media-sphere, as another example, is an elusive, ever-changing entity that orbits throughout the virtual museum and constantly inhabits some other region or precinct arbitrarily. This museum is an architecture where the parameters of the Internet and its implicit condition of digital flux are tempered by new potentials for occupying a landscape of space-time and transforming events.

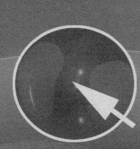

DEO ART / 1990-2000

THE FLUXSPACE PROJECTS

Recently Asymptote completed two installations in a series titled FluxSpace, one in San Francisco at the California College of Arts and Crafts Institute, and the other at the 2000 Venice Biennale. The two projects are full-scale built works using digital technologies in both their design and manifestation. The aim of FluxSpace is to blur the distinction between the virtual and the actual through an exploration of digitally augmented architectural constructs. FluxSpace 1.0, an installation whose size lies somewhere between that of a large model and a small building, was modeled in the computer and constructed using full-size computer-generated templates. The computer's ability to create a model with a high degree of accuracy and then to output it to exacting specifications afforded us the opportunity to create both a virtual object and a one-to-one scale constructed counterpart. An augmentation of the "architectural reality" of the installation was created by manipulating the wireframe assemblies and projecting these transformations onto the constructed objects in the gallery. These "images" were then triggered by embedded sensors sensitive to movement and proximity, which created the effect of a structure under a constant state of mutation and distortion in real-time and real-space. By approaching this built artifact or by passing a hand over its surface one stimulates the object to respond immediately by means of its electronic counterpart. A soundtrack derived from the same algorithmic structures that were being deployed to manipulate the form accompanies each physical transformation to complete the multidimensional experience.

Where FluxSpace 1.0 sought to create an architecture that responded to physical presence through a chance operation tied into a computer data feed, FluxSpace 2.0 sought to move the experiment in another direction, that of architecture as intermediary to an on-line or Web-based spatial experience. The project was somewhat larger than the San Francisco proposal, measuring 100 feet long and standing over two stories high on the grounds of the Venice Biennale. A computer-generated steel framework that dictated the configuration of the interior cavity supported a pneumatic envelope. Inside the structure, two large, rotating discs incorporating one-way mirrors measuring eight feet in diameter were located at two "focal" points at opposite ends of the space. At the center of each semireflective, semitransparent mirror, a 360-degree camera was housed to capture the ever-changing interior space and relay that information to the Internet. As these cameras recorded the interior condition of FluxSpace 2.0 at 30-second intervals for the duration of the five-month installation in Venice, more than 1.6 million different spatial configurations could be viewed and virtually occupied on the Web. What was experienced on the Web and in the actual space was a continually mutating spatiality. This double occupancy elicits a new understanding of architecture in a state of simultaneous virtuality and augmented reality. Virtual architectural environments as augmentations of physical space offer the opportunity for unique spatial experiences and challenge our definition and understanding of what constitutes "real" experience and "actual" space. The evolution of these fluid architectures will be interesting to follow as architects become less concerned with differentiating between physicality and virtuality, and increasingly explore beyond the conventional boundaries of spatial, formal, and aesthetic concerns to redefine what actually constitutes space, architecture, and event.

DISCUSSION 1

CATHERINE INGRAHAM To begin, I want to address some remarks to the panel. The first concerns architecture in relation to the issues of time and the economics of architectural equity – how, for example, the slow transfer of a building from parents to children, or from public to private, is tied to the transferability of that building from one use to another, throughout its history. This transfer presents interesting urban and architectural opportunities for intervention – there are moments in that transfer when everything can be resituated; and moments after everything has been blown to smithereens (here I'm thinking of Romi Khosla's work in Kosovo) when you can restart the process or rebuild conditions of equity again, bringing in external financial resources so as to engage in architectural acts that subsequently attract people.

This also has many parallels to what Saskia Sassen talked about in terms of trying to think through a different idea of centrality and the liminality of time and space. Equally, questions of time in this kind of economic condition of transferability pertain to Fred Jameson's presentation, with respect to what I might call a kind of method of oppositionality – the flexibility of historical contradiction that Fred spoke about functioning as an operational method. The ways in which the treatment of time as infinitely flexible and open to future reinterpretation of the opposition is interesting, given that the Any conferences, and this one in particular, are future-oriented.

One could also consider Bernard Tschumi's reference to passing time and space, or Hani Rashid's gathering of diverse servers into one virtual place, as affecting, in some way, the questions of transferability, opportunism, centrality, and ways of repairing damage and restoring cities.

SASKIA SASSEN Let me just confine myself to two points. The first (and this relates to Hani's presentation) concerns the idea that architecture inhabits more than one space – that is, it's either virtual or real. Here, I find myself coming back to Catherine's comments and the idea of operating within a liminal, or border, zone. But when you spoke about the transferability of buildings, Catherine, and about ownership and use as forms of transfer, I think that something else is also occurring. Building is not simply the physical building, regardless of ownership or use. It is also something constructed in other kinds of spaces. The most obvious example would be those financial instruments that actually capture the building, so that the building is constantly circulating, becoming totally liquid. If one extends this example to other aspects of the transferability of the urban environment, one could come up with a whole series of very interesting issues. In my own work, I'm confined to seeing these innovations only through finance – for example, how finance liquefies and then transforms the entity – but I'm sure that one could take these ideas and expand them into a broader realm.

My second point relates to the idea of the digital. As I imagine architects in their studios, designing with new technologies, they are restricted only to the digital space of their own creations. But looking at the economy, there is no single firm, no single economic sector, that can confine its operations to digital space (including those that produce digital goods, circulated digitally throughout the world). Rather, there is a far more complex topography that weaves in and out of digital space, producing, again, these liminal zones, edges, borders, and frontier zones, where much of the stuff is happening. The issue is how to capture

this topography in terms of a different set of categories, because ultimately we are talking about the need to build a new conceptual architecture. We are prisoners of older categories. I do think, though, that architects have a great advantage over social scientists because social scientists are deeply embedded in canons. At least the architects that I've met at Any are far more experimental and prepared to jump between categories.

FREDRIC JAMESON One could talk about new kinds of time and so on, but the last presentations showed us the spatialization of time and the control of time by space. Contextualizing this issue, in part through an allegorical framework, I was very pleased that in her introductory remarks Cynthia Davidson quoted the comment William Gibson made at Anyone, because it seems to me that the entire panel has been devoted – maybe not my presentation, but all the other ones – to disproving it and to taking another position on this. [See page 45, note 1.] One of the great ideological oppositions of the last years (expressed through a whole set of terms) has been that of dispersal versus centrality, nomads versus the state, **différence** versus presence, heterogeneity versus homogeneity – in short, the idea that what we want is the multiple rather than any need for centralization. But when this opposition turned out to be the market versus planning, maybe people began to feel that it wasn't quite such an obvious thing after all.

Here today I sense the return of certain notions of centrality as opposed to fantasies about absolute decentralization and so forth. When Romi spoke about a new kind of space that comes into being in these buffer zones, it seemed to be a very exciting way of talking about a return of public space

– a once forgotten public space that emerges on both sides of a border, and from which it is possible to construct in new ways something public that is also central. One of the benefits, I think, of Saskia's recent work has been to remind us that digitalization is not this totally dispersed thing, but that it needs its nodes and its centers, which it constructs. Similarly, we mustn't forget the material reality of centers despite the whole transformation that's involved in the global system. Bernard showed us how a new kind of building such as an airport can really be a center of time in which all kinds of events are contained rather than dispersed throughout spaces that have no link to one another, functioning as a kind of operator of the production of these events within a single totality. Equally, Hani's presentation showed how even the so-called virtual is a form of centralization and spatialization by the way in which it allows a unified representation of a whole set of things that are dispersed both in space and in time – a way of holding these things together so that the people it involves can suddenly get a sense of what's happened the whole day, or how they're connected to things that are going on technically in New Jersey or wherever. And so it seems to me that we've developed some arguments that might cause us to rethink notions of centrality, notions of public space, and maybe even notions of planning.

AUDIENCE Hani Rashid's presentation seemed, in a way, really perverse. His virtual stock exchange is actually much more difficult to navigate than it is to navigate conventional charts and information sheets. Rather than a stock exchange, I think that we could look to an MTV video, for example, as a far more interesting and effective representation of information. My

second point concerns how digitalization doesn't transform or find its way back to digital infrastructure. Rather than defined notions of the center, the periphery, the digital, and media, I think we're looking at things that are shifting. Instead of talking about the "real thing" we're talking about things that we feel are current, but which we, as architects, are not part of. So why should we feel that there has to be a center **and** a periphery? They're not exclusive. There are centers and peripheries that have nothing to do with civilization but with the homogeneity of space – that is, I can trade stocks in Tel Aviv or in New York City. The world looks the same everywhere. All experiences are the same. As architects why aren't we reacting through differentiation instead of actual visualization?

INGRAHAM I think that the real question is, what are the new categories for architecture? I mean, you can't both have the center and not have it. That's the power of the center. The power of the center is to exclude anything that throws it into question.

SASSEN My concern is with trying to understand all of this beyond these either/ors. For me, the fact is that there is a space of centrality, but it no longer occupies the geographies that we have associated with it. It intersects with the nonspace of centrality in very different ways. There's a lot of stuff happening at the edges (the edge, not the periphery, which I find to be a problematic category). But when you speak about homogenizing and one of the impacts of the digital being that you can get what you want anywhere, I think that this idea, to a certain extent, is mistaken. This would be to suggest that there is just one digital space. Rather, there

are whole worlds of private digital networks that no Internet service provider is ever going to give you access to – for example, the digital spaces of private finance. These spaces are constituted, digitally speaking, in radically different ways from the space of the Internet that is accessible to the paying consumer or the nonpaying cruiser. And even within the Internet you have enormous cyber segmentations.

When I speak of digital space, what I'm really talking about is its software – that it's much more the software than the hardware that is shaping our experience of the digital. What dominates its production today are those applications that facilitate firm-to-firm transactions via tunneled encryption through the World Wide Web. When you look at the history of the production of software, you get an understanding about digital space that explodes this notion that it is somehow a space. It's as diversified, as complex, as structured as the nondigital space that we walk through in the streets of New York.

BERNARD TSCHUMI As an architect, I've been thinking, more generally, of the paradoxical way in which the more architecture expands, the more it also contracts – that any discussion of real space necessitates a specific debate about the confines of virtual space. Hani's work has been very important here, defining architecture not only as the real space of the physical walls but also as the virtual space that populates it. But this distinction isn't necessarily one unique to today. In the 19th century, in the earliest department stores filled with consumer goods, the architecture was not only the beautiful cast-iron structure but also the merchandise that filled it. Looking further back, one could take Palladio's Villa Rotunda and analyze not only the beautiful sequence of rooms but also the light that holds and transforms those spaces. Architecture is never unitary; it's never just one thing. Architecture is never just about the walls. However, the more it expands, the more definitions of architecture embrace other things. With this expansion, the role of the architect seems to be more and more involved with the manipulation of surfaces — when we talk about doing digital spaces, we mean surfaces, surface mapping, and so on. Other people also just deal with surfaces. For example, when the graphic designer Bruce Mau designed a group of cinemas in Toronto, he designed surfaces. In other words, when architecture takes over other territories, these territories also engulf architecture. This shifting colonization is quite fascinating because it indeed reveals that existing categories are not important anymore.

INGRAHAM I want to address the audience comment to Hani. In what way does architecture contribute to the location of information, particularly in terms of advancing something new?

HANI RASHID I want to thank the questioner for her compliment — perverse is a fantastic word. We architects should be looking to embrace other territories. The questioner asked, "Why not do MTV?" I think that architects can embrace these territories without necessarily just doing videos or entertainment — territories that appeal to sensibilities, to taste, to individuals, and to the public realm. For example, it's become very apparent to us that our clients (the New York Stock Exchange, the Guggenheim, and others) are increasingly turning to us to develop mechanisms of branding, mechanisms for under-

standing their business models, their intervention in the world. Architects like us are now being commissioned to expand the capabilities of businesses and institutions to reach people, and then to help them respond to the various things that they need to respond to. The New York Stock Exchange, regardless of whether you like spreadsheets or not, has adopted the work we did for them as their basic image-generating model. Currently, we are working on a large Web initiative for them, so that ultimately you can get rid of your spreadsheets altogether and move inside different kinds of data worlds. I don't know whether this has anything to do with getting out of the center, but it's definitely getting us architects out of a certain kind of closed, almost myopic, traditionalism, and allowing us to develop new roles and to begin to probe other territories.

INGRAHAM Hani, I would go quite a bit further than you have. I think that architecture contributes to the New York Stock Exchange the principles of transferability that the exchange implicitly rests on, and that the presence of the body — even if it's a virtual body, and therefore slightly clumsy (as the virtual always is) — actually introduces the slow time that the exchange always references. This goes back to the question of centrality, to the idea of location.

RASHID We once sat in a meeting at the New York Stock Exchange with the vice president of operations, which is the exchange's strategic marketing group, and a more powerful body than our actual clients. After we presented our work, we spoke about publicity for the project and which journals it should feature in. They said, "No, no. We have absolutely no interest in architecture. We're interested in the

Financial Times. We're interested in the **Wall Street Journal**. We're interested in the kinds of places where we are." It was an ironic and kind of surreal statement coming from a group that is inside a very famous façade, which they photograph and disseminate all over the world — a building that is extraordinary, but which they pay no attention to whatsoever by virtue of the action on the trading floor. Their comments also revealed a kind of negative, closed mentality, as if architecture is working in opposition to what they want to do. I thought that this was a very interesting problem. But then this same group came back to us, with their tails between their legs, and said, "Okay, we're putting you in the annual report, we're going to promote this," and so on. So this is what we are up against. We are introduced to these projects as architects offering something different, but it's as architects that we are also being stereotyped and repelled to a certain extent.

ROMI KHOSLA I see a great many parallels between the ideas and realities of the nation-state and the terms we are now using to describe architecture — transferring equity, liquidizing, virtual reality. I would argue that we are witnessing the reformation of many of the things on the ground. Virtual architecture has become confined to a certain medium, but it doesn't seem to be able to step outside of this medium and into some real, physical arena. The irony of the reality of nation-states is that we are going through a process of producing virtual nation-states. These are the nation-states of no fixed definition; they have no fixed boundaries; they have no fixed notions of organization or ethics or values. Huge areas of the world are currently going through phases of virtual nationhood, but these are being enacted on the ground, in real space. In a sense you could try to replicate it on a computer in virtual reality, but what we are witnessing is a reality that is virtual. Countries are being liquidized and reformulated.

Within this context the traditional moorings of architecture have become a little less secure because we are no longer sure what is real and what is virtual. If, for example, you are living right now in Sierra Leone or Kosovo, the boundaries between reality and virtuality have become blurred. Given this blurring, and in regard to issues we've discussed today, you realize that architecture has become completely insignificant because it is no longer able to connect – virtual architecture is virtual architecture. But when reality and virtuality get mixed up in real life, then there develops a crying need for architecture to address these issues and intervene in these situations.

INGRAHAM So we're confronted with the usual, failing paradox – is architecture essential or is it irrelevant? To perhaps continue with these dichotomies, I want to ask Fred whether he thinks we're experiencing the spatialization of time or the temporalization of space. It would, for example, be very difficult to say definitively that the economics of building, or the financial principles that govern the transfer of buildings, are architectural. They could be categorized as spatial, but they also concern time. Current theories about the spatialization of time just don't seem to be so clear anymore. This is also true for the uses of history and the seeming inability today to adopt oppositional strategies as ways of arguing these points.

JAMESON I think it would be a very long discussion, but let me put it this way (and maybe this is a less controversial way to begin talking about it anyway) – let's talk about the control of time, the organization of time, the management of time, and so on. If we approach it this way, then things like speculation become ways of organizing the future, controlling the future, making it somehow manageable or reputable. The virtual images that we've seen also seem to be functioning this way – time is this threatening flow that we're now able to work on and do something with and so on. Certainly some of this work can be done through spatialization. Whether one can talk about things like ground and brand in those terms I'm not quite so sure, but it seems to me that this kind of thing is very definitely a way of managing temporality, of making it into something which is tangible, usable, and able to be replayed, stretched out, and miniaturized, which does seem to have a spatial character to it.

SASSEN I agree with Fred, but I would also like to add one more thing. Look at the architectures we have seen this morning. If you take a given building or a given architectural situation, you could say that one of the things happening today in a way that is different from the past is that we have multiple temporal orders looping through a building. In his presentation, Hani kept alluding to what in some strange way was located somewhere in his building, but what he couldn't say was that a different temporal order is looping through what you are, and what you constructed, and what that physical building is. I think the same things are happening in our domestic environments today. Take a house, a household – there are now multiple temporal orders circulating through the home through computer modems, telephones, televisions. Everything now is global

because time has become instantaneous. This time can also be simultaneously accessed from other places. So one way of thinking about the question of temporality, in addition to the transfer of the building and what Catherine spoke about, is to look at the temporal orders that actually circulate through a particular space. This circulation is not something we haven't seen before, but today it is constituted with its own specificity. This is interesting in addressing issues of temporality, which seem more difficult to grasp and understand than questions concerning space.

AUDIENCE Fred, your talk was quite different in that it explicitly addressed allegory. Would you say, in light of your former work, that this is a kind of voluntaristic move on your part, out from under the spatial blanket that covered all the other talks? For example, in Hani's presentation with its rhetoric of invasion, control, morphing, mutation – various spatial terms employed to discuss the alleged temporality of virtuality – you have a sort of false or faux temporality being talked about in a spatial way. My question then is, why allegory now?

JAMESON Well, there's another aspect of this discussion which brings it up to the present, and that is whether one can still talk about contradictions in the same way and read allegorical things in terms of contradiction. This is the question that I would ask myself. My presentation looked to a moment from the past, specifically a modernist moment from the past, and the way somebody like Manfredo Tafuri reads that. But my question to myself, to supplement yours, which I won't answer anymore than I answer my own, is whether those methods are still appropriate to the present situation.

"likes to build s"

"the is to get well"

SPACE FOR CHANGE

WOLF PRIX

UFA Cinema Center, Dresden, and Groningen Museum (above left).

The people that you mentioned, I know them. They are quite lame. I have to rearrange their faces and give them all another name. – Bob Dylan

The discovery of actual building as a new paradigm for our work happened simultaneously with a moment of change in the character and development of the Western city; a change dominated by the gradual privatization of urban public space, which has had profound effects on contemporary architecture as a whole. Faced with a complete lack of public funds, cities and local authorities have found themselves increasingly unable to play an active role in urban planning proposals and instead have sold out to investors, who helped themselves to the biggest and best pieces of the city. It is a game whose end is easily predicted: architecture will end up as infrastructure built to maximize the profits of a global economy.

A mode of resistance to this instrumentalization of our profession lies in an architecture that regards itself as agent to a new philosophy of urban planning. The impulse of architecture to play an active role in urban planning is vital here, because otherwise urban planning will no longer exist. The master plan is dead; but this, as we know, has its advantages. The grid-patterned urban space of the 19th century only really exists on paper; the actual dynamics of today's urban transformations have long prevailed over such idealized visions of order. Today, our urban interventions take place in an amorphous and imponderable space, analogous to chess figures moving horizontally across blurred TV screens. But the grid of the chessboard has disappeared and along with it any predefined rules determining how its surface figures are to be moved. Yet the figures have remained; a castle is still a castle. And its moves are still significant, even though the coordinates of this movement can no longer be plotted within an abstracted frame of reference (B5 to C6, for example).

The more the background recedes, however, the more distinct the figures can become. For in the wake of the implosion of the old order, it is these figures that make a city. Their coming together creates force fields of great tension and, in so doing, creates space. This process is infinitely more complex than the ordained decision to lay down a grid on a peninsula and then fill it up, step by step, with architecture. Space is no longer predetermined (if it ever was). Rather, it develops through the tensions and interrelationships of figures created together, forming the basis for a vigorous urbanity.

This agenda has left visible traces in our architecture, as a comparison of the Groningen Museum (1993–94) and the UFA Cinema Center in Dresden (1994–97) clearly illustrates. The museum represents the final chapter of a phase of our work going back to the 1980s that was characterized by the fractalization of objects. In Groningen we were first able to realize on a large scale a conception of space that exploded into a thousand pieces the confines of the functionalist box. And in contrast to loft-building projects in Vienna, in Groningen we were first able to digitalize our models and build them with the help of modern computer-aided manufacturing technologies developed for ship building.

The UFA Cinema Center, on the other hand, is the first of several projects dedicated to the creation of public space through architecture. The model of a building as object is replaced by the idea of an urban transistor. By this we mean an architecture that is capable of amplifying the urban spaces adjoining it through its own transistorlike spatial organization. In the case of the UFA Cinema Center, this concept resulted in an architecture whose main element was not its function as a cinema. Instead, we made use of its critical mass, giving it a spacious lobby and creating a roofed-in urban space for showing films. Moreover, the cinema volume was raised to allow for a public passageway below that connects two important city spaces.

In order to keep the size of the property needed for the building as small as possible (air rights were cheaper than property prices), we let the vertical volume of the glass crystal protrude obliquely into the space. By this, a different view presents itself from every side; the facade continually mutates with unexpected maneuvers. In the interior, a vertically ascending spatial sequence – best described as Piranesi goes MTV – unfolds, abandoning once and for all the idea of a centrally perceived spatial perspective. The empty volume of the glass hall is also broken up by sculptural elements that appear to float motionlessly in space, like the inside of the refrigerator shooting through the air in slow motion at the end of Michelangelo Antonioni's film Zabriskie Point, exploding together with the entire building again and again.

For us, the UFA Cinema Center represented a new paradigm of spatial definition and formal design based on two interconnected ideas: the free configuration of three-dimensional figures (closely related to the chess figures on the blank screen) united by an overarching cover. In successive projects we have continued to develop this paradigm further, particularly in our current project, an urban entertainment center in Guadalajara, Mexico. It is part of an enormous urban development proposal outside the city, and involves many well-known architects (notably Thom Mayne, Jean Nouvel, Toyo Ito, Tod Williams and Billy Tsien). Our project is approximately one million square feet, consisting of 16 cinemas with a total of 10,000 seats, a shopping mall, restaurants, bars, entertainment malls, and a media center.

In order to spatially organize such a large number of activities, we have broken up the main body of the building to

JVC Entertainment Center, Guadalajara.

an even greater extent than in Dresden. The building is opened up, revealing a landscape of sculptural volumes distributed in space. Here, the cinemas, which in Dresden were still incorporated in the cement block, are liberated and serve as individual, space-forming elements. In contrast to Dresden, the physical unity of the figures has been dissolved even further. While the public space of the lobby in Dresden is still surrounded sculpturally by the body of the crystal, in Guadalajara the lateral parts of the space-cover are raised high, like wings, and define a planar roof that floats over the ground like a flying carpet. A microclimate forms under this cover, both in a literal and figurative sense. The roof fulfills very real climatic requirements, protecting the space underneath it against strong sunlight and high temperatures (which are also reduced by Persian cooling, waterfalls, and other such means). This microclimate also operates in a spatial sense — it is an urban space that stands out from its surroundings without offering too extreme a contrast. Unlike the traditional urban typology of public squares and piazzas, the "walls," which serve a decisive space-forming function here, are not positioned vertically (the façades of the surrounding buildings) but rather horizontally: the bottom level is located 11 meters below grade, and the flying carpet high above everything. The empty space sandwiched between the two levels is the urban space. The sides have been left open to allow it to interact with its surroundings like a transistor.

The spatial distribution of the various programs creates a continual sequence of activities on several levels (the cinemas, for example, are connected with each other on different floor levels). When in use — the idea is to show films continuously — the space will be animated by the constant flow of movement through it. The spatial sculptures, on the other hand, serve to differentiate this general movement. They mark critical points where this continual flow is arrested for brief moments, only to be stirred up again. The sculptures are strategic points that differentiate the flow of space — by stopping it, redirecting it, or intensifying it. We believe that a vigorous urban architectural experience results when both qualities of space are linked, creating a rhythm of dynamism and concentration.

Ultimately, breaking up the architectural object to create a spatially differentiated eventscape makes it possible to transcend the common cliches associated with the shopping mall and the urban entertainment center. Anchor stores are no longer needed to support the less attractive programs, as they are in Victor Gruen's classic concept of the shopping mall. Rather, the project as a whole is more like a buzzing beehive of activity, in which a number of local points of attraction combine to form a vibrating field of energy. This field develops such a critical mass of action that the concept of the anchor store becomes obsolete.

In addition to Guadalajara, which is to be completed in 2005, we have realized three large residential building projects in Vienna. Instead of simply taking the residential program itself as our starting point, these designs were also conceived through an urban planning perspective. The Gasometer residential building provides a clear example. Built in the 19th century to provide the city of Vienna with gas, the four huge gas tanks had long been out of operation before their present transformation into a large-scale complex of apartments, shops, and recreational facilities began. While the proposals of three other architectural teams involved are limited to filling the interior of each of the structures, our gasometer looks to destroy the conventional masquerade of historical reconstruction of an interior hidden behind a sympathetic facade. In order to unmistakably reveal the new interior of the building to the outside, we have materialized the empty volume inside the cylindrical gasometer as a space, rolled it out like dough, and placed it in front of the gasometer in the form of a shield (in this way we also achieve the highest density of all of the projects, which in turn is what makes it possible to finance the entire development). Formally, the project is similar to those in Dresden and Guadalajara, characterized as it is by the same return to a sense of certain primary volumes, which can be understood as a response to the now exhausted formal differentiation of deconstructivism, and because it falls back on certain archetypes of our understanding of form — for example, through Frederick Kiesler, Constantin Brancusi, and Le Corbusier.

While this phase is gradually taking shape — the gasometer will be completed in 2001 — we are currently working on a new method of formal design. To date, the clearest expression of this is our design for the competition for the Science Center in Wolfsburg (a competition we lost to Zaha Hadid). Here we strove to redefine the facade, to make it more than simply the outer shell of the interior space. Instead, we conceived of it more as a membrane between the outer and inner constraints, which are expressed in the form and material of the surface of the façade. The morphed form is the intermediary between these different forces, resulting in a friction between the concept of the building and the situation of the project within the space of the city. As we know, friction generates warmth, causing the façade to melt and allowing it to flow over all of the different forms of the building. This project, unfortunately, will never be realized, but since the projects that we have constructed typically have to wait at least a decade before they are considered socially acceptable, we imagine that the Wolfsburg Center will provide a model for what our built buildings will look like in ten years time.

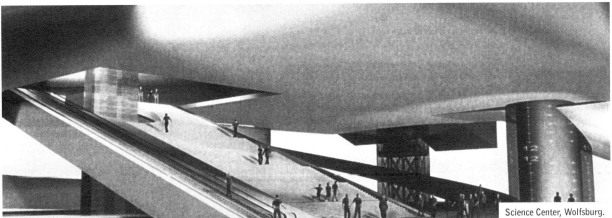

Science Center, Wolfsburg.

GPA Gasometer B, Vienna.

OPEN-ENDED SKILL: SIX POINTS

OSAMU ISHIYAMA

Tree House, Chichibu.

1. Architecture's basic premise is that it offers a tool for people to improve their lives. Into this general definition I would like to introduce the concept of "open-ended skill," as something by which people can create and design their own environment.

Rias Ark Museum of Art, Kessenuma.

2. In Japan, the concept of open-ended skill is particularly important because of the serious housing problems the country suffers from, both in terms of cost and architectural style. The majority of houses look terrible and lack flexibility; an existing architectural model that open-ended skill looks to challenge.

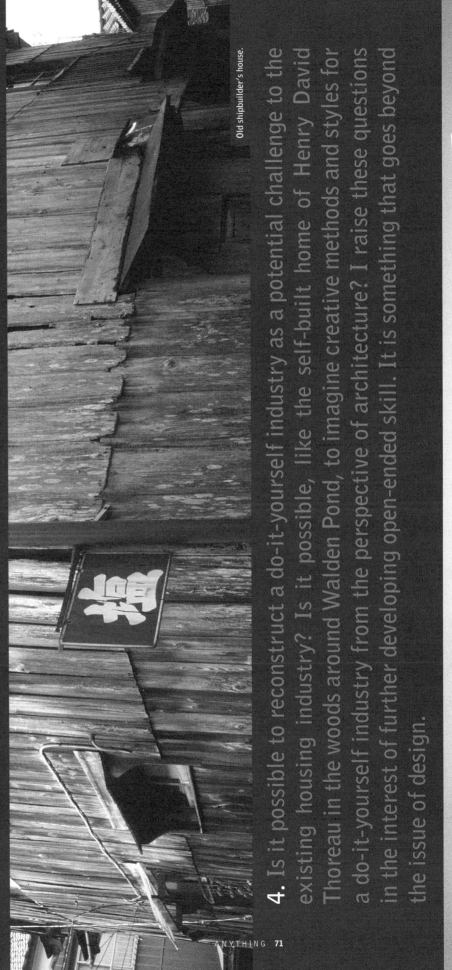

Old shipbuilder's house.

3. Today people want to live in their own private houses. Accordingly, houses become extremely expensive commodities. But through the self-built homes made possible by open-ended skill, this escalation of the housing market can be offset.

4. Is it possible to reconstruct a do-it-yourself industry as a potential challenge to the existing housing industry? Is it possible, like the self-built home of Henry David Thoreau in the woods around Walden Pond, to imagine creative methods and styles for a do-it-yourself industry from the perspective of architecture? I raise these questions in the interest of further developing open-ended skill. It is something that goes beyond the issue of design.

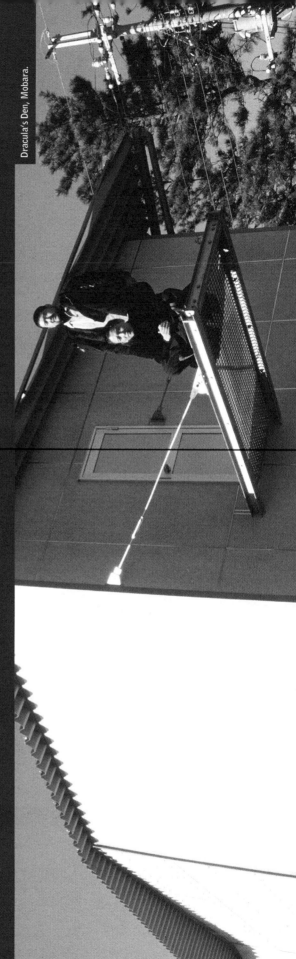

Dracula's Den, Mobara.

002

1999
2000
2001

早稲田Hバウハウススクール Waseda-Bauhaus School

CREEK RESEARCH CENTER
クリークリサーチセンター

5. Open-ended skill methods enable individual builders and architects to broaden their potential and, in the process, to reconstruct the marketing process of design.

6. Open-ended skill, including such activities as carpentry, gardening, and interior decoration, enables and empowers diverse groups of people from all over the world to change the landscape of our towns and cities.

REMOTE
CONTROL
MARK C.
TAYLOR

All distances in time and space are shrinking. Man now reaches overnight, by plane, places which formerly took weeks and months of travel. He now receives instant information, by radio, of events which he formerly learned about only years later, if at all. . . . Distant sites of the most ancient cultures are shown on film as if they stood this very moment amidst today's street traffic. Moreover, the film attests to what it shows by presenting also the camera and its operations. The peak of this abolition of every possibility of remoteness is reached by television, which will soon pervade and dominate the whole machinery of communication. – Martin Heidegger, "The Thing." **1** Martin Heidegger, "The Thing," in *Poetry, Language, Thought*, trans. Albert Hofstadter (New York: Harper and Row, 1971), 165.

We are called to gather one last time. The decade in which we have been meeting has been remarkable in ways we could never have anticipated in Los Angeles in 1991. As we meet to look back and perhaps ahead, who calls, what calls us to gather? Any, of course; Any once again calls – this time in the name of Anything. The call of this seemingly anonymous voice (though from the beginning, we have all suspected we know whose voice it is) raises endless questions: the final Any conference, Anything, is a gathering (What does it mean to gather?) to deliberate the condition (What does it mean to condition or to be conditioned?) of architecture and its relationships to contemporary (Can *anything* be contemporary?) culture. Anything literally means (Does *anything* mean literally?) "any *thing* whatever." During the ten years of Any conferences, it has increasingly appeared that anything – *anything* whatsoever – goes. But there are in fact (What is a fact?) constraints (What constraints?) to thought (What is called thinking?) and action. (Who acts?) Constraints that change *anything* to *this thing*. (Is *this thing* ever *the thing*?) And what is this Any thing anyway? How can a series (Why a series? What is a series?) of conferences framed (What does it mean to enframe or to be framed?) by the idea of undecidability (Is undecidability an idea or the impossibility of the idea?) ever conclude? (Is concluding ending?)

The call, which seems to be anonymous, is indebted to a proper name: Martin Heidegger, whose thing, we shall see, is not anything but the thing. In ways that are not yet clear, we are gathered around the thing. Heidegger's influential essay "The Thing" begins with the words with which I began. Writing decades before the explosion of information and telematic technologies that define our era, Heidegger foresaw our condition on the cusp of the 21st century with uncanny accuracy. From Heidegger's point of view, the "machinery of communication" is a devastating expression of the will to mastery or the will to power, which has inspired Western metaphysics from its beginning in ancient Greece. The dream of what he labels the onto-theological tradition, on display in the globalization of television, is remote control

or, more precisely, to control the remote. If Heidegger were here, he would, I believe, argue that what is out of control today is the will to control. In attempting to think the thing, he struggles to think that which cannot be controlled and thus forever constrains the will to power. While the call that has led us to gather invokes Heidegger's name, the title of this panel – "Thing as Object" – betrays his sense of the thing. For Heidegger, *the thing is not an object*. More precisely, the representation of the object hides the thing whose proximate withdrawal clears the opening in which objects as well as subjects emerge. In the wake of this approaching withdrawal or withdrawing approach, *not* everything goes. Indeed, if we can understand the *difference* between the thing and the object, we will see that the claim that anything goes can only occur when the thing is forgotten.

What, then, is the difference between the thing and the object? And what, for Heidegger, is so objectionable about the object? As always for Heidegger, etymology provides clues to his argument. The German word *Gegenstand* implies that the object is that which stands (*stand, stehen*: to stand) against or opposed to (*gegen*: against, opposed to, contrary to, over against). This principle of opposition is also evident in the English word *object* (German: *Objekt*), which derives from the Latin *obicere* (to throw against, oppose: *ob*, toward + *jacere*, to throw). When understood in oppositional terms, the object is inseparable from the subject. Subject and object, in other words, form a binary opposition, which is not symmetrical. During the modern era, which for Heidegger begins with Descartes's turn to the subject, objectivity is constituted, constructed, or posited by subjectivity. By reducing truth to certainty, Descartes initiates a regime of representation (*Vorstellung*) in which the subject places (*stelle*) the object before (*vor*) itself. This foundational gesture constitutes "the essence of the modern age." In "The Age of the World Picture," Heidegger writes, "When man becomes the primary and only real *subjectum* that means: Man becomes that being upon which all that is, is grounded as regards the manner of its Being and its truth. Man becomes the relational center of that which is as such. But this is possible only when the comprehension of what is as a whole changes." **2** Martin Heidegger, "The Age of the World Picture," in *The Question Concerning Technology and Other Essays*, trans. William Lovitt (New York: Harper and Row, 1977), 128. As Nietzsche realized long ago, with the death of God, the locus of creativity shifts from the divine to the human. For modernity, man, not God, creates the world through the power of representation.

This objectifying of whatever is, is accomplished in a setting-before, a representing, that aims at bringing each particular being before it in such a way that man who calculates can be sure, and that means certain, of that being. We first arrive at science as research when and only when truth has been transformed into the certainty of representation. What it is to be is for the first time defined as the objectiveness of representing and truth is first defined as the certainty of representing, in the metaphysics of Descartes. **3 Ibid., 127.**

Insofar as the object is placed before the subject by the subject itself, knowledge of the object is actually the self-knowledge in and through which the subject becomes certain of itself. When the object is posited by the subject, "the world stands at man's disposal as conquered and the more objectively the object appears, all the more subjectively, i.e., the more importunately, does the *subiectum* – rise up, and all the more impetuously, too, do observation and teaching about the world change into a doctrine of man, into anthropology." **4 Ibid., 133.**

Far from idle abstraction, the epistemology and metaphysics Descartes initiates, which is to say the epistemology and metaphysics of modernism, are concretely realized during the last half of the 20th century in science and technology. Modern science and technology are distinguished by the instrumentality of reason through which subjects as well as objects are subjected to machinations and calculations intended to serve human interests. Heidegger insists that the calculations of instrumental reason are the expression of a "subjective egoism," which is not only destructive but also self-destructive. He continues, "In the planetary imperialism of technologically organized man, the subjectivism of man attains its acme, from which point it will descend to the level of organized uniformity and there firmly establish itself. This uniformity becomes the surest instrument of total, i.e., technological control over the earth." **5 Ibid., 152.** In the world of "planetary imperialism" anything goes. When truth is reduced to certainty and certainty is always self-certainty (norms and criteria by which judgments are made and desires constrained) it becomes impossible to distinguish obligation from inclination.

It would seem to be a small step from Heidegger's "planetary imperialism of technologically organized man" to the processes of globalization, which have spread at warp speed during the decade of Any. Heidegger first presented his essay "The Thing" almost 50 years ago to the day: June 6, 1950, in a lecture given at the Bayerischen Akademie der Schönen Kunste. Though he recognized the radical implications of "instant information" made available by a new "machinery of communication" and was wary of the abolition of distance and remoteness by televisual technologies, he could not have imagined just how tight the telecommunications web would be drawn by the end of the century. And yet, this web is not seamless but is riddled with gaps. These gaps, which are incommunicable as such yet render all communication possible, are traces of what Heidegger names "the thing."

The thing, I have claimed, is not an object. In Heidegger's own words: "No representation of what is present, in the sense of what stands forth and of what stands over against as object, ever reaches to the thing *qua* thing." Subject and object, we have seen, form a hierarchical binary opposition. The thing forever eludes this and every other oppositional structure. The example Heidegger selects to define the thing is a jug (*Krug*: pitcher, mug, pot, jar, urn). "The jug's thingness," he avers, "resides in its being *qua* vessel." **6 Heidegger, "The Thing," 168–69.** But what is a vessel? A vessel is something that holds – in this case something that holds, significantly, wine. On closer inspection, it turns out that the something that holds is actually nothing. "When we fill the jug with wine," Heidegger writes, "do we pour the wine into the sides and bottom? At most, we pour the wine between the sides and over the bottom. Sides and bottom are, to be sure, what is impermeable in the vessel. But what is impermeable is not yet what does the holding. The empty space, this nothing of the jug, is what the jug is as the holding vessel." **7 Ibid., 169.** If the jug's thingness resides in its being *qua* vessel and the vessel is the empty space that is nothing, then *thingness resides in nothingness*. The thing, it would seem, is no thing or nothing. This nothingness is not an absence nor is it a presence; neither absent nor present, nothing is ever near or proximate. Always near without being present, the thing, which is no thing, is not an object and can never be objectified. It cannot be conceived, controlled, calculated. Rather, the thing constrains, confines, and conditions anything and everything.

If we let the thing be present in its thinging from out of the worlding world, then we are thinking of the thing as thing. Taking thought in this way, we let ourselves be concerned by the thing's worlding being. Thinking in this way, we are called by the thing as the thing. In the strict sense of the German word *bedingt*, we are the be-thinged ones, the conditioned ones. We have left behind us the presumption of all unconditionedness. **8 Ibid., 181.**

Once again the argument turns on a word. *Bedingt*, which, of course, contains the word *thing* (*Ding*), means determined, conditioned, caused. Insofar as we are *bedingt* – determined, conditioned, caused, or in Heidegger's neologism, be-thinged – we are not self-determining. Though subjects might posit objects, both are radically, indeed primordially, conditioned by some thing that is incalculable and out of control. So understood, the thing subverts the modern subject and marks the limit of modern science and technology.

Science makes the jug-thing into a nonentity in not permitting things to be the standard for what is real. Science's knowledge, which is compelling within its own sphere, the sphere of objects, already had annihilated things as things long before the atom bomb exploded. The bomb's explosion is only the grossest of all gross confirmations of the long-since accomplished annihilation of the thing: the confirmation that the thing as a thing remains nil. The thingness of the thing remains concealed, forgotten. The nature of the thing never comes to light, that is, never gets a hearing. **9** Ibid., 170.

Heidegger's argument at this point deserves careful consideration. If the annihilation of the thing confirms that the thing as thing remains nil, then the fullest expression of modernity's will to power affirms the very thing – or nothing – it is designed to negate. Heidegger's argument is virtually Hegelian. Though time and space do not permit a consideration of the issue, it is instructive to note that Heidegger's interpretation of modern science and technology is actually drawn from Hegel's analysis of utility in his *Phenomenology of Spirit*. **10** "Utility," Hegel argues, "is still a predicate of the object, not itself a subject or the immediate and sole actuality of the object. It is the same thing that appeared before, when being-for-self had not yet shown itself to be the substance of the other moments, a demonstration which would have meant that the Useful was directly nothing else but the self of consciousness and that this latter was thereby in possession of it. This withdrawal from the form of objectivity of the Useful has, however, already taken place in principle and from this inner revolution there emerges the actual revolution of the actual world, the new shape of consciousness, *absolute freedom*." The "actual revolution of the actual world," is, of course, the French Revolution. When freedom becomes absolute and, therefore, is not constrained by anything other than itself, it quickly becomes "absolute terror" which is manifested as "the fury of destruction." For Hegel, this fury of destruction led to the Reign of Terror; for Heidegger, it led to the dropping of the atom bomb. (G. W. F. Hegel, *Phenomenology of Spirit*, trans. A.V. Miller [New York: Oxford University Press, 1977], 355–56.) For the utilitarian, the being of the object is being-for-the-subject; there is no object-in-itself but only an object-for-me. The subject asserts its essentiality by negating the object upon which it nonetheless depends. In this way, the modern subject negates itself in and through its very affirmation, thereby allowing the return of the repressed thing.

If we understand modernity to be inseparable from the notion of subjectivity that begins with Descartes and comes to closure in Hegel, then Heidegger points toward a postmodern world in which anything *does not* go. Contrary to widespread opinion, major figures commonly – and often misleadingly – labeled "postmodern" do not prescribe a banal nihilism in which anything goes. On the contrary, human thought and action are always conditioned and constrained by some thing that can be neither conceived nor controlled. By now it should be clear that this "thing" is actually the name of the unnamable. This thing renders certainty impossible and truth undecidable. Far from undercutting the possibility of thinking and acting, such impossibility and uncertainty are the conditions of the possibility of words

and deeds tempered by the salutary awareness of what we do not and cannot know.

Though the thingness of the thing remains hidden, it does not disappear but remains as the specter haunting modernity. We can begin to conclude by returning yet again to the missive with which this gathering originated – this time slightly rewritten. "Thinking in this way, we are called" to gather one last time "by the thing as thing." Thinking is never original but is always indebted to something that forever escapes its grasp. This elusive thing is what gathers us without bringing us together. More precisely, the thing not only gathers but also is gathering.

To be sure, the Old High German word *thing* means a gathering, and specifically a gathering to deliberate on a matter under discussion, a contested matter. In consequence, the Old German words *thing* and *dinc* become the names for an affair or matter of pertinence. They denote anything that in any way bears upon men, concerns them, and that accordingly is a matter for discourse. The Romans called a matter for discourse *res*. **11** Op. cit., 174.

For a decade, we have been gathering to deliberate and discuss a contested matter. Regardless of our objectives for entering into this discussion, by now we should realize that the thing is anything – "anything that in any way bears upon men, concerns them, and that accordingly is a matter for discourse."

Over the years, we have heard many names – none the same and none proper – for this thing, which is no thing: the real, the uncanny, *différence*, fold, body, flesh, tear, crypt, specter, death, infinity, Being, the disaster, the infinite, sacred, even God – the list is as endless as thought itself. Pondering these echoes from the past, we begin to suspect that the Any thing has always been about the thing. What we have learned – if we have learned Anything – is that our conclusions are inevitably inconclusive. Far from a failure, this inconclusiveness is what has kept us coming back again and again. And it is what will keep us coming back again and again – even if this is the last time we will ever gather.

STRESS

BRUCE MAU

Stress is the inevitable outcome of a system that incorporates every gesture into a global competition for resources.

Stress imagines every rule and limit to be infinitely flexible, open to constant recalibration as faster, cheaper, and better.

Stress is a post-natural ecology aimed at the ultimate fusion of nervous system and economy.

Stress is the phenomenon of ever-expanding proportions.

A culture that pushes the limits of social, ecological, biological, intellectual, emotional, and psychological capacity in almost every endeavor is a culture of stress.

Looking back over the 20th century, over all modernity in fact, what one discovers is an almost continuous and totalizing cycle: establish a threshold, push beyond it, experience stasis, repeat. One of the central arguments of STRESS is that a culture that can produce the concept of "the envelope" — and then proceed to "push the envelope" in almost every endeavor is a culture of stress. Only a culture of stress could have imagined a flexible boundary and imaginatively cast that boundary around virtually everything.

When we were commissioned by Hortensia Völckers to produce a work for Wiener Festwochen, a performing arts festival in Vienna, the organizers initially wanted a piece that concerned dance or performance. We began there, but the idea gradually evolved. For a time, it took on the name Panorama. It had to do with the notion of being embedded in the image, in this case, a protocinematic space. In traditional, 19th-century panoramas, the spectator always remained at a distance from the image, viewing it from a panoptic platform. STRESS remains a panorama of sorts but the effect is distributed over eight large video screens, 12 feet wide and 18 feet high. The overall image is now fragmented and mobilized within a space where the viewer circulates freely. In the viewing situation set up by STRESS, the viewer is embedded in the space of the image. We have interpreted the techniques of book development and conceptualization through the medium of cinema, using digital projection to create a cinematic experience for the viewer.

The piece has 24 episodes, each one presenting an aspect of the condition of stress. The episodes range from the openly documentary to the abstract. We have, for example, taken a character from the history of stress development, Colonel John Stapp, and let him stand as an emblematic figure. He is the man on the cover of Marshall McLuhan and Quentin Fiore's book The Medium is the Massage, and a central figure in the history of stress. By strapping himself into a rocket sled and hurling his body at breakneck speed down a track in a series of experiments beginning in the late 1940s, Stapp placed himself at the center of research to test the human capacity to endure the forces of gravity. The enterprise was scrupulously recorded by the United States Air Force. They filmed the preparations, the site development, the technicians prepping him for the ride, and the medical examinations afterward. Stapp's encapsulating adventure represents the collision of biological capacity, speed, and cinema.

STRESS is a video-based installation, designed in collaboration with André Lepecki and John Oswald for the 2000 Wiener Festwochen, that explores forces of impact and disfiguration in a series of short episodes. For approximately 40 minutes, and in a large, blackened room, viewers venture into the choreography of stress. They are exposed to the forces of modernization that have, in Marshall McLuhan's words, "worked us over." STRESS takes us to the thresholds of life by exploring our maximal capacities for pleasure and pain, speed and attention, consciousness and endurance, bodily integrity and incorporation.

Assembled in a space surrounding the video installation chamber are 26 "stress objects." In a deployment that invokes the explosante-fixe of the surrealists 70 years ago, these mute monuments, divested of their familiar functions, are positioned as extracts from the late-20th century.

G-FORCE
He thought of himself as matter: mass, surface, density, opacity. He thought of himself as measurable: height, weight, age, pulse. He thought of himself as structure: bone, ligament, muscle, cartilage. He thought of the world as pure force against which he would collide. Once, he thought the world had turned purple—it was only his eyes flooding with blood. He always looked like a child after each experiment. He was constantly being photographed.

RUPTURE
Poachers, mercenaries, militias, hijackers, terrorists, vigilantes, assassins: central characters in the ecology of stress. When market forces go beyond what the market can bear, the result is a rupture of the membrane of power.

Violence spurts in the rent. Poachers, terrorists, assassins step in, not as alien forces but as intrinsic players in the economy and ecology of stress. They complement and guarantee the flow of information, goods, capital, power, and the violent images they help generate.

ZERO
At the zero point of energy, when all should be at perfect rest, particles still endure infinitesimal vibration. In this sense, vibration is the last threshold of the persistence of reality. As vibration permeates zero, the sign of all which is not is finely crisscrossed, fissured, animated. Zero announces not the beginning, nor the end, but the constant, microscopic, vibratile motion toward endless modification.

WALK
ON
DANIEL

I am a so-called artist, not a sculptor, and the pieces that I create focus largely on three dimensions. My work deals more or less with architecture, but then most art deals with architecture, even if only subconsciously. Many artists have traditionally found this architectural influence overbearing, feeling somewhat victimized by its impact, and have looked instead to the complete autonomy of their own artistic creations. My work is not autonomous. It has always been the result of interactions with several things and ideas, but especially with architecture.

The project I want to present here was in fact a collaboration between myself and the architect Christian Drevet for a competition for La Place des Terraux in the heart of Lyon, France. From the air, the square itself appears to be a cutout in the urban fabric of the city, a kind of corridor or channel that links the Rhône and Saône rivers. In researching the history of this site, it was interesting to examine at what moment the square, which was built piece by piece over the centuries — from the 17th through to the 19th — became an ensemble. It is a place of ancient fortification, but it is also expressive of the whole city and its two major axes: the east-west axis that structures the history of the city, between its past and its future; and the north-south axis that follows the city's geography, both in terms of the flow of its two rivers and the economic, social, and urban demarcation between the city's southern peninsula and the Croix-Rousse hill to the north.

As the intersection of these two axes, La Place des Terraux appears to be the most important junction in the city. On a symbolic plan, it seems to combine and oppose the four components of city life: the authority of the city government with the city hall; the authority of the church in the Palais St.-Pierre (a former monastery that is now the Beaux-Arts Museum); the commercial shops in the Massif des Terraux; and the people, or citizenship, with the façade of the Croix-Roussienne. These four components revolve around a fountain by Frédéric Auguste Bartholdi that is said to be "a work of art."

In our proposal for the redevelopment of the site, there was nothing to invent; it was enough simply to reveal and express the obvious qualities of the square. The long façade of the Palais St.-Pierre is punctuated with pilasters that are spaced 5.9 meters apart to create a strong continuous effect. On the other hand, the Hotel de Ville feels like a single monument. Therefore we used the bays of the Palais as a regulating device with which to demarcate the space and to project over the entire square a framework, or grid, with a 5.9 by 5.9-meter dimension. Laid out on the ground, the grid becomes the longitudinal axis of the plaza, linking the entrance to city hall with the entrance to the galleria, and prolonging a thruway connection between the two rivers.

The imposition of this gridded framework within a singular granite texture blankets the entire plaza, considerably enhancing the singularity of the square, and of the public's experience of that space. The uninterrupted grid also exaggerates a perspectival appreciation of the monuments that border the plaza while offering a constant point of positional reference for anyone standing within the square. Acting like a veritable mise en volume, the space formed by the grids on the north façade together with that of the ground creates the impression of an interior volume in which all of the elements take on three dimensions: architectural figures appear like urban furniture, or sculpture.

Principal among these figures is the Bartholdi fountain. Even though the competition brief prohibited any change to the position of this fountain, we proposed moving it. In its original siting on the west side of the plaza, it completely blocked the entrance to the Massif des Terraux, and physically and symbolically prevented a natural circulation between the Saône and Rhône rivers. To liberate the plaza's long east-west axis, we proposed sliding the fountain to the middle of the square, turning it 90 degrees, and backing it up against the north façade of the space. In this new situation a whole new set of consequences was introduced: one rediscovers the beautiful façade of the Massif des Terraux, previously hidden behind the Bartholdi fountain; now orientated to the south, the position of the fountain symbolically represents the birth of a river, paralleling the flow of Lyon's two rivers, from the mountains in the north to the sea south of the city; the contrast between the three ennobled façades (the city hall, the Palais St.-Pierre, and the Massif des Terraux) and the more commercial architecture on the north side becomes immediately obvious; and with the "king," the "curate," and the bourgeoisie on three sides, and "the people" on the fourth, these four façades represent a social history of France's four estates.

Relocated to the north side, the power of the Bartholdi fountain and the specific urban siting of the plaza between Lyon's twin rivers, suggested to us an installation that played with water. In that spirit, we placed small, individual fountains at the center of each square that makes up the grid, and that could act, in some way, as the confluence of the Saône and Rhône. In total, 69 fountains were installed, leaving certain areas in the plaza free for circulation and cafes. Placed within a shallow basin of black granite, only two centimeters deep, small water jets in each of the 69 squares allows them either to project a fountain, to turn each individual square into a static reflecting pool, or to drain and vanish completely in order to return the surface to another use. When all of the fountains are operating, Bartholdi's triumphal equestrian monument seems to be floating above a shallow sea, while to people sitting in the surrounding cafes, anyone crossing this aquatic Place des Terraux appears to be walking on water.

Fountains on and off at the Place des Terraux, Lyon.

DISCUSSION 2

JEAN-LOUIS COHEN I want first to turn to Mark Taylor's presentation, which attacked the founding assumption that "the thing" and "the object" had something in common. Mark, how could you develop this notion in relation to some of the architectural issues that are surrounding us today?

MARK TAYLOR Looking back at the presentations of work-in-progress this morning, I think one could make a case that when notions of the digital and the virtual (and they are not the same) are expanded, they necessitate a reconfiguration of "the object" in such a way that it takes on more of the characteristics of "the thing" as perceived by Heidegger. That is to say, the distinction between thing and object, as Heidegger described it, is that the object is always that which can be represented or represented in an oppositional structure that allows for a certain kind of definition and control, whereas the thing can never be set up in terms of the kinds of binary structures that the subject/object presupposes. It seems to me that if one begins to see what I would call an expanded notion of information – that is, information and data processes that are not limited to the screen but that in certain ways obscure the line between the immaterial and the material, or the physical and the ostensibly nonphysical – then the kind of oppositional structures presupposed by the notion of object begin to be rendered problematic. So, it may well be that digital and virtual objects are more thinglike than objectlike in terms of this distinction. With this shift, of course, goes a certain, precarious hold on control – in other words, objects might not be as objective as they appear to be once you're in that virtual environment.

COHEN I was struck by the fact that in all the talks we heard this afternoon, perhaps with the exception of Bruce Mau's, there were implied notions of surface and skin. One could see this in a number of the projects of Coop Himmelb(l)au, and also in how Osamu Ishiyama worked with the envelopes and skins of his buildings. Could we say then that "thingness" in architecture today is identified with a skin, given that the discourse has traditionally celebrated structure, celebrated components or networks or systems inside of a building?

TAYLOR I think that as infrastructures become increasingly problematic (regardless of how those infrastructures are understood philosophically), one begins to get a sense that the skin extends all the way down, all the way within, so that skin itself becomes complicated. In a way this touches on what Fred Jameson was talking about this morning – that a loss of depth leaves a superficiality. Depth is there to simplify complexity, at one level, but part of what seems to happen when depth itself becomes another layer of surface is that surface becomes complicated in such a way that it cannot be reducible.

One of the ways that I've been trying to think of this lately has been in terms of the difference between the figure of the grid and the figure of the network. You can picture a grid, but a network is very hard to visualize. One of the fascinating things about Wolf's cinema project is that what might have been a classically modernist type of structure gets warped in interesting ways. It maintains a rectilinearity and undergoes a kind of warping of the structure. Wolf, how do you see the grid functioning within this apparent simultaneity?

WOLF PRIX Do you mean the grid on the surface?

TAYLOR I mean the grid on the surface, and yet the building itself destroys a grid structure.

PRIX The only grid we used was for the glass skin, but that was more for reasons of economy than anything else.

TAYLOR What would you have done without financial constraints?

PRIX We would have invented an energy field which protects us, because skin in architecture is just a medium, as I said earlier, to protect us against the overcooling or overheating of our bodies. If we could replace the skin with an energy field, I would do it immediately. This is my hope for digital architecture – that it can create fields and forces that could replace materials (not everywhere and at anytime, but just sometimes).

You know, sometimes we say architecture starts where space ends. This could be a reason for trying to get rid of all materials. On the other hand, after reading the latest research about space – that something in our brain signals space as an area that you can move through – it brings me back to the idea that architecture also has to have materials you can touch, surfaces you can feel as material.

GREG LYNN That's the topic for tomorrow morning.

PRIX Oh, I'm sorry!

COHEN Overlaps are the best thing that can happen here. I have a question for Daniel Buren – Daniel, you introduce grids into a number of city settings. Have you been aware of the seemingly obsessive work that has been carried out in architectural discourse on grids over the past decades, so that working on grids, distorting grids, reinterpreting urban and architectural grids becomes referenced to an architectural discourse outside of an artistic one?

DANIEL BUREN I think the desire to stabilize something is a very old and natural impulse. Of course, over the last ten years I have seen the kinds of distortion games you describe played by architects with grids. But I don't think this relates to what I do, because I don't see my work as architecture. I just see myself as working with existing material, in front of buildings but not connected to them, in ways that are both conceptual or more obviously physical. For example, in the Place des Terraux project, we simply tried to clean the space instead of adding a new object. The result was something almost empty — making a wonderful, existing space visible again by cleaning it of all the clutter that had gathered there over the years.

AUDIENCE There have been so many different kinds of reality presented here today, but in contrast to the hectic images of Bruce Mau's video presentation, or to the intensity of the world that Romi Khosla confronts, I felt so much more comfortable with Daniel Buren's world, because he has a greater sense of introspection and a sensibility for our origins, for water and history.

COHEN Sanford, as a sort of adjacent observer to the field of architecture, how do you respond to these issues — yourself as Sanford Kwinter, not as Bruce Mau's proxy?

SANFORD KWINTER I've been waiting for ten years for somebody to quote Bob Dylan at an Any conference and I'm very jealous that it was Wolf and not me. Now I'm a bit uncertain of what to say so let me begin by working through a couple of initial

ideas. The first is that I too share a profound and spontaneous compassion when water and history are elicited as places where one might rather find oneself today. The second, though, concerns the impulse to flee. What I refer to here is the struggle that we, as moderns, must engage in, but that we must also learn to triumph over. This, more than anything, is our work. We must overcome the impulse to flee the incredible and undeniable ugliness of the present. It is our responsibility to embrace it, and to at least pretend to love it, if for no other reason than because it is ours. I have spent many years trying to reconcile the ugliness of what is ahead of us, of what approaches, with the beauty that one is allowed to imagine as part of where we have come from. I'm fully aware that this is a romantic posture, but I am convinced that it is one that we need in order to live. I have found increasingly over the last years that history — as much as we may love it and take consolation in it, and as much as we may realize that it offers a better place to be — has become something of a hindrance to a responsible way of grasping and dealing with the problems of the present. I absolutely do not plan to spend the rest of my working years entirely engaged with the vulgar future and present, but for now I have consciously left history behind. The history that consumes us today, I would argue, is being made for us in and as a default scenario. Humans, I fear, no longer really make their own world. We are living in troubled times, and I feel that we should be careful about taking solace in the bath of history. Please do not think that I am accusing you [the questioner] of cowardice. I'm just telling you that this is a problem that we all face, and we all choose different ways to deal with it. Perhaps cultural work today should resemble a kind of mili-

tary service. You need to put in some of your best years for the nasty defense of liberties, and only then can you disengage in order to pursue subtler, more refined ends. But the second pursuit without the poignantly mitigating influence of the first invariably falls into complacency and decadence.

AUDIENCE I want to return to Mark Taylor's comments, because I'm trying to think how one could reconceptualize this new notion of the thing — the thing not necessarily operating in a kind of binary differentiation from the object but as something different. I have in mind some of the work that Rem Koolhaas did early in his career with respect to the Berlin Wall and later with the Bibliothèque Nationale in Paris on the void, and the notion of emptiness in architecture now becoming a kind of surrogate for the thing.

TAYLOR I've also been thinking a lot recently about the figure of the Berlin Wall and its collapse as a trope for examining many of the changes that have occurred over the last decade. I don't particularly like the notion, or metaphors, of collapsing walls, but maybe in their place (and this is stuff that I'm trying to work through) we could shift from the notion of the wall, which in a certain sense creates a slash between a whole world of binaries, to the notion of a screen or of screening. **Screen** is a nice word because it signifies lots of different things. Screens also seem to be a more apposite way of looking at these things today, as walls that were once secure appear to be transforming more into permeable screens. This isn't to suggest that they just disappear, but that things are more permeable. Nietzsche says somewhere (and I can never remember where) that when reality disappears we aren't left with appearance because appearance and reality are a packaged deal – when one goes, the other changes, is reconfigured. Similarly, the screen can mean both to hide and to show. So I don't think that we are necessarily seeing a move toward the immaterial today, because at one level a lot of the processes that we have taken to be material are rather information processes that increase a kind of permeability, and therefore they break down the oppositional structure of the **Gegenstand** or object into a kind of screening that both reveals and conceals at the same time.

COHEN I just want to make two brief comments in conclusion. The first, I would argue, is that common to many of the works we have seen today is a sense of playfulness – architecture as a playful and sometimes cheerful experiment. Equally, and somewhat ambivalently, though, the works and discourses surrounding them also all revealed a certain tension: a tension between art and architecture in the city with Daniel Buren's work; a tension and opposition between thingness and objectness in the discourse of Heidegger as interpreted by Mark Taylor; tension inside and outside the skin in the buildings of Wolf Prix; a tension between images, narratives, and buildings in the work of Osamu Ishiyama; and the tension of daily life as the central focus of Bruce Mau's **STRESS** installation. I say this not to diminish them or to try to smooth out their contradictions but rather to highlight their fruitful differences.

"use this"

"avoid fatty s"

IN THE MOOD FOR ARCHI-
TECTURE

JEFFREY KIPNIS

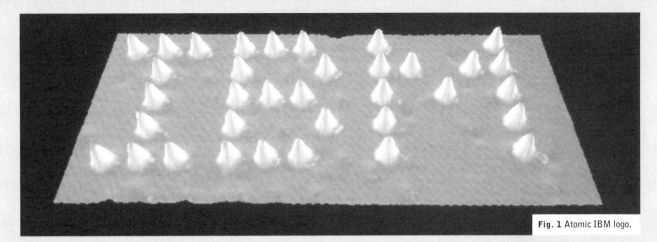

Fig. 1 Atomic IBM logo.

Fig. 2 Jacques-Henri Lartigue, **Car Trip, Papa at 80 kilometers an hour**, 1913.

Fig. 3 Gilles Deleuze, **Bergsonism**, cover design by Bruce Mau.

I was looking over ten years of Any – it's pretty amazing. And I was asking myself what questions are left, because in a sense what I was hoping to do here was to bury Any by praising it. Any has accomplished an extraordinary feat: it has exhausted the problem of representation, of theory in architecture, in every domain – semiotic, Marxist, Freudian, diachronic, synchronic, new and old criticism. But we should now see what questions are left over, and imagine where we could go from here.

The first unanswered, yet to be broached question, I would argue, is, how can architecture be political? I mean, given that architecture is a self-conscious art form (and not a kind of mythology of "good building" in the hands of an architect), how does architecture behave politically? I raise this in response partly to Fredric Jameson's argument over the last ten years, that in every way that architecture tries to be political, it fails. Second, how does architecture produce irreducible effects? How does it produce effects that belong entirely to architecture and that in some sense are a version of the form of its own autonomy? This in turn deals with why architecture is considered special as a practice. The third question is still open-ended: How is architecture essential? This, I would argue, belongs to a much larger problem that theorists are considering today, and that is, how do we think about art in terms of techniques that are no longer part of the "added-value problem?" This problem states that there is life, art adds quality to life, and therefore it is invaluable, but it is not essential to life. So a way of thinking about art practices in general, and architecture in particular, through systems that are no longer based on added-value models but on essential models, would, I think, be interesting. This then raises the last problem: What is the question of architectural expertise?

To essentially launch a discussion of these questions, I want to begin with an image from an important moment in history. It is an image of atoms manipulated into the form of a logo – an astonishing moment in the impetus of representation. [Fig. 1] Here we are, able to move atoms; we have power over matter (which is almost incomprehensible); we have a power to do things with matter that has incredible promise, and all we can think of is to make an IBM logo out of it. This, for me, is really telling. (I think that this is also where Any is at too – we have an enormous amount of power but we don't know what to do with it.) About a year later, the same atomic scientists were continuing to move atoms around. But instead of making them line up to form a kind of logo for IBM, they made the first artificially constructed molecule, and all of a sudden, entirely new properties are discovered from the manipulation of the material. The implications of this study are that material thought is

no longer going to be just phenomenological. It's no longer going to be looking at the essential properties of the material effect, and then exploring them. It suggests that the manipulation of the material itself, as a kind of atomic semiotics, is possible.

Walter Benjamin, as we all know, considered that architecture is observed in a distracted state. This has always been a challenge to architects in the sense that they thought that he was attacking architecture, and that they needed to fight through the distraction. Hence, Colin Rowe's argument that architecture needed to be understood in close reading, in a state of high-tension – that one needed to regard it as if Benjamin were arguing that all of the detail, all of the expertise, and all of the formal and material relationships that existed in the distracted state were ignored. I think, however, that Benjamin's argument was something really quite different. All of that expertise operated in its most powerful form in a relationship of "in the mood of distraction." So one of the discussions that we have had at Any that I see as shaped by materiality is this debate between close reading and distraction – or what I would call a debate about mood.

In this regard, I remember the first conversation at the first Any conference, when someone said, What about the materials of architecture? I was on a panel, and I said that just like a writer, the materials of architecture are not the letters. You don't analyze Faulkner by analyzing how he uses r's and s's. You analyze Faulkner through the tropes of writing; his figurative language. I said this because at that time I was arguing that architecture is primarily about meaning; to understand architecture one had to look at its semiotic abilities. It then occurred to me, though, that when you read a book by Faulkner, the mood of the book, the materiality of the book, has also been designed. It's been designed by an expert – the graphic designer. So the cover of the book, the choice of paper, the fonts of the letters, the spacing, the justification – these have all set up a distracted meaning that's not part of the intentional consciousness of the meaning, and is perhaps where the materiality of the book starts to have effects more powerful than the actual text. So I decided to refine my argument a little. Architecture does, like all material practices, have the ability to represent and to act in a tropic structure, but it also has the ability to produce these other kinds of effects – and I see graphic design as the ideal example.

There is a very famous Jacques-Henri Lartigue photograph of motion. [Fig. 2] I am referring to it because it provides the background image of Bruce Mau's cover design for Gilles Deleuze's book *Bergsonism*. [Fig. 3] Now *Bergsonism* is really a discussion of matter and duration and time. One of the issues Henri Bergson was interested in was different concepts of time. (The Any conferences, by the way, are one of the most amazing places to understand Bergsonism, because at Any you can sit in a room for 20 minutes and it can feel like a century; you can come to Any and actually live forever.) What is incredible about this book is the degree to which there is expertise and intellection. But you are not reading this from the cover of the book. The design sets up a mood of reception through a color spectrum – the transition from red to green, and the elongation of the image. Technically, this reveals a high level of expertise, and is full of meaning, but it is not meaning that you are really required to pay close attention to; rather, it sets up the receptive space of the work. In the end, this means that we have to look at something else (and this is the argument that Sanford Kwinter has articulated about the culture of the image), because the prevailing model of close attention, the production of new meaning, and, in fact, the whole issue of criticality, draw on the diagram of collage. Essentially, all of the productions of Any have been to theorize various versions of collage – collages of program, collages of signs, collages of forms. It has become the ubiquitous and most powerful organizing principle in 20th-century society, and it has organized architecture to the point where we know no alternatives.

Collage requires a certain mood of receptivity: we pay close attention, we begin to understand the various critical junctions and disjunctions, it dematerializes in a certain way, and deterritorilizes. What is important here is not the specific materials of these issues but the image of the issues in their new juxtaposition. So the effect of collage is to support ideas, and close reading, and to suppress material effects. And it has a fantastic power – it produces new knowledge. One collage has saved hundreds of thousands of lives: it is the collage that launched the first National Science Foundation studies that found that smoking causes cancer. [Fig. 4] What is especially interesting to me is that this image creates a mood that one has to fight through to get into the objective frame of mind to actually understand the knowledge. The mood of it, however, is something that I am also interested in – what it takes to get through the mood, to the collage, to read the consequence. Now, we have fantastic powers because of this – because of our studies of collage effects, ideation, and semiotics, we can do incredible things. I can take a fairly banal image of a still life, and then through a series of tricks, give it new meaning. And give new meaning to the idea of still life, as if it's *still* life. On the other hand, this misses the fact that the painter has also done something – the painter has used the luminescent qualities of the paint, and the gray tones, so that every time the light changes at every gray scale, the luminescence and iridescence of the light changes, and so it moves through the day in a spectacular fashion. The material properties and the material effects, then, actually overwhelm the production of meaning (that close attention), and produce a mood. The more we frame it and analyze it for its ability to produce meaning, the more we lose relationships that, I think, also make it more interesting.

In looking recently at two images of the brain – one showing ordinary brain waves, the other showing the brain stimulated – two things occurred to me. The first was that I liked the image of the ordinary brain much better. The second was that this image appeared to have more information in it. What is happening is that a single surface (the video surface) is indexing all the information in a body (because it's an electroencephalograph); every thought, every bit of information, is indexed into a single surface or a single material frame, so that hyperindexicality produces an effect over and above any reading (that is, anything we might term "voluptuous" or "iridescent"). So this alternative model for producing new affects and effects by hyperindexing single surfaces is a way that we can use to connect issues like the treatment of surfaces involved in contemporary architectural debate (luminescent projects, distorted form, complex surface projects, etc.). Hyperindexicality, therefore, becomes a way to work with technical expertise to produce material effects that are no longer either phenomenological or critical. Again, illustrative of this idea is a dew garden. It is particularly interesting because in looking at it, we're not especially interested in the pattern but in the fact that it was created by a person who is applying a hyperindexical relationship to the material properties of dew to create these patterns, and then they're gone two hours later.

Lastly, I want to compare two films to see if I can offer some sense of the possibility of mood-changing affect as a project for architecture as opposed to criticality. This is a still from a very familiar film to architects – it is from the set of *Rear Window*. [Fig. 5] *Rear Window* is, as you know, a spectacular film by Alfred Hitchcock. It is amazing how many architects have written about it (including the Finnish architect Juhani Pallasmaa, who tried, impossibly, to draw an analytical plan of the set). What is particularly interesting about this film is that it summarizes all of the achievements of Any; every form of critical analysis and semiotics is put into play, whether it's the Athletic Club collage of programming, or the collage of the federalist style, or the syntax of the windows, or even Bernard Tschumi's "necessity of committing murder to appreciate architecture" – the film is the very essence of architectural theory. It is constructed entirely out of signifying elements that actually are about dematerialization. The use of materiality in this film is suppressed entirely into the favor of signification. For example, the sets are completely reconstructed; the apartments are thin so that the back wall is close enough to the front window to act like a

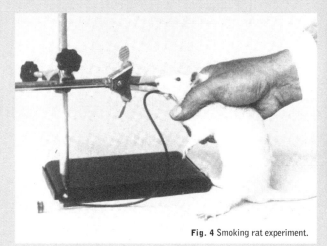

Fig. 4 Smoking rat experiment.

Fig. 6 Richard Brooks, **In Cold Blood**.

Fig. 5 Alfred Hitchcock, **Rear Window**.

painting; there are constant numbers of references. It was impossible to light this film with natural light and artificial light normal to an apartment, so the entire lighting stock at Paramount Studios was used to create the artificial lighting effects of the film.

Rear Window begins with the thermometer reading 92 degrees Fahrenheit, to let you know that it's hot. This is really important for two reasons: Hitchcock wanted to symbolize the murder, because he had heard a theory that most murders occur at 92 degrees. Just to reemphasize the heat, Jimmy Stewart's character, Jeff, is first introduced in the film sweating. You never see sweat again in the entire film. (Obviously you couldn't have Grace Kelly sweating in an Edith Head outfit, but under lights, through nighttime dinners, there is no sweat and no bugs.) But the heat is important. Why is the heat important? Because you need to have the windows open. Why do you have to have the windows open? Because you can't film through glass (the reflections would interfere with the shot). And in fact, the Chicago-style window used in the film has no glass. So the great thing about *Rear Window* is that in order to use the sign of the window and create the critical effect, it has to eliminate the window. There are no windows in *Rear Window*.

In looking at the construction of the film's symbolism, I don't mean to impugn *Rear Window*, because it is an astonishing critical accomplishment in representation. I do mean to suggest that the way we have exhausted representational thinking can be seen in the film. Notice, for example, the binoculars that Jeff uses early in the film; but as he gets more and more erotically involved in the panoptic, voyeuristic issue, it turns into an "erect" lens of sorts. Technologically equipped this way, of course, he represents Hitchcock; he represents the filmmaker. Seen through this guise, one then gets the most wonderful overlaying of roles – the filmmaker (or rather, Jeff, the symbol of the filmmaker), seeing the actual filmmaker (Hitchcock, in one of his famous, brief cameo appearances), at the same time as being under the direction of the filmmaker. The film's central visual motif is Jeff's open window. But as I said earlier, there is no window in the middle frame, and several times in the film Hitchcock has someone actually pretend as if they're looking in the middle frame – through nonexistent glass.

The last image I want to examine is from a scene at the end of Richard Brooks's film, *In Cold Blood*. [Fig. 6] In this famous shot, the refraction of rain water on the pane of window glass projects tears down the face of Robert Blake – that is, the window does all the crying. What is interesting to me is that as you're following the film, the effects that are producing the affect of the film essentially make it irreducibly filmic. You could not produce the same effect with slides –

you have to show the film, you have to hear it. It works like Mau's book cover. It is irreducibly filmic; it requires film expertise. It is not the auteur model of the director because this was an effect discovered by Conrad Hall (the cinematographer) by accident, because the stagehands sprayed too much water onto the glass. They didn't even discover it until they saw the rushes. The whole process of different forms of expertise coming together to produce material effects that produce meaning at the level of affect over and above signification, is, I think, a valuable model for us to explore.

LIGHT SCORE

Properties of light also provide the organizing concept for the Museum of the City we designed for Cassino, Italy. We attempted to model the light on computers and quickly realized physical models were necessary. In fact, light should be modeled full size as it falls off a wall at the square of its distance to the source. The galleries are organized in interlocking light sections. Between each section is an interval, which is the equivalence of silence in music and which forms a reversible sequence that can be "played" by bodily movement. Each exhibition area begins as neutral space individuated through its specific quality of light.

THE THINGNESS OF LIGHT

STEVEN HOLL

MUSEO CASSINO, KEY TO THE SCORE

c	curve-shaped light
l	linear light
cl	curved and linear light
cl.dr	curved and linear light with dropped ceiling
cl.md	curved and linear light with round slit
clS	curved and linear light with superimposed slides
rc	reversed corners
g	grabbed light
sqsq	two squares grabbing light
gg	double grabbed
ggS	double grabbed superimposed slides (to be superimposed)
gg?	double grabbed superimposed box
gg.dr	double grabbed with soffit
t.sq	center square cut out with tinted glass
oo.up	two round spaces stacked, upper view
oo.und	two round spaces stacked, under view
s	spiral space
/s	semi-circular space with slit on side
b	shell space (double s)
sqb	center square cut-out shell space
sqbS	center square cut-out and shell space superimposed slide
sq	center square cut-out
o	center round cut-out
orc	center round cut out and reversed corners
orcS	center round cut out and reversed corners superimposed sides
obx.und	round space stacked on a square space, under view
obx.up	round space stacked on a square space, upper view
ŏbx.und	round space with slit roof stacked on a square space, upper view

As we enter the 21st century, we find that the boundaries and horizons of our fundamental experiences have expanded and continue to expand. We experience and think differently than we did 100 years ago, even 20 years ago. Should we therefore feel differently? How elastic are our minds? How can we stretch them? As a potential vehicle for this expansion of thought, the luminous power of light aligns architecture with the poetry of phenomenal experience and the physics of optics. Light is the haiku of architectural building materials; it achieves the most with the least. Yet the physics of light are complex – scattering, polarization, reflection, refraction, diffraction, and interference can all be understood as the substance with which we can build new spatial experiences.

The presence of light is the most fundamental connecting force of the universe. According to current scientific thinking, light first appeared around half a million years after the Big Bang, in the period known as "decoupling." Before decoupling, the universe was an opaque, shadowless, plasmalike material; after, it became transparent to light. Light is visible electromagnetic radiation that measures between 400 and 700 nanometers, but the boundaries of light are not as precise as its scientific definition would reveal due to our varying perceptions of it. Light can be read both as a phenomenon (typically recorded in words) and as a pressure (as it is seen in science). Similarly, language without structure, like natural light, has essences that transcend specific meanings and purposes. Language can then become a form of light in itself, just as light can become a language. In a contained volume pierced with openings, light makes the space luminous, dreamlike, with its own language. For the viewer, a moment of intense sensibility ignites the intuition. Sideways, forward, backward . . . the empty words of light are spoken in utter silence.

As light travels greater and greater distances away from its source, it grows dimmer and its beam begins to flatten out. There is, however, a limit to how thinly light can be spread before it begins to flicker. Eventually light becomes "lumpy." At its most diffuse, the ultimate lump or "atom" of light is a photon. If our eyes were strong enough, we could "see" photons striking the retina, creating a discontinuous flickering beam.

Light's wave/particle duality is a mystery like that of the fundamental paradox of modern physics. The two fundamental theories of General Relativity (for the large scale) and Quantum Mechanics (for the smallest scale) are not yet reconcilable. We can analyze light, but no scientist has yet been able to describe clearly what light exactly is. It seems today that light is remarkably and irreducibly of a dual nature. As the history of ideas continues, the enigma of light is an ongoing episode.

The speed of light at 186,000 miles per second – a constant so fixed as to become an astronomical measure in light years – has recently been called into question. In an experiment at Harvard University, light has been slowed to a speed of 17 miles per second using a system of laser beams with electromagnetically induced transparency. (In optics, it would seem, geometry is destiny.) Lene Vestergaard Hau, who worked on the Harvard experiment, has said that light will be slowed further to one mile per hour, and predicted that it might be possible to get atoms to surf on the front of a light pulse. At another extreme, an experiment by Anedio Ranfagni, Rocco Ruggeri, and Daniela Mugnai, for the Italian National Research Council in Florence, has pushed light to 300 times beyond its "constant" of 186,000 miles per second. Given such speed, one can imagine a radical change: rather than being electrically driven, for example, computers could be light driven. The nanotechnology of the optical switch, crucial for this new "after electronics" revolution, has already been established.

The different properties of light provided the organizing concept for the Museum of the City we designed for Cassino, Italy, in 1994. To illustrate our ideas, physical models were necessary, but unlike standard architectural models, light should be modeled at full size in order to see how it falls off a wall at a square of the distance from the source. Using the results of these studies, the galleries of the museum were organized through interlocking light sections. Between each section is an interval. We saw these intervals as equivalent to rests in music and as forming a reversible sequence that can be "played" by the passage and procession of bodily movement. Thus each exhibition area presents itself as neutral space, individuated through its specific quality of light.

A museum space, in this way, has been filled with a desire to "represent." But if we imagine the mystery of how light feels, could we also imagine its exact natural, vocalized representation? Perhaps architecture could begin to make sense here as a score. [See previous spread.] For example, if we characterize a property of an interlocking light section, L is very valuable. G and S are quite useful. The interval – which may be the most important reflective space – is the all-important blank. We imagine that we can move forward or backward in the spaces of light. A sense of the theater comes through as it holds in the rhythms of architecture's light. The psychological effects of light can lead to extremes of feeling with direct repercussions. We can speak of light as in a dream.

The Light Laboratory, functionally established as the new entrance vestibule of the renovated Cranbrook Institute of Science, utilized light technologies in an experimental project employing glass lens techniques never before constructed at this scale. In the Laboratory, every day is different. The low winter sun refracts in luminous waves while a prismatic rainbow washes the blank wall in unpredictable iridescence. Gentle waves of diffraction suddenly merge with pulsing shadows, which appear near the ceiling as inverted dancers. The speed of shadow is vibrant. Similar studies in light have informed projects in Helsinki and Seattle. In Finland's Kiasma Museum, the building captures the low angle of the Helsinki sun (which never rises above 51 degrees) with its double-warped curve tracing a reverse curve of the sun's directional path. At the Chapel of St. Ignatius in Seattle, the concept of a gathering of different lights, or seven bottles of light in a stone box, forms chromatic space. An eclipse of white clarity suddenly gives way to a pulse with color – light here is contingent, its shadows intermittent. Another experiment made in chromatic space is at 410 Sarphatistraat on the Singel Canal in Amsterdam. As a large "Menger Sponge," the spaces of the building were made parallel to a composition method of the composer Morton Feldman, who looked "not to compose but to project sounds into time." The pavilion, plan, section, and elevations of the building, all equally perforated, are an experiment in designing what Feldman calls "patterns in a chromatic field" via chance operations.

Through these kinds of studies, a new field of vision is opening to the pressure of light and the speed of shadow propelled by science's phenomenal discoveries in the last part of the 20th century. These experiences of light and shadow are moving from the simple umbra of shadow to the penumbra of extended sources. Light's once fixed "constant" speed is being slowed in some experiments and increased in others. For example, "Red Shift" measurements have allowed us to ponder the paradox of the acceleration of the expanding universe. We think and see differently, therefore, we should feel differently.

There is, then, a "thingness" of light which may be scored and given phenomenal order. This would not be a verbal order as light is not verbal – rather, we need spaces and images. Light's "thingness" embraces the paradox of wave/particle duality. Like the gap between relativity and quantum mechanics, these central mysteries characterize modern physics. Here is where science metamorphizes into poetry and art; this is architecture's territory.

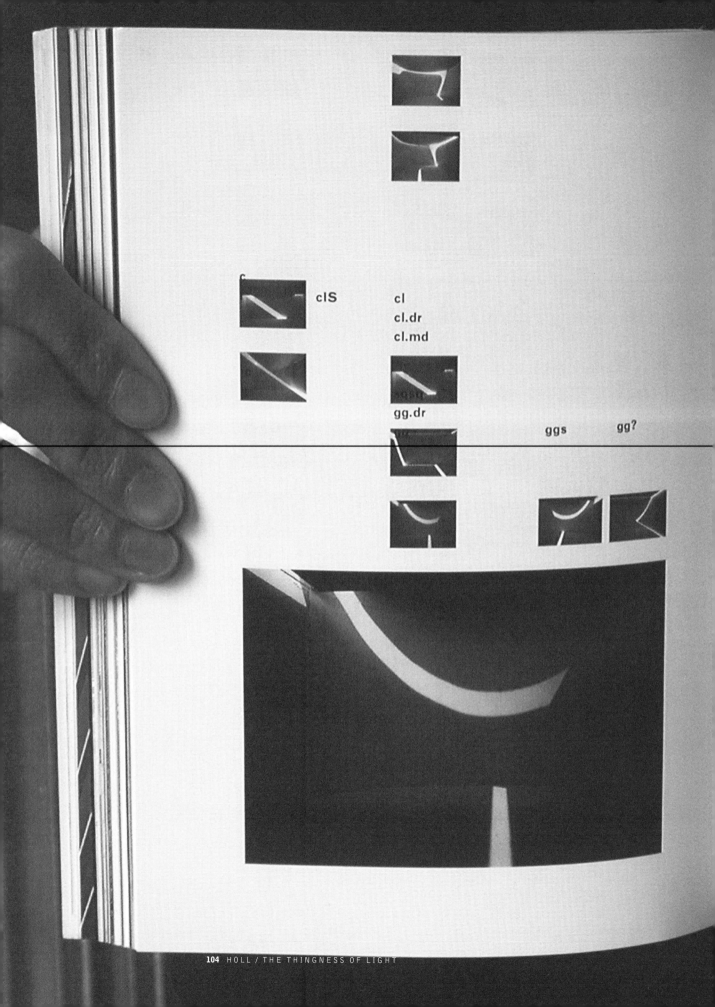

clS

cl
cl.dr
cl.md

gg.dr

ggs   gg?

c

  clS

cl.md

rc

g

gg.dr

o   oo.up   oo.und

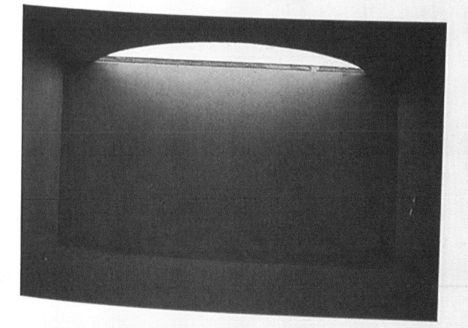

RADIANT
SYNTHETIC
EFFECTS

BEN VAN
BERKEL/
CAROLINE
BOS

Aarnhem Transfer Hall.

To make an architecture that is truly utilitarian, we need to know, calculate, and direct its effects. But how does one define architectural effect? Effects are felt but cannot be grasped; effects are not bodies, facts, or properties. Effects are not standardized and categorized. Effects include sensory experiences of the external world, experiences of the inner world, and experiences of emotion or affect. An architectural effect synthesizes these three aspects.

Some of the most liberating effects that architecture can achieve today spring from new understandings of time and space. Time and space are no longer seen as homogeneous. Through synthesis and visualization, mathematicians and physicists have gradually worked toward new conceptualizations of space as differential; space has black holes in it, it is curved, it expands and contracts, it changes with time. Space is seen as topologically formed. New visualizations of space arise, like the imaginary phase space. With these new conceptualizations comes an increased malleability of substance. Factors relating to the organization of space, such as allocation, division, and appropriation, become elastic. The spring structure is a new spatial effect, consisting of a line that transforms itself as it writhes through space, coiling, supercoiling, and uncoiling as it twists and flattens itself out again, stretches itself widely and narrows once more in an uninterrupted sequence of deformations. The Seifert surface is an orientable surface of which one boundary component is embedded in such a way that it forms a knot, resulting in planes changing direction and flipping over. Mathematically, orientability implies that a surface has two distinct sides. Orientability therefore pertains to a spatially obvious situation.

Under the influence of time, the pliability of space becomes even greater, especially when time is itself seen as an entity subject to transformation. Time, while irreversible and thus only susceptible to change in one direction, is increasingly thought of as differentiated. Time is variable in many ways, not through acceleration alone. It has intervals, as shown by periodic systems; it is a factor in entropy; it generates uncertainty and unpredictability. The subjective experience suggests that time varies constantly; there is regulated time and there is time that is boundless, there is long time and short time, quality time and catastrophic time.

The volatile, differentiated aspects of time enhance the realistic potential of topological knots for architecture. Topology, as the study of the properties of surface structures under deformation, is the hybridization of differential space and differential time. When the continuous deformation of the surface leads to the intersection of interior and exterior planes, the transformability of topological surfaces results in nonorientable objects. The perfect continuity of nonorientability initiates new categories of surfaces and effects. The Möbius band, used architecturally, makes a thematic connection operate differentially in a field of time. The surface integrates distribution of the programs, infrastructure, construction, events, and time. The mathematical proposition of the Klein bottle gives rise to even more far-reaching architectural effects. As an edgeless, nonorientable geometric structure that intersects itself, it has no closed interior. It can be used to achieve an integral construction that works like a landscape acted on by dynamic force fields. The surface of the Klein bottle can be translated into a channeling system, incorporating all the ingredients that it encounters and propelling them into a new type of interrelated, integral organization.

Topologically inspired diagrams like the spring structure, Seifert surface, Möbius band, and Klein bottle are not applied to architecture in a stringent mathematical way, but neither are they mere metaphors or themes. These orientable and nonorientable organizations provide unifying, abstract, three-dimensional models that can be wholly or partially projected onto real-life locations to integrate the imagination and the policy at the basis of the project and its programs, techniques, organization, and public utility. They provide direction and introduce into architecture the effects of differential space and time.

SILK CUT EFFECT

Territorial effects are among the most direct manifestations of time and space in an orientable situation. In the field condition of the beach, the towel is the orientable mediator that is used to make territorial organizations. In an urban grid, building blocks and streets are the mediators. They too are orientable – a house has its interior and exterior surfaces. The urban grid is a stable and meaningful pattern of organization. However, when dynamic territorial claims that counter the planned structure are introduced, the effects that result are less stable and straightforward. The Silk Cut cigarette advertisements demonstrate the effects of dynamic territorialization in the field of communication because they create a complex loop structure to communicate their message. The indirect, layered approach generates an abstract visual/commercial statement, leaving out all references to the product itself. The message is both literally and diagrammatically founded on slashing the orientable surface, revealing how tenuous and open to transformation the distinction is between the planes of being and of representation.

The Silk Cut effect shows that some of the strongest, most successful contemporary effects are related to the destabilization of structure, meaning, and image. Working

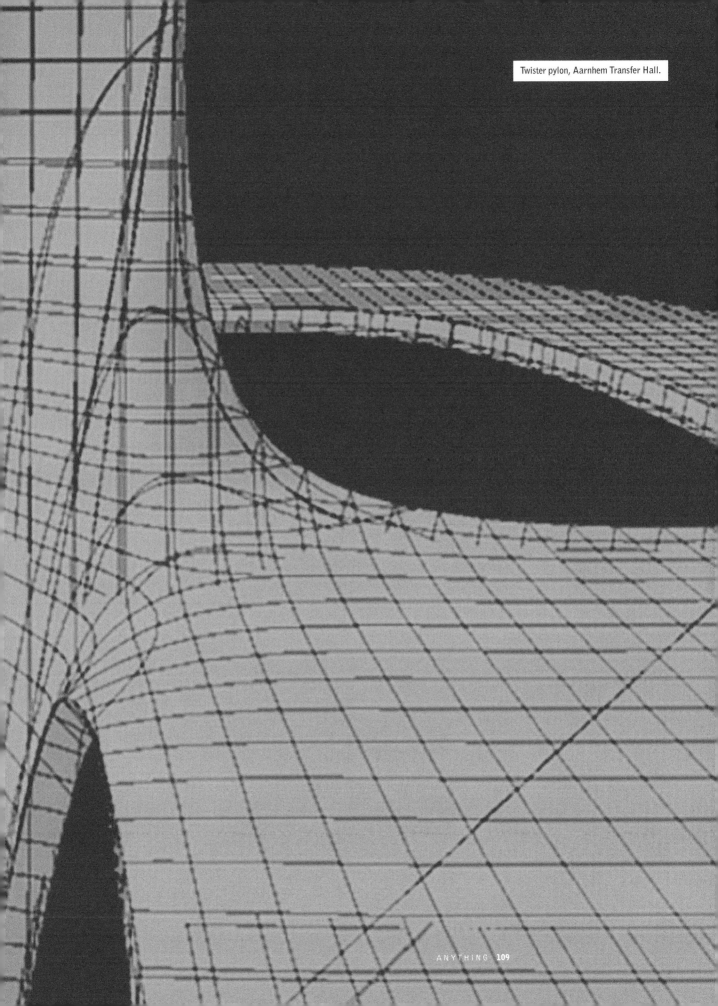

Twister pylon, Aarnhem Transfer Hall.

Interior, Aarnhem Transfer Hall.

with many layers in response to a complex situation does not necessarily generate multiplicitous and complex effects. On the contrary, layered strategies, incorporating diffuse structures and diffuse messages, result in stronger architectural effects. The reading of pattern organizations as the stable consolidation of the relation between structure and image becomes impossible under the pressure of dynamic territorial claims; the whole idea that form has significance disappears.

MADE IN HEAVEN EFFECT

Fashion and advertising are united in their celebration of the product – this being primarily an immaterial package of styling, marketing, and display. Its special effects are universal recognition and positive sensations. Its seductiveness is a form of utility. The familiar luxury of the product has an uplifting and spiritual effect.

It does not matter who has made a product; names matter only insofar as they are brands. An architect's desire to be nameless is no false modesty; on the contrary, it is an expression of the highest ambition. We invest in the infrastructure of a name and an organization only to produce; the product itself is the thing that is launched into the world, into history, to stretch its existence, which is only effect, as far as possible. In architecture, the Made in Heaven effect is expressed most purely in perfectionist buildings that give you a rich feeling that causes you to gaze continuously upward and from side to side. To enter their hollow bodies with your own body enlightens you. To move through them is to walk through a painting; you see what you choose to see, your gaze swerves and orients you through color, shine, light, figuration, and sensation.

AIRPORT EFFECT

Airports are places of floating, noncommittal comforts that have their source in numbers. Continuous logistics, compounded by the liberating sensation of imminent departure, culminate in a smooth and anxiety-repressing effect. Numerically, the airport is situated at the extreme end of a transport-junction scale, which also contains bus terminals, railway stations, and motorway service stations: that is, places where qualities emerge from quantities. Here, separations are not so much spatial as temporal. In the airport model, mathematical nonorientability is paralleled by time-based continuous difference, which inhibits the fixed orientation of programs – movement is the program and the program is moving. The time-based topological organization requires a vast input of information. Mediation technologies are used to assimilate the logistics and the policies forming the basis of the project into a model or diagram that is more timetable than masterplan.

FACIALITY EFFECT

Everything comes together in the face; the effect of faciality lies in the utility of integration. Modernism was responsible for making possible an understanding of the outer surface of a building as four or five elevations, rather than the façade-mask. Now we can see beyond elevation to the black hole and white wall system that produces an integral effect, irreducible to a single meaning. Faciality transforms the building into a unified landscape that we read like a face; there is no point in separating its parts. Faciality implies subjectification; the face, the organization, is undeniably subjective. No other organization is quite like it. Utility and outward appearance are intermingled in the unique face. There is no mask to pull off; the skin does not "represent" some rigid presumption about functionalist goings-on behind it; it is what it is, inside and outside.

BACK TO ZERO EFFECT

Today, a good building is a work of art – a silent, abstract sculpture. It looks just as good without people as it does with them because it has its own life; the contemporary building does not need external events to come to life anymore. How does one achieve a building that is as useful as a work of art but is still the manifestation of a public science?

We need to start again at zero to move to the questions of organization: How can we instrumentalize the global imagination into contemporary organizational structures, and how can we instrumentalize the new public, mediated space into contemporary architectural effects? To coordinate informational layers into an abstract architectural organization is similar to the activity of a sound technician mixing musical layers; the input of numerous instrumental recordings leads to a coherent musical system possessing synchronous frequencies. To move through a structure like this is to experience cinematic effects as the structure unravels in time, coils back in on itself, engenders spin-offs, bumps into itself, and ties up loose ends. Empty, reduced, and abstracted, the organization can absorb more information.

Effects act on many levels and there are always many of them at work simultaneously. The effects that we describe here do not operate in a pure and undiluted form but, at best, take part in a kaleidoscope of utility, in which the vividness of each individual effect is moderated by the simultaneous presence of other effects. Effects are actions and they emanate from relations. The best effects which architecture can produce in the contemporary world are those that are proliferating and moving, effects that are anticipatory, unexpected, climactic, cinematic, time-related, nonlinear, surprising, mysterious, compelling, and engaging.

THINKING OF GADAMER'S FLOOR

JACQUES HERZOG

A few years ago, the Centre Georges Pompidou in Paris invited a small group of architects to think about an exhibition on architecture that would feature new media rather than traditional architectural objects such as models, plans, and photographs. Despite the subsequent cancellation of the show due to a lack of funding, we had already started developing a concept based on the idea of interviewing four people from different fields and different generations, and asking them the very basic question, "What is architecture?" Among the four, we wanted to ask a child; we wanted to ask an artist; and we also wanted to talk with a philosopher.

Our philosophical interview, which took place four years ago, was with the then 96-year-old Hans Georg Gadamer [seen opposite], who studied under Martin Heidegger and became one of the greatest figures in German philosophy in the 20th century. The interview was especially interesting because Gadamer's words sounded as if from another time and world, a period when architecture had a kind of unbroken quality, and a now lost sense of the real. We asked Gadamer to describe what he saw architecture to be in the most general terms, and without reference to any specific architectural works. In his response he did not offer any theoretical explanations but instead told us a story from his childhood, growing up in the town of Breslau.

In the home of his parents, which was one of the *Gründerzeit* bourgeois villas in the town, there was a wonderful parquet floor in the formal reception room, into which the children (including the young Hans Georg) were not allowed to enter except on special occasions like Christmas. Describing the piano and billiard table that stood on this bare floor, Gadamer spoke of this surface as something magical – a wonderful wooden floor, immaculately well-kept and polished so that it filled the space with the smell of wax. Every once in a while a friend of his father's would come to visit, and because it was often raining in Breslau, he would enter carrying his dripping raincoat and umbrella. The man, like his father a professor at the university, always appeared to be immersed in his own thoughts, and would, upon entering the forbidden room, always place his coat and soaking umbrella right down on the magical floor. As a child, Hans Georg would be horrified that a friend of his father's would do such a thing. He still vividly remembers the image of the polished wooden floor decorated with water droplets from the sodden umbrella.

I often think of the Gadamer story because of its idea of the real. Gadamer's floor describes a concept of reality that does not exist anymore – the artisanal and traditional background of the floor itself has been lost for quite some time – but what makes this surface so interesting is its architectural potential for today. In this sense, Gadamer's floor can become an emblem for a very powerful design strategy in its emphasis on materiality, gravity, and maintenance, and its focus on the floor as a floor.

One of the most important architectural elements that makes the Tate Modern in London such a successful building with artists, curators, and the visiting public is the wooden floor that we introduced on almost all of its levels. Irregular and untreated, the oak floor planks are simply nailed down onto their joists. Brutal and beautiful at the same time, it is both rough like a piece of industrial architecture and soft like fashion designer Vivian Westwood's hyper-sophisticated fabrics. We wanted to introduce a specific floor surface so as to ground or root people within this huge building, to exaggerate the sense they have in standing up vertically in front of the works of art. So, unlike Gadamer's parquet, the Tate Modern floor is an intellectual rather than an artisanal product. We were not interested in the nostalgia of revitalizing long gone methods of traditional production, but we were interested in the physical result, in the physical reality of traditional architecture. To achieve this sense of the real, we developed and tested full-scale mock-ups of almost every major detail in the building as part of a process driven by thinking, discussing, and trying, rather than rehearsing individually the necessary technical skills.

In this way, the Tate Modern floor became a prototype for our conceptual and strategic approach to architecture; an approach that is often masked with the traditional costume of architectural elements we all seem to have somehow seen before – comfortable and familiar. This wooden surface is, of course, not a single and isolated piece in that new museum. It is bound to the overall concept of the whole building, based on what we like to call *aikido* strategies. This is a system through which we try to take the pre-existing as a quality that, like in the techniques of the aikido martial art, you use for your own purposes, transforming it into your own energy. So what once seemed to be alien, hostile, and insurmountable, all of a sudden becomes a field where you can act and dictate the architectural and urbanistic scenarios.

The importance of these strategies became obvious to us when we were first faced with the huge brick mass of the existing Bankside power station. What could we possibly do? We could not propose tearing this huge brick mountain of a building down, or destroy any of its obvious architectural elements, such as the chimney (which initially we did not see as relevant to a museum of contemporary art). Another paradox of the existing structure was the obvious intention of its architect, Sir Giles Scott, to connect the building to the brick tower of the cupola of Saint Paul's

Cathedral immediately across the River Thames – a building that has a particularly strong urban and symbolic power in contrast to Bankside, which becomes more secluded and unpublic the closer one gets to it. Scott's design had been prominent and concealed at the same time; people had to be kept away from it. This was something we had to change, and in a way reverse, without destroying or losing the powerful energy of the existing structure. So we decided to drastically cut away the low-rise additions to the main body of the building that were literally masking the site. After these first operations we then added, piece by piece, elements such as the north entrance, the ramp, and the light beam, in a kind of genetic surgery that would incorporate the new pieces into an existing architectural family, all speaking the same language, almost as if they had been there all along.

Inside the building we decided to remove all of the machinery of the former power station, in order to reveal the structure in its most naked state. We became aware that the building was nothing but a huge envelope for that machinery: there was not a single space designed to be different from another; everything was filled with steel structures, platforms, boilers, valves, turbines, engines of every kind. With all of its generators removed, the turbine hall immediately struck us as a space of enormous potential; a volume that in an almost archaeological way could be dug out so as to become visible to an approaching public. People, we felt, should be able to reach the lowest point on the museum site, where all the existing structures could perform internally even more powerfully than the way they reveal themselves externally. At the same time, we wanted to achieve a nonhierarchical layout of the different levels in the museum, avoiding basement and main levels, and to suggest a more democratic treatment of space for a building that looked to become one of the leading museums of the 21st century.

Once we dug out the turbine hall we found the resulting space to be incredible and overwhelming, but it was almost too big and too industrial to serve as a public entrance to the new museum. In particular, we hated the domination of the vertical steel structural columns, and felt that we had to find something that both enhanced the power and logic of the churchlike interior while diluting its monumental impact. We tried many things until we found the light boxes, which, like the large glass piece on top of the building, seem to float, to be unstable in some way, and to cut through the steel columns. The fact that they are mounted in front of the steel structure (and not behind or in between) makes the columns appear less powerful than the light and glass. These light boxes have multiple functions,

which are both dynamic and static: as quiet, more intimate spaces for visitors to rest; as windows that look both from the galleries into the turbine hall and from the hall into the galleries; as illuminating beacons for the main entrance; and, in a strange way, as almost cinematic monitors that project the movement of people.

In the gallery spaces we looked to continue to play with these various dichotomies, framed, the whole time, by the hard physicality of the wooden floor. Interestingly, a number of the artistic works that fill the completed galleries in the Tate Modern also allude to this overlapping of contradictory elements, notably Gary Hill's video installation, *Between Cinema and a Hard Place*, from 1991. As described by Sophie Howarth in the Tate exhibition catalogue, Hill uses video images to explore the metaphors, rhythms, and intonations of language. In a darkened room, 23 television monitors, both black-and-white and color, are stripped of their outer casing and arranged in lines like stones marking a boundary. Across the screens visual sequences unfold and fragment, moving from left to right. Initially it seems as if the images are triggered by a voice reading from "The Nature of Language," an essay by Heidegger. However, as the work continues, the precise correlation between sound and image becomes increasingly unclear. Monitors switch on and off; images flicker and blur. Scenes are transferred from screen to screen or extend across multiple monitors. The images explore the relationship between domesticity and landscape, and reflect on concepts of emotional and geographical closeness, which are the heart of Heidegger's text. Some were filmed from a moving car, and include houses, windows, bridges, fences, and signposts – the frontiers that define or delimit space. As its title suggests, the work also questions the relationship between cinematic and real space. The physical presence of the hardware contrasts with the immateriality of the video imagery, the immediate gallery environment with the televised landscape. The spaces between the monitors insistently fragment the flow of images, underscoring the sense of dislocation expressed in the text.

For us, the title and description of Hill's installation read like a formula for understanding the spatial concept for our Tate project as well as for the design of a number of other projects currently being developed by our office, notably the Kramlich Residence and Media Collection in Oakville in the Napa Valley north of San Francisco. The Kramlich project is conceived as a superimposition of three types of spaces: an immaterial (cinematic) space below grade; a hybrid of material and immaterial space on the garden level; and a real and material space in the attic and along the roofscape. The first of these is a suite of dark rooms specifically

Gary Hill, **Between Cinema and a Hard Place**, 1991.

Gallery floor, Tate Modern, London.

Kramlich Residence and Media Collection.

designed to project and present media installations from the Kramlich collection, such as Hill's *Viewer* or Bill Viola's *Greeting*. A labyrinthine system of interstitial spaces connects the different dark rooms, creating a kind of soft and flowing corridor between the various artistic installations.

The whole below-grade area of the building is a kind of immaterial and shapeless architecture in which no architectural form or particular material should be visually active. The visitor is exposed to the radiating light of the artist's work rather than to the material world of walls, ceilings, and floors delimiting the galleries. In approaching the building, imagine yourself walking or driving through the lush vegetation of the Napa Valley, with the intense smell of trees and bushes and the glaring daylight. All of a sudden you find yourself in a totally artificial world below grade. Your perceptions of reality will then literally shift into something cinematic and almost immaterial.

On top of this hidden dark space sits a glass house entirely built of curved, intersecting glass walls. Living spaces, bathrooms, guest rooms, pool, and master bedroom are all woven into each other like a labyrinth of flowing transparent spaces. Maintaining some sense of the cinematic, certain parts of the curved glass walls can be decorated with the projection of films, videos, and other electronic media, which, unlike paintings and sculptures, can be switched on and off, alternating, in the process, between the material and immaterial. The transparency of the glass walls also provides spectacular views into the landscape and lush Kramlich garden. These views into nature enhance the physical aspect of the glass house, while the electronic images projected onto the glass walls seem to dematerialize the architectural space.

The roof is the third and most physical part of the Kramlich Residence. Structurally and architecturally it is totally different from the below-grade area and the glass installation; a seemingly expressive architectural style that derives from the wide spans and large canopies that we wanted to create. Exaggerating this sense of difference, the steel beams and girders are clad in a translucent Teflon membrane that can be lit at night, transforming the whole roofscape into a huge lantern. Within the roof structure we also left empty certain spaces between the large girders so that we could excavate and create intimate rooms, like the irregular shapes of a domestic attic. In this sense, these chambers are very traditional rooms, decorated with wooden floors and wallpaper, and with conventional doorways opening out onto the roof terrace, heightening a feeling we wanted to create of the real.

In this way, the Kramlich Residence offers a variety of different spaces far beyond the traditional needs and program of a private residence. But the most interesting thing for us is not so much this variety but the shifting concept of reality inscribed in its sequence of rooms. These shifts are based both on our architectural strategies and on the almost subversive curatorial idea we developed of placing art objects everywhere, mixing functional everyday domestic devices with technically sophisticated art installations. In fact, the whole house is characteristic of our approach to architecture, inspired by a concept of evoking and merging issues of the natural and artificial, the material and immaterial, art and nonart, the public and the private.

THE THING CALLED ARCHITECTURE

RAFAEL MONEO

Having followed the previous Any meetings, from Anywhere to Anyway, from Anyplace to Anybody, from Anyhow to Anytime, I now find myself confronted with Anything. For some reason, I am reluctant to adopt a Heideggerian reflection on "thingness," contemplating the essence of building in favor of simply seeing "the thing" as architecture; our profession, our interest, our life. So I have identified "the thing" that informs this conference plainly with architecture, and have prepared some ideas that reflect on the state of the art in architecture today.

Critics and historians of architecture (as distinct from its theoreticians) have consistently tried to legitimize the so-called "modern architecture," born between the two world wars, by relating it either to new techniques of construction or to the new figurative style with which it was contemporaneous. It was argued that this new architecture would contribute to the consolidation of a new society, rejuvenating cities and inspiring new ways to conceive the built world. Critics like Sigfried Giedion celebrated this architecture and its new techniques, declaring the necessity for, and inevitability of, a new built environment. Similarly, historians such as Bruno Zevi saw in this architecture a reinvention of space and a reassessment of ideals of beauty. This legitimation of modern architecture was fueled in part by its sympathetic relationship to the work of avant-garde artists, and for its exploitation of the latest technologies – a connection seen as proof of this architecture as a product of the zeitgeist, the spirit of the time. Neither theory nor history was seen as relevant or necessary. It was enough to be in contact with the moment, developing architecture with the work of the avant-garde artists and building in consonance with the innovations of industry.

This justification endured until the last third of the 20th century, until finally, in the 1960s, the legitimacy of modern architecture was for the first time severely questioned, and its status as the inevitable and only product of the true historical development of architecture came under scrutiny. Team X and the architects gathered around Alison and Peter Smithson were among those who first called for a more solidly founded modern architecture. They sought an architecture with more structure; an architecture less concerned with purely visual and stylistic issues; an architecture based more on method and less on fashion. This theoretical approach also produced attempts to rationalize the design process, for example, in the work of Christopher Alexander, and led to more sophisticated attempts to provide methodological guidelines for design, such as in the work of Geoffrey Broadbent (now a much less known theoretician). While today this work seems surprisingly ingenuous, at the time it was understood as an advanced theoretical approach to functionalism. Other architectural theoreticians also attempted to establish links with linguistic studies, in anticipation of the definition of a possible new architectural language. Books such as Renato De Fusco's *Il Codice dell'Architettura*, or the chapter on architecture in *The Absent Structure* by Umberto Eco, in many ways looked to establish norms and rules that would provide the foundation for a new architectural theory.

In the mid-1960s, new critiques of modern architecture emerged. On the one hand, Aldo Rossi challenged modern architecture by referencing the traditional city, while on the other, Robert Venturi decried the rigid norms of modern architecture, celebrating instead those examples where anomaly prevailed. Each presented a new approach to architecture, and their influence quickly spread. Following quite a different direction, and supported by formalist critics such as Colin Rowe, the New York Five architects (Peter Eisenman, Michael Graves, Charles Gwathmey, John Hejduk, and Richard Meier) claimed that true modernity had yet to be realized, and attempted to further develop those earlier principles. By the end of the 1960s, modern architectural theory had lost its authority.

These new attitudes broke with the respectful view architects had typically maintained for historical continuity, and as a result, critics and theoreticians attempted to develop a comprehensive view of architecture. Having lost contact with artistic trends, and skeptical of the relevance of industrial progress to architecture, the new critics turned their attention instead toward other fields: for the most part, theory was to be left in the hands of historians. One key figure here is the Italian architectural writer Manfredo Tafuri. Educated within a highly emotive, Marxian environment, Tafuri used history as a means to understand the present. He sought to transform the present by discovering the true reasons, the social reasons, behind the more apparent realities of events and styles. In the process, Tafuri tried to explain architectural history within the framework of universal history, and reached the conclusion (aided by the nihilism of the Frankfurt School) that architecture in the current world was only a fantasy nurturing the idealistic goals of the profession. There was no longer any possibility for architecture to serve a social purpose. Tafuri's texts were tremendously influential and, as a result, many Italian architects of his generation suffered from a distrust of the practice and its seemingly inevitable compromise. Later, Tafuri abandoned this approach and ended his career as a more canonical historian, but his preeminence had a definitive impact on the role of theory in subsequent architectures.

One consequence to this renewed interest in history was the reuse of established stylistic features in the architecture of postmodernism. In effect, the late-1960s and early-1970s saw an architecture based upon the misuse of historical references, which produced a built world in which fiction prevailed. The failure of postmodernism in the early-1980s brought a strong reaction against history and its dismissal as an alternative to theory. Abandoning history meant an anxious search for new alternatives. This change also coincided with a renewed interest in theory, particularly in America. From the beginning of the 1980s, then, one can see a shift that brings the study of architectural theory from the Old World to the New. But curiously, American architectural scholars often based their work on a superficial reading of European thinkers, predominantly the French poststructuralists. Following Tafuri's precedent, critics and theoreticians began to fill their texts with quotes from Michel Foucault, Georges Bataille, Félix Guattari, Gilles Deleuze, Jean-François Lyotard, etc. But ultimately it was Jacques Derrida who would be the guide for a new understanding of architecture, or more precisely, his writings would determine the role architecture could play in society. *Deconstructivism* became the label. Its metaphorical content, implicit in the operation of an independent and autonomous reading performed by the deconstructivist critics, was adopted by architects seeking to justify a new style. The potential of dismantling conventional construction was very attractive, exuding the appeal of a new radicalism, a worthy complement to the new trends of literary criticism. Success seemed guaranteed. In retrospect, one sees in the Museum of Modern Art's "Deconstructivist Architecture" show of 1988, a desire to proceed with new schools and styles. A nostalgia for the avant-garde revealed itself through an eagerness to coin new labels. Deconstructivism represented an effective label, but a very broad and vague tag when one considers the diversity of approaches represented in the exhibition.

This attempt to see theory as an explanation of what architecture could mean in the context of universal history was extended to other disciplines in order to explain wider social issues. As a result, theories of architecture developed in order to explore the discipline's reaction to broader issues, such as gender and race. Theory was employed as a means of reflection, not action. In this way, theory had evolved into a position antithetical to the concept of *critica operativa* that the Venetian critics and theoreticians around Tafuri established in the early 1960s. One sees in much recent criticism, based on the manners of the deconstructivist literary critics, texts in which a personal reading overwhelms any more specific or relevant reference. As with literary criticism, architectural criticism in the late 1980s and early 1990s was more a token of individual creativity than an effort to explain or clarify the architect's world.

It can be argued that there is a common ground on which today's architectural attitudes are based. While risking reductiveness, one can see this consensus as recognizing that there are no more shared values allowing a universal language; that architecture is very rarely used today to represent power because of its uncertain role in society; that today building techniques are less restrictive than they were, and as a conse-

quence it is difficult to develop an architectural theory based on the logic of construction; that the city has dissolved physically with the explosive growth of communication and transportation. Such a dispersion brings with it new encounters with nature. Without confidence in an urban theory based on modern architecture, people do not accept the utopian descriptions of the city. The connection between social justice, fear, and appropriate urban design is no longer accepted. Today, society seems to be more the result of considering each and every individual rather than an abstract entity with a collective character.

Without shared values, without any clear expectations of architecture, with the easy application of sophisticated technical tools, and with the awareness that the old city is gone, architects no longer believe in an architecture founded on disciplinary principles inspired by other work in the visual arts. Architects do not believe that today's world is represented either by artistic trends or by a common figurative language that might give form to a universal culture. Without such help, yet eager to participate in the extremely active and energetic world of the present, architects immerse themselves in the search for an architecture able to reestablish links with the world around them. Architects once again are urgently seeking the spirit of the time, the zeitgeist.

Today there are no more theoretical approaches, no more French philosophers at the inception of a project, and no more obscure quotations. Architecture wants to find its inspiration in the currents of social and economic energy. This lack of confidence in an architecture more consonant with language and figurative experience in turn introduces us to an architecture that is more direct, more spontaneous, and more connected to daily life. A wave of pragmatism then (more or less veiled) runs throughout current architecture. Even though today's critics and theoreticians do not emphasize the importance building techniques have had in the past, contemporary architecture can be seen through the lens of the building industry. Today's trends, such as minimalism, can be understood as an aesthetic based unconsciously on new building techniques that emphasize the cladding of the building, the wrapping of the skin. This increased value given to the skin explains why architecture oscillates between the most elementary volumes and a fragmented composition of abstract pieces. In either case, there is a reluctance to admit form or iconography. Having said this, one should add that new technology today is more about computers than the building industry. Computers are increasingly present in architecture, mostly in the design process. Computers are indeed enlarging the universe of available forms by allowing for the description and representation of any volume or surface, including forgotten geometries lost to us because of the difficulties of their representation. Moreover, computers help to handle the transformation of familiar forms, introducing innovation and a broad range of operations. As a result, design itself becomes the most important moment in the production of architecture, while its sophistication obscures the more mundane issues related to the architectural site.

Without the earlier desire for a universal architectural language, individuality prevails in the architecture of today. As a consequence, architecture is either tempted by the ambition of becoming a work of art, or it falls directly into anarchy. Both positions are apparent today. What has been abandoned is the fantasy of a new architecture as nature's replica. The temptations (so present in modern architecture) of an organic architecture still inspired by Aristotelian cosmology have been forgotten. Today, architects constantly enter some kind of personal domain. It is no longer possible, therefore, to speak about schools or about styles; instead, one speaks only about individuals.

Even though contemporary architects tend to neglect modern architecture, they do work within the confines of this earlier movement. In the same way that mannerist and baroque architects were dependent upon Renaissance forms while aspiring to a quite different architecture, late-20th-century architects still maintain an intimate contact with modernism — working with Corbusian elements as if they were reminders of an inherited and inevitable language.

If architects have lost interest in an architecture that maintains a continuity with the past, if they ignore today's figurative models but are looking for a direct and mandatory representation of the world today, then what issues are attracting them? How do they intend to reflect the world around us? Architects, it seems, are now concerned with capturing the mobility and fleeting, unstable condition of a world that appears to resist the idea of any fixed image. Form, something always associated with architecture, is seen now as something static; something that, because it endures, has little to do with today's fluid culture. Our world today is mostly conveyed by electronic screens; witnesses to the ways we live that change every instant, belying, in the process, any sense of stability. Waves express this representation of form over time; waves that blend with the landscape in apparent camouflage, attempting to avoid any sense of consolidation. Architecture should be able to reflect this mobile condition. Reality presents itself as fragmented and broken, discontinuous and incomprehensible. In the past, architecture looked to the opposite; it seemed to long for an identity, for buildings that possessed their own autonomy and independence. But the model that scientific knowledge offers us today suggests the opposite: a world interconnected, discontinuous, and diverse, multiple and fragmented.

Many questions, then, are raised by this ingenuous way of representing today's visual culture. Principally among these, one could debate whether or not this "direct realism" (such as waves embodying unstable forms) is a legitimate way to represent the current world. Could our contemporary condition be expressed more naturally in a less contrived way? Curiously, today's latest architecture does not emphasize its ephemeral quality, or true mobility, as the works of Archigram looked to do in the 1960s. Today's architectural attempts to recapture the zeitgeist are too direct and too literal. Perhaps by backgrounding theory, a more direct, more specific expression might express itself less self-consciously.

What will the issues be in the near future? I want to insist on the fact that architecture is not dictated solely by the pressures of different local conditions, but rather we should see the prerogative of the architect as being able to choose the formal conventions with which to build. This implies a certain reflection and a certain theoretical commitment. One should also ask some generic questions, such as, What is the appropriate continuity with the built surroundings? This immediately emphasizes the importance of a shared language that might go some way to overcoming the wild individualism of today. In other words, this questioning leads us to consider the specific features that define this activity, or this thing, called architecture. To insist on this point may sound unusual, but I am compelled to remind architects today about the relevance of some more explicit theoretical conditions of this much beloved activity called architecture, with which so many of us are so passionately involved.

DISCUSSION 3

DAVID CHILDS I want to begin with a quick question for Ben van Berkel. I thought one of your earlier comments about using the sun as a material was particularly evocative. What other thoughts on the possibilities of the immaterial, or natural forces, do you have?

BEN VAN BERKEL The whole idea of material effects should be seen primarily in terms of how they can start to organize something. We use whatever we can in terms of material organization to enhance the qualities of public life. I consider even the way one sits on a material organization, or how one triggers or moves a material organization, as being part of a natural force that can be directed and manipulated.

JEFFREY KIPNIS Ben, in all of your projects there is this process by which you take a kind of single, flexible substrate, whether it's the structure or the graphing device, and then you saturate it with high levels of information so that it deforms in a very fluid fashion. So I want to know two things. Is it simply the rigor of the process that interests you, or do you expect the process to rebroadcast the information? In other words, when I look at a seven-dimensional work, am I supposed to be able to read the information in it? Or looking at the force diagram, does it appear as a Candella-like project in which I'm reading the expressive possibilities of complex structure? I understand the rigor of the work but not its ambition.

VAN BERKEL The ambition is clear — the work looks to allow organizations to liberate themselves. For me, the most striking problem in architecture right now is that we use amazing words and concepts and ideas, but nobody is stretching the actual architecture into new forms of organization. That's the ambition.

KIPNIS But isn't it like building a machine and then wondering what it can do?

VAN BERKEL No, because it's not even related to the machine. I see the surfaces of my architecture more in terms of a face: there is nothing to explain about the face. Everything is in it – there is emotion in the face, there is desire in the face, there is the landscape of the face.

CAROLINE BOS I think that we do spend a lot of time trying to come to grips with a certain reality that we encounter, and this is maybe what you mean by the enormous amount of information that's being brought together in our work. With all of this material, we then try to find within it relations that turn things around, to look at it again from different angles.

KIPNIS But in your mind do you expect people to read the information back out of the architecture?

BOS No.

VAN BERKEL People decide themselves how to read the architecture.

CHILDS Ben, the similarities of thought that Jacques Herzog was discussing with his Kramlich Residence in relation to your thoughts about continuous movement and materiality were particularly interesting. Do you have any reaction to what Jacques was saying?

VAN BERKEL What I really like about that house is that the glass is both organizational and immaterial at the same time. But if you look at the notion of the floor, which Jacques introduced his talk with, I wish that this idea of the flexible ground could find its way into the flexible section of the glass house and instrumentalize the space. I wish I understood it a little bit better because I don't really see the importance of the archaic element of the floor. I find it almost classical and representational.

JACQUES HERZOG Well, Ben, I think that's obviously the difference between us. But if you go and see the new Tate in London I think you will change your mind. I back Rafael Moneo's statement; I don't like architectural debates that are just words. I like the freedom that we have in architecture now more than ever, and I don't feel the slightest regret that all the theory, distinct from everything else, seems to have gone out of the discipline. For me, the theory and the thinking must be in the architecture itself. This is the only way architecture can survive, because so many things are more powerful and more interesting theoretically than architecture. Architecture rests upon material, physical, and sensual qualities, and the effect they have upon your body. A floor is one of those things. As long as I don't have wings to fly but have feet to stand on, I must say that a floor is a really important element in a building.

VAN BERKEL But Jacques, that's not really answering the question about the instrumentality of the immaterial that you spoke about. I wasn't criticizing the floor so much as questioning what is representational and what is more instrumental in the way that you use materials.

HERZOG But I'm not interested in the instrumental or in representation. It's simply that you stand somewhere and you feel it or you don't. That's the difference.

VAN BERKEL But what about the glass that you designed, for example, in the Prada store – curved and with the possibility of actually touching the products? There it became a generator for a particular kind of movement and action. In the house, too, the glass starts to trigger mobility.

HERZOG Absolutely, but I don't see this as a contradiction, and even if it is a contradiction, I think it's wonderful to have these kinds of ambiguous moments in a house. This is ultimately what we try to achieve.

RAFAEL MONEO I would like to use the work of my friends around the table here to demonstrate the point I was trying to make in my talk. The work of Ben van Berkel and Caroline Bos very clearly shows the attempt to transform the description of certain phenomena within the architecture itself. I like the images they showed and their attempt to capture a much more complex geometry from these nonorientable pieces. I also like the research they do on these new geometries, and that the computer is opening our eyes wider. But I find it quite ingenuous and difficult to believe that simply by taking this system of fluxes you can directly produce the architectural form.

Ben, you also said something a moment ago that I found appealing and really quite touching – that you want organizations to liberate themselves. It seems to me, though, that you are actually liberating the architect from making the commitment to what he or she designs by being so directly tied to the description of the phenomenon. But people are not freed, not liberated that way. It seems to me still pertinent to emphasize ideas of functional difference, and that through this difference buildings are much more able to allow people

to be free. But having said that, I am not trying to ignore the extent to which we have been permeated by a new world. Because for sure, today's architecture is much more dematerialized or deterritorialized (to use two of architecture's current, favorite descriptions of itself), and I understand that these processes are happening. And maybe these new sensibilities, these new meanings, are the result of the collaging of a broader set of theoretical ideas that have invaded architecture in such a positive way. One can see the value of these ideas in Herzog's work, for example, in the quite compelling way he uses new materials or new solids.

I don't, however, think that the way Steven Holl presented his work helps us to understand its basis. He doesn't need to connect new theories of light with his architecture. This seems to me misleading, because his work very beautifully and powerfully deals with light by using old, established architectural devices. Steven just seems to be trying to legitimize his work by illustrating it with images and light constellations from a number of scientific magazines. [Steven Holl drums his fingers on his microphone.] This seems to me a bad way of relating contemporary thought to today's architecture, because his architecture, as good as it is, is related much more clearly to a traditional way of thinking about light and architecture. Architects today appear to be blind to the former theoretical principles that they have been using as the starting points for their work. So, I just don't see the dematerialization that we have been talking about. It seems to be simply a graphic device, limited only to the transformation and fluxes of an architectural pattern. To be permeated by a deeper sense of context, or by deeper, more informed feelings provided by the new culture and the world around

us, would be a more positive basis for our work, rather than such a direct and literal acceptance of the images of this world, or what we recognize as the images of this world.

STEVEN HOLL Naturally I have to refute. I would agree with the criticism of being too literal about the interpretation, but I think this is another discussion. In terms of my own architecture, let me bring out a couple of salient details. For example, at Helsinki, the use of white glass with the translucent installation wall had never been done before at that scale, and the use of those large lenses (ten by ten), liquid-filled and economically constructed, couldn't have been attempted had I relied on traditional architectural methods.

I also want to make a point about desire (and this, Rafael, is where we have a large gap between us). Consider the membrane walls that were built in the 1930s, when the intention was for very thick white stucco. When you cut through these walls, all you see is brick – they were built in brick, but the desire was there to do something else. And then I think of the opposite in the 1980s, of postmodernism and all those fake brick walls – brick skins just hanging there. What I want to bracket is the desire. I think that this moment that we occupy has potential that we have never had before, but we should not put ourselves in the wrong frame of mind, like we were in the 1980s (and by the way, what was built under the rubric of postmodernism was a lot more damaging to America than anything built under modernism). Obviously, I can not design a project that's going to slow the speed of light, but I think what's fascinating is the frame of mind that we can be in now and how it can inspire us to create more interesting things.

KIPNIS This is an incredible panel to be in; the passion and the integrity, the intensity and the insanity of it. Steven is a really bad physicist, so I think Rafael should relax a little bit. I want to respond to Rafael's argument because I feel that it touched us all, and I'd like to outline how a new discourse emerges from it. I opened my discussion with a question that we need to keep taking up, and that is, how is architecture political? Rafael kept asking the question, how can architecture become not just politically responsible but how is it political? His formula was no more French theory, no more obscure quotes, take your inspiration from sociology and economics. I thought this is interesting because now I'm supposed to no longer begin a project with French quotes or obscure quotes; I'm supposed to begin a project with economic quotes and sociological quotes. In a sense, he finds himself in exactly the same trap: the example he wants to use is modernism, the most self-conscious moment of all, but the effect that he wants to produce is an architecture that's less self-conscious. I think Rafael's problem is this: he doesn't understand that mood and atmosphere and autonomous architectural effects are in fact the best way for them to be political. When painting tried to be political by taking up political, representational themes, it failed, but when painting understood its practice as a part of material practices in an ecology of practices (for example, in abstract expressionism), it found its most poignant political moment. So we have to really let go of the idea that we obligate architecture as a self-conscious art form to a social responsibility, to representation and efficacy, that it has never been able to fulfill. And just like in mathematics, and just like in painting, and just like in every other material practice, as it

develops the mechanisms by which it advances its own internal processes, and therefore explores the forms of new consciousness, it becomes genuinely political. So actually, I think the most political work that we saw today was the work that had abandoned the representation of political life in order to explore those issues.

SASKIA SASSEN In this little transaction between Rafael and Jeff I find myself on Jeff's side. But Rafael, I really understand what you are looking for, and maybe I can show this by invoking Steven's notion of desire. I heard in your speech a desire for an engagement with a project that can be articulated in socioeconomic terms (the way Romi Khosla yesterday began the discussion), but that in a way the political instantiation of the architectural project has to come from its own vocabulary and its own complexities, rather than by ushering in the complexity, so to speak, of the economic and the sociological. I want to reiterate the idea that the desire for this economic-sociological project can actually be filtered through the complexities of certain architects, but I don't think that this is the most likely form for architecture to be political. (I also feel the same way about art, in much the same way that Jeff described.)

In my own work, and in many of the presentations today, I feel that one of the issues we're dealing with is the location of complexity. Much of the art of the 1980s and '90s typically located complexity in the ability to assemble rather elementary elements. What I find so enjoyable in the work presented here is that the location of complexity shifts away from assemblage and traditional installation and onto something that becomes, in Ben's terms, an organizational form that can encompass a growing amount of diversity. The notion of scale is also a

significant issue, and one that seems to relate both to my work on global markets and digitalization and to the architectural work of Ben and Caroline: for example, the organizational form of their projects encompassing what used to be separate units. This scaling-up is, in a way, what Jeff was trying to describe when he invoked the question of liquidity in his beautiful slides – that is, the extension that sort of explodes all of the boundaries. Together with this relocated complexity and scale change, the idea of uncertainty has also taken on a real importance. (Hani Rashid's presentation yesterday, for example, showed how the New York Stock Exchange introduced this idea into their negotiations.) As an economist, I've also been looking at how economic institutions handle uncertainty – which they do principally by bringing more and more data into the situation, despite the fact that this still doesn't solve the problem. Ben and Caroline's presentation highlighted the complexity of the engineering issues that they have to consider, so I'm wondering if uncertainty is a presence in the work, or whether architecture eliminates uncertainty. Is the act of creating architecture the act of neutralizing uncertainty? If so, then architects are way ahead of economists.

VAN BERKEL I think that your ideas of scale could relate to what we call the nonexistence of scale as it pertains to many structures. If you allow a set of parameters to work with the organization (for example, public flux, economics, political and cultural implications), then it is possible to play with the organization to the extent that we almost become nonscalar. But the whole idea of uncertainty is an interesting one, and something you have to constantly deal with as an architect. In the project we are working on for our latest client, for example, we were asked after just one week to produce financial calculations for the design because the client wants to know every risk in the development of the project. This uncertainty can also reveal itself in the organizational articulation and expression of a building – our station project in Aarnhem, for instance, is column-free, because the client wanted to be able to change and extend the building. I showed the client that this more free-flowing organization would be more flexible and allow for more uncertainty than a rigid, boxlike organization.

MONEO I would like to say something more about this sense of freedom that we have been talking about. It seems to me that it is actually the spaces that appear to be formally consolidated and clearly defined that ironically are more open-ended due to these uncertainties of use. In a way, I am a little apprehensive that the attempt to incorporate all of these new tools and new technologies for building the world returns us again to a phase of over-defined cost-effectiveness. As Jeff Kipnis said earlier of a particular Hitchcock scene, "This is a very irreducible filmic episode." I guess that for our cities and our built world we need to provide the freedom to liberate architects' forms in the way Ben was describing – but this relies upon a direct cost-effectiveness relationship. There is also a lot of contemporary architecture today that in effect retraces earlier, more ingenious precedents; for example, the Archigram work of the 1960s. By looking at these kinds of precedents one can see how new designs and visions of the world can be generated out of technical research into new materials, for example, and that this is very much architectural research. But over the last five years or so we seem to have

lost contact with certain theoretical ideas, and this has thrown us into a somewhat less clear atmosphere for producing architecture that isn't liberating and that isn't allowing for uncertainty. I would argue that paradoxically this uncertainty could develop in more well-structured form. I just wanted to reiterate this point.

BOS Maybe you are right, Rafael, maybe we lose some of the richness of architecture by involving ourselves less in theory. On the other hand, in place of that loss are the gains we make in our communication with other fields. I think this is what Saskia was appreciating in this contemporary work. In response to Saskia's comment about uncertainty, I would say that one of the dangers of architecture is that it is terminally optimistic. But by trying to increase communication, and by seeing architecture more and more as a platform for different specializations, we can dissipate the insecurities of this optimism. But there is a risk here too (and this is one of the dangers of what Jeff seems to be promoting) that architecture's most powerful aspects relate to a specific discipline outside of architecture (in Jeff's case, film). Rather, I think we should bring these things back into architecture and see this communication as a powerful thing, not as something that has been lost.

KIPNIS I didn't say we don't communicate with other fields.

HERZOG At the end of the day it is very simple. Rafael, you mentioned Aldo Rossi earlier, whose best line was that "architecture is architecture." Strangely, perhaps, I think this is the only way architecture survives as something that is really culturally important. Of course we are open to all kinds of disciplines, and we have

collaborations with artists and many people from different fields – relationships, I think, that are absolutely crucial. But Saskia, you work far away from the physical world in many ways. The difficult thing for us is to make our ideas happen as architecture. I know this sounds so easy, but it's ultimately a very difficult thing to do. For example, in the Virtual House Competition, [see **ANY** 19/20, "The Virtual House"] I tried to enhance the old aspect of pushing the material world to such a sharp edge (like in ancient Japanese and Chinese cultures) that it released an almost spiritual quality. This is ultimately what architecture can do in its best realization. But if architecture doesn't maintain this essential specific quality, then it just becomes boring, like Tati's **Mon Oncle** France of the 1950s, with everybody trying desperately to be more modern than everybody else; or today, with architects battling over who is the most contemporary.

CHILDS Jeff?

KIPNIS Let's eat lunch.

IGNASI DE SOLÀ-MORALES To say that architecture is architecture is just a tautology. It means nothing, it's a self-repetition, a statement closed in on itself. It's like saying a shoe is a shoe, a man is a man, etc. It doesn't leave architecture open to any kind of debate. If architecture is architecture forever, maybe we shouldn't be having any discussion at all. But Jacques, you did allude to something that for me is very important, and that is the material condition of architecture – something that I see as the key point of discussion for this panel, and for contemporary architectural debate as a whole. However, in setting this discussion up in terms of the dichotomy between the material and immaterial,

I think we have fallen into a huge trap, because what exactly is the immaterial? Again, it's a kind of reverse tautology – immaterial is what is not material. I think a better divide would have been the classical distinction between the material and the ideal – a distinction between what we perceive through our senses (concerned as they are with physical, bodily experiences) and what is related to our mind, and our capacity to produce abstract thoughts. Seeing the distinction this way also relates to Saskia's notion of uncertainty, because uncertainty could be understood in terms of material conditions, and also in terms of the abstraction of economics – counting, for example. In this sense, combining uncertainty with materiality could precipitate an architectural debate that advocated both difference and variety as well as the irreducibility of primary forms. References to Aldo Rossi could then be very useful, because Rossi's neoclassicism demanded an adherence to a primary order, yet he permeated this order, internally, with the uncertainty of everyday life – an ambivalence that was famously revealed in his Nîmes Arena. This idea of having fixed structures that convey a sense of identity in physical terms, but which on the inside allow for a variety, a diversity, an uncertainty, seems to me quite distinct and original.

KIPNIS I have one response before we go to lunch. The point I'd like to make about this discussion is that there is no such thing as an abstract idea in the brain. The brain is a material organization of dynamic processes. For me, this whole issue of ideality, and of it being ahistorical and antievolutionary has suppressed the question of the possibility of a material practice in its own right. When Jacques says, "architecture is architecture," it is not a tautology, or at least it's a

tautology as an instrument, in the same way that "a tree is a tree is a tree" becomes a poem – it's an instrument that causes an effect. When you talk about an idea, you're talking about a material effect. You're not talking about a preexisting platonic condition that somehow arrives in your brain. So the whole debate about material practices and the ways in which they produce new effects is at the very essence of how architecture discovers its new possibilities. It cannot be driven by the representation of ideas.

VAN BERKEL I just want to respond to Rafael's comments. I really don't understand your almost romantic idea, Rafael, of theory and architecture. I find it so reductive, so unexpectedly narrow, in the ways in which it sees the almost dialectical relationship between how the two could influence each other. There is so much after theory. You proposed an almost counter-theory of the way in which, since the 1960s, we can now look to new approaches to dealing with contemporary techniques. But in the '60s we didn't have the possibility to use these techniques. Of course we studied the Smithsons, and all these guys; we followed them incredibly closely. But they were not equipped with the tools that we have now. They were not able to visualize public forces. So I really think that your contemporary understanding of political, cultural, architectural, and urban proliferations, and of the ways in which we can free ourselves from restricted ideas, is not as open as you suggest. I think we should allow our profession to free itself from its own possibilities.

CATHERINE INGRAHAM I know you're hungry, but I can't quite believe what I'm hearing from this incredibly distinguished panel of architects and

thinkers. Every single one of you is a theorist. As theorists, you confront the material information that is before you – material, social, political, whatever – and are opportunistic in the face of it, grasping it. And then, as Jacques Herzog said, you're not interested in the nostalgic positioning of that material as some kind of untouchable artifact that you situate in a vitrine. No, you reach out for it, you theorize it, and by so doing, you become an architect. This transition seems to me true of everybody's work in different ways and with different kinds of details at work – from the accidental knowledge of light, to the accidental knowledge of the raindrops on the floor, to the accidental knowledge of how orientation torques buildings in the direction of the cantilever, etc. There's an incredible opportunism in the face of all this, which makes you then the architectural theorist.

To "blur" is to make indistinct, to dim, to shroud, to cloud, to make vague, to obfuscate. Blur is equated with the dubious. A blurry image is typically the fault of a mechanical malfunction in a display or reproduction technology. For our visually obsessed, high-resolution, high-definition culture that measures satisfaction in pixels per inch, blur is understood as a loss.

Yet blur can also be thought positively. For the Futurists, the motion blur was a technological virtue, as revealed by the photographs of Anton Giulio Bragaglia, documenting the discrepancy between the speed of a body in motion and the shutter speed of a camera. Dynamism is caught in a metaperceptive mode. Motion blur is a special effect currently built into most high-end video cameras and video editing programs. The latest version of Photoshop, for example, offers Gaussian blur, radio blur, and smart blur. In contemporary Japanese photography, **bokeh** identifies the quality of blur coherence in the optics of a lens. Bad bokeh has a doubling effect, good bokeh has a smooth Gaussian falloff. Bokeh, then, is the art of constructing de-emphasis.

What, however, can the construction of de-emphasis mean in architecture? The Blur Pavilion for Swiss EXPO 2002 is an experiment in de-emphasis and the immersive potential of blur on an environmental scale. Blur is located at the base of Lake Neuchâtel in the town of Yverdon-les-Bains. The cloudlike building measures 300 feet wide by 200 feet deep and hovers 75 feet over the lake. Filtered lake water is shot as a fine mist through a dense array of high-pressure fog nozzles. The fog system is composed of 12,500

wind: 8.2 knots humidity: 52% temperature: 60°F

wind: 1.1 knots humidity: 25% temperature: 91°F

wind: 0.8 knots humidity: 92% temperature: 81°F

wind: 1.2 knots humidity: 48% temperature: 42°F

Various meteorological states of blur.

nozzles spaced 1.2 meters apart in every direction along 24 kilometers of plumbing lines. Following Fujiko Nakaya's fog-engulfed geodesic dome for the Osaka World's Fair of 1970, Blur uses the inherent ambiguity of the fog to foil the conventions of heroic EXPO or world's fair architecture, to engage substance without form, and to stage a slow event.

Blur is smart weather. A built-in weather station reads actual climatic conditions such as shifting temperature, humidity, and wind speed and direction, and sends the data to a central computer where control algorithms regulate the system's response across 13 zones. The form of Blur is dynamic — a constant play of natural and technological forces.

The public can approach the structure from the shore via a 400-foot-long pedestrian ramp. As the visitor nears the fog mass, visual and acoustical references are slowly erased. The ramp deposits the public in the middle of an exposed platform of open grating across which people are free to move; what remains is only an optical "whiteout" and the "white noise" of pulsing fog nozzles. On the platform, which is roughly the size of a football field, movement is again unregulated. This is the site of Babble, a media event that uses wireless transmission and the challenge of navigation. In addition to the artificially produced natural sublime in the disorienting and scaleless fog mass, the project aims to create a technological sublime: to make palpable the unfathomable speed and reach of the data cloud.

As an interruption to Babble, a fog-free zone at the center of the fog mass enables another form of communication with a six-sided glass box speared by a dense array of animated vertical LED signboards. Messages appear to emerge from nowhere, penetrate the glass box, come into sharp focus, and then disappear again into the haze. The array of LEDs is linked to the Internet and functions effectively as a three-dimensional chat room. Messages sent out to the Net by participants climb up the field of LED columns; responses rain down. Architecture and technology exchange properties: while architecture is dematerialized, media becomes physically tangible.

The public can leave the media platform and continue the ascent to the Angel Bar at the summit, emerging like an airplane piercing a cloud layer. Bar service is located along a depressed ramp sandwiched beneath an upturned sunning area. To push the aesthetics of nothing further, the bar serves only water. A large variety of waters from various global sources are available, including a selection of commercially available bottled spring waters, artesian waters, mineral waters, sparkling waters, distilled waters, as well as rain waters and municipal tap waters from international cities, and an exclusive collection of glacial and polar waters.

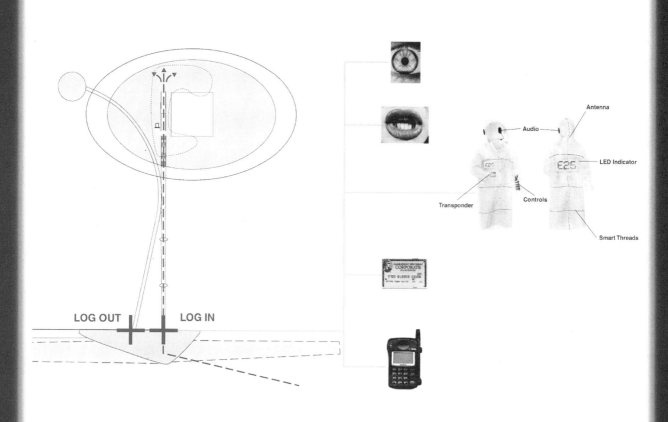

Braincoat diagrams.

EXPOs and world's fairs are predicated on mass spectacles. The term **spectacle** privileges vision. Seen from the shore, Blur will form a seductive visual icon whose image will undoubtedly feature in numerous advertising campaigns, but as a physical experience it will offer little to see. It is an immersive environment in which the world is put out of focus, and so provides a perfect context to put our visual dependency into focus. Blur/Babble redefines the spectacle as indifferent to vision. The focused attention of spectacle is replaced by an attention dispersed across the fog mass and sustained by a sense of apprehension. The relation between attention and mobility is prompted. A range of movement is offered, from aimless wandering to curious trolling or grazing, to motivated browsing or shopping, to aggressively focused hunting.

Unlike entering a building, entering Blur will be like walking into a habitable medium — one that is featureless, depthless, scaleless, spaceless, massless, surfaceless, and contextless. Disorientation is structured into the experience. As an alternative to the new orthodoxy of high definition, Blur exploits low definition and impaired vision, and exchanges visual immersion for an immersive acoustic encounter.

At the base of the access ramp on the shore, every visitor logs in to the system. The visitor crosses the entry with the swipe of a credit card and receives a "braincoat" (smart raincoat), equipped with a portable CPU and integrated tracking and sound technologies. From there on, the building knows you and your whereabouts. The electronics embedded in the skin of the coat electronically extend the body's natural system of navigation. Rather than rectifying the loss of vision, the coat acts as an acoustical prosthesis to supersensitize the sense of hearing.

Babble is the acoustical equivalent of blur. As vision is out of focus in the building, so too is hearing. Sound is atomized like water; it's a granular extension of the climatological system. In this space of disorientation and unregulated movement, a very precise spatial logic is invisibly mapped: the entire media platform is acoustically digitized and can only be comprehended through physical movement. Intelligible words and sounds in the babble can be discovered by following invisible axes. A visitor wandering through the fog can navigate along these text tracks and discover intersecting links that lead in new directions to new content. In this way, each participant becomes an acoustic interface to the audio database, scanning the surface of the platform like a cursor. As the visitor slows down, speeds up, or changes direction, so does the sound. The audio database will change dynamically as visitors leave acoustic traces behind that are incorporated into the babble.

Sound is carried on you, beamed to you, and is present in the ambient space. At times, a voice will emanate from your coat. This omniscient navigator/narrator will

The Angel Bar.

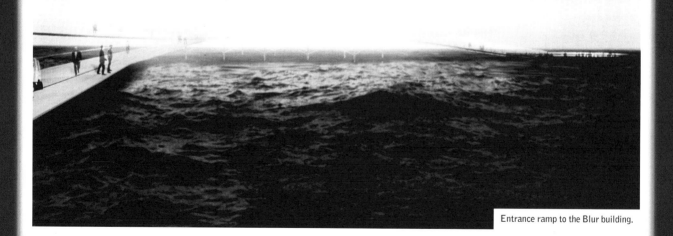

Entrance ramp to the Blur building.

know your name, who you are with, which way you are walking, and the length of your attention span. It will accompany you everywhere. At any time, 400 wandering bodies will be tracked; their complex patterns of flocking and swarming will depend on the play of attentions and the mutating relation of the variables.

World expositions have not changed fundamentally since the 19th century; the exposition survives as a spectacle of national and corporate display. From the earliest expos onward this display is typically one of abundance and proliferation, where nations and corporations join in a celebration of consensus, unity, and shared purpose, yet are exhibited within a scenography of competition and rivalry. The fiercest competition is the competition for the future. The history of these world exhibitions is a history of speculations about the future and the role of the sponsor in forming that future. The pavilion, capable of articulating a compelling image of the future, is therefore understood as a serious contender for inheritor of the future. Typically the future is portrayed as a site of emergence, organic growth, and technological advancement. The future usually seems to be a lot like the present only better, made possible by technology.

Blur takes on the uncertainty of the future epitomized in the weather. When we speak about weather, it is assumed that we are talking about nothing, or that more meaningful forms of social interaction are being avoided. But is not the weather, in fact, a potent topic of cultural exchange, a bond that cuts through social distinction and economic class, superseding geopolitical borders?

Contemporary culture is addicted to weather information. We watch, read, and listen to weather reports across every medium of communication, from conventional print to real-time satellite images and Web cams, to the round-the-clock, real-time, meteorological entertainment of the Weather Channel. Weather is also at the center of a technological debate. Our cultural anxiety about the weather can be attributed to its unpredictability. As a primary expression of nature, the unpredictability of weather points out the limitations of technological culture. While advanced methods of detection and tracking help to warn and thus protect us from the ravages of an indifferent, tempestuous nature, the weather is unstoppable. It is beyond our control.

At the same time, global weather disturbances, like global warming, are proof that weather and climate are not impervious to human intervention. If, through technological recklessness, we can alter the weather inadvertently, then we can also alter it willfully. We can play God. Weather modification has long been seen as a political and economic weapon, even a war crime. As with our power to affect genetic structures, both our dread and fascination with weather stems from the possibility of actually controlling it.

Blur/Babble will be an epic, interactive, and serialized weather opera.

THING AS FEELING: EMOTION PICTURES

GIULIANA BRUNO

Motion is Emotion. – Douglas Sirk

Douglas Sirk goes to the heart of the "matter" of motion pictures, condensing it into a single word that also offers a clue to understanding cinema's bond to architecture and geography. Following the path sculpted by this film director, let us then explore the nature of "emotion pictures" through the tangible, tactile links between architecture and film.

As Greek etymology tells us, *haptic* means "able to come into contact with." As a function of the skin, then, the haptic – the sense of touch – constitutes the reciprocal contact between us and the environment, both housing and extending a communicative interface. But the haptic is also related to kinesthesis, or the ability of our bodies to sense their own movement in space. Developed through this observational logic, one could take the haptic to be an agent in the formation of space – both geographic and cultural – and, by extension, in the articulation of the spatial arts themselves, which include motion pictures. Emphasizing the cultural role of the haptic, I would like to pursue a theory that attempts to make tangible sense of mnemonic space, and to address the diversity of this habitable space.

ATLAS AND THEORIA

In looking at this haptic mapping, a haptic image of theory is needed, open to architectural premises. This "archaeology of knowledge" comes from an iconology developed for theory by Cesare Ripa in 1593. In Ripa's influential treatise, *Iconologia*, theory itself transports us into a haptic realm. *Theoria*, the figure the Greeks associated with vision and contemplation, is instead pictured here architecturally and redefined in spatial terms.

Theoria is an allegory – a figure that deserves particular attention today for the potential inscribed in its mode of depiction, which features webs of historical and spatial narratives, and in so doing, enables a reinterpretation of the conjunctions of history and space itself. The allegory of theory that concerns me here is depicted in the form of a woman's body, as is also the case for certain female geographic allegories contained in atlases. For example, in the frontispiece of Jan Barend Elwe's *Atlas* (1792) the representation of spatial knowledge is dominated by two women who appear to be creating geography. 1 See Jan Barend Elwe, *Atlas*, Amsterdam, 1792. One stands, holding a compass over a large globe with one hand, as she touches the surface of the globe with the other. She is making a map or, rather, charting the globe: "designing" the earth. The atlas "fashions" space with, and as, a female subject.

In Ripa's own iconological treatise, the image of Theoria is associated with other female allegories such as those

embodying geography, choreography, and geometry, whose mappings are tactile. "Geometria," he writes, measures with one hand "the movement, the rhythm, and the materiality of the body," and with the other, its "line, surface, and depth." 2 Cesare Ripa, *Iconologia* (Rome: Heredi di Gio. Gigliotti, 1593). The citation on *Geometria* (my translation) is taken from a contemporary Italian edition (Turin: Fogola Editore, 1986), 1: 184. Seen in this context, Theoria herself becomes a mapping. She has not only been "fashioned" with cartographic and architectural accoutrements but has also been provided a *location* for her activity: a set of steps. In Ripa's own words, "Theoria can be aptly represented in the form of a young woman who looks and aims upward, joining her hands together and holding on her head an open compass that points skyward. She is nobly dressed in blue, and is in the process of descending from the summit of a staircase." 3 Ripa, *Iconologia*, 2: 294. In this representation of Theoria, a tension is created between two opposing forces. The woman's body is the seat of this oppositional movement, from which theory is produced. "Dressed" for theory, with her toga holding the torsion of two vectors, this spatial, epistemic tension in fact defines her theoretical plight: her figure negotiates a movement between a drive for geographic ascent, which measures, points upward, and aims high; and an architectural descent, which tends downward, toward the material world and perhaps even to the unconscious. Ripa's understanding of Theoria, therefore, is haptic. The compass, literally implanted in her head, becomes a cognitive prosthesis. This epistemic headset is quite spacious, for the compass is wide open to the world. Looking like a set of pointers and receptacles, it becomes, figuratively, her theoretical antennae – her "feelers" of space.

A THEORIA OF FILMIC SPACE: FROM FLÂNEUSE TO VOYAGEUSE

Along the route fashioned by this Theoria, we can conceive a different theory of cinematic space, one concerned less with sight than with site. In elaborating upon this "site-seeing," I am following the path of a theoretical wandering, a "streetwalking" enacted to link the filmic anatomy of movement to modern urban architectures. 4 See Giuliana Bruno, *Streetwalking on a Ruined Map* (Princeton: Princeton University Press, 1993). Along this trajectory, I have looked to move away from the perspective of the Lacanian gaze, dominant in film theory, into diverse architectural motions, and the haptic rather than the optic. In this way, the fixed optical geometry that informed an old cinematic *voyeur* becomes the moving vessel of a filmic *voyageuse*. Here, then, we can travel with motion pictures – a spatial form of sensuous cognition that offers tracking shots to traveling cultures.

MOVEMENTS OF THE HAPTIC

In site-seeing, we first pass "Montage and Architecture," the essay written by Sergei Eisenstein in the late 1930s. [5] Sergei M. Eisenstein, "Montage and Architecture" (c. 1937), Assemblage, no. 10 (1989), 111–31. The text was originally to have been inserted in a book-length work. Here, the figure of the filmic promenade evokes Le Corbusier's own "architectural promenade," as the link between the architectural ensemble and film is developed along the observer's route. But architecture and film share more than the framing of space and the succession of sites organized as shots from different viewpoints, adjoined and disjoined by way of montage and shifting viewing positions. The filmic/architectural promenade is an actual map – a construction experienced by its users. As evidenced in Toba Khedoori's architectural paintings, space is the frame of one's lived experiences, a lived space. Dwellings, narrativized in motion, construct an intersubjectivity, as the bodies that occupy them leave traces of their history on the wall and on the screen.

Architecture and film are constantly reinvented by stories of the flesh. Layers of cultural space, densities of histories, haptic transiti are all housed in their traveling-dwelling. In their habit of habitation, they house the erotic materiality of tangible interactions – a complex of socio-sexual mobilities. Their geometry is the connection between public sites and private spaces: doors that create a passage between interior and exterior, windows that open this passage for exploration, they are "moving" sites. Site-seeing is thus an actual means of exploration: at once a housing for, and a tour through, our narrative and geography.

TRANSPORT

By arguing that this form of "transport" includes psychogeographic journeys, we can investigate the genealogy of emotion pictures, mapping a geography of intimate space itself – a history of movement, affect, and tact. The major premise of my forthcoming study Atlas of Emotion is that motion produces emotion, and that, correlatively, emotion contains a movement. [6] Giuliana Bruno, Atlas of Emotion: Journeys in Art, Architecture, and Film (New York: Verso, forthcoming, 2001). It is this reciprocating principle that informs my work, shaping its haptic path through various cultural journeys, moving between the map, the wall, and the screen. The Latin root of the word emotion speaks clearly about a "moving" force, stemming as it does from emovere, an active verb composed of movere, "to move," preceded by the suffix e, "out." The meaning of emotion, then, is historically associated with "a moving out, migration, transference from one place to another." [7] Oxford English Dictionary (Oxford: Clarendon Press, 1989), V: 183.

Extending this etymology, we can create our own theoretical emotion, enhancing the fundamentally migratory

sense of the term as it employs, in practice, the haptic affect of "transport" that underwrites the formation of cultural travel. It is there, in this very emotion, that the moving image was implanted, with its own psychogeographic version of transport. Cinema was named after the Greek word kinema, which, interestingly, connotes both motion and emotion. This vision of film as a means of transport understands transport in the full range of its meaning, including the sort of carrying that is a carrying away by emotion, as in transports of joy, or in trasporto, which in Italian encompasses the attraction of human beings to one another. It implies more than the movement of bodies and objects, as imprinted in the change of film frames and shots, the flow of camera movement, or any other kind of shift in viewpoint. Cinematic space moves not only through time and space or narrative development but also through inner space. Film moves, and fundamentally "moves" us, with its ability to render affects and, in turn, to affect.

THE CULTURAL JOURNEY OF EMOTION

Cinema provided the modern subject with new tactics for making "sense" of a cultural movement which includes the motion of emotions. In its haptic site-seeing, there is room for mobile, emotional habitation. As a house of moving pictures, film maps this habitable space. Its "architexture" not only fashions bio-history (a map of bios, or life-mode) but draws on its emotion to circulate this history. And does so tangibly.

Retracing the steps of the cultural history that generated this "moving" image – our modern, mobile cartography – we can see that neither voyeurism nor perspectivism can envision a filmic site-seeing or even account for it. We need to theoretically access a different genealogy of space, a "theoria" activated in "moving" topographies, especially those written off as sentimental or feminized, and hence marginalized. Searching for movies before cinema, we thus go in search of a language of affects, beyond its psychoanalytic manifestation, and follow its course as an unstable map of "transports."

Historically, the activity of site-seeing developed largely through garden strolling, especially through picturesque gardens in which women took an active interest. [8] The literature on the picturesque as landscape aesthetics is vast. For an introduction see, among others, John Dixon Hunt, Gardens and the Picturesque: Studies in the History of Landscape Architecture (Cambridge, Massachusetts: MIT Press, 1992); and ed. Monique Mosser and Georges Teyssot, The Architecture of Western Gardens: A Design History from the Renaissance to the Present Day (Cambridge, Massachusetts: MIT Press, 1991). For a view of gender difference, see Sylvia Lavin, "Sacrifice and the Garden: Watelet's Essai sur les jardins and the Space of the Picturesque," Assemblage, no. 28 (December 1995), 17–33.

In this space, one was taught to feel through motion. As

1 Jan Barend Elwe, **Atlas**, 1792.
2 **Jeux de l'amour à Tivoli**, from Pierre-Jean-Baptiste Nougaret, **Paris métamorphosé**, 1799.
3 Apparatus used for rolling panoramic wallpaper, 19th century.
4 Imperial Institute Cinema, London, a movie house designed in the 1920s as a museum gallery.
5 Emotions painted on glass for magic lantern shows, c. 1750–1800.

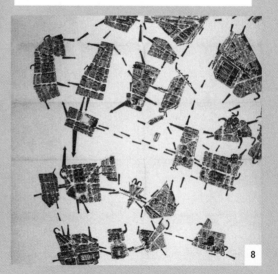

6 Jan Brueghel, **The Senses**, 1618.
7 Madeleine de Scudéry, **Carte du Pays de Tendre**, 1654.
8 Guy Debord and Asger Jorn, **Guide psychogéographique de Paris**, 1957.

Christopher Hussey put it in 1927, the force of the picturesque was "to enable the imagination to form the habit of feeling through the eye." 9 Christopher Hussey, *The Picturesque: Studies in a Point of View* (London: G.P. Putnam's Sons, 1927), 4. Here, the eye is epidermic; it is a skin; sight becomes a sense of touch. Picturesque vision is then haptic imaging. Its architectonics, creating a drama of changing sets, act as a medium for emotional responses. Combinatory permutations of feelings are impressed on a landscape of the surface. It was this emotional habit – the haptic "fashioning" of movement that is emotive – that was to become embodied in the filmic sense.

In the garden, as in the cinema, one could traverse series of imaginative states of mind in the form of living pictures. A memory theater of sensual pleasures, the garden was an exterior that put the spectator in "touch" with inner space. As one strolled through it, a constant double movement connected external to internal topographies. The garden was thus an outside turned into an inside; but it was also the projection of an inner world onto the outer geography. In a sensuous mobilization, the exterior of the landscape was transformed into an interior map – the landscape within us – as it was itself culturally mobilized.

It was principally the 18th century that advanced the idea that motion could expand one's sensate universe, and craved movement as a form of physical and "sensational" stimulation. Geography became the shifting experience of a "sense" of place. This was a fluid, emotive geography, which, associating the local and topographic to the personal, enhanced the passionate voyage of the imagination. Diversely shaped by associative philosophies, 18th-century landscape design embodied the very idea that motion rules mental activity and generates a "fancying" – that is, a series of relationships created on imaginative tracks. The images gathered by the senses were thought to produce such "trains" of thought. 10 Barbara Maria Stafford, *Voyage into Substance: Art, Science, Nature, and the Illustrated Travel Account, 1760–1840* (Cambridge, Massachusetts: MIT Press, 1984), 4. It was the emergence of such sensuous, serial vision (a vision of affects) that made it possible for the serial image in film to make sense, and for trains of ideas to inhabit the tracking shots of emotion pictures.

FROM THE WINGS OF DESIRE TO TENDER GEOGRAPHY

The type of emotional sensibility laid out in garden design was foreshadowed and set in place by an influential map. In 1654 Madeleine de Scudéry designed the *Carte du Pays de Tendre*, a map of tenderness, for her novel *Clélie*. 11 *Carte du Pays de Tendre* [the map of tenderness] was published in Madeleine de Scudéry, *Clélie* (Paris: Augustin Courbé, vol. 1, 1654), engraving by François Chauveau. For general information on this map, see Claude Filteau, "Le Pays de Tendre: l'enjeu d'une carte," *Littérature*, no. 36 (1979), 37–60. Salons directed by women, such as Scudéry's, were open to the world of gardens, and her taste for them may even explain the foundation of this map. 12 See Michel Conan, "The Conundrum of Le Nôtre's *Labyrinthe*," in John Dixon Hunt, ed., *Garden History: Issues, Approaches, Methods* (Washington, D.C.: Dumbarton Oaks Research Library and Collection, 1992). The *Carte de Tendre* was its own landscape, comprised of land, a sea, river, and lake, and included some trees, a few bridges, and a number of towns. This map visualized, in the form of a landscape, an itinerary of emotions that in turn formed the topos of the story. Mapping the passing of emotional time in space, the *Carte de Tendre* makes a world of affects visible to us.

Landscape design and the emotional map met along a haptic route. This too was "designed" as a place that evoked emotion in the shape of motion as one traveled through it. In fact, Scudéry's map designed a landscape of emotions to be experienced as a series of sensational movements. In this "moving" way, it made "sense" of the place of affects. It also made sense of sentimental displacement. The emotional map produced an *emotion*, and the motion inscribed therein was not only kinetic or kinesthetic. As in garden design, there was a liminal passage which made it possible for the exterior world of the landscape to be transformed into an interior landscape, and vice versa. Emotion materialized as a moving topography.

A tender geography was put into place: transforming *ekphrasis* from a descriptive mode of representation into a narrative mapping of places and people, this map envisaged the kind of geography that Gertrude Stein would call a geography of "inhabitants and vessels." 13 Gertrude Stein, *Geography* (1923), in *Printed Lace and Other Pieces* (1914–37), *The Yale Edition of the Unpublished Work of Gertrude Stein* (New Haven: Yale University Press, 1955), vol. 5, reprinted in *A Stein Reader*, ed. Ulla E. Dydo (Evanston: Northwestern University Press, 1993), 470. To traverse this land is to visit the ebb and flow of a personal and yet social psychogeography. Scudéry, in this way, turned intersubjectivity into a map by which one might navigate interpersonal relations. The *Carte de Tendre* made a geographic document of relational space in the form of a map.

The map creates an itinerary for anyone who travels with it, or for those who navigate its landscape. It is made up of multiple narrative routes that in ways that are ultimately protofilmic can be navigated forward and backward, at accelerated speed, or even in slow motion. There are no rigid directives for this map tour. Several movements are possible and encouraged in a touring that produces a cumulative emotional effect. The spectator/passenger is at times even led astray in this garden of emotions.

The *Carte de Tendre*, part map, part *veduta*, depicts a terrain that keeps spilling over a cartographic "off-screen." As in a filmic frame, the sites on the map are in constant touch with the territory off the map. The open land of amorous *terrae incognitae* might lure the traveler to wander well beyond the landscape of the map. Driven by amorous "curiosity," one is beguiled by the epistemic seduction of swimming in the unknown.

In Scudéry's tender landscape, there is an interplay between natural and architectural settings. As noted in the novel, for instance, she "had not placed any villages along the banks of the River of Inclination [an inclination of feeling], which runs with such a rapid course that there can be no lodging along its shore."[14] The citation (my translation) is taken from a contemporary French edition of the novel. Scudéry, *Clélie* (Turin: Giappichelli, 1973), 1: 309. In other cases, a steadier inhabitation of the *emotion* is possible. Villages, and even cities, are designed on the map to *house* this sentiment. They function as resting places along the map tour, places of lodging for the emotional movement.

Going "back to the future," different "movies" can be projected on this map. Let me, for example, recount one of them, but one not conforming to any Hollywood story. It is the movie with no happy ending. In the unfolding of relationships, things, of course, may go wrong. That is, they may go the wrong way and terminate in the Lake of Indifference. The only enclosed site on the map, this enormous lake is a visibly disturbing sign of deadly amorous stillness. The Lake of Indifference is a still-life portrait of terminal love. Swimming in it is as lethal as navigating the haptic insensitivity of ending a love affair. In the Lake of Indifference, there can be no more touching between people.

ZOOMING IN ON A CARTOGRAPHY OF EMOTION PICTURES

Scudéry's map established an entire trend of emotional cartography that has extended through to today. Many contemporary configurations of mapping acknowledge a direct inspiration from the *Carte de Tendre*. They include the Situationists' dynamic maps of urban affects, such as the chart of *The Naked City*, named after the 1948 American film noir of the same title, and the *Guide psychogéographique de Paris*, both of which were produced in 1957 by Guy Debord and Asger Jorn.[15] On situationist cartography, see, among others, Thomas McDonough, "Situationist Space," *October*, no. 67 (Winter 1994), 58–77. Artist Annette Messager's *Le jardin du tendre* of 1988 also makes the connection clear in its very title.

If this type of geo-psychic map continues to be "re-collected," it is because it itself followed the architectural legacy of the art of memory, which enabled the transformation of topographical *savoir* into an art of mapping.[16] On the history of the art of memory, see Frances A. Yates, *The Art of Memory* (Chicago: The University of Chicago Press, 1966). Today this architecture of memory comes to us in the form of moving pictures. It bears the palimpsestual wax texture of filmic celluloid – a

"set" of constant redrawing, a place where many stories "take place" and take the place of memory.

If memories are motion pictures, it is because cinema documents cultural sites and imagined geographies that are bound up in the physiology of spectatorial life. Its archival renderings are transported to the viewer, who, in turn, is transported by them. In this way, cinema carries with it the mapping impulse and the "transport" inscribed in emotive cartography, which charted the motion of emotion. The "motion" picture has turned this particular landscape into an art of mapping, charting the collapse of mnemonic time on the surface of spatio-visual "architextures." Now the fabric – the screen – can "emove." This field screen, home to a heterotopia of reinvented rhythms, is a permeable, reversible site, where the geo-psychic fragments of an inner world not only take shape but make room. Exhibited inside out, exposed to light in the darkness, they are, reversibly, turned outside in.

In this emotional cartography, a history is written on the physiognomy of space and mobilized in its geo-psychic rhythm. It is written between the flesh and the map – on the map that is our face, and on the filmic facade, which is our map of history and the screen of memory. In the genealogical journey that the Greek term *kinema* – as both motion and emotion – took to become "our" cinema, pathognomic research "features" large. It constructed emotional views that, as revealed in 18th-century lantern slides of the movements of passions, even look like filmstrips. This form of mapping offers a mnemotechnical apparatus to travel a library. It creates an archive of emotion pictures, bound to the surface of the architectural wall and the film screen.

THE COURSE OF EMOTION

What is mobilized in film's own emotional mapping is the plan of an unconscious topography in which emotions can "move" us, for they are themselves organized as a course. In film, as in the emotional course mapped by Scudéry, sentiments come to be mapped as physical transformations, written as a moving physiognomy. Indeed, emotional cartography is about an itinerary, the carnal knowledge by which one comes to know beings. It is the kind of cosmography that draws the universe in the manner of an intimate landscape. This is a drawing whose texture is the text of our inner fabric: a place where pictures become a space, an architecture.[17] In the words of the artist Gerhard Richter, "Pictures will become an environment or become an architecture," a dream he realized in his *Atlas* (1962–present). See Dorotea Dietrich, "Gerhard Richter: An Interview," *The Print Collector's Newsletter*, vol. 16, no. 4 (September/October, 1985), 130. The place in which a filmic-architectural bond is pictured, figured as a map – a chart of emotion, taking hold of the movement of life with life in motion. Not just a cinema, but a *kinema*.

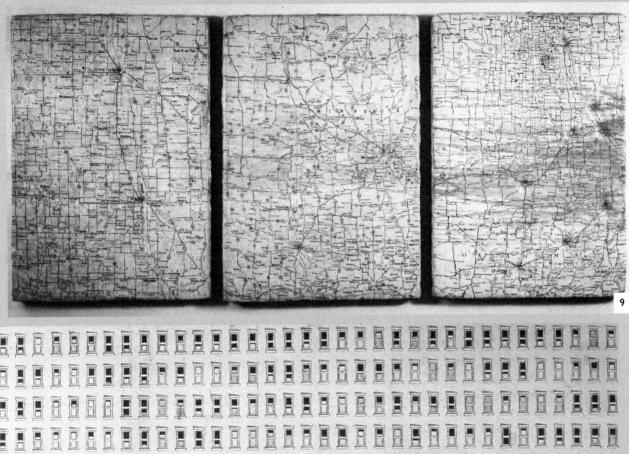

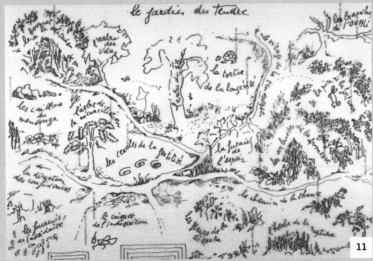

9 Guillermo Kuitca, **Untitled** (**Roads**), 1990.
10 Toba Khedoori, **Untitled** (**Windows**), 1994–95.
11 Annette Messager, **Le jardin du tendre**, 1988.

Nara Centennial Hall.

A CONCISE GENEALOGY OF THE THING

AKIRA ASADA / ARATA ISOZAKI

TRANSLATED FROM THE JAPANESE BY SABU KOHSO

A–1

In modern philosophy, especially since Immanuel Kant, the concept of "the thing" has come to be split in two: the thing we perceive and the thing-in-itself. According to Kant, we represent a thing as an object by filtering it through the web of associations that it projects. Yet this results merely in the thing-for-us (*das Ding für uns*), leaving the thing-in-itself (*das Ding an sich*) to survive beyond this web and the limits of our understanding. While the thing as object belongs to the phenomenal world of representation, the thing-in-itself belongs to the noumenal world beyond it.

Having taken this split as its starting point, modern philosophy followed dual paths, oppositional yet complementary. One path rejects the thing-in-itself, considering it a metaphysical fiction, and deals instead only with the thing as object. In a sense, this is a regression from Kant to David Hume, but at the same time it is the advancement toward the information society described in 1968 by Jean Baudrillard in his first work, *The System of Objects*. As a result of what Baudrillard saw as an information overload, things as objects became deprived of their fundamental weight and functional characteristics,

and floated instead upon the surface of consumer-information society as serial signs and simulacra.

The second path continues to pursue the thing-in-itself, in the process sinking deeper and deeper into some kind of semantic abyss. Following this path, we would pass from Kant to Arthur Schopenhauer and reach Sigmund Freud and Jacques Lacan (and finally Slavoj Žižek as a postmodern reincarnation of Lacan). Therein the "real" – notably the (maternal) thing (*das Ding/la chose*) – is deemed an excess that cannot be subsumed within the (paternal) symbolic order; rather it might be seen as a hole or rupture in that order. For Lacan, art, including architecture, is that which is organized around this hole or void (*le vide*).[1] See Jacques-Alain Miller, ed., **Le séminaire de Jacques Lacan**, vol. VII (Paris: Seuil), 162. It is also worth noting that the Japanese term **mono** contains a nuance that is close to the thing-in-itself. As revealed by the title of the famous Japanese animé, **Princess Mononoke**, or by the expression, **mono ni tsukareru** (possessed by the thing), **mono** indicates the reality embedded within the deepest level of our minds.

There are two phases of the thing – the information overload and drift of the thing as object; and the retreat of the thing-in-itself.

How, though, do they appear in our problematic of architecture and urbanism? In a 1962 essay titled "The Space of Darkness," Arata Isozaki examined the comparative concepts of void (*kyo*) and darkness (*yami*) in the context of analyzing both Japan's ancient architectural tradition and the urban reality of the 1960s, set adrift by the waves of imagistic excess. Void describes the modern city where everything becomes subsumed in a flow of signs and symbols, while darkness points to an unnamable thing that lurks in the deepest corner of architecture (in the crypt, so to speak, where no information can reach). Forty years after Isozaki's initial observations, in today's architecture and urbanism the polarization between the void as an escape from the thing and darkness as a condensation of the thing seems to be more highly charged than ever.

Postmodern consumer-information society has accelerated the advance of the void. Architecture and urban infrastructure as physical matter have progressively retreated into the background, while a flood of signs and simulacra, and the information network that hosts them, have moved to occupy the foreground. In the Japan of the 1990s, the main actors in the theater of

our cities are seemingly transient young men and women adorning themselves with the mobile prostheses of Discmans and cell phones. To these urban nomads the reality of cities is no more than an animated backdrop. Seeing in this new youth culture a complete lack of any kind of depth, artist Takashi Murakami has called their consciousness "superflat."

Conversely, in 1995 the Hanshin Awaji earthquake and the terrorism of the Aum Supreme Truth Cult (which peaked in an attempt at unconditional mass murder by sarin gas in the Tokyo subway system) not only forced open a crack in the city surface, exposing the frailty of the urban infrastructure, but were also traumatic incidents that marked some kind of "return of the real." As the literary critic Kojin Karatani argued at the Anywise conference in 1995, and as Isozaki and Osamu Ishiyama presented in their Japanese Pavilion at the Venice Biennale in 1996, the literal destruction of the earthquake surpassed the superficial mode of the semiotic destruction and made it totally obsolete. Meanwhile, the Aum incident represented a pathological, blind leap from the ever-expanding void behind the superflat surface of consumer society down into the

real (though certainly this was no more than an illusion of the real).[2] It is significant that the Aum cult had no interest in the architectural design of its facilities. The believers lived in barracks with no decoration whatsoever, single-mindedly striving for salvation. In this way, the consequences of the earthquake and the terrorists dissolved at once both the postmodernism and deconstructivism that had been making up the surface of cities.

After experiencing these opposing forces in the 1990s, Japan now appears to be teetering on a tightrope, precariously trying to avoid a descent into either extreme. But this problem is not unique to Japan. In the West, one finds oneself similarly suspended, as if in a comical and cruel farce, between the electronically amplified procession of simulacra (Jean Baudrillard) and the return of the real (Hal Foster). How can we escape this suspension, escape being torn between opposites? We have to resist polarization somehow; perhaps we have to discover, by theoretical scrutiny or historical retrospection, a third element that precedes this dichotomy. If Isozaki is seeking a retrospection today, it is not an aesthetic return to Japanese tradition but a risky challenge necessitated by the actual problematic.

Arata Isozaki, **Transcendental architecture of meditation**, Venice Biennale, 2000.

I-1

In correspondence to Akira Asada's concise account of "the thing," I would like to present two exhibitions I curated, one that began before the Anything conference, and another that was shown shortly after.

I came to New York City for the Anything conference in June 2000 via Stockholm, where the first exhibition, "Utsu," was taking place. "Utsu" (which also means "void" in Japanese) was a kind of revision of a previous exhibition that I curated 20 years ago — "Ma: Japanese Space and Time." After Stockholm, Utsu returned to Japan, while I continued on to Venice for the second installation, Transcendental City, which was part of the 7th International Architectural Biennale, "Less Aesthetics, More Ethics." The subject of the first exhibit was ghosts, and that of the second was consciousness. In English, neither concept seemed to concern "the thing" directly, yet they do in the Japanese sense of the term mono. The Japanese equivalent of "thing," mono suggests both thing and matter; it involves not only the teleologically identified object, but also the dynamism of event. Therefore, seen from the vantage point of mono, both ghost and consciousness could be thought of as "things."

UTSU

In medieval Japan, painters confronted the unprecedented and seemingly impossible task of representing the invisible. Japanese gods had previously been conceptualized only through their manifestation as indications and suggestions, and never anthropomorphized; it was forbidden to imagine their concrete features. In this way, icons had not been revealed in any visual, material form since ancient times. Yet, confronting the then growing necessity to represent these gods, a number of painters developed a way of depicting their own shadows as ghostly apparitions – a type of representation subsequently called yogo-zu. In many cases this specter was captured in the tense features of a host's body at the very moment it seemed to be possessed by a spirit, while other scenes depicted the ghost, or shadow, of a god seen floating immediately before possession. Behind the idea of gods as apparitions, and of the spiritual possession of earthly bodies, was the assumption that the body was a hollow receptacle. In Asia, these ideas were expressed in Buddhism as emptiness (sunya) and in Lao-tsu as void (kyo); in ancient Japan, they were referred to as utsu.

Utsu signifies the void inside something: a cave in a rocky mountain; the hollow of an old tree; the space of the dugout, or canoe; or the cavity of a pit dwelling. All of these voids were thought to house the sacred spirit. As people's ideas of the void became more and more ritualized, even a solid gemstone was believed to internalize a void; and a sack of cloth, without holes for hands and feet, was thought to host the sacred God. The more removed an object was from exteriority, the more sacred was considered its internal void. When a certain thing was sanctified, it was then thought to contain an internal void – an imagined void. Spirit (hi) is absorbed into utsu. While the concepts of Buddhism and Taoism were transcendent, utsu was concrete and practical (described more precisely in German as sachlich).

The exhibition featured the work of four artists: Issey Miyake's work can be defined as utsu (void) + hata (fabric) = utsuhata, which according to ancient records means a piece of clothing that has been made without being sewn. A prime example of this would be Miyake's "A-POC." The furniture designs of Shiro Kuramata similarly can be seen as utsu (void) + hari (beam) = utsuhari. His principal work is Miss Blanche. My own recently completed architecture can be defined as utsu (void) + fune (boat) as in the ancient, sacred dugout, which contains a hollow space inside. An example of this kind of work is the Nara Centennial Hall. The work of the sculptor Aiko Miyawaki was featured in the exhibition titled "Utsuroi" (meaning transition) – a compound of utsuro (void) and hi (spirit, or in Chinese, qi). Her wire sculptures exemplify this idea.

These contemporary artists all conceptualize their work (perhaps unwittingly) on the relationship between utsu and hi. In this way they reveal a similarity to the invocation of the Platonic chora as the concept of productive place. But utsu, I would argue, is more concrete than the vibrating winnow in the Timaeus. Utsu is fed by the dynamism of paradox in seeing everyday things as containing a vacuum, or conversely, in visualizing a vacuum as things, as everyday objects.

A-2

Modern philosophy beginning with Kant more or less sustained the dualistic program – form (eidos) shapes substance (hyle) – deriving from antiquity. Gilles Deleuze and Félix Guattari later introduced a new tertiary idea: form shapes substance, yet matter exists on a level that cannot be accommodated by the form/substance schema; furthermore, matter is not invisible like the Kantian thing-in-itself but morphological through its self-organization. Overturning the stance of conventional epistemology that sought to grasp matter as a surplus of form/substance, Deleuze and Guattari insisted that a temporary order of form/substance is generated by way of the self-organizing morphologies deriving directly from the flow of matter – as in a model of the "dissipative structure" presented by Ilya Prigogine. It is also possible that the chora Jacques Derrida extracted from Plato's Timaeus assumes a similar position, becoming the topos of a third form/substance term, and is thought to render morphogenesis by rhythmically vibrating like a sifter.

Isozaki's architectural approach to rereading Japanese tradition is not dissimilar to these philosophical investigations. What he is seeking to grasp through the examination of such traditional concepts as utsu and ma (interstice) is no less than this topos. These concepts assume a retrospection of the virtual topos that, preceding the form/substance dualism, provokes their derivations.

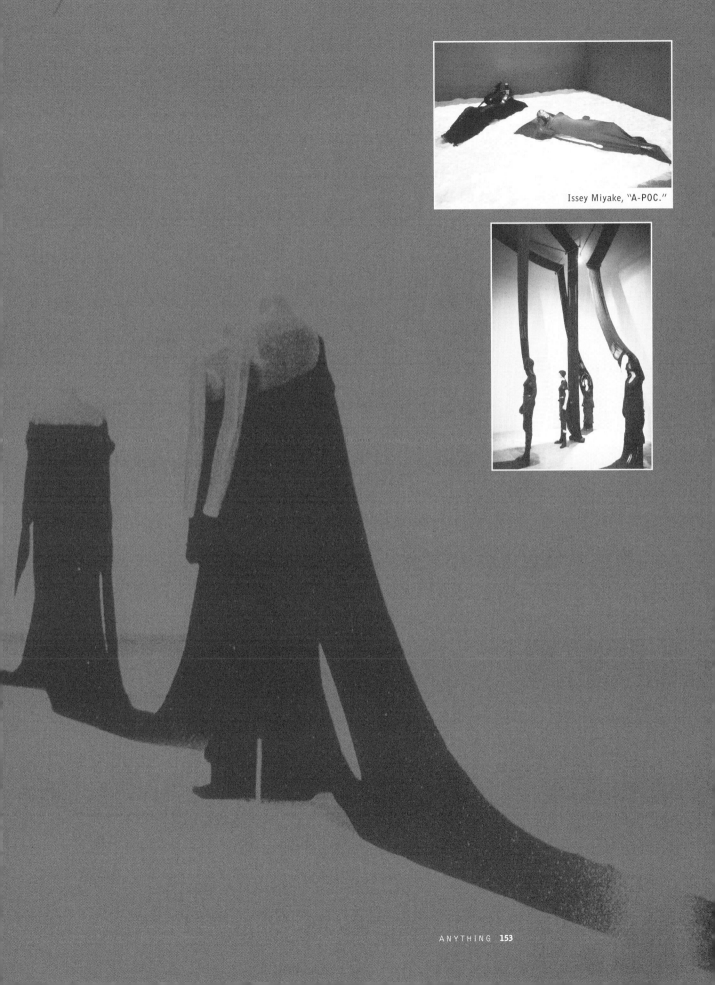

Issey Miyake, "A-POC."

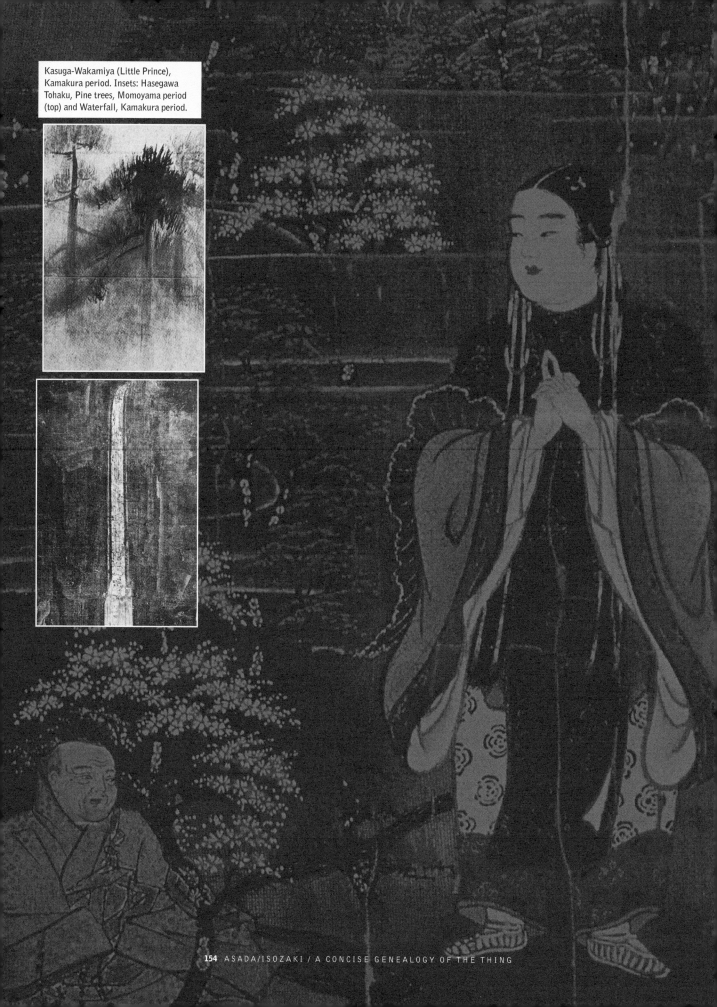

Kasuga-Wakamiya (Little Prince),
Kamakura period. Insets: Hasegawa
Tohaku, Pine trees, Momoyama period
(top) and Waterfall, Kamakura period.

This certainly risks an occultist reification — a danger shared by the French philosophers. If, for instance, the virtual topos that precedes the form/substance schema is ontologically hypostatized, it would be just another mono (thing). Rather, it should be treated as *koto* (event). In Japanese, *koto* is indivisible from *kotoba*. That is to say, *koto* alternates between mono (*les choses*) and kotoba (*les mots*), presence and absence, the imaginary and the symbolic.

On the other hand, when we intend to grasp the virtual topos directly, that is, by the intuition precedent to and beyond language, the risk of reification drastically increases. (During the past decade of Any conferences, we have observed a tendency to shift from the linguistic model to a computer-generated model, hand in hand with the theoretical shift from Derridian deconstruction to Bergsonian/ Deleuzian *Lebensphilosophie*. Understandably, the conventional linguistic model of the symbolic order and its deconstruction are not enough today. At the same time, there is a danger in this tendency that the intention to advance from the conventional model results in a return to the imaginary.)

How can we install the virtual topos that precedes the form/substance schema and vibrates in between presence and absence, the imaginary and the symbolic, architecture and urbanism? It is a philosophical question par excellence, as well as the most substantial problematic for architects and urbanists who confront architecture as event and city as event.

I - 2
TRANSCENDENTAL CITY
1. The World of the Archipelago

One representative image of our world could feature islands floating over three different kinds of oceans — actual, virtual, and trance. These islands could then weave a relational network by communicating with each other, forming a kind of archipelago. The oceans have always been the locus for certain kinds of interaction.

In the actual world, the islands are communities called cities or states; in reality they float over the ocean. The physical means of transportation between them includes journeys on foot, ship, car, and airplane. Here, time appears as distance.

In the virtual world, the islands are equivalent to terminals, floating over an ocean of liquid crystal. Bodies are transmitted as images of digitalized information, and because the transmis-

sions are instantaneous, time disappears while only order remains.

In the transcendental world, the islands are a consciousness (read also as *life*) contained in individual bodies floating over an ocean of cosmic awareness (life) that is ruled by natural law. Communication (transference) between individual consciousnesses (life) is mediated by the ocean of cosmic awareness into which individual consciousnesses dive. Time is a succession of instances; states of trance and flying yogi imply that the body exists in a state of intense receptivity.

2. The Vibrant Universe

Sunya permeates every corner of the universe. Physically it forms utsu (vacuum or void) but it also becomes ma (a gap) that supports the immanence of matter. It is this ma that generates *vibration*, the origin of all difference, which then forms waves that suffuse the universe.

—Language: Languages, or names of things, are transmitted as waves of different vibrations: this is a secondary communication between the consciousnesses (lives) contained by bodies. The main form of communication is alingual and is transmitted via cosmic awareness.

—Architecture: The contour is drawn by the

negotiation between the waves of consciousness expanding from within bodies and the waves of vibration suffusing the universe; the visualization of the embryonic stage of this aura is the halo or nimbus.

—The City: The visualization of cosmic architecture suffused with various types of waves is the so-called *mandala*; sensing the composition motivates individual consciousness to be incorporated into cosmic awareness; meanwhile, in its formation, the city as a community mimics the mandala.

—The Mandala: A kind of cosmic model that when contemplated incorporates individual consciousnesses into the universe; in other words, individuals can live in the universe. The world is structured as a nesting box of cosmos, mandala, city, architecture, and individuals, based upon natural law.

3: Invincible Power

When cosmic awareness is incorporated into meditation, it forms an invincible barrier around the body. On earth, the most effective wave is generated within the atmosphere approximately two hours after sunrise — that is, when the invincible power becomes the strongest. Places for mass meditation — "possessed *isola*" (islands) — are positioned in the 12 time

zones separated by two-hour time differences. This invincible power covers the whole earth by forming a chain that would stabilize regional conflicts, realizing peace. The shelters that cover the places for mass meditation are configurations of the contours drawn by the negotiation between the waves of consciousnesses. Originated in the auras generated around bodies, they are held in place by the tension between heaven and earth.

—The Actual Cities: The 12 time zones and the positions of the islands are marked on the Dymaxion map.

—The Virtual Cities: The Mirage City (*Haishi*) Project illustrates the becoming of islands of this category.

—The Transcendental Cities: The Great Seer's Site is an ideal model for all islands, floating over the oceans of cosmic awareness, real water, and the liquid crystal of cyberspace.

The central podiums are for meditation, a "possessed architecture." The positions taken by the ascetics assume a mandala as a cosmic model, and the emanation of aura around their bodies is visualized as a configuration. This assumes city, architecture, the ascetics' sitting positions, and also a diagram of the body.

MAKING
ZAHA

STRANGE
HADID

The title of this conference, Anything, obviously has a double edge. Anything could imply a degree of corruption and decadence and yet it also suggests a degree of freedom and liberty, like the liberty to take judgment on a certain thing, pushing the boundaries of the social project.

Doing my own thing, or "thing as feeling," is in defense of radicalism. Doing my own thing (and letting others do their thing) does not mean to be self-indulgent or oblivious to collective purposes. Doing your own thing means first of all to do things differently, to experiment, to resist the normal, to upset, to suspend the already known in order to give the new a chance. To me, feeling implies the freedom to work intuitively rather than via well-known and well-rehearsed reasons – the new as **felt** rather than known. Doing your own thing means being a catalyst for innovation, being an agent for mutation, a mechanism for evolution – selection and reproduction.

The avant-garde embraced the importance of mutation in the evolution of culture. To do things differently means making strange. To this end, I have started experimenting with strange drawing as an engine of invention. But now that our office is moving, hopefully, toward actual building, the question I want to raise here is, Is it still legitimate to experiment radically with full-fledged building?

The public domain should invest in experimental buildings as catalysts of self-transformation so as to create a new wilderness of fertile ground for further social evolution. This means letting some of us do our own thing without resorting to all of the already well-established "best" practices or standards. To imply that these experiments should be seen as not entirely successful if only half of them are fully achieved is fundamentally wrong. I have personally suffered from this kind of thinking and have been trying for many years to really push, not only for myself but for others, the boundaries of the possible.

There comes a point when I think it is especially critical that one not only negate but actually question either typology or functionality in the hope of discovering a new functionality, a new kind of nontype embedded in existing typologies. Here, land formation (a kind of going into the wilderness) and drawing techniques can begin to superimpose a number of trajectories or projections from which to extrapolate a spatiality that is not always evident. Abandoning methods that are familiar to us, like axial symmetry or other conventional ways of organizing space, enables us to search for a new kind of mutated or mediated space; a space that also fundamentally implies an open system of organization.

Acting on many of these instincts, our project for the Contemporary Arts Center in Cincinnati is a kind of aggregation, or perhaps an implosion, that borrows from the

Mind Zone, London (above and previous spread).

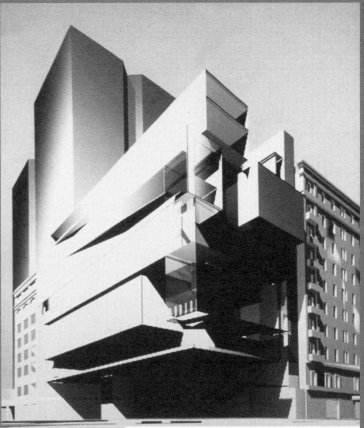

Contemporary Arts Center, Cincinnati (models below).

Contemporary Arts Center, Cincinnati.

scale of the landscape of the city and implodes it into the interior. The new building will provide spaces for temporary exhibitions, site-specific installations, and performances. To draw in pedestrian movement from the surrounding areas and create the sense of a dynamic public space, the entrance and lobby to the building's circulation system are organized as an "urban carpet." As it rises and turns, this carpet leads visitors up a suspended mezzanine ramp and through the full length of the lobby space, which during the day functions as an open, sunlit, "landscaped" expanse that reads as an artificial park. In contrast to this polished, undulating circulation system, the galleries are expressed as if they had been carved from a single block of concrete, hovering over the lobby space. Varying in size and shape, these solid and void gallery spaces interlock like a three-dimensional jigsaw puzzle. Enveloping the whole space is an undulating, translucent skin, through which passers-by can see into the life of the arts center.

The Millennium Dome in London was also an exercise in experimenting with a kind of interior urbanism. Of the 14 thematized exhibition zones within the dome (with titles such as Body, Play, and Work) we were asked to create the Mind Zone. We first approached the design of this space by thinking about how to represent the mind when its physical manifestation as the brain is so inadequate a signifier of its complexities. If the mind is essentially an experimental consciousness, then its physicality can only be seen as a host mechanism. These were the ideas that informed our design. The structure of the exhibit, of folding continuous surfaces, is therefore seen as a host, within which the physical presence of its contents can be located. The folding structure also offers a spatial interplay and confrontation with the subject matter, which strives to evoke the participants to think.

It was also very important for us within this interior exploration to invite a number of artists into the space of this "mind" to offer their own interpretations and installations. The zone itself is organized around the propositions of these artists, which lead the visitor through the space via conditional stages: from the question of what constitutes intelligence to perceptual inputs; through the mechanisms of thought to speculations on individual and cultural malleability. This organization revealed the importance we placed on avoiding the restriction of definitions, allowing, in the process, the mind to evolve and progress. The structure and materiality of the space also highlighted this lack of rigidity — the use of glass-fiber skins and a honeycomb, resin floor structure — creating an ephemeral, temporal quality befitting a space whose lifespan was to be just one year.

ANYTHING
INTERVENTION
GARY HILL /
PAULINA
WALLENBERG-
OLSSON

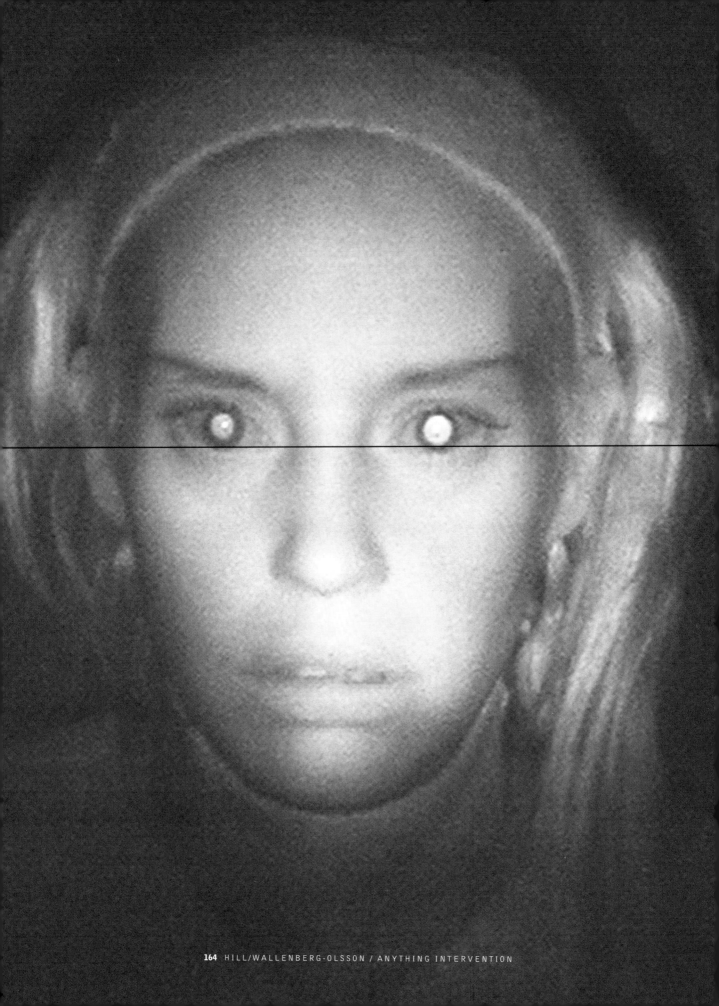

Where have you been
Hvar har du varit
for such a long time,
så länge,
Sven in the Garden
Sven i Rosengård?
of Roses?
Jag har varit
I have been in the stable,
i stallet,
our Dear Mother.
kära Moder Vår.
You'll await me sooner
I vänten mig sent eller
or never.
aldrig.

What have you done
Hvad har du gjort
in the stable,
i stallet,
Sven in the Garden
Sven i Rosengård?
of Roses?
Jag har
I have watered
vattnat fålarne,
the horses,
kära Moder Vår.
our Dear Mother.
I vänten mig sent eller
You'll await me sooner
aldrig.
or never.

Hvi är ditt svärd
Why is your sword
så blodigt
so bloody,
Sven i Rosengård?
Sven in the Garden
Jag har slagit
of Roses?
min broder,
I have killed
kära Moder Vår.
my brother,
I vänten mig sent eller
our Dear Mother.
aldrig.
You'll await me

sooner or never.
Hvart skall du

då ta vägen,
Where will you go now,
Sven i Rosengård?
Sven in the Garden
Jag skall rymma
of Roses?
av landet,
I shall leave the country,
kära Moder Vår.
our Dear Mother.
I vänten mig
You'll await me sooner
sent eller
or never.
aldrig.

What will you do with
Hvad gör du då
your wife,
af din hustru,
Sven in the Garden
Sven i Rosengård?
of Roses?
Hon får spinna
She may spin for
för födan,
the food,
kära Moder Vår.
our Dear Mother.

What will you do with
I vänten mig sent eller
the children,
aldrig.
Sven in the Garden
Hvar gör du då af
of Roses?
barnen små,
They may beg at
Sven i Rosengård?
each man's door,
De få gå för hvar
our Dear Mother.
mans dörr,

kära Moder Vår.
When will you return?
I vänten mig sent eller
When the swan
aldrig.
turns black.

When does the swan
När kommer du tillbaka?
turn black?
Näs Svanen han Svartnar.
When the crow

turns white.
När Svartnar Svanen?

När Korpen han Hvitnar.
When does the crow

turn white?
När hvitnar Korpen?
When the granite float.
När Grästenen Flyter

And when do the
Och när Flyter
granite float,
Grästenen,
Sven in the Garden
Sven i Rosengård?
of Roses?
Stenen,
The granite never float,
den Flyter Aldrig,
our Dear Mother.
kära Moder Vår.
You'll await me sooner
I vänten mig sent eller
or never.
aldrig.

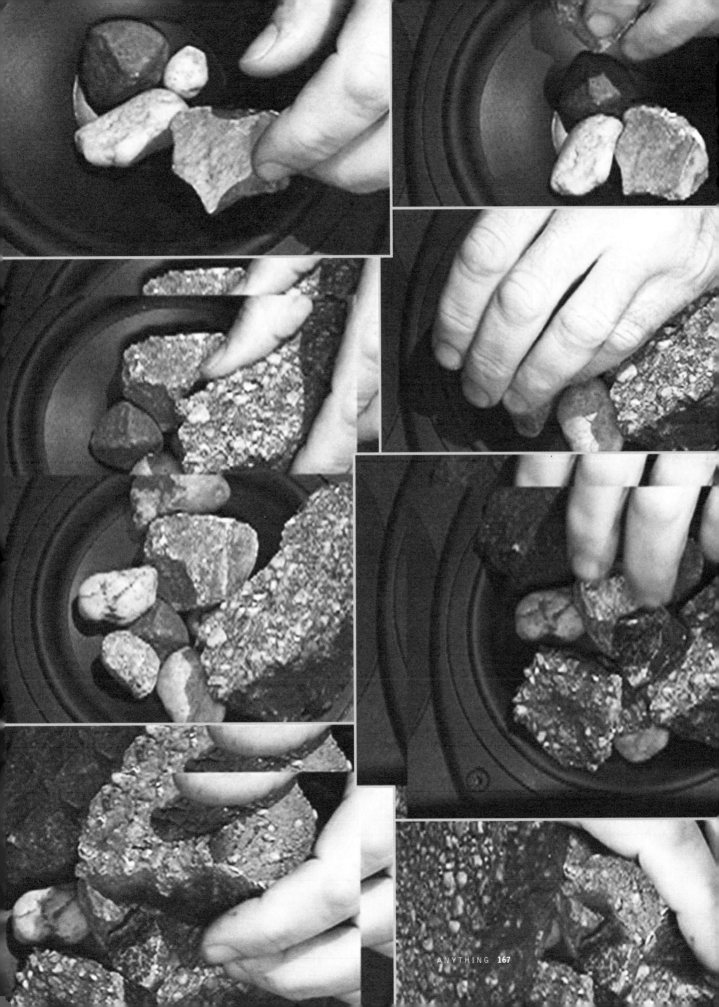

DISCUSSION 4

PHYLLIS LAMBERT Ten years ago at the first Any meeting we talked about Plato and not Heidegger; we talked about simulacra; we talked about Benjamin; we talked about the demiurge and not blur; we talked about deconstruction, not flux. These differences revealed themselves in the discussion this morning – the concrete practice of architecture and its theory confronting the use of science and different types of technologies. The location of theory in relation to architecture and its practice is perhaps an issue that we can reintroduce to this afternoon's discussion.

IGNASI DE SOLÀ-MORALES After listening to the presentations and discussions, my first thought is how many of our concerns today, at the threshold of the 21st century, are related to the production of art. This perhaps reveals that the connection between architectural production and artistic thinking is not lost, but that both architecture and what we call fine arts or art (with or without a capital **A**) have changed in quite important ways. The relationships between production and thinking, and between production and theory, are in the process of change. In the presentations this afternoon, very different relationships appeared, from Arata Isozaki's piece, which was fully immersed in a philosophical body of thought concerning the idea of emptiness and what that means in architecture, to other experiences in other fields – for example, the fantastic presentation by Gary Hill and Paulina Wallenberg-Olsson, which I'm sure many people here considered as something that typically hasn't been regarded as part of architecture. In this sense, it's not strange that the status of theory is also in the process of changing. There is no longer one space called theory, one space

called production, one space called art. Maybe the collapse of this compartmentalism is a good development. In this regard, Liz Diller's work is especially interesting in that it erodes, confuses, and blurs architecture's traditional boundaries. Similarly, for me, the relationship between theory and practice is something generated not through the academy but through our everyday work. It's a kind of permanent tension and interrogation rather than something that could be separated academically into different classrooms, so to speak. During this morning's session, I thought we were presented with very academic definitions – "this is architecture," "architecture is architecture," "too much theory," "the wrong kind of theory." Because of these divisions, I thought the session was not particularly interesting. This afternoon, though, we have heard talks that deliberately looked to confuse and blur these divisions – a confusion that I see as essential to the enrichment of our future work.

AKIRA ASADA Ignasi mentions the relationships between art and architecture – maybe we can also think specifically about the relationship between cinema and a hard place, to borrow a Gary Hill title. Giuliana gave us an insightful lesson about cinematic/kinematic space, which is both motional and emotional. But what particularly interests me, Giuliana, is not so much this cinematic/kinematic space as such, but the gap or distance between this space and its outside – between cinema and a hard place. I think that this is the real problem for architecture and urbanism in relation to cinematic art.

GIULIANA BRUNO I agree with Ignasi. One of the interesting things

for me as a film theorist is the blurring of the disciplinary boundaries between cinema, art, and architecture. I focused my talk on the relation between motion and emotion, but I think the slides also revealed a dialogue about an art form – a fluid, genealogic, historical, and very contemporary discussion that I feel film theory has not gone into enough. The spatial dynamics of this debate also have clear links with architecture – for example, moving in and out of the space of viewing painting, the picturesque, and different ways of conceiving, framing, editing, moving, etc. In this sense, although my talk specifically addressed the movement of emotion, it also alluded to the movement of the representation of place and displacement. One of the ways in which displacement functions is as an emotional displacement, which is an addition, in a sense, to a kind of history of the representation of how we intersect, live, conceive, and perceive space. I would argue that it is precisely at the intersection of architecture, art, and film that theoretically a lot of this work can take place (Gary Hill's work also shows the richness of this intersection in practice).

Interestingly, rather than art and architecture, film theory has been much more receptive to psychoanalysis, to literary theory, the Lacanian gaze, and a certain kind of linguistic-semiotic model, which, in a sense, tried to account for something that I don't think can be accounted for. Instead of literature and English departments, I see film theory in the university as locating itself closer to the departments of art and architecture, because I would argue that it is precisely in what architects and artists do that we can find a theoretical, practical, and historical genealogy.

ASADA But it seems to me that what is important for architecture is not only what is happening on the screen, within the frame, but outside the screen, outside the frame. This, I think, is what Gary's **Between Cinema and a Hard Place** is about — a video installation consisting of 23 monitors, with the projected images split over the distance of the monitors. Its images are composed of typically flawless Gary Hill editing, almost frame-by-frame, so there is no continuous flow. And the images are scattered in space. It's always a little hazardous to speak about a work in front of its author, but what seems to me particularly important in this piece is not only an impeccably crafted cinematic/kinematic space but also the way in which the images are cut, split, and scattered in time and space, making us sensitive not only to what is happening on the screen, within the frame, but also outside the screen, between the frames. I'm emphasizing this aspect precisely because the problem of today's architecture is its seeming infatuation with graphic images on the computer screen. In this computer-generated world the shape is always changing; it's full of motions and full of emotional appeal, but when you freeze it and build it, it suddenly loses all the charm it had on the screen. In the physical realities of built space, what is important is not only the concretized image, but also the relationship to its outside, which you can't see on the computer screen. In other words, architecture includes not only cinematic/kinematic space on the **imaginary** dimension but also void space on the **real** dimension. Of course, I'm critical of a certain Lacanian authoritarianism (which, by the way, is not so much about the gaze and the image as it is about the void), but I still have to say that it's not so

easy to get rid of the real, which cannot be represented on screen.

GARY HILL I want to first comment on Giuliana's presentation in which she talked about the etymology of the words **motion** and **emotion**, and got there through the move from kinesthesis to cinema. I've also traced this etymology starting with the words **sight** and **insight**, which lead us along the same path. This then also has a reciprocal relationship to actual speaking, so not only perhaps is there a relationship between motion and emotion but also between motion and speaking as something to **incite**, to actually move an image. Without this speaking, the image becomes something closer almost to spectacle, in which our experiences are completely privileged by the eye. This leads me to a second thought, that so many of the presentations today concern the deprivileging of the eye. In fact, Liz Diller's entire project is an incredible dematerialization of vision in some sense. Similarly, Arata and Akira spoke about void spaces — even the actual architecture we saw appeared almost like empty eye sockets; the vision had been emptied out into some other space.

ELIZABETH DILLER I found Gary and Paulina's presentation to be the most architectural contribution to this conference. It took up the actual space that we're in, the actual architectural space. Of course its rules and the way in which it played with genres were also incredibly strong and spatially, architecturally, rich. I can't, though, leave Akira's statement behind because I find in it a tremendous confusion between thinking and comparing the computer screen to the film screen. We are in a screen culture and are used to looking at all kinds of

screens all the time — TV screens, computer screens, movie screens, etc. — and I think it's critical to make a distinction between each of their spatialities. Certainly, when one reflects on the change in the relationship between architecture and technology, the computer screen is a critical tool for thinking about architecture in a different way, in a way that we couldn't before without these tools. But one doesn't necessarily expect that screen to deliver anything else. It's all to do with the way a project is thought outside of any methodology and any tool. I just want to make that distinction. Now that architecture is no longer the dominant voice of cultural expression and has been replaced by technologies, the question for me is, how, while under the all-encompassing embrace of that technology, can architecture find some small corner to say something other than lament its small role? This is a question that our work is dedicated to; to finding perhaps some interesting opportunity to intersect technology and architecture in which these two conditions are not kept apart or thought of as being engaged in some kind of warfare.

BRUNO The dematerializing vision that Gary mentioned is also part of the project that I'm taking on. This dematerialization has a particular significance in film theory because the discipline has been dominated for so long by the idea that film is just a visual medium conceptualized around notions of the Lacanian gaze. For me, to move outside of this, and in a sense dissolve, dematerialize, and move elsewhere, is precisely how I see my own project developing.

I also agree with Liz that the computer screen cannot be analyzed in the same way as the film screen. My presentation looked at the film screen and tried to show a certain kind of blurring and mapping of the architectural wall into the film screen — the cinematic screen as a sort of skin that has borders and connects to the outside. Cinema then is a house of moving pictures; it's a form of dwelling. It's not just the frame of a painting, and even in that respect there is always a kind of border that speaks to all four sides. Narrative cinema has always been organized in the form of dialogue between outside space and inside space. There is also a certain kind of liminality to the movements of the filmic screen. It passes before us at 24 frames per second, it's silent, and it's dark; it is a still image that creates the illusion of movement by way of diffraction, so in a sense it is also part of this silence, if you like — the silence of the eye. The black part of the frame is also the thing that makes it possible to exist, and this, in a sense, is what attracts me to film because there is a constant movement between placement and displacement. The fabric of this dichotomy, this texture, is also what distinguishes the filmic screen from the workings of the computer monitor. In relation to this liminality, I also had in mind one of Gary's works, in which a kind of brain enters in and out of a house, changing the way in which the house is organized. In a sense, this is precisely the kind of movement that I was trying to map out in my presentation; a borderless and yet bordered kind of moving fabric that for me constitutes the house of moving pictures.

LAMBERT I would like to take this discussion a bit out of **le cadre du boudoir** and ask Kurt Forster if he would be good enough to place this debate within a broader intellectual and historical perspective.

KURT FORSTER This is a pretty tall order at this hour of the day. I'm coming out from behind this strip of yellow plastic that has been wrapped around the reserved seats and on which it says, "Caution, Do Not Enter" (of course this precaution could perhaps be read both ways). I'm also not sure whether we are treading on the thin ice of theory or the already broken ice of history, floating down an accelerating torrent of demonstrations. What can be done to get rid of both of them?

One thing which struck me, and which I believe has been addressed by quite a number of people today, has to do with what one could, perhaps very approximately, describe as "atmosphere." It has to do with the various induced states that either have to be created or brought about or are chosen among the innumerable possible states in which the world presents itself to us — that atmospheric state that has been alluded to many times through light, through emotion, motion, through a transformative capacity now seemingly vested in the things themselves. But how does this atmosphere really come about? I call it atmosphere because it extends around and beyond us, yet does not coincide with any of the things necessarily contained within an atmosphere. In fact, the atmospheric dimension seems itself to relate to an induced state of visualization — namely, the way things behave when we turn them in front of our eyes: that we can fly through them, that we can take a view from any kind of distance, pass right through them, or arrest our relationship at whatever distance we wish. This atmospheric quality, I would argue, was first engineered at an extraordinary scale at the precise moment when the natural sublime was being discovered: the park landscape, a nature completely manipulated so

as to induce certain emotional responses, to offer, in fact, a kind of laboratory of experience — you go through a dark grotto, suddenly the sunlight cuts out; you enter a damp and dripping tunnel; you emerge on the slopes of a volcano; or you walk over a bridge that, under the very impact of your own weight, starts to move and shake precariously. The park (and Woerlitz near Dessau, the largest and most elaborate "English" park in Germany, would be a wonderful illustration of this) produces a sort of atmospherically induced, emotional laboratory in which water spouts, artificial waves, darkness, and light belong as much as the shaping of the topography.

So when I saw the machinery proposed by Diller+Scofidio to terminally vex my compatriots over Lake Neuchâtel, I thought it was a marvelous demonstration of accomplishing a third (previously unknown) thing of which we know one and two. We know the natural sublime, within which Switzerland has played an undeservedly large role; we know the technological sublime, which we associate much more with work done in the United States; and now perhaps we have in the technologically induced cloud, created in order to pull all organ stops in the atmospheric register, the technological sublime gradually dissolving into a simulation of the natural sublime. The natural sublime in the end reveals itself progressively and contradictorily to be an induced state — a state that we can experience while immersing our feet in pure, clear liquids, and whatever thirst we may have is quenched by the mineral waters of the experience.

I was also thinking of the extent to which Zaha Hadid's wonderful drawings and representations induce in the existing city (where some of her work will be located) a kind of altered state of reality, and then how her work is able to channel through itself these particular induced states. I am somewhat at a loss for words for describing this, although it's something that the images appeared to articulate.

And of course there was also that moment in the Japanese pavilion at the 1996 Venice Biennale, when the return of the real earthquake seemed suddenly to endow the natural sublime, in its most destructive capacity, with some of the power that the 1755 earthquake of Lisbon had on the entire Enlightenment in Europe. Suddenly all intellectually induced states – the unknowability of the thing and the ever-changing shadings of its experience that separate the subjective state of some perception from the objective being – in a sense collapsed, in that the thing killed the very subject trying to apprehend it. In this way, I would argue that the Biennale pavilion had an extraordinary wake-up call quality in that it suggested, not by chance, and in terms that Akira formulated so sharply, that the Kantian dilemma has not been completely removed from knowledge simply by extended strolls through the park.

In the end, I think that it is simply futile, if not outright stupid, to constantly try to establish the borderlines of the discipline: what belongs to sculpture; where does architecture begin; whether that leg hanging out of the ceiling, or coming out of the painting, is invading this space or that; whose visual field does drawing occupy, etc. The entire range of experiences, with all of their categorical definitions of academic origin, has been completely swept into one experiential reality. By the same token, we should also remind ourselves that this collapse has in the past been subject

to extremely severe criticism – what was called baroque sham or theater fakery – and that what followed was a call for the immediate return to the essentials of each one of the different fields of activity.

BRUNO This is really interesting for me, because one of the possible connections between cinema and architecture is of course the materiality of the atmospheric – not only as a kind of genealogy or archaeology but also because movie palaces in the past were called "atmospheric theaters." To me, this perhaps reveals the ways in which the archaeology of cinema is connected to the form of the atmospheric. There is also the parent of the sublime – the picturesque – working within this atmosphere, which is why I evoked a garden in my presentation not simply as a topography but also as a place where all these hydraulic, fluid mechanisms and technologies (which became the fluid technology of motion pictures) took place in picturesque settings such as London's Vauxhall pleasure gardens. These gardens opened at six o'clock at night and were spaces of lightness radiating in the dark, where all of these spectacles were projected onto screens and backdrops. In things like Vauxhall's **eidophusikons**, or precinematic spectacles, there is a kind of archaeology of fluid, hydraulic mechanisms projected onto screens that I see as evolving into the atmospheric screen of the cinema in the 1920s.

HUBERT DAMISCH I am very interested in the presentations and discussions today because in a way they serve as confirmation of something that I have been trying to argue for all my life. They showed that real theory comes from the art itself. As a historian of art, as a supposed

philosopher, as a theoretician, I learn from the art. I don't try to theorize it but to learn what is at work in the art and how it was thought out. For instance, I think that Gary Hill's presentation was extraordinary because it was not a narrative but a succession of modalities of thinking, which I found particularly interesting. I would like to hear him comment on this – on the way in which it dealt first with the voice, and then with material, with matter obliterating the sound with pieces of stones, before finally returning again to sound and the specter.

HILL I first want to point out that this was a total collaboration with Paulina Wallenberg-Olsson. The work began when **ANY** magazine asked me to contribute to its last issue, dealing with ideas of zero, the erasure of sound, and the north. These were some of the themes that they suggested, and knowing Paulina, I asked her if she wanted to take part in this project. We did a graphic work for the magazine and then decided to do this intervention for the conference today. So I guess part of the content of this work came out of the magazine's themes. The song that Paulina sang is one that she has known for a long time. It's a ballad from the 12th century. What was interesting about it for me is its lyrics. As long as there is another metaphor following the previous metaphor, then the song can continue to be sung, there's the possibility that the sun may return. So it had to do with this kind of division, of going toward a zero with the possibility of perhaps never getting there, yet also with the inevitable possibility that this would collapse. These then were some of the internal ideas that we threw around, but we weren't really sure about how to go about doing it. We had been working with infrared and the idea, or feeling, of something very present, but at the same time we wanted an image that would produce a kind of distance, or relative distance, next to a kind of absence – a kind of simultaneity of presence and absence, again as something that we saw as closer to our understanding of zero. Our final thoughts concerned the problem of translation because we wanted the words to be understood. It made sense to sort of translate it this way and then produce a kind of physicality based upon the same content, in which the division takes place by the destruction of the voice with a materiality. In the last 24 hours we added the final projected elements, in a sense to have a sound that would penetrate a given architecture, a given context of speaking. I don't know if that does anything to help, but . . .

DAMISCH No, thank you, that was very revealing, very enlightening. I think your answer showed that I was right to ask the question. For me, the most important idea, and it is one that I will return to tomorrow in my presentation, is the notion of projection. Elizabeth Diller spoke about not confusing different types of screens, and I agree with her, but for me the more general point is the overriding relationship of the screen to projection. In France at the moment there is great debate over this issue – the Cinémathèque in Paris, for instance, sees the process of transferring all 35-millimeter film stocks into digital media as highly contentious because it would signal the end of projection. It will totally transform the idea of the film and its reception. But what does the computer screen have to do with projection? In the computer monitor there is no projection in the optical sense, but there is projection in the perspectival sense, in the geometrical

sense. The image on the computer screen is produced through a technological transformation, but this transformation is still based on a very simple trick of perspective. So Akira may have been wrong in confusing the different types of screens, but he was right in raising the issue of the relationship between the screen and the frozen image.

ZAHA HADID Part of the problem is that when you see an image on the screen it has a sense of depth, perhaps falsely, that printed images do not have. There is also the issue of light and luminosity, which I think is especially critical in terms of cinematography and film. For me, the lighting that illuminates the screen and then radiates out is very seductive. I'm curious that in all of the presentations, the speakers seemed to reveal a similar kind of seduction in the acceptance of other mediums, notably cinema and art. These mediums are attractive because they have different degrees of permanence. They can last for a few minutes or an hour. I think people have a resistance to the same kind of emotional indulgence in architecture. Today we are surrounded by cries for a kind of aesthetic of neutrality that seems to fulfill all those politically correct needs of restraint and so on. My argument, though, is that we're so emotionally charged when we see beauty and strangeness in film that we need to invest architecture with these same qualities, so that we can feel propelled to architecture in the same way we are drawn to other mediums.

DAMISCH Zaha, you speak of the difference between an image projected onto the screen and an image printed on the screen, but in being part of the culture of the screen, you must not

forget that there is another type of screen – the screen image, the image that obliterates. This is a Freudian concept. It suggests an image that screens, or impedes, your vision; that there is something behind the screen that you cannot see because the image on the screen prevents you from seeing it. An image that you think of, in order not to think of something else.

HADID But this is too perfect in a way . . .

DAMISCH It's too perfect?

HADID . . . I think that we are too fascinated by mutation – it leads us into a predictable world. The elements of error and randomness are very critical to our being productive as opposed to just repetitive. This perfection implies a repetitiveness because you can multiply it many times, but it does not signal a life. What is interesting about this animosity is that it leads one to think about a life beyond what you immediately see; contemplating what kinds of spaces might be appropriate to this other, imagined life. What intrigues me about the boundaries between architecture and film is not how we understand each other, but how we can spatially occupy these other spaces.

DILLER I hadn't thought about it until you mentioned it, Hubert, but this distinction between looking at a source of light, staring into a source of light like a TV or a monitor, and seeing an image projected onto a screen is very important. It's a spatial difference. The source of the image and the point at which that image is cut and thrown in and out of focus is a space that is usually occupied. So there is a kind of extra immersion that takes place, aside from the filmic content that happens in that space — rear projection films **feel**.

DAMISCH You're right, there is a big difference. The light coming from the screen and the light coming to the screen are completely distinct. Going to the movies, finding your seat, one always appears as a shadow on the screen. But when you watch TV, you can walk around it and it doesn't matter. The image is always there. There is no interference.

HILL I want to add a few, what may turn into very nonlinear, thoughts on these screen issues. As Liz said, there is projection and there is emission, but even the metaphors of these two distinct processes introduce all kinds of continuous thoughts. Film projects at 24 frames per second, but the interesting thing for me is that video does not even exist as frames per second, but rather as sequences of light going on and off at very high speeds. If we think of immersion, or what it might do to a viewer or a participant, then we must also think about what this kind of left-to-right scanning emission does to a person. I feel that it actually has a lot to do with the cycle of the way the brain goes on and off with its neuronic pulses — and maybe this is something that we can begin to achieve some kind of conscious control of.

Anyway, screen technology is in an incredible state of flux now, and becoming more so. Related to this flux, and an issue that I see as very important but which we skirted earlier, is the question of computer animation and its relationship to other kinds of image making. As we move "forward" through the technological advancements of computer technology toward something that is closer and closer to real time (with no delays in render-

ing), the space of mediation begins to disappear. With this disappearance also develops a sense of power, of ultimately being able to do "anything" with the image, with the idea, with the points, with the lines, with the perspective, with whatever you want. This may have been the point Akira was getting at.

Some time ago my first experience with computer animation was through a friend who was working as an animator. He had been an architect but then decided to switch to computer animation because he wanted to be able to show people moving images to best illustrate what the thing was going to look like. I always used to say, "Wouldn't this be great if it was real time?" And he would say, "No it would not be great. I like to do something, sit back, and watch it render, so that I can think about what I am doing." It's this thinking, I think, which goes back to the earlier discussion on the Heidegger thing — not the Heidegger "thing" but another Heidegger "thang" — that has to do with what Heidegger called the "nature of language," in which poetics and thought relate to what he termed a "neighboring nearness," rather than with quantitative ideas of time and space. It's not then a question of how close they are in time and space, but that their neighborliness is a spatial metaphor for the ways in which poetry is related to thinking. This might have been the space that Akira was somehow referring to in bringing up the question of computer animation.

ASADA Yes, although I was thinking of spatialites in the sense of Maurice Blanchot rather than Heidegger.

DILLER Again, I think that these things need to be clarified — the

difference between the computer screen as a site of the construction of an idea, like the construction of an animation or a model, and display as a system. The potential feedback between one and the other is the charge. I think that what you're asking for is the correspondence between the technology that's used for production and the final display of the project, which is the architecture. The most compelling part about the piece that you [Gary] performed for us today was the feedback in the system, both in terms of the acoustics and the visual display devices, such that they canceled each other out. I was waiting at the edge of my seat to see what would happen with the videotape that you shot of Paulina singing. There is something so potentially fascinating about the relationship between all these modes of display and construction and the ways that they start to interfere with the screens and display devices. They can develop spatialities and various intersections with architecture.

"has a
about"

"the

""

THE
OF ¥€$
KOOL

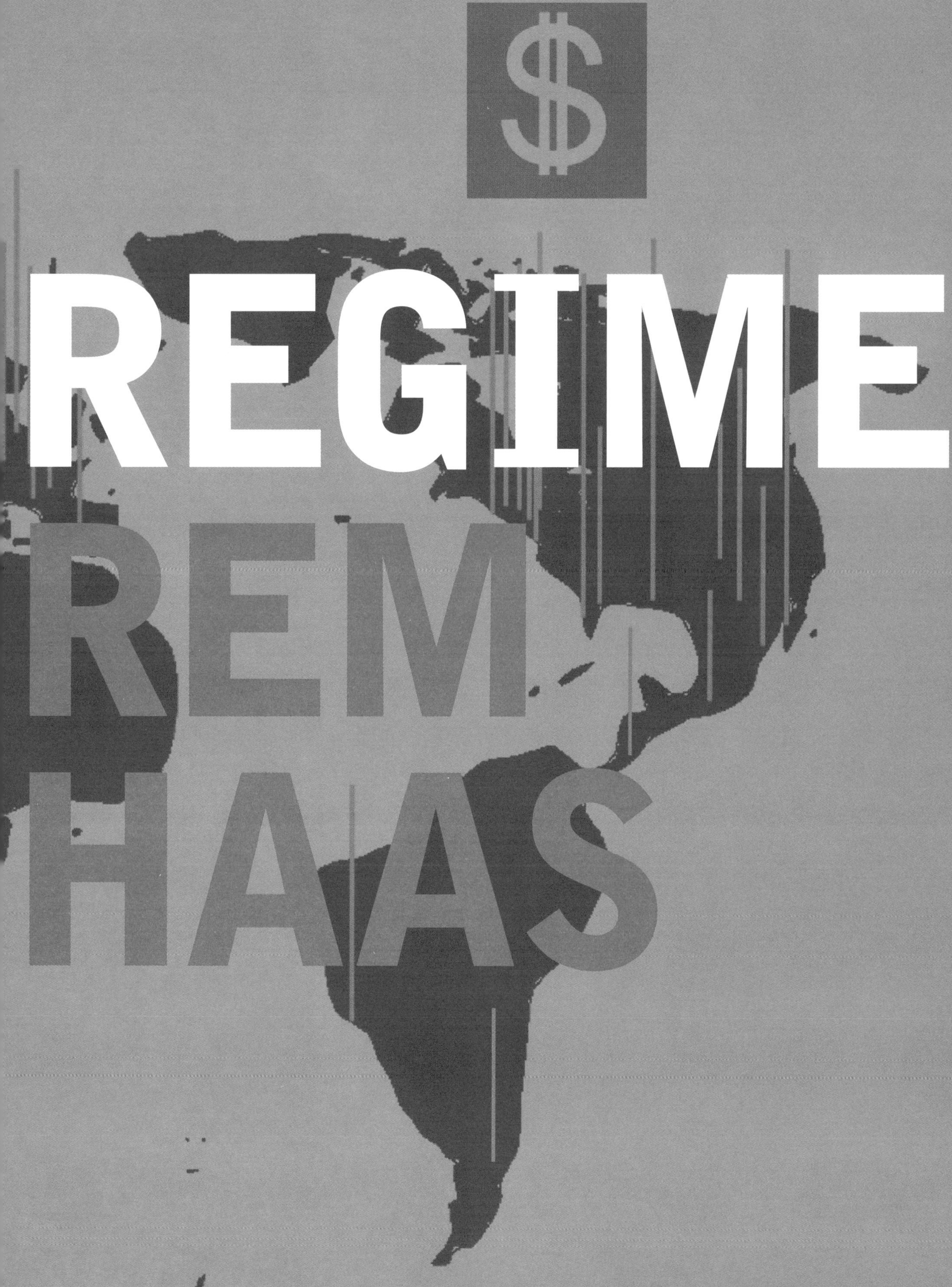
$
REGIME
REM
HAAS

Fig. 14

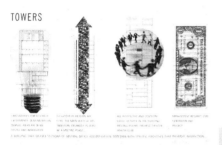

TOWERS

Fig. 5

Fig. 15

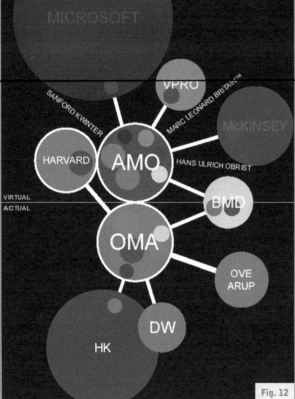

MICROSOFT

VPRO

SANFORD KWINTER

MARC LEONARD BRITAIN™

McKINSEY

HARVARD

AMO

HANS ULRICH OBRIST

BMD

VIRTUAL

ACTUAL

OMA

OVE
ARUP

DW

HK

Fig. 12

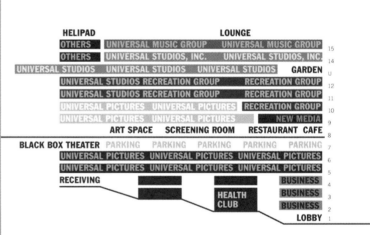

Fig. 6

	HELIPAD			LOUNGE		
	OTHERS	UNIVERSAL MUSIC GROUP		UNIVERSAL MUSIC GROUP		15
	OTHERS	UNIVERSAL STUDIOS, INC.		UNIVERSAL STUDIOS, INC.		14
UNIVERSAL STUDIOS	UNIVERSAL STUDIOS		UNIVERSAL STUDIOS		GARDEN	U
	UNIVERSAL STUDIOS RECREATION GROUP			RECREATION GROUP		12
	UNIVERSAL STUDIOS RECREATION GROUP			RECREATION GROUP		11
	UNIVERSAL PICTURES	UNIVERSAL PICTURES		RECREATION GROUP		10
	UNIVERSAL PICTURES	UNIVERSAL PICTURES		NEW MEDIA		9
	ART SPACE	SCREENING ROOM		RESTAURANT CAFE		8
BLACK BOX THEATER	PARKING	PARKING	PARKING	PARKING	PARKING	7
	UNIVERSAL PICTURES	UNIVERSAL PICTURES	UNIVERSAL PICTURES			6
	UNIVERSAL PICTURES	UNIVERSAL PICTURES	UNIVERSAL PICTURES			5
	RECEIVING				BUSINESS	4
				HEALTH	BUSINESS	3
				CLUB	BUSINESS	2
					LOBBY	1

Fig. 10

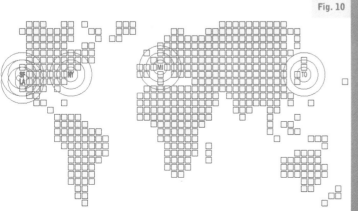

Fig. 9

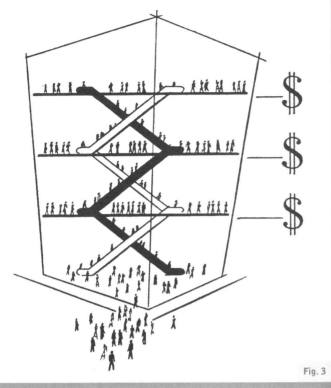

Fig. 3

Fig. 2

Fig. 4

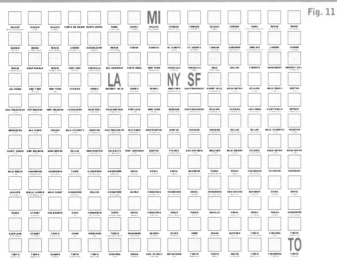

Fig. 11

Fig. 13

Fig. 7

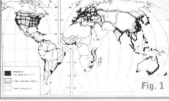

Fig. 1

Fig. 8

Looking back on a number of conferences, certain images represent for me a state of architecture that has disappeared, if not forever, then certainly for the time being. One of these was drawn 30 years ago by Constantin Doxiadis and represents the world according to his vision of the near future; it indicates that as recently as 1970, architects could be confident and unembarrassed in presenting their visions on a global scale. [Fig. 1] According to this particular vision, the world is described through only three conditions: black represents the universal city, gray is other habitats, and white is thinly populated. It is clear that a diagram with this kind of simplification can only be made by a professional culture that is entirely confident in the precision of its own diagnoses.

Through our work, it has become apparent that we now live in a completely different condition. Providing some kind of trademark for this change is an acronym formed from the three major currencies of the world – the yen, the euro, and the dollar – which together spell the word ¥€$. It is important to realize that we no longer operate in a state of absolute confidence but that we are laboring under the regime of ¥€$. My contributions to the Any conferences over the past couple of years have been to try to identify what the consequences of this ¥€$ are for the urban condition, on the one hand, and, on the other, for architecture itself.

I have to make an admission: I am not an unconditional lover of architecture. Therefore, for me, certain aspects of architecture's decline implied by the ¥€$ have been very welcome. This has, I think, accounted for an apparent cynicism in my description of the consequences of the ¥€$ regime in architecture. As opposed to my conditional love of architecture, however, I have an unconditional love for the city. I have used this fondness to mobilize the city against architecture according to a formula that was perhaps overly simplistic, defining the city, the urban condition, as something that generates potential – unlike the activities of architecture, which exhaust potential and are greedy and preemptive.

I want to examine here the consequences of ¥€$ for the urban condition. At the Anyhow conference in Amsterdam, I showed this condition at its most rampant, in the Pearl River Delta area around Hong Kong. My presentation offered an inventory of what the new conditions of the city there might be. It is clear, for example, that when one looks at the simultaneity of rice fields and major road intersections in an image of the center of Shenzhen in China, that this degree of contrast and

heterogeneity has never occurred before in combination with such a scale and apparent maturity of building. [Fig. 2] So we have something that is interesting in its hybridization, in the sense that it is embryonic and at the same time ancient in terms of its typologies. It is also clear that this kind of heterogeneity could never have been invented by a single urbanist; nor would any urbanist want to claim credit for such a coexistence of buildings. Just as Greg Lynn has spoken about networks and the consequences of adaptation – of even the smallest elements changing the whole – one of the bizarre consequences of globalization and the ¥€$ regime is a new kind of organicism. In the Pearl River Delta – a network consisting of the cities of Hong Kong, Shenzhen, Zhuhai, and Macao – there is no longer the sense of a single complex or a single composed entity but rather a sense that the incentives of globalization, economics, and the market economy have produced a relentless competition between each and every element. This has created the City of Exacerbated Difference, where each change in any of its components necessitates the conceptual adjustment of the entire system: if Hong Kong becomes denser and more urban, Zhuhai has to become more suburban to maintain its contrast.

For me, this represents a particular reading of what the ¥€$ regime and market economy mean for the city. These consequences are equally powerful for architecture, and it is these consequences that my students and I have tried to define in the Harvard Guide to Shopping. This project investigated a number of phenomena according to a very simple basis. First, we looked globally at the amount of shopping that each citizen of the world currently has to support, either as an involuntary taxation or as a voluntary ownership. (In certain countries, America among them, this is a very considerable burden.) The second thing we noticed is the infiltration of shopping into even the most sacrosanct elements of architectural consciousness. For example, at the souvenir shop in the Barcelona Pavilion, this infiltration clearly speaks for itself. Is it then possible to resurrect architecture as a tourist attraction? And what kind of architectural resurrection is possible in a market economy?

Critically, through shopping, and according to the pervasiveness of shopping, the architectural profession relearns its diagrams. We are all still imprinted with the image of Le Corbusier's Maison Dom-ino, but I would argue that the multistory mall is a more important, more relevant diagram, and has been for a very long time. [Fig. 3] Ignored as it is, this architecture is about the multiplication of floor space and the smooth connection between those floors, to the extent that movement between them becomes like a new unconscious. The enormous expansion of shopping, the direct and inevitable consequence of the market economy, has now clearly infiltrated every category of building. Shopping on its own will tend to survive less and less, and is therefore forced to combine itself with activities such as churchgoing and education, or with major infrastructural elements such as airports. This increased pervasiveness over the past ten or twenty years has completely transformed the status of architecture, in the sense that architecture (in spite of what you might think from this Any conference, where we still continue to present individual buildings) is becoming increasingly limitless – that in many cases in contemporary architecture, it is impossible to say where a building begins or ends. It is impossible to discern whether or not the architecture is the result of a single gesture of creation; it is also impossible to say whether each part is equally alive. There are clear examples of architecture where certain parts of a building are gangrenous, while other parts of the same building still function properly.

I have tried to imagine what this architecture could be called, or how it could be identified, and the term I have come up with is **junkspace**. Junkspace is defined as the corollary of space junk – the debris that mankind leaves on the earth. What is critical about junkspace is that it is spatially extravagant, architecturally ambitious, and incredibly intricate, yet at the same time utterly unmemorable. This shift from the memorable to the literally unmemorable is something that has happened on our watch, and in this sense I continue to find it bizarre that a project like Any can be so independent of these kinds of developments. In a not untypical section of the architecture of junkspace, large parts of a building appear to be in a permanent process of conversion; intestinal ducts emerge from cavities in the ceiling, cladding panels are peeling away, as if the architecture is being X-rayed so that you can suddenly see how it is made. In this respect, perhaps the key aspect of junkspace is its massive erosion of architecture's core values of stability and materiality. I am convinced that we are not isolated from this process, and that we maintain a much stronger connection to these architectures than we would like to believe.

Our architecture has tried to adjust and come to terms with these conditions, among them the undecideability of each program at this moment, the shift from public to private clients, and the inevitable engagement with the values of corporations. I want to describe a number of projects where this shift is most evident, beginning with a project for the new headquarters of Universal Studios. Our client was the grandson of the man who commissioned Mies van der Rohe to design the Seagram Building in New York, so this was therefore an architectural operation at a high level of ambition and tradition. What was most interesting was how the diagram of the components that had to go into the building when we began the operation in 1995 changed: only six months later 30 percent of the components had disappeared – they had either shrunk or been sold or had expanded to such a size that they could no longer be part of the building. What was especially critical to us, and increasingly apparent, was that architecture's relationship to program and its engagement with the needs of the client had become much more vague, while at the same time there was now an almost complete separation between program and form. We then had to incorporate this somehow in our thinking. [Figs. 4 and 5]

So if this was the program, it had already been completely surpassed by the time we went into design development. [Fig. 6] We soon realized that we were, in fact, not working on a specific program but on the amalgamation of a number of autonomous firms – that we were in effect fabricating a new corporate entity. If we understood it as such, however, and if we accepted all the turbulence that went with this kind of fabrication, were we going to be even remotely successful? We would need to develop a single identity for an empire established on whiskey, which had then imagined that it could marry a company dedicated to film, and then decided that music was at least as interesting, if not more so, and then had felt that connections to the Internet were also absolutely essential. All of this had to be part of our brief; but we were also required to play an important role in helping the client understand this and to give a kind of gestalt to these kinds of accumulative operations, an identity to that work. It became clear that we could do this only by offering a generic and infinitely flexible chunk of office space where any one of these programs could happen. But the generic or the Miesian is, of course, no longer enough; it has no identity, or at least is not seen to have one. So we had to devise a way to generate specificity for the client. We imagined that the generic could be a series of horizontal planes, intersected at four points by vertical tower elements: one tower constituted laboratories for thinking, for having ideas; a second tower was for circulation;

a third tower was for community and interaction; a fourth tower was for money (or supervision). [Fig. 7] It was only when we developed this other kind of communication, which had nothing to do with architecture (despite the fact that we had at the same time actually been covertly designing a building recognizable in architectural terms), that we decided to present it almost as a graph of an urban condition, with all the flexibilities and potential for mutations that the urban diagram has — the infinities, for example, that the urban diagram has over the fixity of architecture.

A second project, currently in development, is the public library in Seattle. I want to describe this project not in detail but in terms of the steps we had to take in accommodating certain drastic shifts in current culture. It is clear that the library is one of the last remaining bastions of social good, a status that has made librarians on the whole overly self-satisfied and moralistic; they are confident that they are one of the rare professions that is doing good. This is the self-image of the librarian. But the librarian now has to compete with a public realm that is now utterly transformed and radicalized, with packs of consumers that need iconography and entertainment rather than enlightenment. So a critical part of our approach to the library became not to make the mistake of accommodating this kind of moralism.

We read the program presented to us in such a way that certain elements would remain relatively stable, allowing others to be flexible; we were also simultaneously working on a Web site so that the two could be complementary, treated as a single presence. [Fig. 8] It was clear that a library needed books. But it was equally clear that a library needed parking, that a library needed office space, that a library needed a newly defined kind of catalogue; this we imagined as a kind of trading floor, an electronic process that in itself could have entertainment value. In between, there were entities that could not yet be defined very clearly. Reading became the incentive for the library itself, which featured a series of highly contained and stable platforms for this purpose. Diagrammatically, a series of public spaces fill the residue between the platforms, as spaces where public life, or the mutations of public life as they are suggested by the library and its current unstable configuration, can unfold. The platforms and the unstable spaces between them are made into a single entity by cladding the entire thing in a skin of structure that both breathes and performs all the necessary technical tasks. [Fig. 9]

An even more highly developed abstraction is evident in a project we are currently working on for Prada. Over the last two years, Prada has opened 200 stores; they felt that they had reached the limits of the current definition of the Prada brand. They asked us, then, to strategize, on a purely technical level, what they could do in this situation. We were asked to look at stores in Milan, Los Angeles, New York, San Francisco, and Tokyo. Because it is undeniably a global company, we needed to look first at Prada on a global scale. So, through the back door, we have returned again to the global consideration of Doxiadis, though in a much more modest — and perverse — way. [Fig. 10] We first made a Prada atlas, initially plotting the location of Prada stores in relation to gross domestic product. From these studies, one could see that the world is composed of a series of economically inflated and deflated countries; Russia, for example, in Prada terms is shriveled to insignificance, as obviously Prada stores only exist in the inflated portions of the globe. [Fig. 11] We then looked at Prada and climate, at first sight not a very direct or important connection, until one realizes that most Prada stores are in the moderate zone of the world, since only in this zone are two collections a year a necessity. (There is a tropical exception, which accounts for a region of the world where air conditioning is a highly developed necessity.) We continued by looking at Prada in relation to the main centers of world population; here a drastic discrepancy appeared, which could also be a reason for optimism in commercial terms, in the sense that there is room for a lot more Prada. Finally, we addressed the issue of what a store could be in this condition. Obviously the universal store cannot work at this scale. The ingenuity was to make these exceptional stores — not reflexive stores, which would be vulgar or simply redundant, but more context-centered stores that could destabilize the message of Prada and, therefore, in spite of its relentless global expansion, maintain an aura of experimentation, even theory.

We saw these studies as experiments in how to engage a completely new condition for architecture and a new constellation of clients and priorities. It also became important for us to rethink the way the architectural office considered these commissions. For instance, when Greg Lynn and Jean Nouvel present the technical abilities of their respective offices, it is something of a shame that there is no possibility for combination or cooperation between them. If we combine our respective technical insights, contexts, and delivery systems, architecture could at the very least become a more vigorous presence among contemporary forces. On a modest scale, this is what we are trying to do with the formerly (or soon to be) antithetical office of Herzog & de Meuron in a project in New York City. It is possible that any one of the architects at Anything could also be part of a future cooperation. A more developed model would be one where we, as authors, would remain relatively small entities, but each would have a shared domain of competence that, in being constituted as a project rather than as a series of competing identities, would make the impact and power of what architecture can do much more visible. This is not a grab for power but, on the contrary, the reimagining of a territory.

In the same way, we can also deal finally with the sense of inferiority that we have felt for a long time relative to those with a frequent and pleasurable access to the virtual world. We can finally realize, as the Eameses expressed it, that everything is architecture, and that architecture is defined as organization. There is a rather sad situation that I think is part of the persistent unwillingness of architecture to align itself with particular cultural conditions: namely, the fact that there is no domain at the moment that doesn't use architecture as its dominant metaphor. Whether it is computer programming or corporate reengineering, everyone talks about "the architecture of" followed by almost any word – the architecture of media, of the virtual, for example. But we remain so stuck in our own traditions and history, and are so proud to be stuck – so proud to be still thinking about form and building – that even some of the most virtuoso productions of the computer are still ultimately intended to be translated into building. In Lynn's case the translation may be proceeding according to plan; but at the same time one wonders whether this is really a necessary step. The irony is that architecture is the one profession that does not benefit from this explosion of interest in architecture in terms of its other organizational capacity, its other structuring capacity.

For these reasons, we have divided the field into two parts, the actual and the virtual. In addition to our Office for Metropolitan Architecture (OMA), we have established its reverse (AMO) to deal with all those demands that do not need to be articulated in building demands that are either too fast or too abstract or too fluid, but that nevertheless benefit from architectural thinking. In all of this, Harvard acts as a very convenient think tank and permanent incentive, with the idea that everyone moves between all of these entities. [Fig. 12]

So far so good. These were all frank engagements with the world of ¥€$. Of course they were not always comfortable, not frivolous in a certain way; a permanent questioning of our motives. (I would say that what is often read as cynicism in our work is actually very often innocent; the Harvard Project, for example, is not really about thinking about what would hurt the architecture of the nervous system most – like shopping, or cities in the process of insane acceleration – but more an incentive that starts with ignorance and the need, in the course of architectural activity, to gain knowledge about certain phenomena – one of the more difficult aspects of the profession.) But there was always a nagging voice about the rightness of all of this – a nagging expectation that sooner or later the realm of ¥€$ would either end or be replaced, adjusted to, or adapted by, other forces. One of the most pernicious implications of the market economy is its unconscious faith in its own immortality. But there is no reason, statistically at least, to believe that; I am 55, and in my life I have lived through four or five different economic systems. In this sense, I felt it was becoming increasingly important to look at different things, as a counterpoint to the incredible gloating over money. It felt important to begin to investigate the accommodation of the city to globalization and poverty; and for that, through Harvard, we began to look at Africa.

In order to visit Nigeria, for example, you need 12 injections. In my case, the 12th went wrong and I developed meningitis. This was a drastic moment that changed my character for a certain period; this also became the period in which we looked at Lagos with a particular kind of receptivity. Nobody knows whether Lagos has 13 or 20 million people. [Fig. 13] I have now been there three times, and with each visit one thing is becoming increasingly clear: that Lagos is not about the chaotic, not about poverty, but about other forms of organization. For example, recently I looked at a particular market, which could also be described as a particular traffic jam. [Fig. 14] But the traffic jam is permanent. The reason for the congestion is that during the slowdown – the "go-slow" as it is called in Nigeria – there is an infinite expansion of the number of transactions possible between the stuck and the unstuck. This is part of what these economies are all about: not major transactions, but an urban realm made up of a permanent field of miniature transactions that cumulatively lead to an infinite number of survivals. Aerial views of these go-slows reveal certain patterns, complicated by an adjacent railroad line.

Bread, tomatoes, meat, and all the other produce in the market are arranged along the rail line. When the occasional train rolls through, the market simply opens temporarily, like the Red Sea, and then closes immediately afterward. An even more dramatic example of this patterning is revealed by the restless system of highways that dead-end in a completely degraded area of Lagos. It is in these areas that the city takes part in the global economy, but it is a participation on a totally different level. Lagos's highway infrastructure, built in the 1960s, culminates in a swamp used partly for agriculture and partly to house a crust of criminal inhabitants. Nine months after I first encountered this dead-end, the entire area had been transformed. What at first sight looked like a rubbish heap was actually an endlessly creative sorting field, where apparent garbage was transformed into piles of selected elements. The space underneath the highway is now used for manufacture and fabrication. There is the beginning of a kind of technological rescue operation, in which even Microsoft is now hiring Nigerian programmers because of their particular ingenuity and shamelessness in combining different systems. What only nine months ago was an area dominated by crime is now turning into a highly organized recycling center. This, for me, is the advantage of these intermittent visits: what at first seems stable may actually be much more radically submitted to change than anything in our situation, where in less than a year, a swamp can be transformed into a relatively ordered condition.

As a footnote to this African study, six weeks ago I returned to Russia for the first time in 30 years. I had been there in the late 1960s and early '70s, very involved in research on Russian architecture. Going back, I was stunned by a confrontation with another kind of architecture; even now in St. Petersburg (formerly Leningrad) one is still surrounded by communist architecture, an architecture at an incredible scale that made up the city in the late '60s and '70s – an architecture that was based on equality, that openly dealt with issues like brotherhood and other good intentions – whatever aberrations we now know and have always known the communist system maintained. [Fig. 15] This was another shocking confrontation with everything that we (and I) have abandoned, but at the same time it is, in terms of its timing, perhaps significant – an indication of what might eventually be recuperated in a new form.

15

INFORMATION OBSESSION: MULTISCREEN ARCHITECTURE

BEATRIZ COLOMINA

1.

We are surrounded today, everywhere, all the time, by arrays of multiple, simultaneous images: in the streets, airports, shopping centers, and gyms; on our computers and on our television sets. The idea of a single image commanding our attention has faded away. It seems as if we need to be distracted in order to concentrate. As if we – all of us living in this new kind of space, the space of information – could be diagnosed en masse with attention deficit disorder. The state of distraction in the metropolis, described so eloquently by Walter Benjamin early in the 20th century, seems to have been replaced by a new form of distraction, which is to say a new form of attention. Rather than wandering cinematically through the city, we now look in one direction and see many juxtaposed moving images, more than we can possibly synthesize or reduce to a single impression. We sit in front of our computers on our ergonomically perfected chairs, staring with a fixed gaze at many simultaneously "open" windows through which different kinds of information stream toward us. We hardly even notice it. It seems natural, as if we were simply breathing in the information.

How would one go about writing a history of this form of perception? Should one go back to the organization of television studios, with their walls of monitors from which the director chooses the camera angle that will be presented to the viewer; or should one go to Cape Canaveral and look at its mission control room; or should one even go back to World War II, when so-called situation rooms were envisioned with multiple projections presenting information from all over the world side by side for the instant analysis by leaders and military commanders?

But it is not simply the military, or war technology, that has defined this new form of perception. Designers, architects, and artists were involved from the beginning, playing a crucial role in the evolution of the multiscreen and multimedia techniques of presentation of information. While artists' use of these techniques tends to be associated with the "happenings" and "expanded cinema" of the 1960s, architects were involved much earlier and in very different contexts, such as military operations and governmental propaganda campaigns.

Take the 1959 American exhibition in Moscow, where the government enlisted some of the country's most sophisticated designers. Site of the famous Kitchen Debate between Richard Nixon and Nikita Khrushchev, the exhibition was a Cold War operation in which the Eameses' multiscreen technique turned out to be a powerful weapon. To reconstruct a little bit of the atmosphere: in 1958 the USA and USSR had agreed to exchange national exhibits on "science, technology and culture." The Soviet exhibition opened in the Coliseum at Columbus Circle in New York City in June 1959, and the American exhibition opened in Sokolniki Park in Moscow the following month. Vice President Nixon, in Moscow to open the exhibition, engaged in a heated debate with Khrushchev over the virtues of the American way of life. The exchange became known as the Kitchen Debate because it took place – in an event that appeared impromptu but was actually staged by the Americans – in the kitchen of a suburban house split in half to allow easy viewing. The Russians called the house the "Splitnik," a pun on the Sputnik, the satellite the Soviets had put into orbit two years before.

What was remarkable about this debate was its focus. As historian Elaine Tyler-May has noted, instead of discussing "missiles, bombs, or even modes of government. . . [the two leaders] argued over the relative merits of American and Soviet washing machines, televisions, and electric ranges."[1] For Nixon, American superiority rested on the ideal of the suburban home, complete with modern appliances and distinct gender roles. He proclaimed that this "model" suburban home represented nothing less than American freedom.

The American exhibition in Moscow captivated the national and international media. Newspapers, illustrated magazines, and television networks reported on the event. Symptomatically, Life magazine put the wives, instead of the politicians, on its cover. Pat Nixon appears as the prototype of the American woman depicted in advertisements of the 1950s: slim, well-groomed, fashionable, happy. In contrast, the Soviet ladies appear stocky and dowdy, and while two of them, Mrs. Khrushchev and Mrs. Mikoyan, look proudly toward the camera, the third one, Mrs. Kozlov, in what Roland Barthes may have seen as the punctum of this photograph, cannot keep her eyes off Pat Nixon's dress.[2]

Envy – that is what the American exhibition seems to have been designed to produce (despite vigorous denials by Nixon in his debate with Khrushchev: "We do not claim to astonish the Soviet people"[3]). But not envy of scientific, military, or industrial achievements. Envy of washing machines, dishwashers, color televisions, suburban houses, lawnmowers, supermarkets stocked full of groceries, Cadillac convertibles, makeup colors, lipstick, spike-heeled shoes, hi-fi sets, cake mixes, TV dinners, Pepsi-Cola, and so

1 Elaine Tyler-May, Homeward Bound: American Families in the Cold War Era (New York: Basic Books, 1988), 16. See also Karal Ann Marling, As Seen on TV: The Visual Culture of Everyday Life in the 1950s (Cambridge, Massachusetts: Harvard University Press, 1994).

2 Life, 10 August 1959.

3 Khrushchev: "You Americans expect that the Soviet people will be amazed. It is not so. We have all these things in our new apartments." Nixon: "We do not claim to astonish the Soviet people." U.S. News & World Report, 3 August 1958, 36–37.

The Kitchen Debate of Nikita Krushchev and Richard Nixon.

Charles and Ray Eames, **Glimpses of the USA**, Moscow, 1959.

Buckminster Fuller's dome, Moscow, from **Life** magazine.

COLOR: THE MOSCOW FAIR

NIXON ON THE STUMP IN RUSSIA

FAR OUT AND WAY UP:
FAD FOR SPORT PARACHUTING

MMES. MIKOYAN, NIXON
KHRUSHCHEV AND KOZLOV

AUGUST 10, 1959

Charles and Ray Eames arriving in Moscow.

on. "What is this," the newspaper *Izvestia* asked in its news report, "a national exhibit of a great country or a branch department store?"[4]

It was in this context that Ray and Charles Eames produced their film, *Glimpses of the USA*, projecting it onto seven 20-by-30-foot screens suspended within a vast (250 feet in diameter) golden geodesic dome designed by Buckminster Fuller. More than 2,200 still and moving images (some from Billy Wilder's film, *Some Like it Hot*) presented "a typical work day" in the life of an American citizen in nine minutes, and "a typical weekend day" in three minutes.[5] The thousands of images were pulled from many different sources, combined into seven separate film reels, and projected simultaneously through seven interlocking projectors.

The Eameses did not simply install their film in Fuller's space. They were involved in the organization of the whole exhibition from the beginning. George Nelson, who had been commissioned by the United States Information Agency (USIA) to design the exhibition, and Jack Masey from the USIA brought them into the team. According to Nelson, it was in an evening meeting in the Eames House in Los Angeles, culminating three days of discussions, where "all the basic decisions for the fair were made. Present were Nelson, Ray and Charles (the latter occasionally swooping past on a swing hung from the ceiling), the movie director Billy Wilder, and Masey."[6] According to Nelson, by the end of the evening a basic scheme had emerged:

(1) A dome (by Fuller).
(2) A glass pavilion (by Welton Beckett) "as a kind of bazaar stuffed full of things, [the] idea

being that consumer products represented one of the areas in which we were most effective, as well as one in which the Russians . . . were more interested."

(3) An introductory film by the Eameses, since the team felt that the "80,000 square feet of exhibition space was not enough to communicate more than a small fraction of what we wanted to say."[7]

The multiscreen performance turned out to be one of the most popular exhibits at the fair (second only to the cars and color televisions).[8] *Time* magazine called it the "smash hit of the Fair,"[9] and the *Wall Street Journal* described it as the "real bomb shell."[10] Groups of five thousand people were brought into the dome every 45 minutes, 16 times a day, for the duration of the fair.[11] Close to three million people saw the show, and the floor had to be resurfaced three or four times during the six-week exhibition.[12]

The Eameses were not just popular entertainers in an official exhibition. *Glimpses of the USA* was not just images inside a dome. The huge array of suspended screens defined a space, a space within a space. The Eameses were self-consciously architects of a new kind of space. The film breaks with the fixed perspectival view of the world. In fact, we find ourselves in a space that can only be apprehended with the high technology of telescopes, zoom lenses, airplanes, night-vision cameras, and so on, and where there is no privileged point of view. It is not simply that many of the individual images that make up *Glimpses* have been taken with these instruments. More importantly, the relationship between the images reenacts the operation of the technologies.

The film starts with images from outer space on all the screens: stars across the sky, seven constellations, seven star clusters, nebulae, etc., then moves through aerial views of the city at night, from higher up to closer in until city lights seen from the air fill the screens. The early morning comes with aerial views of landscapes from different parts of the country: deserts, mountains, hills, seas, farms, suburban developments, urban neighborhoods. When the camera eyes finally descend to the ground, we see close-ups of newspapers and milk bottles at doors. But still no people, only traces of their existence on earth.

Not by chance, the first signs of human life are centered upon the house and domestic space. From the stars at night and the aerial views, the cameras zoom to the most intimate scenes: "people having breakfast at home, men leaving for work, kissing their wives, kissing the baby, being given lunchboxes, getting into cars, waving good-bye, children leaving for school, being given lunchboxes, saying good-bye to dog, piling into station wagons and cars, getting into school buses, baby crying."[13]

4. Quoted in Alan L. Otten, "Russians Eagerly Tour U.S. Exhibit Despite Cool Official Attitude," *Wall Street Journal*, 28 July 1959, 16, col. 4.

5. John Neuhart, Marilyn Neuhart, and Ray Eames, *Eames Design: The Work of the Office of Charles and Ray Eames* (New York: Abrams, 1989), 238–41. See also, Hélène Lipstadt, "Natural Overlap: Charles and Ray Eames and the Federal Government," in Donald Albrecht, ed., *The Work of Charles and Ray Eames: A Legacy of Invention* (New York: Abrams, 1997), 160–66.

6. Stanley Abercrombie, *George Nelson: The Design of Modern Design* (Cambridge, Massachusetts: MIT Press, 1995), 163.

7. Ibid., 164.

8. "The seven-screen quickie is intended as a general introduction to the fair. According to the votes of Russians, however, it is the most popular exhibit after the automobiles and the color television." Max Frankel, "Image of America at Issue in Soviet," *The New York Times*, 23 August, 1959.

9. "Watching the thousands of colorful glimpses of the U.S. and its people, the Russians were entranced, and the slides are the smash hit of the fair." "The U.S. in Moscow: Russia Comes to the Fair," *Time*, 3 August 1959, 14.

10. "And Mr. Khrushchev watched unsmilingly as the real bomb-shell exploded – a huge exhibit of typical American scenes flashed on seven huge ceiling screens. Each screen shows a different scene but all seven at each moment are on the same general subject – housing, transportation, jazz and so forth. U.S. officials believe this is the real pile-driver of the fair, and the premier's phlegmatic attitude – not even smiling when seven huge Marilyn Monroes dashed on the screen or when Mr. Nixon pointed out golfing scenes – showed his unhappiness with the display." *Wall Street Journal*, 28 July 1959.

11. Max Frankel, "Dust From Floor Plagues U.S. Fair," *The New York Times*, 28 July 1959, 12, col. 3.

12. Pat Kirkham, *Charles and Ray Eames: Designers of the Twentieth Century* (Cambridge, Massachusetts: MIT Press, 1995), 324. From interview of Billy Wilder by Pat Kirkham in 1993.

13. Taken from the working script of *Glimpses*, Eames Archives, Library of Congress, box 202.

As with the Eameses' later and much better-known film *Powers of Ten* (1968),[14] which, incidentally, reused images of the night sky from *Glimpses of the USA*,[15] the film moves from outer space to the close-up details of everyday life. But in *Powers of Ten*, the movement will be set in reverse, from the domestic space of a picnic spread with a man sleeping beside a woman in a park in Chicago out into the atmosphere, and then back down inside the body through the skin of the man's wrist to microscopic cells and to the atomic level. Even if *Powers of Ten*, initially produced for the Commission on College Physics, was a more scientific, more advanced film, in which space is measured in seconds, the logic of both films is the same. Intimate domesticity is suspended within an entirely new spatial system – a system that was the product of esoteric scientific-military research but that had entered the everyday public imagination with the launching of Sputnik in 1957. Fantasies that had long circulated in science fiction had become reality.

Glimpses, like the "Splitnik" house where the Kitchen Debate took place, displaced the USA-USSR debate from the arms and space race to the battle of the appliances. And yet the overall effect of the film is that of an extraordinarily powerful viewing technology, a hyperviewing mechanism, which is hard to imagine outside the very space program the exhibition was trying to downplay. In fact, this extreme mode of viewing goes beyond the old fantasy of the eye in the sky. If *Glimpses* simulates the operation of satellite surveillance, it exposes more than the details of life in the streets. It penetrates the most intimate spaces and reveals every secret. Domestic life itself becomes the target, the source of pride or insecurity. The Americans, made insecure by the thought of a Russian eye looking down on them, countered by exposing more than that eye could ever see (or at least pretending to, since "a day in the life of the USA" became an image of the "Good Life" without ghettos, poverty, domestic violence, or depression.)

2.

What kind of genealogy can one make of the Eameses' development of this astonishingly successful technique?

It was not the first time they had deployed multiple screens. In fact, the Eameses were involved in one of the first multimedia presentations on record, if not the first. Again, it was George Nelson who set up the commission. In 1952 he had been asked to make a study for the Department of Fine Arts at the University of Georgia in Athens, and he brought along Ray and Charles Eames and Alexander Girard. Instead of writing a report, they decided to collaborate on a "show for a typical class" of 55 minutes. Nelson referred to it as "Art X," while the Eameses called it "A Rough Sketch for a Sample Lesson for a Hypothetical Course." The subject of the lesson was "Communications,"[16] and the stated goals included "the breaking down of barriers between fields of learning . . . making people a little more intuitive . . . [and] increasing communication between people and things."[17] The performance included a live narrator, multiple images (still and moving pictures), and even smells and sounds (music and narration). Charles Eames later said, "We used a lot of sound, sometimes carried to a very high volume so you would actually feel the vibrations."[18] The idea was to produce an intense sensory environment so as to "heighten awareness." The effect was so convincing that apparently some people even smelled things when no smells were introduced, only a suggestion in an image or a sound (for example, the smell of oil in the machinery).[19]

It was a major production. Nelson described the team arriving in Athens "burdened with only slightly less equipment than Ringling Brothers. This included a movie projector, three slide projectors, three screens, three or four tape recorders, cans of films, boxes of slides, and reels of magnetic tape. Girard brought a collection of bottled synthetic odors that were to be fed into the auditorium during the show through the air-conditioning ducts."[20]

The reference to the circus was not accidental. Talking to a reporter for *Vogue* magazine, Charles later argued that "'Sample Lesson' was a blast on all senses, a super-saturated three-ring circus. Simultaneously the students were assaulted by three sets of slides, two tape recorders, a motion picture with sound, and peripheral panels for further distraction."[21]

The circus was one of the Eameses' lifetime fascinations[22] – so much so that in the 1940s, when they were out of work and money, they were about to audition for parts at the circus. They would have been clowns, but ultimately a contract to make plywood furniture allowed them to continue as designers. And from the mid-1940s on, they took hundreds and hundreds of circus photographs, which they used in many contexts, including *Circus* (a 180-slide, three-screen

14 *Powers of Ten* was based on the 1957 book by Kees Boeke, *Cosmic View: The Universe in Forty Jumps*. The film was produced for the Commission on College Physics. An updated and more developed version was produced in 1977. In the second version the starting point is still a picnic scene but it takes place in a park bordering Lake Michigan in Chicago. See Neuhart et al, op. cit., 336–37 and 440–41.
15 See handwritten notes on the manuscript of the first version of *Powers of Ten*. Eames Archives, Library of Congress, box 207. The film is still referred to as *Cosmic View*.
16 "Grist for Atlanta paper version," manuscript in the Eames Archives, Library of Congress, box 217, folder 15.
17 Neuhart et al, op. cit., 177.
18 Owen Gingerich, "A Conversation with Charles Eames," *The American Scholar* 46, no. 3 (Summer 1977): 331.
19 Ibid.
20 Abercrombie, op. cit., 145, quoting George Nelson, "The Georgia Experiment: An Industrial Approach to Problems of Education," manuscript, October 1954.
21 Allene Talmey, "Eames," *Vogue*, 15 August 1959, 144.
22 Beatriz Colomina, "Reflections on the Eames House" in Albrecht, op. cit., 128.

Clockwise from top left: Charles and Ray Eames, **Circus**, **Powers of Ten**, **House: After Five Years of Living**, and **Think**, 14-screen IBM presentation.

slide show accompanied by a soundtrack featuring circus music and other sounds recorded at the circus), presented as part of the Charles Eliot Norton Lectures at Harvard University that Charles delivered in 1970, and the film *Clown Face* (1971), a training film about "the precise and classical art of applying makeup" made for Bill Ballentine, director of the Clown College of Ringling Brothers Barnum & Bailey Circus.

The circus, as an event that offers a multiplicity of simultaneous experiences that cannot be taken in entirely by the viewer, was the Eameses' model for their design of multimedia exhibitions and the fast-cutting technique of their films and slide shows,[23] where the objective was always to communicate the maximum amount of information in a way that was both pleasurable and effective.

But the technological model for multiscreen, multimedia presentations may have been provided by the war situation room, which was designed in those same years to bring information in simultaneously from numerous sources around the world so that the president and military commanders could make decisions. A number of the Eameses' friends were involved in the secret military project of the war rooms, including Buckminster Fuller, Eero Saarinen, and Henry Dreyfuss, whose unrealized design involved a wall of parallel projected images of different kinds of information.[24]

A number of wartime research projects, including work on communications, ballistics, and experimental computers, had quickly developed after the war into a full-fledged theory of information flow, most famously with the publication of Claude Shannon's *The Mathematical Theory of Communication* in 1949, which formalized the idea of an information channel from sender to recipient whose efficiency could be measured in terms of speed and noise.

This sense of information flow organized the "Sample Lesson" performance. The Eameses said, "We were trying to cram into a short time, a class hour, the most background material possible."[25] As part of the project, the Eameses produced *A Communication Primer*, a film that presents the theory of information, explaining Shannon's famous diagram of the passage of information. The film was subsequently developed in an effort to present current ideas in communication theory to architects and planners, and to encourage them to use these ideas in their work. The basic idea was to integrate architecture and information flow.

If the heroes of the Renaissance were, for the Eameses, "people concerned with ways of modeling/imaging, . . . not with self-expression or bravura . . . Brunelleschi, but not Michelangelo,"[26] the great architects of our time would be the ones concerned with the new forms of communication, particularly computers: "It appeared to us that the real current problems for architects now – the problems that a Brunelleschi, say, would gravitate to – are problems of *organization of information*."[27]

The logic of information flow is further developed in the 1955 Eameses' film *House: After Five Years of Living*. The film was entirely made from thousands of color slides that the Eameses had been taking of their house over the first five years of its life.[28] The images are shown in quick succession (a technique called "fast cutting," for which the Eameses won an Emmy award in 1960[29]), and accompanied with music by Elmer Bernstein. As Michael Braune wrote in 1966:

> The interesting point about this method of film making is not only that it is relatively simple to produce and that rather more information can be conveyed than when there is movement on the screen, but that it corresponds surprisingly closely with the way in which the brain normally records the images it receives. I would assume that it also corresponds rather closely with the way Eames's own thought processes tend to work. I think it symptomatic, for instance, that he is extremely interested in computers . . . and that one of the essential characteristics of computers is their need to separate information into components before being able to assemble them into a large number of different wholes.[30]

This technique was developed even further in *Glimpses*, which is organized around a strict logic of information transmission. The role of the designer is to design a particular flow of information. The central principle is one of compression. At the end of the design meeting in the Eames House, in preparation for the American exhibition in Moscow, the idea of the film emerged precisely "as a way of compressing into a small volume the tremendous quantity of information" they wanted to present, which would have been impossible to do in the 80,000 square feet of the exhibition.[31] The space of the multiscreen film, like the space of the computer, compresses physical space. Perhaps 50 cloverleaf highway intersections are shown in just a few seconds. So are dozens of housing projects, bridges, skyscraper scenes, supermarkets, universities, museums, theaters, churches, farms, laboratories, and so on.

23 Neuhart et al, op. cit., 91.

24 Barry Katz, "The Arts of War: 'Visual Presentation' and National Intelligence," *Design Issues* 12, no. 2 (Summer 1996): 3–21. I am grateful to Dennis Doordan for pointing out this article to me.

25 Gingerich, op. cit., 332.

26 Notes for second Norton lecture. Eames is referring here to "Professor Lawrence Hill's Renaissance," Eames Archives, Library of Congress, box 217, folder 10.

27 "'Communications Primer' was a recommendation to architects to recognize the need for more complex information . . . for new kinds of models of information." Eames, "Grist for Atlanta paper version," manuscript in the Eames Archives, op. cit.

28 Colomina, op. cit.

29 Charles and Ray Eames won an Emmy Award for Graphics for their rapid cutting experiments on *The Fabulous Fifties*, a television program broadcast on 22 January 1960, on the CBS network. It included six film segments made by the Eames Office. From Paul Schrader, "Poetry of Ideas: The Films of Charles Eames," *Film Quarterly* 23, no. 3 (Spring 1970).

30 Michael Braune, "The Wit of Technology," *Architectural Design* 36 (September 1966): 452.

31 See Abercrombie, op. cit., 163–64.

But the issue was much more than one of efficiency of communication or the polemical need to have multiple examples. The idea was, as with the "Sample Lesson," to produce sensory overload. As the Eameses suggested to *Vogue*, "Sample Lesson" tried to provide many forms of "distraction," instead of asking students to concentrate on a singular message.[32] The audience drifts through a multimedia space that exceeds their capacity to absorb it. The Eames-Nelson team thought that the most important thing to communicate to undergraduates was a sense of the relationships between things, what the Eameses would later call "Connections." Nelson and the Eameses argued that this awareness of relationships between seemingly unrelated phenomena is achieved by "high-speed techniques." They produce an excessive input from different directions that has to be synthesized by the audience. Likewise, Charles said of *Glimpses*:

> We wanted to have a credible number of images, but not so many that they couldn't be scanned in the time allotted. At the same time, the number of images had to be large enough so that people wouldn't be exactly sure how many they have seen. We arrived at the number seven. With four images, you always knew there were four, but by the time you got up to eight images you weren't quite sure. They were very big images – the width across four of them was half the length of a football field.[33]

One journalist described it as "information overload – an avalanche of related data that comes at a viewer too fast for him to cull and reject it . . . a twelve-minute blitz." The viewer is overwhelmed. More than anything, the Eameses wanted an emotional response, produced as much by the excess of images as their content.

The multiscreen technique goes through one more significant development in the 1964 World's Fair in New York. In the IBM ovoid building, designed by the Saarinen office, visitors board the "people wall" and are greeted by a "host," dressed in coattails, who slowly drops down from the IBM ovoid; the seated 500-person audience is then lifted up hydraulically from the ground level into the dark interior of the egg where they are surrounded by 14 screens on which the Eameses project the film *Think*.[34] To enter the theater is no longer to cross the threshold, to pass through the ceremonial space of the entrance, as in a traditional public building. To enter here is to be lifted in front of a multiplicity of screens. The screens wrap the audience in a way that is reminiscent of

32 Allene Talmey, "Eames," *Vogue*, 15 August 1959, 144.

33 Gingerich, op. cit., 333.

34 Mina Hamilton, "Films at the Fair II," *Industrial Design* (May 1964): 37–41.

35 Arthur A. Cohen, *Herbert Bayer: The Complete Work* (Cambridge, Massachusetts: MIT, 1994), 292. Mary Anne Staniszewski, *The Power of Display: A History of Exhibition Installations at the Museum of Modern Art* (Cambridge, Massachusetts: MIT Press, 1998), 25–28.

36 Script of the IBM film, *View from the People Wall* for the Ovoid theater, New York World's Fair, 1964. Eames Archives, Library of Congress.

37 "U.S. Gives Soviet Glittering Show," *The New York Times*, 25 July 1959.

Herbert Bayer's 1930 "diagram of the field of vision," produced as a sketch for the installation of an architecture and furniture exhibition.[35] The eye cannot escape the screens because each screen is bordered by other screens. Unlike the screens in Moscow, those in the IBM building are of different sizes and shapes. But once again, the eye has to jump around from image to image and can never fully catch up with all of them and their diverse contents. Fragments are presented to be momentarily linked together. The film is organized by the same logic of compression. Each momentary connection is replaced with another. The speed of the film is meant to be the speed of the mind. The "host" welcomes the audience to "the IBM Information Machine": ". . . a machine designed to help me give you a lot of information in a very short time. . . . The machine brings you information in much the same way as your mind gets it – in fragments and glimpses – sometimes relating to the same idea or incident. Like making toast in the morning."[36]

In addition to the multiscreens, the dome in Moscow housed a huge RAMAC 305 computer, an "electronic brain" that offered written replies to 3,500 questions about life in the United States.[37] The architecture was conceived from the very start as a combination of structure, multiscreen film, and computer. Each technology creates an architecture in which inside/outside, entering/leaving, meant entirely different things and yet they co-existed. All were housed by the same physical structure, Fuller's dome, but each defined a different kind of space to be explored in different ways. From the "Sample Lesson" in 1953 to IBM in 1964, the Eameses treated architecture as a multichannel information machine. And, equally, multimedia installations as a kind of architecture.

3.

All of the Eameses' designs can be understood as multiscreen performances: they provide a framework in which objects can be placed and replaced. Even the parts of their furniture can be rearranged. Spaces are defined as arrays of information collected and constantly changed by the users.

This is the space of the media. The space of a newspaper or an illustrated magazine is a grid in which information is arranged and rearranged as it comes in: a space the reader navigates in his or her own way, at a glance, or by fully entering a particular story. The reader, viewer, consumer, constructs the space, participating actively in the design. It is a space where continuities are made through "cutting." The same is true of the space of newsreels and television. The logic of the Eameses' multiscreens is simply the logic of the mass media.

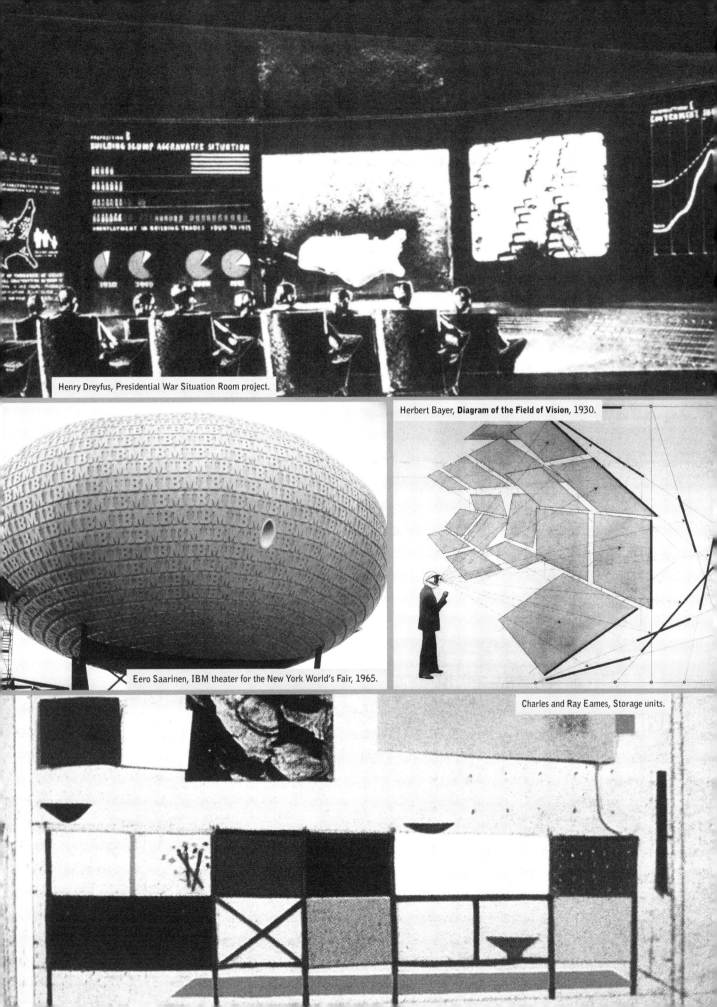

Henry Dreyfus, Presidential War Situation Room project.

Eero Saarinen, IBM theater for the New York World's Fair, 1965.

Herbert Bayer, **Diagram of the Field of Vision**, 1930.

Charles and Ray Eames, Storage units.

Charles had already spoken in 1950 of our time as the era of communication. He was acutely aware that the new media were displacing the old role of architecture. And yet everything for the Eameses, in this world of communication that they were embracing so happily, is architecture: "The chairs are architecture, the films – they have a structure, just as the front page of a newspaper has a structure. The chairs are literally like architecture in miniature . . . architecture you can get your hands on."[38] In the notes for a letter to Italian architect Vittorio Gregotti accompanying a copy of Powers of Ten, they write: "In the past fifty years the world has gradually been finding out something that architects have always known, that is, that everything is architecture. The problems of environment have become more and more interrelated. This is a sketch for a film that shows something of how large – and small – our environment is."[39]

In every sense, Eames architecture is all about the space of information. Perhaps we can no longer talk about "space" but rather about "structure," or more precisely, about time. Structure for the Eameses is organization in time. Their technique of "information overload," used in films and multimedia presentations, as well as in their trademark "information wall" in exhibitions, was not used to "overtax the viewer's brain" but precisely to offer a "broad menu of options," and to create an "impulse to make connections."[40]

For the Eameses, structure is not linear. They reflected often on the impossibility of linear discourse. The structure of their exhibitions has been compared to a scholarly paper, loaded with footnotes, where "the highest level of participation consists in getting fascinated by the pieces and connecting them for oneself."[41] Seemingly static structures, like the frames of their buildings, or of their plywood cabinets, are but a framework for positioning ever-changing objects. And the frame itself is meant to be changed all the time. These changes, this ever-fluctuating movement, can never be pinned down.

The multiscreen presentations, the exhibition technique, and the Eameses' films are likewise significant not because of the individual factoids they offer, or even the story they tell, but because of the way the factoids are used as elements in creating a space that says: "This is what [the space of information] is all about."[42]

Like all architects, the Eameses controlled the space they produced. The most important factor was to regulate the flow of information. They prepared extremely detailed technical instructions for running even their simplest three-screen slide show.[43] Performances were carefully planned to appear as effortless as a circus act. Timing and the elimination of "noise" were the major considerations. Their office produced masses of documents, even drawings showing the rise and fall of intensity through the course of a film, literally defining the space they wanted to produce.

The experience for the audience in Moscow was almost overwhelming. Journalists spoke of too many images, too much information, too fast. For the MTV and Internet generation watching the film today, it would not be fast enough, and yet we do not seem to have come that far either. The logic of the Internet is already spelled out in the Eameses' multiscreen projects.

Coming out of the war mentality, the Eameses' innovations in the world of communication, exhibitions, films, and multiscreen performances transformed the status of architecture. Their highly controlled flows of simultaneous images provided a space, an enclosure – the kind of space we now occupy continuously without thinking.

38 Gingerich, op. cit., 327.

39 "Powers of Ten – Gregotti," handwritten notes. Eames Archives, Library of Congress, box 217, folder 11.

40 Ralph Caplan, "Making Connections: The Work of Charles and Ray Eames," in Connections: The Work of Charles and Ray Eames, catalogue of an exhibition at the University of California, Los Angeles (Los Angeles: UCLA Press, 1976), 43.

41 Ibid., 45.

42 In an article about the Mies exhibition at the Museum of Modern Art, Charles Eames claimed that the space of the exhibition itself communicated better than any object in it, the idea of space in Mies: "The significant thing seems to be the way in which he [Mies] has taken documents of his architecture and furniture and used them as elements in creating a space that says, 'this is what it's all about.'" Charles Eames, "Mies van der Rohe," photographs by Charles Eames taken at the exhibition, Arts & Architecture 64, no. 12 (December 1947): 27.

43 "To show a 3-Screen slide show," manuscript in Eames Archives detailing the necessary preparations for an "Eames 3 screen 6 projectors slide show" with "sound" and "picture operation procedure," illustrated with multiple drawings, 14 pp. Eames Archives, Library of Congress, box 211, folder 10.

OBSESSION ≠ FASCINATION

JEAN NOUVEL

TRANSLATED FROM THE FRENCH

BY JEAN-LOUIS COHEN

I want to discuss a rather introspective and indiscreet topic – the issue of obsession as it relates to architectural creation. Obsession is something that I am not especially attracted to: I do not like the idea of being represented as an obsessed person, whether inside or outside architecture, but especially from within the discipline, because the architect is ideally located to impose his own obsessions upon others. One is not forced to withstand the fixations of painters or writers, for instance, because in art obsession quickly turns into monomania. But architects always seem to respond to any question with the imposition of their various obsessions.

I have often thought that the idea of style imposes itself through the repetition of the same kind of manias, of the same tricks. For example, in the various artistic explorations of the 20th century, it always seemed to be enough simply for the painter or sculptor to identify his or her thing (even if it is a very small thing) in order to be considered a major artist, complete with the guarantee of immediate, direct identification. The signature of the artist becomes, in this way, much more significant than the work itself. In short, obsession typically leads to the systematization of all artistic creation, and to subtle, subsequent declinations that tend to lead me into deep sleep.

However (and in an apparent contradiction to what I have just argued), there are certain obsessions that fascinate and interest me when they can be merged with an idea, or with the work itself. For example, I know an artist who every day photographs his face from the same position and angle. The effect of this artistic rigor is that as he gets older his hair becomes whiter, and so the images he produces each day also become lighter and lighter. In a way, his own life is becoming a work of art, not in the hedonistic terms of Michel Foucault, but still very similar to his idea of a life as art. I cannot think of any parallel examples in the field of architecture (except, perhaps, for Postman Cheval's Ideal Palace in Hauterives), but it is something that is difficult to talk about here, in an architectural setting. So, rather than **obsession**, I prefer the term **fascination**, and will mention here some of the things that fascinate me.

I am fascinated by the unique character and dimension of places and circumstances, both in space and time. I am fascinated by plaques that announce, for example, that "Napoleon stood here" or "Rousseau lived here." I am fascinated by the idea of modifying architecture's state of things by making or staging the apparent disappearance of fragments of reality that do not belong to me. It might seem illusory in respect to planetary questions but it is nonetheless essential. It is important because at this precise moment, in this precise space, changing the physical world really depends on our own interventions. I can be moved by feelings of very deep tenderness for this particular microcosm and everybody within it, so that all my intellectual

Lyon Opera House.

Foundation Cognacq Jay, Rueil Malmaison.

Office building for Interunfall, Bregenz, Austria.

energy is mobilized in order to transform, in some small way, this tiny piece of the world. Through this transformation, I am able to maintain the illusion of actually being of some use.

The functionality of a built thing also reinforces this illusion. This seeming usefulness reveals itself through the architectural program only as an excuse, a pretext. But at the same time the program is also the trigger, the initial factor in any design, the answer (as all architecture is) to a question that was never in fact asked. In the course of our working lives as architects, we are simply required to build several hundreds of thousands of square feet within a particular frame of time. Countering this expectancy, one of my fascinations is that every piece of architecture I produce be based rather on a process of **détournement** — a hijacking of architecture's conventions. There is a sort of fatal dimension, or hazard, to these quasi-automatic buildings that leads to cultural invention. Is it possible to work without an architectural intentionality — of fundamental, or primary, ideas — to work without a specific and contextual conceptualization in order to build? Because in fact what we are building is a sort of typical building that, with the exception of certain changing parameters, is already designed, is already installed on the hard drives of engineering firms.

Here I cannot help but think of Robert Venturi and Denise Scott Brown and their rejection of architecture as made by architects and their celebration of a certain form of banality over the heroism of supposedly great architecture. My obsession, then, becomes one of trying to escape both the trivial and the ridiculous. There are only a few interesting architectural solutions among thousands of lousy ones — you have to find the correct one, and to do that you need a proper strategy. But in refusing to be obsessed by form, I realize that I have become obsessed with strategy. I admit it. Strategy, as I understand it, means analyzing data — geographical, historical, topographical, typological. It means going into a sort of brainstorm so as to detect the traps, detect the easy solution. It means establishing two distinct lists — attitudes to be avoided and targets to be met.

I am, in this way, a diagnosis addict. The strategies I employ look first not to the object itself but rather to the resonance, interference, and contradiction created by its presence. I am not looking or longing for integration, but for the discovery of conditions within which an architecture will improve, or that will enhance its surroundings. It is a distant dialogue, an exchange that is fed by the images of everyday life: images produced throughout this century by technology, science, and art. These images, which produce powerful effects in a photographic sense, are the food for thought for architects, and have direct influence over the forms that architects develop in their

Clockwise from top left: stadium, Saint Denis; Cartier Foundation, Paris; convention center, Tours; holiday homes, Cap d'Ail; Museum Quai Branly, Paris; Hotel Les Thermes, Dax; Peking Opera House.

architecture. However, in absorbing these ever-present and somewhat obsessive images, one must also avoid their oversimplification – we should look instead to blur and collage their use to produce a truly polysemic architecture.

In this saturation of architecture with image there is also the unavoidable contamination of cinematic culture. Architecture in this sense is all about image rather than space, in that it is perceived and experienced essentially through the eye. Seen, so to speak, this way, the classical notion of framing is revealed as an architectural device that easily predates the introduction of cinema. In responding to the influence of movies in today's architecture, the sequencing of frames has become an especially familiar trait – manipulating depths of field, seeing alternately what is focused and what is blurred, what is revealed, what is hidden, what is living, what is inert – so as to create an architecture of cinematic montage.

The other principal fascination of modernity today is the differentiation in programming objects through the use of light – playing with materiality and with light so as to emote both the permanent and the fugitive. How can one conceive on the same spatial base, on the same spatial support, various ranges of projects? How can we use darkness, clouds, rain, mist, cars, trees, people to form some kind of strategic perspective? How can we promote the simultaneous awareness of both the instantaneous and of eternity, of fragility and solidity, of the unplanned and the preprogrammed? How, also, are all these elements and ideas to be positioned or inserted into a dialogue with the preexisting so that they can radiate?

In terms of ideas everything is possible. What is needed is an original hypothesis. In terms of desire everything is possible. What is needed is an absolute passion. In terms of change everything is possible. What is needed is both a metamorphosis and a becoming. In terms of otherness everything is possible – conviviality, instant communication, and networks. What is needed is a truer form – both antagonistic and irreducible.

Saïtama Arena, Tokyo.

Kiryat Arieh, Tel Aviv.

A FLEXIBLE ARCHITECTURE

GERMANO CELANT

TRANSLATED FROM THE ITALIAN

BY MATTEO CAINER

In the course of the 20th century, the practice of architecture was typically based on a rigid allegiance to an ordered and harmonic hierarchy of elements, formally bound to functionalism and to a sense of integration without difference. The goal was always to organize a building's spatial, volumetric, and environmental properties according to an established orthodoxy that legitimizes its existence; to come to a rational, linear, abstract, and absolute statement in which the architectonic articulation branches out as if it were a scientific constellation of how one should live. This aesthetic orthodoxy was tied to an unthinking respect for technology, but in its eagerness to elevate the technological to the level of the spiritual, and for all buildings to be machines for living, architecture lost all sense of the value of the anarchic, the imaginary, the provocative, and the iconoclastic.

Only in the last 30 years, with the emergence of architects like Gaetano Pesce and Frank Gehry, has an architecture that moves between a kind of zoomorphism and figural atrophism come to be expressed and receive a certain amount of attention. What once seemed irrelevant to modernist architecture (the organic, the ephemeral, the surreal, and the sensual) has now begun to be incorporated into the architectural canon. Through their designs, Pesce and Gehry have objectified a kind of architectural lyricism. A counterpoint to the impersonal architecture that preceded them – a relic dictated by functionalism and technology – they have created a fantastic and plastic architectural language; exuberant buildings that flow through varying forms, colors, and materials, always pushing the limits of established architectural expression. This architecture works through instability and contingency and holds to the sanctity of the first expressive idea; an idea only later bolstered through a series of technical processes, rather than the processes themselves informing the architectural vision.

Gehry cloaks his architectural constructions with an almost reptilian skin. Freely articulated over the surfaces of his most recent buildings, titanium scales are manipulated with a sculptural intensity, as walls undulate and detach from the primary structure, creating plastic spaces located somewhere between those of Donald Judd and Richard Serra. From Bilbao to Seattle, Gehry's architecture offers itself as a series of distinct exteriors, of flowing outer skins that barely touch or graze their own interiors, so much so that these wriggling surfaces render themselves as alternatives to the culture of the inside, giving importance to their spectacular superficiality. This semantic redistribution of architectonic elements (interior and exterior, surface and structure, building and city) highlights the visibility of the built form, pushing it to extremes through the theatricality of its constructions. The introduction of principles of disorder and the figural that both Gehry and Pesce have in fact been exploring for more than thirty years is characteristic of this new architecture.

Since 1967, after studies in cinematics and dynamic projection, Pesce has looked to stimulate multiple tactile senses in the design process; processes that he ties to some kind of architectural eroticism that can be seen in the physical metamorphosis of his forms. For example, the "blood" that continuously flows in his performance piece, Pièce per una fucilazione (1967), completely floods the whole floor space on which the audience is seated. This work inspired a number of subsequent studies, like his wounded-hand ashtray, Manodidio (1970), or his couch made of sacks that transforms itself into a residue of blood, also from 1970.

Design, as revealed through these pieces, shows itself capable of overlaying multiple expressive models, connected only by a certain anthropomorphism and the celebration of the human figure in all its sensual corporeality. Continuing to canonize the messiness of the body, in part as a reaction to the polite, impersonal formalism of Italian design in the early 1970s, much of Pesce's work has looked to create increasingly expressive and suggestive emblems of the body's sexual and fluid materiality. For example, in an untitled 1970 installation, a Brion Vega radio and a Kartell piece of furniture are covered by blood from a flowing catheter. Likewise, bas-reliefs placed at the entrances of two of his architectural works take the forms of a human face and ass, titled Autoportrati (1970) and Porte (1972).

The sensuality of this corporeality subsequently led Pesce into using softer, more flexible materials, like polyurethane and rubber, and into exploring an iconography of male and female figures as reflected in three of his later installations: Museum for a Young Industrialist (Basel, 1986); Maison des enfants (Parc de la Villette, Paris, 1985); and for Chiat Day in New York (1994). The first is a museum designed around the idea of the medieval crest or emblem as some kind of gift or homage to the magnificence of the rich prince or powerful lord behind it. Removing all the conventional trappings of a museum, Pesce designed instead a building as emblem, representing only the microcosms of the personal and private life of its patron. There is no sublimation, no ascetic absoluteness or functionality. Here the private and the personal overcome all historical and cultural statutes in creating a portrait architecture. This cult of personality is further exaggerated through the anthropomorphizing of its architectural forms: the tower eye, the polyhedral nose, and the loading bay ears. The face therefore becomes a system of both communication and functionality within a complex and accessible architectonic body.

The introduction of the corporeal into more pragmatically habitable, architectural forms has inevitably led Pesce to an architecture in which materiality and mobility, transformation and mutation are the defining principles. Aided by the flexibility and tactility of his favored materials of rubber, felt, and resin, Pesce has created objects and structures that blur their conventional functional associations – his Up 5 armchair and Up 6 footrest designs, for example, appear to be made from the skin of a soft belly, while his Green Street Chair (1987) exudes a seductive air, like some kind of siren. These objects tend to adapt to the circumstances and occasions of their use, balancing (literally and figuratively) the bodies that come into contact with them. Through this dialogue, Pesce dissolves the actual forms of the pieces, as well as the absoluteness and conformity of much of modern design, beneath a unique and poetic fragility.

These kinds of images and associations are also apparent in the interiors that Pesce designed in the apartment of Marc-Andre Hubin in Paris (1986), at the Galerie Mourmans in Kokke-le-Zoute (1993), in the Dujardin store in Brussels (1993), and for the offices of the New York advertising company Chiat Day. In each of these designs, Pesce layers the spaces with elaborate architectural narratives and an exuberant use of color, material, signs, and symbols that seem to bury any kind of stylistic logic beneath a singular, artistic visual expression. Hidden beneath this apparent chaos, however, are detailed and highly articulated conceptions of space. At the Chiat Day offices, for example, Pesce removed the ubiquitous culture of individual computer work stations in favor of an open piazza of telematic communications to which workers could connect without having to occupy a specific, limited space. This idea of people and images in motion corresponds to a nomadic vision of design and construction that thrives on irregularity and flexibility, and distinguishes all of Pesce's various projects (buildings, interiors, furniture,

and lighting designs) as distinct and evocative flashes of innovation.

In continuing to dismantle the rigidities of design, Pesce's more recent architectural works have projected this sense of movement vertically through the structure. For example, in his Organic Building in Osaka (1990), the façade of the building has been transformed with the vertical planting of both trees and flowers, in an attempt to arrive at a more obviously organic architecture. Similarly, at the beach house he designed in Bahia, Brazil, Pesce looked to create a kind of dreamlike space in which bodies could bounce (both metaphorically and physically) across its flowing plastic forms and through its exuberant, multicolored spaces. The idea is always to create architectural and sculptural constructions that enchant and entice not through their rigorous adherence to a set of materials (typically concrete and glass in contemporary architecture) but through the less tangible, ephemeral sensuality that they exude. At the same time, in responding to the particularities of site and to the personalities and idiosyncrasies of each of his clients, Pesce creates distinct and individually tailored works. In contrast to the anonymity of much modern design, Pesce personalizes architecture with character, tactility, and flexibility to such an extent that he seduces and induces new, loving, and heartfelt feelings for the living.

Gaetano Pesce, doorway.

REFUGEE REPUBLIC

INGO GÜNTHER

The philosopher Paul Feyerabend understood scientific progress as linked to a fundamental breaking of the previously established rules. This has been condensed into the idea that "anything goes" — a rule that suggests "there are no rules." Much of my work fits neatly into this category. But on another level, "anything" is potentially all-inclusive, so "anything" can also be understood as a selective totality. One such totality is the global, and it is the selective framing of the global through a project of thematic globes titled *Worldprocessor* that I have been working on since 1988.

On traditional globes, the world is outlined in common, recognizable codes: lines represent borders and specific colors depict mountains or forests. The globes that form the *Worldprocessor* project, however, depict a broad spectrum of statistics, ranging from political conflicts, socioeconomic studies, and environmental problems to technological developments and the spread of disease. It was through this geography of information that I was ultimately led to the apparent "discovery" of an entire country — a country that exists, so far, only in the intangible dataland of statistics. I call it the Refugee Republic. This is not a metaphor but a construct that has recently started to take hold in the circles of policy makers and scholars. The project, sanctioned to a certain extent by Joseph Beuys' notion of social sculpture, looks to place the problematic issue of refugees on its feet. But it is not quite walking yet, despite many art installations, Web sites, critical reviews, awards, and, perhaps most importantly, encouraging responses from refugees themselves.

The Refugee Republic project seeks to establish an experimental, transglobal, supraterritorial state as an instrument for refugees to represent themselves worldwide and to fuse their experiences into a global cooperative. The result would both accommodate investors as well as meet the need for a socioeconomic, political, and ideological avant-garde, and perhaps simultaneously serve as a structural model for the rest of the world.

We are fed media images of refugees that provoke an overwhelming sense of pity and sympathy. These images, however effective and necessary for mobilizing the donation of money and goods as well as political help, do not reflect the reality in most of the camps, which are characterized more by boredom and desperation than by any immediate physical dangers. Today, a refugee spends an average of five years in a camp. We need to address the situation of time that remains after the initial chaos — about one percent of time spent in the camps — has been managed by such able organizations as Médicin Sans Frontiers, the International Red Cross, and other nongovernmental organizations (NGOs).

REFUGEE = CAPITAL

Refugees and migrants represent not only a problem but also a solution. If configured as a transglobal net that would inculcate its own form of statehood, the world's refugee population would become the best candidate for a socioeconomic, political, and ideological avant-garde. The refugee republics of modern history, principally the United States, show that a steady influx of foreigners is an essential ingredient for becoming an economically successful country; nonetheless, public consciousness of this correlation seems to be at an all-time worldwide low. And refugees suffer through crises of identity. At the same time, national borders all over the world have become ever less permeable, as partly revealed by the easy availability of surveillance electronics and passive war machinery — notably land mines. Borders now can be projected at whim. On the other hand, ethnic, national, and geographical zones of tolerance have fallen victim to the transportation and information explosion. Wars are now easily started but are more difficult than ever to end.

Officially, as recognized and registered by United Nations agencies such as the United Nations High Commissioner for Refugees (UNHCR), there have been approximately 20 million refugees in the world over the last 20 years — a population larger than that of Australia — the majority of which have been housed in UN camps. Unofficially, as reported through organizations such as the United States Committee on Refugees, the estimate is more than double that figure: unregistered displaced persons now account for one percent of the world population. If it were possible for refugees to pack and carry with them a proportional part of their country's land (measured at approximately 37 people per square kilometer), they could piece together a state the size of France, Germany, England, and Italy combined. Configured as an intercontinental federation, it would circle the globe.

The original refugee states developed partly because there were still large, sparsely inhabited areas to be discovered and conquered. Today all of the world's territories have been located, charted, and populated. Even in the recent past, traditional refugee republics like the United States, Canada, Australia, and Israel actively sought refugees and competed for the right to absorb them. Today, however, it is industries that are lured from one country to another through tax incentives and other inducements, while refugees are regarded as an economic and social burden and a cultural liability. Recognized as refugees by the UN (and several international conventions), they survive in camps as prisoners of international charity. The simplicity of the generic term *refugee* does not, however, reveal the wide diversity of this population. This group is not just

supranational but also multilingual, multicultural, and multireligious. It commands neither territory nor capital. It has neither democratic structure nor any suitable form of political representation, or even any kind of government. A next generation refugee republic, then, would have to evolve as an experimental supraterritorial state that would be able to anticipate socio-ideological and economic challenges. It would both force and enable solutions.

Refugees from World War II were mostly European and were absorbed relatively quickly into other Western nations. Today's more heterogeneous refugee population is a global phenomenon comprising widely divergent cultures that resist simple assimilation.

In the 1980s, this group was the fastest growing segment of the world's population, increasing by an average of between ten and twenty percent each year. If represented as a state, it would be ranked within the top ten percent of the world's most populated countries, immediately above Turkey and just below Italy and England.

NATION, STATE, AND TERRITORY

If one is to accept the definition of *nation* as an integral territory with a common culture and language (and thus identity), then there is hardly a country today that is not multinational. There are, however, nations that exist without country or sovereignty – the Kurds, the Navajo, the Palestinians, and many other groups. In this way, a refugee republic of the next generation does not require the delineation of a traditional, territorial national boundary. Sinti and Roma, for example, are two nations that neither have nor demand their own land but whose people have created a nation while circumventing the occupation of an exclusive territory. Singapore, Hong Kong, and Liechtenstein are also highly successful countries, despite the fact that they control negligible territories. Geostrategic position can therefore be more important than size, just as education and communication infrastructures are more important than raw space. The enormous physical territory covered by the former Soviet Union, formerly the largest country on earth, contributed to its ultimate collapse rather than guaranteeing its survival. The only token territory that the Refugee Republic would need could be leased by the UN from larger countries or those which have few opportunities to profit from their land. Alternatively, segments of the electromagnetic spectrum could qualify as a quasiterritorial area. "The Network" could then become a home. Refugees, just like anybody else today, could claim a right to information and to telecommunications access. Such rights could easily be derived from the Universal Declaration of Human Rights, the UN Mass Media Declaration, and other conventions and treaties. Ironically then, refugees, always the last to have access to network technologies, would as victims of territorial borders benefit most from the borderlessness of these technologies.

GOVERNMENT

Refugees lack self-representation, and this has always been a problem. Even though this may make them more manageable for those agencies that decide their fate, they end up without democratic exercise – an inevitable liability when being repatriated or admitted for permanent resettlement in a democratic country. An international refugee network would help in developing democratic modalities inside and outside the camps. In addition, the Refugee Republic's sphere of influence would be structured by migration routes and communication structures. Conceptually, its "citizenship" would be defined not so much by passports as by a universally acceptable worldwide transit visa and by the ownership of shares in an "owner-operated" country. At a certain point this country could make an Initial Public Offering (IPO) for itself, offering the potential of reaching more than 100 million eyeballs. The Refugee Republic's stock price would reflect the success of this corporate country.

ECONOMY

Calculating both the existing and potential world refugee economy is more than just a statistical challenge. For example, the income generated by the approximately two million Egyptian migrant workers could serve as a reasonable indicator of the economic potential of the migrant economy – a figure that equals 75 percent of Egypt's annual exports. Similarly, Bangladesh would not be able to survive without the financial support of its emigrants. Even the emigrants from the former Yugoslavia constitute a significant 30 percent of its country's export, making them the single largest export "article." In addition, there are countries profiting directly from the existence of refugees in their territory. For example, in order to house the Cambodian refugees in 1979, the UN was forced to lease land from the Thai government for more than ten years. All relief care for the 300,000 refugees was to be purchased in Thailand, greatly benefiting the Thai economy.

The Refugee Republic, alternatively, could significantly benefit from, rather than simply reinforce, the advantages of global power. It could develop without a clearly defined territory and currency, but with infrastructural network connections and NGO and UN support; without physical trade but with transnational knowledge and contacts not affected by laws and borders; without historical and political structures but with a strong sense of peace and freedom; without a common language but with common fates, interests, and experiences.

THE MODEL STATE

The United States adopted and benefited from the constitutional and philosophical ideals of Europe, and then reframed these ideals, independent and unencumbered by historical baggage, as a model for the rest of the world. Today, Europe is still reaping the fruits of this American perspective, which provides a plausible reflection of Europe's own present and future. But because those countries that used to accept immigrants have now reached saturation and are no longer capable of representing the global spectrum, America, and indeed the entire world, would actually benefit from a new refugee republic.

This republic would be a mirror of a world which, to some extent, is partly pre- and partly postpolitical – a world where diverging trends of globalization have led to retribalization (ethnification and regionalization). Geographical isolation has virtually vanished in the fog of the information and transportation explosion. As a hypercultural, hyperlingual, multiethnic, transglobal net-state, the Refugee Republic would present an opportunity to fine-tune international law and ordinances as well as to implement the decisions and ideals embodied by the UN. Above all, it could pioneer a contemporary and overarching understanding of human rights and duties – the state of being human under adverse conditions; a situation that increasingly threatens to become the norm for the multipolar world.

FEASIBILITY

But will it really happen? The Refugee Republic project was originally intended to have the effect of an advertising campaign for refugees. However, as recent technological developments have outpaced their conceptual use, the project looks less outrageous and less utopian by the day: second and third generation computer systems are waiting to be recycled and can be revitalized with Linux, Berkeley Software Design (BSD), and a host of other free software products that have become available under public license; companies like Xerox are embracing concepts such as "knowledge communities"; long-distance learning and e-commerce are the buzzwords of e-entrepreneurs and e-educators; geographical distance is no longer a significant obstacle to business, education or social interaction; Internet communities have superseded the populations of many countries (America Online/Compuserve); Microsoft is issuing electronic passports (could the loss or rejection of such a passport constitute exile?); Hong Kong and Singapore have started to export themselves as success packages along with banking laws, civil codes, education systems, and industries;[1] For example, after initially being invited by the Chinese government to help develop the economy in Zhuhou, the Singapore administration was subsequently asked to provide social engineering and establish compatible administrative services. Oracle, the software company noted for database applications, has developed a Government Online/Electronic Management System ("GOLEM"); according to the *Economist*, illegal immigrants are now the contraband of choice – it is less risky and more profitable to traffic in them than to engage in cross-border drug trades.

Statistics, technologies, and necessity may all suggest a refugee republic but the perspectival shift required not only to embrace the idea but also to actively pursue it would, it seems, only come naturally to members of post-Aristotelian societies – not exactly the typical locale of refugees. The further we move away from an American point of view, the more arcane and outrageous the concept appears. Globalism, I have come to understand, is really a Western, if not American, invention that can be replicated, more or less, by other Western nations – but this replication does not come easily. I have yet to find a culture that has the same total, or indeed global, definition of space and its sphere of action. Using a fixed point at the center, monotheism lends itself to and encourages all-encompassing ventures. Muslims, as observed by the Harvard-based Syrian scholar Bassam Tibi, empowered by a similar monotheistic viewpoint, suffer the most as they watch the West act in and dominate what they see as their own domain: the entire world, a totality, a globality. China and Japan, for example, have had throughout their histories designs on their neighbors, but neither of them was ever truly global: former Japanese Premier Nakasone even saw the need to initiate a government-sponsored *Kokusaika*, or internationalization of Japan.[2] The Greater South East Asian Co-Prosperity Sphere was to liberate the South East Asian countries from European colonial rule and create a common market under Japanese leadership. The sphere was to cover roughly the territory occupied by the Japanese forces in World War II.

Without this initiative, it was feared, Japan would have remained hopelessly parochial and thus unfit to take on the global marketplace.

It is no coincidence that the first globe on record was made just over 500 years ago by the Portuguese navigator Martin Behaim. Globalism just does not seem to be one of the default settings in the cosmologies of other cultures, and therefore will be something which can, at best, be simulated by tracing the deep imprints of the West's footsteps on this globe. The globalist perspective will always be a thing of the West and only imitated by the rest.

Of course, for the project to be successful, a Refugee Republic would never emerge.

THE NEW GENERIC

GENERIC

GREG LYNN

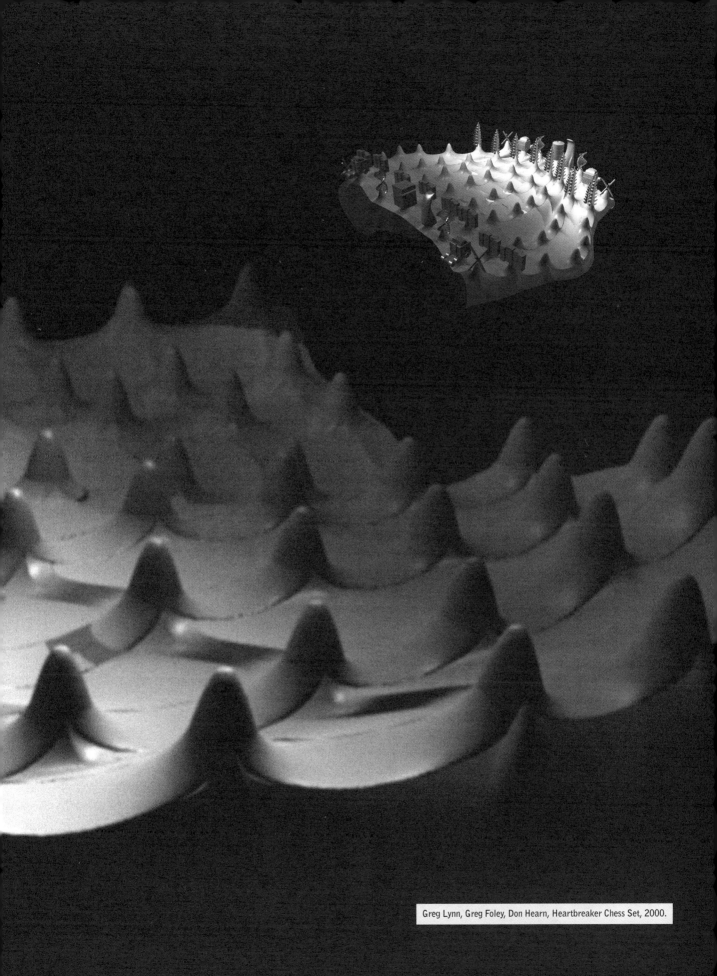

Greg Lynn, Greg Foley, Don Hearn, Heartbreaker Chess Set, 2000.

Partial mock-up of an Embryological House, Venice Biennale, 2000.

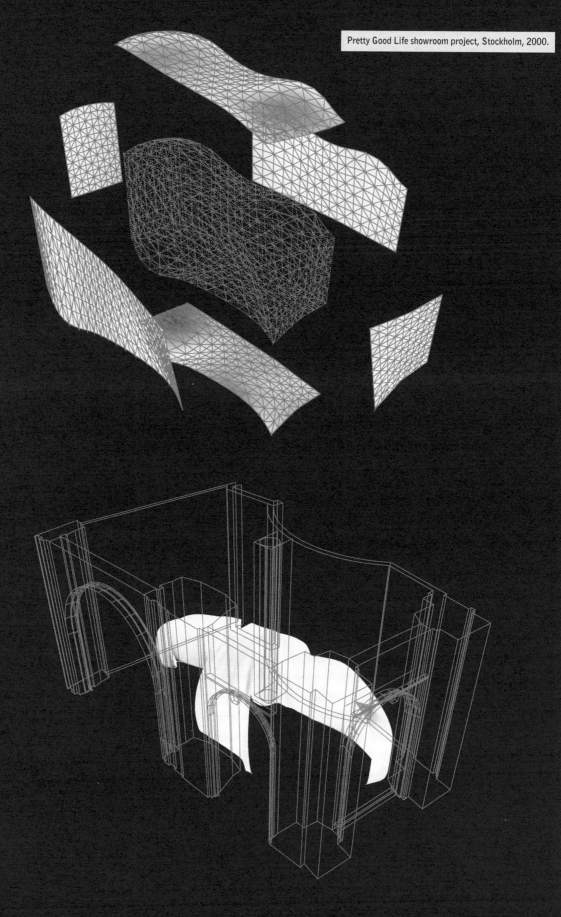

Pretty Good Life showroom project, Stockholm, 2000.

DISCUSSION 5

THOMAS KRENS I think that the best way to begin this discussion, given the rapt attention of the audience, is to open it up right from the beginning and see what kind of thoughts have been provoked by the presentations this morning.

KURT FORSTER I was very intrigued by Rem's divided world, between the virtual and the real, but I was thinking whether their opposition, which seemed to extend into the two halves of his presentation, has not in fact already been completely dissolved. For instance, one of the most important economic and social aspects of Prada is the massive manufacture of surrogate Prada, sold within a stone's throw of every Prada store by the people who come from those most populous areas of the globe and who represent, in a sense, the inverse image of Prada itself. So to imagine, as you presented it Rem, how Prada could possibly extend its reach, one approach would be to jack up its products to a more exclusive and almost purely art level, while at the same time also taking in hand the production of surrogate Prada, so as, using a pharmaceutical analogy, to be both the manufacturer of the generic drug and the name drug.

Also, as I was listening to Rem's explanation of the relationship between the short list of programmatic schemes and the seemingly long list of architecture, I suddenly wondered whether the statement that "everything is architecture" should not also be considered in connection to its virtual contradiction – namely, that as a consequence of all of this, there is almost no architecture left.

REM KOOLHAAS Kurt, what I find interesting is that you, the director of a cultural institution, have just laid out a program to help energize Prada's survival. I also think that to

a certain extent their survival is insured, because according to rumor Prada actually produces its own fakes. But more importantly, in response to these ideas of everything or nothing being architecture, I think we have been limited to definitions of architecture as something that embodies ideals in built form, or intentions in built form. By giving up these conventions, architecture expands into developing ideas for organizations, coexistences, and communities, so that its claim to be everywhere is reinforced rather than weakened.

GREG LYNN One of the things that I found very interesting about this panel is how media and information in architecture are no longer antithetical to one another, as everyone was talking about it a few years ago, but are in fact intricately linked. For example, Beatriz showed how media and architecture came together to form a very particular identity for a whole series of events. Rem's Prada work and definitely the showroom strategy are both projects that have media but are also looking for some kind of relationship between a physical environment, as temporary as it may be, and a media definition. I think that the notion of identity is now situated very much between media and physical infrastructure. Architecture now occupies a very particular place in that whole exchange. So, I didn't see Rem's OMA/AMO distinction as oppositional but rather as just a way to sort out the particular tasks and to put them together in a new kind of expertise. But as Beatriz showed, this is something that has been going on for some time.

BEATRIZ COLOMINA For at least half a century. This is what is interesting about the Eameses and why I spoke about them today. As Greg said, these questions of media transforming archi-

tecture have been around for a long time. But this statement that "everything is architecture" makes me nervous, too, because at a certain point one has to compete with the megalomaniacal ambition of the architect to approach or to appropriate every single possibility of our own intervention. I want to clarify this in relation to the Eameses. People constantly ask why they abandoned the practice of architecture – an architecture that people typically understand only in terms of the house that they built for themselves in 1949. The Eameses spent their entire life explaining to everybody that everything they were doing was architecture – that a chair is architecture in miniature; that in its structure a film has architecture; that the layout of a page is architecture. Even in thinking about the Mies exhibition at the Museum of Modern Art in 1947, they saw another kind of architecture. In an article he wrote in **Arts and Architecture**, Charles Eames makes very clear that what is important is not the individual buildings represented by Mies in the form of models and drawings but rather the way in which Mies organized space; that is, Miesian space. So the exhibition itself is an architecture communicated in real time; an architecture that you can hear as your foot treads on the step, an architecture that you can smell.

KRENS I want to pose a series of questions, and they're addressed to either someone on the panel or the audience. In thinking about Rem's talk, which began with the analysis of shopping, and of Beatriz's notion of information, and Hani Rashid's presentation yesterday about the creation of virtual spaces, it seems to me that technology has clearly had an enormous input. But equally important is market research – trying to figure out not so much what people want, but what their wants and desires are on a visceral and intuitive level. One of the implications of technology is that all of our attitudes and decisions, conscious and unconscious, are being assembled into a grand database somewhere, whether embedded in our credit cards or telephone bills or whatever – that this database of desire and satisfaction exists. Architects, particularly as a class, not to mention marketeers and others, then appear to be tapping into this database and using this information to create spaces. I'm thinking specifically about Rem's image of the changing building program in the Universal project, and Jean Nouvel's comment about strategy; that strategy as embedded in architecture is an important aspect of the discipline. But what happens when the program constantly changes? What if you don't know what the program actually is in its unconscious? And if this information is available and can be grasped, will this somehow change the shape of architecture? Does it give architecture a form that we don't expect, one that is driven neither by aesthetics nor formal concerns but by a whole series of unconscious decisions as preface to a kind of universal architecture of daily decisions and unconscious needs? Do formal considerations – the shape of the building, the romance of the building, the image of the building – matter at all at the end of the day?

GERMANO CELANT I want to go back to this idea of everything being architecture. For people in the world of fashion, architecture **is** fashion now – but this is architecture understood not in terms of space but only as time. What is important in Rem's collaboration with Prada is that they're dealing with the speed of time, which is related to an object in time, not an object in space. The shop is a speed element, the object is a speed element; it is only

a situation for consumption. The strategy is to connect with the idea of time. Time is no longer a virtual element but a physical product, and a product that has to be shaped in order to be sold or distributed. The change for architecture is that it's no longer dealing with space but with time. That's why architecture is fashion, or fashion has to do with architecture, and that's why the two things come together.

AUDIENCE A number of the presentations today on the relationship between media and architecture dealt with physical infrastructures and with virtual "thinfrastructures," but while everyone is discussing time and fashion, no one is speaking about the political implications of the gap between these two constructs. For example, what is the difference between those countries that don't have an infrastructure and are now adopting this thinfrastructure, and those situations in which there is an equal growth of the two? These thoughts are especially addressed to Rem, because you've spent so much of your career working on infrastructures or enabling infrastructures in a political space. What kinds of infrastructures can we speculate on to bridge or address this gap?

KOOLHAAS The whole notion of bridging is in some ways redundant because it implies that the same conditions would eventually prevail everywhere. Rather, what is becoming increasingly clear is that globalization will not lead to a homogenous condition.

AUDIENCE I'm not talking about homogeneity, but of the gap in between. Why aren't we using this gap for additional things or ideas or . . .

KOOLHAAS I think we will be using it very soon. There are many indications in Nigeria that this is actually

happening. It is clearly revealed by the electronics market in Lagos, which consists of one-story buildings that all are like garages, with garage doors – two-meter-high buildings with 30-meter-high antennas on the roof for mobile phone connections. Entering these garages, one finds a kind of technological abattoir inside. So this simultaneity of contradictory things that you spoke about is in a sense already in place.

LYNN I just want to shift the discussion a little bit, partly because this is a retrospective conference, but also because I think that it's not as simple as mapping the market and mapping the public realm and trying to adapt to it. I think it's also not an issue of being megalomaniacal about assuming that we could manage it politically. Over the last ten years a group of people at this conference have developed particular critical theoretical tools – tools that are particularly good at working with identity. In terms of Rem's project, Prada has clearly recognized an opportunity (provoked through Rem's research); it's not as if they were shopping around for architects. They were actually going to organizations with very particular techniques. This also brings up the question of identity. We have seen recently that the Eameses' work is now coming back as fashion. When I saw those images of the Moscow exhibition, it was incredible how fashionable they are right now. The aesthetics of modernism as a whole is also coming back as a very fashionable thing. So more than organizational techniques, what I see as especially important is the development of very particular formal and stylistic identities.

SANFORD KWINTER Intervening here from the floor, I would like first to thank the panelists for their presentations, which were extraordinary, provocative (so strange and uncustomary for an Any conference), and for their remarkable cohesiveness and sustained reflection on a fairly constant theme. Having seen myself relegated in one of the slides to the realm of the virtual, I'm left wondering whether I'm condemned to spend the rest of my life up there. [See page 182, fig. 12.] You see, it was a surprise but not altogether a surprise. For I think it's one thing to talk about obsession in a personal sense, but it's another thing to talk about obsession publicly and together as one has done here, because it suggests the question as to whether there might exist a historical structure to obsession. In this context, I feel compelled to address Greg's comments because, more than anything else, I couldn't help hearing behind all of the presentations today the echo of Eisenhower's famous farewell speech. In that speech, Eisenhower pointed out that what had taken place in the United States after World War II had been inevitable; there had been a huge growth in the armaments industry, which already then employed over 3.5 million people. He could only warn people against the profound transformations, especially in our social structure, that we would soon begin to see.

I would suggest that one begin to think about all of the work today, about the structure of the particular kinds of obsessions that were presented to us, through the optic of this admonishment. The pervasive theme of information that came up in the presentations, as a direct development from the information theory first articulated during and immediately following World War II, is little more than the ultimate argument and justification for what is really our world's, and today's, principal obsession – the obsession with markets. I'm asking you all to consider the possibility that

we are all participating today in a huge collective hallucinatory obsession. Our thinking and our thought patterns have been overtaken and dominated by the terms and conditions of the market. I'm wondering whether anybody sees, whether anyone even believes in, the possibility of standing outside of the market mentality and imagining a reality different from the one we are living today. These thoughts have been provoked, to a certain extent, by something Rem said to me earlier. Sitting in a cab on the way up here this morning, he turned to me and asked, "How long has it been since you have thought about brotherhood and the good?" This, I thought, was a real plea for collaboration. A "howl" in fact, as Alan Ginsberg would put it, "for the best minds of our generation" and how they have been lost. So, this is just a preamble to my point that it's perhaps a little dismissive to see these serious issues in terms of identity – to see the problem of identity engineering and the obsession with identity today as something that we have chosen for ourselves.

LYNN No, no, I was just saying that identity is our particular expertise. It's actually not market research. I can't think of a thing that I would be worse qualified for than market research. Rem, do you think that's what you do?

KOOLHAAS I think Sanford's question is about whether we have a choice in being like we are.

INGO GÜNTHER I think there **is** a choice, that you have to differentiate between motivation and rationalization.

KRENS But market research is not a negative thing.

LYNN I'm not saying it's negative. I'm just saying that I'm not an expert in it.

KRENS I see market research as an intrinsically and deliberately democratic thing. It's a function of technology; it's a function of communications and the fact that things are wired together, and then with the free exchange of ideas, more and more people can enter into the dialogue and resources can get allocated. Market research is there to try and figure out who buys Prada and where they live. It doesn't make sense to build Prada stores in the Amazon jungle and to charge $200 for a pair of pants – there's no audience, no market there. So there's a natural selection process. Market research follows the population; it follows the wealth and it also tracks the architects. Why then does Prada hire Rem Koolhaas to design its stores and do its analysis? Because . . .

LYNN They've got an image problem.

KRENS . . . yeah, and they think it'll be cool, and that ultimately it will increase sales.

PHYLLIS LAMBERT I think the question is, Why does Rem consider doing it?

KRENS Because they're going to pay him. And because it gives him the opportunity to work within the system and to shape its values by trying to understand how its mechanisms work (I would assume, not speaking for Rem).

AUDIENCE I think that the questions of rationalization and motivation still stand. In this room we are all well-groomed and well-dressed; we are all consumers. But the degree to which we integrate ourselves in the consumer environment is still a question of choice and of distance. As architects, does this consumerism allow you to be the architect you want to be, or does it suggest the limitations of what you can never be?

CELANT I think that culture is changing. It is now becoming an industrial process. Culture produces commerce because it produces goods and gadgets. So it's not strange that now commerce produces culture. Commerce wants to connect with high architecture, to art, and to intellectual and artistic creativity. There is a shift in the last five years around art and fashion, art and design, art and architecture, and so on, because of this kind of osmosis between culture becoming commerce and commerce becoming culture. The reason an architect has to work for shops, or why shops have to have architecture, is really the interface between the two.

GÜNTHER In advertising, branding is understood as the total control of every aspect of consumer interaction. This is why these companies hire architects, because architects are very good at the control of that environment and the control of that interaction. Architects can also provide a greater sense of permanence, in that a brand lasts forever, as opposed to the products themselves, which can be copied within ten months or so. This is the standard in the advertising industry.

AUDIENCE This is a question for Greg Lynn. It seemed to me that in the Eameses' project in Moscow, the choice of the seven screens appeared to be something rather important insofar as it limited or questioned human perception in terms of how many are too many and how few would be too few, and in that way placed technology parallel to some kind of human condition. In terms of the variations that you spoke about, how do you place yourself so that you

can gauge the precise number, if, in fact, there is a fixed number?

LYNN To a certain degree I willfully abdicate a lot of the questions about scale and articulation to machines. With the house, you can see that it starts off as a very generic thing, but then it gets aesthetically tuned or refined. Right now, I'm actually more interested in what the machines are doing to the design process than in developing preconceptions about the number of panels or the degrees of curvature. So most of what you spoke about is abdicated at the front end and then refined through the design process.

I also want to say one other thing. This panel seems to have a kind of dour relationship with the audience, but for me, listening to the presentations and debates, I've never felt more excited about research having successfully been realized. The Any conferences, which I was very depressed about last year, suddenly seem a little more exciting, because a lot of the techniques and tools that were seen as radical and oppositional are now being put into use in a highly cultural, public, and commercial way. And if anybody were to suggest that the embryological houses are being driven by market desire, then I would be incredibly flattered, because I feel that these houses came out of a very particular kind of research and engagement with architectural history and theory autonomous from any kind of market desire. If they have some application, then that, I think, is great, but in fact it's a research. The same thing can be said about most of the work that we've seen here – that it is the result of critical and intellectual research that is now finding a way to embed itself in a wider culture.

JEAN-LOUIS COHEN The Any conferences started with the rejection of a model of architectural practice

defined simply as some kind of service industry in favor of architecture as a field of intellectual inquiry, as a field of radical thought. It seems to me that today we have seen a return to architecture's "servicing" past by widening its spectrum, by trying to deal with those forces that shape society. So my question is, What is left of architecture today as a specific experience after ten years of these meetings and 25 years of radical architectural thought? Are we simply serving or are we learning from the department store, as Rem has been doing? And what are the patterns of learning that we ought to develop to maintain the radicality while not completely negating transformations of the real world?

KRENS Do any of the architects on the panel want to take a crack at defining and defending the profession?

KOOLHAAS I don't think that the profession is being attacked. But I'm happy that you brought this up, Jean-Louis, because I think that from the very beginning of the Any conferences there was a kind of latent tension between radicals and radicalism and nonradicals. My position is that the whole pretension of radicalism expressed in architecture is kind of fictional because architecture in itself can only endorse. I don't know of a single architecture that engages in radical conflict with the assumptions that its client has about it. There has always been this kind of ambiguity that we consider ourselves radicals, but we are tied to the profession. This brings us back to a discussion we had a few years ago at Any in talking about Lille – whether you can be critical as an architect. I think that you can be critical as an architect in every other field parallel to architecture, and next to architecture, but not strictly speaking through architecture.

"the first you think of"

FROM ANY-THING TO BIOTHING

ANTHONY VIDLER

In a review of "The Triumph of the Baroque" exhibition at the National Gallery of Art in Washington, Herbert Muschamp quoted me as stating, boldly enough, that "All architecture is the result of panic." 1 Herbert Muschamp, review of the exhibition "The Triumph of the Baroque: Architecture in Europe 1600–1750," "When Ideas Took Shape and Soared," the *New York Times*, May 26, 2000. I will refrain for the moment from detailing what it was I actually said in favor of exploring the implications of Muschamp's ensuing comparison of the multiple and complex forms of the baroque to a contemporary interest in computer morphing: the scrolls, spirals, trompe-l'oeil, illusion- ism, repetition, and perspectival stretching of the baroque should, he observed, "give pause to those who think that computer-generated, so-called blob architecture has no place in the old bricks-and-mortar world."

The adoption of the baroque as a harbinger and early sighting of modernity has, of course, been around a long time. Heinrich Wöfflin was clear in his discomfort with the way in which the dissolution of Renaissance spatial boundaries precipitated a bodily unease and ambiguity of place that would be characteristic of the modernity evoked first by Piranesi and then by Richard Wagner. (This is what I probably said to Herbert.) Walter Benjamin found in baroque tragic drama the ancestor of the fragmentation, expressionism, and bureaucratic disenchantment that surrounded him in Weimar Berlin. Sigfried Giedion, with a more optimistic tone, saw the merging of spatial transgression and structural expression as prophetic of the space-time and structure treaty out of which Corbusian modernism was forged. More recently, these authorities have been reread as confirming the baroque as a first instance of postmodernism, with its loss of historical faith and its fragmentary, allegorical counternarratives. Now it is the turn of computer morphing, of the blob, to be traced to the baroque.

Of course Muschamp is not the first to make the connection; indeed, since the publica- tion of Gilles Deleuze's *The Fold: Leibniz and the Baroque* in 1984, and then with the serendipitous presence of Bernard Cache in the seminar on which the book was based, the theoretical and formal connection between baroque folding and computer folding has been firmly in place. 2 See Bernard Cache, *Earth Moves: The Furnishing of Territories*, trans. Anne Boyman (Cambridge, Massachusetts: The MIT Press, 1995). I will not trace the epistemological history of this conjunction here – I have elsewhere argued that Leibniz's baroque is perhaps even more interesting as a theoretical starting point for folding than Deleuze's; but for my purposes here, the relationship, if considered on any level, is useful if only as a first way of setting the criteria for interpreting the results of the procedures set in motion by computer morphing programs in architecture.

In developing the comparison baroque/blob a little further, we may well be returned to the notion of "architectural panic" and "architectural anxiety," but not precisely in the way in which early psychological art historians such as Wilhelm Worringer (whom I was quot- ing in the initial statement cited by Muschamp) or late-modern *New York Times* critics have used the concept. Rather, we will find our own special form of anxiety in the face of the blob, and one certainly more suitable for the digital moment than that turn-of-the-century *Platzscheu* or agoraphobia seen by Worringer as the root of all abstraction.

In its paradigmatic schema, as outlined by Greg Lynn in *Animate Form*, the procedures of blob production are compared to the reproduction of forms in nature. They are arrived at through the use of software that not only morphs but also animates and reproduces form, iteration after iteration, as if following the genetic evolution of biological organisms; form for the blob-maker is, so to speak, a product of autogenesis. Now, while the biological analogy has always informed architecture, architecture has not, at least until recently, aspired so directly to the imitation of biological processes or to the formal status of the biological entity. Gaudi may have generated forms that in Dali's view looked edible, emulative of hysterical processes; Le Corbusier may have generated the codes of the Modulor from his measure of man; Mies may have sought an organic form for modern technology commensurate with that found by Raoul Francé in bones and plants, but his metier was the manipulation of I-beams; Wright may have sought a formal "organicity" parallel to that of "growth and form" in nature; but all such references were embedded in the codes of architecture itself. What was being morphed was "architecture" not nature, and, as with the baroque, it was architecture that provided the key to distortion and formal displacement, to what was being rendered fluid and what was being rendered spatially infinite. For the baroque, there was no infinity without reference to the perspectival frame; no anamorphosis without reference to the initial viewing point of the human viewer; no warped façade without reference to one that was not. Indeed, no baroque without Renaissance. And, in turn, for Le Corbusier, Mies, Wright, and the rest, as we know, all modernism was a more or less overt transformation of classicism, which remained the test and the root of even the most radical deconstruction.

But for the animist of animate form, there is apparently no such referent. Against what Lynn calls the "statics" of the discipline of architecture, "Animate form," he writes, "suggests animalism, animism, growth, actuation, vitality, and virtuality." 3 Greg Lynn, *Animate form* (New York: Princeton Architectural Press, 1999), 9. For the biological, thanks to the manipulative potential of software, has now taken on the status of the real, and further, the architectural, far from simply analogically referring to the biological, assumes its own biological character, and becomes, in a way, a biomorphic structure of its own. That this is possible, even to fantasize, is a result of the digital, which reduces, or maps, all phenomena into the same code – the strings of zeroes and ones that indifferently render our human genome or building. Lynn develops forms that for all intents and purposes not only imitate natural organisms but also develop and grow, reproduce and evolve according to the same principles as natural organisms. He shows, for example, the flea and the dust mite at varying scales. When placed side by side with, for example, the Cardiff Opera project, the resemblance is more than organic in affect; rather, there is the distinct implication that the building itself purports to *be* organic in form. The coincidence of animate form and animal form is enhanced in these kinds of schemes by the fortuitous development of the technologies of the skin; if Gehry's earlier "fish" were scaled in imitation of his grandmother's carp, the Guggenheim Bilbao is digitally produced and constructed as if it were a fish; in a further development, Lynn's skins would ideally perform all the functions of a biological wrapping.

In these projects and many like them, the missing link in the traditional chain nature-architecture-building is "architecture": the jump is straight from nature to building – this is perhaps what disturbs Rafael Moneo so much. What was symbolic in classicism, allegorical in the baroque, and abstracted in modernism, is now rendered in the domain of the real – or rather the real-virtual where the "real" now resides – in both natural biological and building terms. Nature and building are merged in an endless digital manipulation of material, inert and living. Digital technology allows for a direct passage from one to the other, so that all domains of the "real" are mapped at one and the same time.

Here then we might want to ask: by what criteria are we to judge these new bio-forms that no longer join us to cultural or historical tradition, but, so to speak, have attained an emancipation from culture that scientific thought has always willed but now has achieved? Certainly there is an affect of somewhat old-fashioned functionalism that so punctually rules, like an updating of the modernist alibi, every transformation and iteration of the systematic evolution of form in the diagrams of Ben van Berkel et al. Certainly "functions" that have never hitherto been calibrated into form can now be injected as percentages of animated force, as warpings of a potentially endless field of forces. Certainly too, the affect of the smooth surfaces and high-technology construction methods, the precision of intersecting geometries so complicated as to seem, finally, non-Euclidian, would offer the image of a modernism accomplished, the utopia of technological functionalism at last achieved by technology. Would we then be in the line of a Summerson, who as long ago as 1949 predicted that "function" in the form of program would be the criteria for all future architecture? Or a Jencks, who as long ago as 1971 presciently observed that the "architecture of 2000" would turn out to be a bio-architecture as the final accomplishment of modernist functionalist utopia? 4. See John Summerson, *Heavenly Mansions, and other essays on architecture* (London: Cresset Press, 1949), and Charles Jencks, *Architecture 2000: Predictions and Methods* (New York: Praeger, 1971).

Such a line of argument would, however, imply that all the iterative moves and all the different kinds of "information" mapped onto the generative model be accompanied by their corresponding criteria of use, of environmental and structural if not social instrumentality. We would then hypothetically be able to measure the input of each programmatic unit in terms of its output, and so on. But this is obviously neither the case nor the intention – the morphological moves range from the technical to the metaphorical to the fantastic; the "lines of force" mapped again and again onto surfaces from the geological to the geographical, from the topological to the geometrical, are often taken from empirical data – the flows of traffic during certain hours, the trajectory of the sun – but equally often also from the "automatic writing" of the context – its magnetic force fields deduced with not a little psychological mysticism (or faith) from topography and geology. Topographies, indeed, dominate these procedures, topographies that have replaced cultural space, or semiotic element, as the ur-form of autogenerated architecture.

Here, interest in the surface, supported by topological enquiries from Deleuze to Jacques Lacan, coincides with the affirmation that architecture is indeed nothing but surface. This would imply, from a traditional humanist standpoint, an apparent reduction of architectural experience from tectonic *effect* to surface *affect*. This shift would parallel the first, from architecture to nature, by a more direct reference to the "body," which has always been theorized and projected as hidden inside architecture, from Vitruvius to the present. But where this body was incorporated in classical form through proportion and composition – that is, by analogy – and in modernist form through ideas of psychological projection – that is, through empathy – its incorporation as "affect" dissolves it into a series of sensations and their intellectual or sensory attributes; that is, the body is admitted only as trace, as hidden in the fragmentary associational mappings of memory and direct apperception. In van Berkel's words, the deterritorialization of the body implied in these mappings leads to the reterritorialization of the face as surface affect – holes, darks and lights, promontories and hollows, rather than eyes, cheeks, and noses. Architecture, once thought to be a monumental body for the body, or at least a psychological home for the mental body, has now been rendered as thin skin for an even thinner skin.

In a recent article confronting this apparent dissolution of bodily humanism in architecture, Brian Massumi argues that rather than seeing an increasing and oppositional rift between our human and "Euclidian" bodies and the new non-Euclidian digital and virtual world being generated for them, we should understand this as a still incomplete transition. The problem, he proposes, lies not in the fact that the new affective skins are wrong for us, but in our own reluctance to assume the full affective nature of our own experience of our bodies. "What if," he asks, "*the space of the body is really abstract?*" Which would mean that the new skins generated by topological analysis, far from being "mutant geometries that don't correspond to anything real," would in fact relate to "dimensions of *lived abstractness* that cannot be conceptualized in other than topological terms." 5 Brian Massumi, "Strange Horizon: Buildings, Biograms, and the Body Topologic," in Stephen Perella, ed., *Architectural Design*, special "Hypersurface II" issue, 1999. Such a homology between architectural form and the intellectual form of humanness would of course demand a special form of postpsychological vision, one that, indeed, transcends the special cases of visual and perceptual disfunction and disjunction cited by Massumi as evidence for his model of the "abstract" body.

But perhaps we should take our cue more directly from the implications of the very term *animate form*, and without any traditional architectural resistance, accept the homology between nature and building there implied. This, of course, would be to accept the new, late-20th-century nature of nature itself and the concomitant culture of its comprehension. Here we would be registering a shift in what Theodor Adorno and Max Horkheimer called the "dialectic of Enlightenment" to what might seem at first sight a regression from Enlightenment rationality to an identification with the "forces" of nature once assumed to be part of a lost past of animism and the uncanny. From Francis Bacon and John Locke to Sigmund Freud, animism was seen to be the enemy; its superstitions were to be routed out of institutions, social practices, and minds in order for a demythologized rationalism to triumph, setting a critical distance for the ordering of knowledge and abstraction of form. As Adorno noted, "The disenchantment [de-mythologization, to follow Max Weber's term *entzauberung*] of the world is the extirpation of animism." 6 Max Horkheimer and Theodor W. Adorno, *Dialectic of Enlightenment*, trans. John Cumming (New York: Seabury Press, 1972), 5. A return to animism, then, would imply, from the standpoint of the Enlightenment, a return to magic, myth, and shamanism, and a decided refusal of reason, science, and the apparently certain "truth" of empirical knowledge. This would also imply, which is often enough stated, a turn away from the formulas of a rational architecture, itself deeply implicated in the Enlightenment project.

But as we know, in Adorno and Horkheimer's terms, this very Enlightenment project, founded on what they call a "mythic terror," simply substituted one fear for another – the fear of the unknown is replaced by the alienation of the human subject from the natural world: "The noontide panic fear in which men suddenly became aware of nature as a totality has found its like in the panic which nowadays is ready to break out at every moment: men expect that the world, which is without any issue, will be set on fire by a totality which they themselves are, and over which they have no control." 7 Ibid., 28. The only escape from such alienation and panic fear was, they argue, the authenticity of the work of art, which "still has something in common with enchantment," in positing its own "self-enclosed area, which is withdrawn from the context of profane existence, and in which special laws apply." 8 Ibid., 19. Herein lay what for Benjamin, and following him, Adorno, called the aura, and hence the almost magical status extended to art in the post-Enlightenment world; hence too, the continual return to, and reliance on, the cultural codes that make art special – the "irrational" rules of architecture, for example, that somehow have been encoded to mirror the "rationality" of the world.

In this context it is difficult to leap to the conclusion that the call for animism in architecture represents a pure return to a pre-Enlightenment condition. For one thing, its generative processes depend entirely on the science that affords enlightenment its ultimate instruments and justification. For another, its appeal is to a nature no longer apprehended by a magical ritual but by scientific experiment. In these terms, indeed, digital animism represents a logical and entirely rational extension of the Enlightenment project. A better formulation than that of primitive regression would then perhaps be modernist functionalism, founded on a myth of rationality, and redeemed by the advent of perfected rationality itself. If, as Lynn argues, "movement" in architecture was once represented by the fictive movement of the frame-by-frame montage of the movie, now movement and force can be integrated as a single process of animation, leading to a form that bears all the traces of these forces, the scars of its inherent animism, so to speak.

This would then be an animism developed out of rather than in reaction to the Enlightenment, an animism with its own special terms of judgment and thus its own position vis-à-vis its human subjects. Here we may have to abandon all pretense of the human-centered criteria of rationalism, of an architecture that embodies the human and is established to give what Wölfflin and Benjamin called a *Spielraum* for the subject, room for it to move, play, and establish itself; a subject that has held more or less constant since the Renaissance, and, despite attempts to destabilize it or even kill it off under modernism and postmodernism, has more or less survived intact to the present. This subject has always been defined in opposition and distinction to the animal. As argued by Adorno and Horkheimer, the "idea of man in European history is expressed in the way in which he is distinguished from the animal. Animal irrationality is adduced as proof of human dignity." 9 Ibid., 245. Following from this, any metamorphosis of men into beasts was seen as a mark of damnation.

And yet the germ of this subject's present dilemma was, by the very same token, seeded in the Enlightenment dream of absolute mastery of nature, the conversion, in Adorno's terms, of "the cosmos into one immense hunting-ground," which as a result has brought the human into dangerous proximity to the inhuman. On the one hand, nature is entirely subordinated to man's reason; on the other, it is thereby manifested in a totality modeled and controlled by the digital that merges the one into the other, setting up a boundary-free zone that no longer clearly distinguishes the human from the inhuman, man from nature.

And, where once the limits of the human and the nonhuman were described in representation by the limits of mimicry, digital representation has for all intents and purposes erased the boundaries that were originally the subject and site of elaborate rituals of imitation and propitiation, or in the modern period, no less elaborate rituals of obeisance to cultural precedent. In architectural terms, it is more than interesting that the kinds of software employed for the morphing, animation, and generation of form are in essence identical to that software now used to develop bio-organisms, analyze and activate DNA and genome practices, and transplant, clone, and engender life forms. The interface between these two realms, consisting of "artificial" natures – sensing skins, autoresponsive environments, photo- and bio-sensitive surfaces – is likewise a product of and manipulated by the digital. And of course there is little interface, or firewall, operating to separate any of these domains from the other; after all, a digital model of a genetic code is more than representation – a simple modification of this code can generate its own re-formed organism.

Such an elimination of boundaries – between, say, architectural skin and our skin, architectural "façades" and our faces, between the morphogenesis of the natural and the human, and, finally, between the evolution of natural forms and the autoreproduction of digital forms – naturally induces a certain anxiety in the (traditionally described) human subject. It is true that the morphed surfaces of the new blobs are infused, so to speak, by affect, and to a lesser degree by effect – both properties that guard traces of the human/emotion/psychic in their allusions. But these traces are themselves simulacra of other, formerly material traces, and entirely subordinated to the surfaces they apparently mark.

The insistent trajectory that digitalization describes toward the convergence of the architectural and the natural is also, at another scale, traced between the human and the inhuman, with the architectural object, once a mediating and protective device between these pairs, now removed in favor of a generalized model of "nature" that not only subsumes the human but is technically controlled by it, yet entirely at its mercy. "As the animate approaches the inanimate," writes Adorno, "and the more highly developed form of life comes closer to nature, it is alienated from it, since inanimate nature, which life in its most vigorous form aspires to become, is capable only of wholly external, spatial relationships. Space is absolute alienation. When men try to become like nature they harden themselves against it. Protection as fear is a form of mimicry." [10 Ibid., 180.]

In this characterization of the project of enlightenment, space interestingly enough emerges as the flux of anxiety and the site of alienation. In post-Enlightenment terms, however, such space is entirely transformed by the digital; indeed, there seems little that is spatial in the digital world, save for its ability to mimic "space" as we know and "experience" it. As architecture moves from a space in which the human composes its relations with nature to a nature in which the human is absorbed through the self-reproducing technologies of animation, we are positioned in a strange limbo of an apparently endless and developmental sequence of forms that, precisely because of their digital composition, are potentially the only "real." Mimicry here becomes a key to the recognition of "form" and an instrument in the simulation of space, even as space itself, at least as we humans have known it, is collapsed into the endless, directionless, placeless string.

Here we are returned to our earlier consideration of panic, but in another register entirely to that fearful panic that Wölfflin felt in the face of the baroque or to the "agoraphobia" cited by Worringer as the first incentive for geometrical architecture. For what I am implying is that another kind of subject identity is constructed by spaces that are auto-generated by a software that knows nothing of a distinction between animal and human, and one that, for the present at least, is more concerned with the morphological and topological transformations of an outer skin or shell than in the humanoid dimensions of the interior. It is not at present clear whether our new identities will fully embrace our newly found digital kinship with nature; nor even whether our own biomorphic forms will endure as presently constituted stable reference points for judgment and contemplation. What is clear is that digital mimicry has given the lie to any claim of the necessary human in the modeling of the inhuman; which is certainly, as Lacan pointed out some fifty years ago, a problem of ethics, if not of aesthetics.

SURFACE INSCRIPTIONS

IGNASI DE SOLÀ-MORALES

A few weeks ago, in one of the terminals of London's Heathrow Airport, I sat down to have a coffee while I waited for my flight to be called. Glancing at the packet of sugar that came with the coffee, I was very much surprised to see printed on it the words *Minimalist coffee*. That packet was the starting point for the reflections set out below.

Throughout the 1980s and into the mid-1990s the terms *minimal* and *minimalist* were used to describe the dominant features of the poetics of a whole current in contemporary architecture. Over the years, the term, which must have struck a chord somewhere, proliferated on all sides. Anything and everything could be minimalist. For certain critics, always inclined to banal and confused trivialization, minimalism could be picturesque, geometrical, technical, repetitive, structural, contextual, and who knows how many other virtually irreconcilable adjectives. [1] See J. M. Montaner, "Más allá del minimalismo" in *La modernidad quadrada: Arquitectura arte y pensamiento del Siglo XX* (Barcelona: Gustavo Gili, 1997), 181–206. So the term *minimalism*, now used not only in journalism but also in the advertising of home decoration magazines and as the name of a brand of coffee, seems to call for a certain necessary distance.

Without conducting an exhaustive study, it seems to me that the connection between minimalism in art and minimalism in architecture was forged during the last few years of The Institute for Architecture and Urban Studies (IAUS) in New York when, through a series of events and texts, the term *minimalism* was put forward as a notion of resistance. At that moment in time, the presentation at the Institute of the "Strada Novissima" by Paolo Portoghesi (1980) and a polemical lecture by Leon Krier on the continuance of Albert Speer's classicism (1981) brought the IAUS into open confrontation with a rampant commercial postmodernism then in the full processes of expansion. This was a time when Kenneth Frampton was trying to open up another front of resistance with critical regionalism, while Peter Eisenman was twisting his solipsistic researches into cubic form ever tighter, arriving at his most charged and complex proposals, House X (1980) and the Fin D'Ou T HouSe (1984).

In the final issue of the Institute's journal, *Oppositions* (24), Christian Bonnefoi published a text titled "Louis Kahn and Minimalism," originally written in 1979. This was the first time that minimalism was invoked explicitly to explain the features of a certain architecture of the moment, relating it to the homonymous currents in the visual arts. [2] Christian Bonnefoi, "Louis Kahn and Minimalism," *Oppositions* 24, 1981. Originally published in *Architecture arts plastiques* (Paris: Corda, 1979). Within these arts, and in architecture too, the feature common to all minimalist poetics is resistance – a silent negation in opposition to the charlatanism of the various artistic languages. Mies van der Rohe's *beinahe nichts* and "less is more" (an expression that, although attributed to Mies, no one is really sure he actually ever used) ring out as a call for decorum and individual dignity in the face of the demands of the market, of the media, and of the headlong consumption of forms and images. The taciturn and impenetrable features of the old architect of the Seagram Building are in stark counterpoint to the glamour of a Robert Venturi, a Michael Graves, or a Hans Hollein immersed in the mechanisms of the production of hedonistic, disposable architectures, nostalgic and trivial.

Minimalism has both conceptual and religious referents. The reduction of architecture to the elementary forms of gestalt perception orients the search for basic vocabularies in the minimalist repertoires. It is a matter of attaining to permanent codes pure experiences. It is the Barthesian pursuit of writing the degree zero and a radicalization of the semiotic discourse of the 1970s in order to convert it into an essential language, a pure poetry, transcending referents, contexts, and imitations. Minimalism opts for complete redundancy, for pure self-referentiality, and for the most elementary levels of abstract form.

This descent into the essential and the basic, which to a certain degree is nothing other than a recuperation of the more formalist avant-garde, has a fundamentally religious (and thus ethical) component. If the psychological techniques of Zen can be explicitly invoked by a Christian mystic such as Thomas Merton, it is because he is interested in the ethics of progressive renunciation, the loosening of the bonds of desire as a vital project, and the reduction of the body and its expression to a sedated atemporal stability. 3 Thomas Merton, *Mystics and Zen Masters* (New York: Farrar, Strauss and Giroux, 1967), and *Zen and the Birds of Appetite* (New York: New Directions, 1968). The Zen *aesthetic* is, of course, also an ethics and a religiosity that in the West occupies the space of austere forms of conduct, the active and progressive abandoning of the transience of empirical experience, and the implicit repudiation of the lack of value in the impermanent. Minimalism in art and architecture is an ethic of withdrawal and the renunciation of a contemporary world filled with contradiction and banality.

In the realm of cultural values, the intentionality of a given poetics is always significant if manifested in the appropriate conditions, under which it evolved and from which it sought to constitute itself as a discourse affirming certain values over others. Paradoxically, architectonic minimalism as framed by opposition and renunciation ceases to have any fundamental power when it is trivialized, confused, and reduced to mere fashion. Minimalism, the poetics of individual resistance, of a quasi-religious ethics expressed through a language of essential forms and gestures, becomes empty of significance, consumable, and ethically void as soon as it is commercialized by the market. Today, when minimalism is emblematized by the cultural products of Philip Glass, Calvin Klein, and Tadao Ando, it no longer possesses anything of either its poetic program or its aesthetic or ethical nuances. Confusion and fashion have dissipated the Oriental renunciation, while the term is manipulated toward other associations that are now likely to be neither abstract nor spiritual.

There is nothing fortuitous about this dissipation of the intentions of minimalism. The central problem of minimalist thinking is that at its root it presents itself as a path leading from the dualism of the contingent to a supposedly absolute, essential synthesis. It proposes to cut back to the barest essence every experience on the basis of the dichotomy between the world and the subject. This is the starting point from which it will be possible to arrive at the pure, sublimated sensation. The subject wants to win the battle with the world, canceling it out, fleeing from it. In the tension between real disorder and the impositions of an ideal order, minimalism will also put forward, with programmatic resolve, simple geometry and pure colors in opposition to the promiscuous complexity of our sensory experience, all as a means of filtering and purifying the channels of our sense experiences through the notions of form and dimension that proclaim the need for synthesis.

Minimalism has indeed been a poetics with a precise theoretical support, with a well-defined metaphysical, ethical, and aesthetic conception. I cannot pursue in depth here the debate about these foundations, but certain basic philosophical objections should be clearly evident. Aesthetic propositions are not neutral, and the ideological messages that these emit may not even be congruent with the purpose of achieving the goals they apparently set for themselves. Minimalism is dead as an expression of the cultural values of resistance and emancipation. Its hermetism goes hand in hand with its trivialization. Its inability to do business in a contemporary scenario of multiplicity and desire means it can subsist only as an exotic and fundamentalist position: something like an exquisitely formalist, aristocratic, and personal stylization of the individual experience of the subject.

Only dual thought can serve to establish a mode of thinking and operating that confronts pairs of concepts and situations: profound as opposed to superficial; apparent as opposed to essential; serious as opposed to trivial. These are the results of a dual conception of reality whose philosophical expression in the modern (and contemporary) age has maintained both the idealist Kantian tradition and that of the subsequent Hegelian dialectic. According to this dialectical tradition, the collision between affirmation and its consequent negation is supposed to lead to a higher synthesis that will in turn reproduce the same movements of permanent antitheses and syntheses.

In the Hegelianism of the Left, in Marxism, this meant that there was a progressive culture opposed to the more stagnant culture of bourgeois power, and that there was a clear and rational use value in contrast to an exchange value dictated by the competition of the market and, also dialectically, by the way employers exploit their workers and their productive labor. In this dialectic between use and exchange value, or between the logic of the master and the slave, Marxism sees the source and basis of the capitalist market and class struggle. It also gives birth to the hope that the market and social relations will finally, some day, be revolutionized, arriving at the final synthesis in which the losers will become winners and reason will triumph over conflict.

The culture of the supposed Left has bowed down in fear and trembling before the might of the market and the negation of the plausibility of its products. Now architecture must disappear, overwhelmed by its status as a consumer durable, or it must take flight and go into hiding rather than linger on as a private, useless, individual activity. Opposition to the market and its seductive and deceptive products, so devoid of rational utility, must lead therefore either to revolution or to that minimalist repudiation which, being practically the degree zero of the persuasive, communicative, and aesthetic action, might manage, by omission, to come close to the ideally defensible condition of independence from the market, effectively escaping its perverse domination.

In Walter Benjamin, Henri Lefebvre, Guy Debord, Fredric Jameson, and in many other prophetic voices of the anticapitalist critique, architecture must renounce any illusion to its capacity to act, to transform reality and come up with something new. The initiative of innovation has been taken on by the market and its lackeys from the standpoint of supply and the side of persuasion. Conversely, on the side of demand, the subject, the social individual of architecture, can only resist the seduction or suffer it, as one suffers a sickness, as an invasion or the arbitrary rule of power. Thus critical resistance appears once again, with no innocent social-democratic alternatives of other architectures or uncontaminated architectures – recriminations and accusations, discreditings and distancings. According to the dualist perspective, this is the position that supposedly has to be adopted in the face of consumer society and the constant manipulation of the market. There is no space for a critical architecture, as Manfredo Tafuri would have said; only a critique of the architecture produced by the capitalist market is possible. 4 Manfredo Tafuri, "Per una critica dell'ideologia architettonica," *Contropiano 1* (January–April 1969), translated as "Toward a Critique of Architectural Ideology," in *Architecture Theory since 1968*, ed. K. Michael Hays (Cambridge, Massachusetts: MIT Press, 1998). The implacable confrontation between the positive moment of the proposition of the market capitalist and the negative moment of the critique is a confrontation between irreconcilable and mutually exclusive positions. The outcome of this negative thinking, of negation as affirmation, is a schism, a critical confrontation, and, finally, silence.

Both the positive nihilism of the Zen Buddhist minimalist tradition and Nietzschean anticapitalist radical negativity stem from this dual conception and from the illusion of a lost unity that must be regained by and for the subject or society. What would happen if, instead of constructing our discourse on the basis of a dual conception of reality, we were in a position to start from the multiple as the initial text, as the field in which a thousand battles are to be fought? Thinking the multiple from the multiple has decisive philosophical, ethical, and aesthetic consequences: philosophical, in the sense that we are reflecting on a reality of which we ourselves are a part; ethical, to the extent that the event is not envisaged as pure chance (as a Mallarméan game of dice) but as the occupation of void spaces, as a colonization whose strategy and plans are generated in the action itself (principles here are not something prior, permanent, and unalterable but are reflexive constructions, the products of earlier intentions and experiences that are mobilized adroitly in the attempt not so much to achieve the good or assume the bad as simply to try to attain the best); and finally from the aesthetic standpoint, where proliferation again means that every artistic construction is inevitably superficial and is produced in the play of appearances. Here, appearance is not to be opposed to essence, or the superficial to the profound. What is, what I am, what the world is, appear only on the surface, achieving sufficient consistency so as to appear in an instant, or at the intersecting of two lines — never eternally, never permanently.

The Deleuzian fold is not defined by the geometrical form of a sheet of folded paper, or by the painstaking ironing of a shirt, as in the brilliant installation by Elizabeth Diller and Ricardo Scofidio. 5 See Elizabeth Diller and Ricardo Scofidio, "Deviants," in *Flesh: Architectural Probes: The Mutant Body of Architecture* (New York: Princeton Architectural Press, 1994). Rather, the fold is the indication of the disjunction in the continuum of what is, of the existing. Reality manifests its differences through the creases of its surface. Metaphorically we might say that every conflict, every opportunity, and even every decision produces a fold. This is the case in science, in ethics, and in aesthetics — a fold is the trace, the inscription of a principle of difference. 6 Gilles Deleuze, *The Fold: Leibniz and the Baroque*, trans. Tom Conley (Minneapolis: University of Minnesota Press, 1992). See also, Alain Badiou, *Deleuze: The Clamor of Being*, trans. Louise Burchill (Minneapolis: University of Minnesota Press, 1999). For art and architecture, the fold is the opposite of the reduction and progressive elimination typical of minimalism. The fold gives rise to accidents and irregularities, and these irregularities inscribe themselves, install themselves, on the surface. An architecture of conflict is an architecture of events that inscribes itself on the surfaces, forming folds. Such superficial inscriptions are the spur and the occasion of all proliferation, of any process of multiplication that will inscribe itself on the surface. Maps, tattoos, contour lines, eruptions, and separations are signs of the differences and multiplicities that underpin a thought that is neither dialectical nor dualist but plural and relational.

Is it really possible, then, to confuse the opacity or the transparency of minimalism with the differentiated and promiscuous ambiguity of an architecture that multiplies its surface effects as the consequence of a perception that is more relational than affirmative, more oscillating than definitive, more full of marks than of forms? When what we are dealing with is the surface, then nothing becomes interior; there is only exterior. Here, the superficial is not the opposite of the profound, because there is no such disjunction. To work the surface, to explain it, to make of it a significant operation from a sensory point of view, is to see in the surface a field of forces, a place where energies come from diverse directions, and where sources cross and collide. Let us hold on to the sensual materiality of these superficial procedures and note that this materiality is not something given but a result, a consequence, of *maîtriser*, of dominating (even if only tentatively) the diversified processes that take place on the surface, on the other side of things. To reiterate, the materiality of the surface is a production, it is something that is decided, projected, invented (all of which could be seen as a consequence of imagining a pluralist conception of reality).

Having spoken of the relational condition of the events that produce folds and leave marks, we must also bear in mind that this does not take place ideally or abstractly but in the concrete particularity of each case, on the totally defined material support on which creases, seams, and eruptions will leave their impression. Those who come from the architectural realms of pure geometrical speculation will not find it easy to install themselves in this territory. The tradition that proceeds from Eisenman through Bernard Tschumi to Greg Lynn suffers from the rigors of abstraction and the immaterial purity of its geometrical discourse. But today it is heartening to witness the heroic efforts of so many architects whose training was grounded in a geometric tradition to endow their works with corporeality, materiality, roughness, and folds, as they seek to embrace the conditions inherent in architecture, such as the tangible, the palpable, the observable. Their most recent projects represent a highly attractive endeavor to break away from abstract solipsism and arrive at the fleshiness of material folds.

Here, once again, it is not a question of setting rationality and sensibility in opposition to one another but of endeavoring to set the latter in continuity with the former. On the other hand, those who come more from a visceral grounding in chance and sensuality than from rationality and geometrical order seem to have started off with a ten-length lead in the race to make architecture a particular event specific to each case and place. In effect, the seductive power of the work of Frank Gehry, Enric Miralles, Thom Mayne, or Jacques Herzog and Pierre de Meuron lies in its sensory immediacy, even if their works do renounce rational intelligibility. As Karl Marx said, "They do not know it but they do it." Opaque or transparent, dematerialized or ecological, these architectures start out with a bonus of particularity, of concrete materiality that positions them directly on the battlefield of proliferations, events, and inscriptions. Even if their lack of discourse means they are often erratic, their material density produces a peculiar fascination.

"I am only my appearance," affirmed the 17th-century Jesuit philosopher Baltasar Gracian in El Discreto. In a time of changing virtuality, permanent multiplication, and the collision of energies, the appeal to superficial appearance as the site of aesthetic action clears the ground for other modes of doing and showing. In much the same way that guerrilla warfare differs from conventional war with a distribution of forces that is not totalitarian but more selective, so too can guerrilla architecture, fighting within the folds of surfaces, prove more productive and stimulating, provoking localized events of variable intensity rather than the old postulates of a supposedly universal rationalization. It is not a question of a general program or a strategy of total occupation. It is no more and no less than a matter of being in permanent and active readiness, on the lookout, for the clefts and creases may be the site of emancipation.

THE THING
ELIZABETH GROSZ

Philosophy should be an effort to go beyond the human state. – Henri Bergson, "An Introduction to Metaphysics."

1 Henri Bergson, *The Creative Mind: An Introduction to Metaphysics*, trans. Mabelle L. Andison (New York: Citadel Press, 1992), 229.

THINGS

I want to look at some issues that I think are preliminary to those regarding new technologies; abstract and philosophical questions more generally about the concepts of matter, life, and technology which frame and preconfigure contemporary technologies. Above all, I want to explore both the thing as condition and effect of technology, and to see if we can understand technology as the thing.

The thing goes by many names. Indeed the very label, "the thing," is only a recent incarnation of a series of terms which have an illustrious philosophical history: the object, matter, substance, the world, noumena, reality, appearance, and so on. In the period of the Enlightenment, from Descartes to Kant, the thing became that against which we measured ourselves and our limits, the mirror of what we are not. While rare, anomalous readings of the thing emerge in post-Kantian philosophy, it is primarily associated with inert materiality. Since the cold war, and through this alienation from the subject, the thing has been associated with an animated and potentially malevolent materiality; a biological materiality that is or may be the result of our unknowing (usually atomic or nuclear) intervention into nature – the revenge of the blob, of protoplasm, of irradiated existence – which imperils man. Nevertheless, through these various permutations, the thing remains identified with immanence, with what we are capable of overcoming, albeit with the input of a technological supersession of the body and its reemergence in virtual form. 2 See, for example, Hanna Fenichel Pitkin's curiously titled *The Attack of the Blob: Hannah Arendt's Concept of the Social* (Chicago: University of Chicago Press, 1998). But instead of outlining this history, paying homage to the great thinkers of the thing, and particularly to the scientists who devoted their intellectual labors to unraveling its properties and deciphering the laws regulating its relations (the thing has become the property of the intellect and of science), I am seeking an altogether different lineage, one in which the thing is not conceived as the other, the binary double of the subject, the self, embodiment, or consciousness, but as its condition and the resource for the subject's being and enduring. Instead of turning to Descartes or his hero, Newton, to understand things and the laws governing them, we must instead begin with Darwin and his understanding of the thing – the dynamism of the active world of natural selection – as that which provides the obstacle, the question and the means by which life itself grows, develops, undergoes evolution and change, becomes other than what it once was. The thing is the provocation of the nonliving, the half-living, or that which has no life, to the living, to the potential of and for life.

The thing in itself is not, as Kant suggested, noumenal – that which lies behind appearances and which can never appear as such, that which we cannot know or perceive. Rather, if we follow Darwin, the thing is the real that we both find and make. The thing has a history: it is not simply a passive inertia against which we measure our own activity. It has a "life" of its own, characteristics of its own, which we must incorporate into our activities in order to be effective, rather than simply understand, regulate, and neutralize from the outside. We need to accommodate things more than they accommodate us. Life is the growing accommodation of matter, the adaptation of the needs of life to the exigencies of matter. It is matter, the thing, that produces life; it is matter, the thing, which sustains and provides life with its biological organization and orientation; and it is matter, the thing, that requires life to overcome itself, to evolve, to become more. We find the thing in the world as our resource for making things, and in the process, for leaving our trace on things. The thing is the resource for both subjects and technology.

This Darwinian inauguration of the active thing marks the beginning of a checkered, even mongrel, philosophical history, a history that culminates in a self-consciously evolutionary orientation: the inauguration of philosophical pragmatism that meanders from Darwin, through Nietzsche, to the work of Charles Sanders Peirce, William James, Henri Bergson, and eventually, through various lines of descent, into the diverging positions of Richard Rorty, on the one hand, and Gilles Deleuze on the other. These are all, in their disparate ways, pragmatist philosophers — those who put the questions of action, practice, and movement at the center of ontology. What these disparate thinkers share in common is little else but an understanding of the *thing as question*, as provocation, incitement, or enigma. 3 As William James implies in his discussion of the thing, or object, the object is that which takes effect, directly or indirectly, on our perceptual responses and motor behavior. The object is the ongoing possibility of perception and action, the virtual trigger for responsiveness: "To attain perfect clearness in our thoughts of an object, then, we need only consider what conceivable effects of a practical kind the object may involve – what sensations we are to expect from it, and what reactions we must prepare. Our conception of these effects, whether immediate or remote, is then for us the whole of our conception of the object, so far as that conception has positive significance at all." William James, "What Pragmatism Means," in *Pragmatism and Four Essays from The Meaning of Truth* (Cleveland: Meridian Books, 1970), 43. The thing, the matter already configured, generates invention, the assessment of means and ends, and thus enables practice. The thing poses questions to us, questions about our needs and desires, questions above all of action: the thing is our provocation to action and is itself the result of our action. But more significantly, while the thing functions as fundamental provocation, as that which, in the virtuality of the past and the immediacy of the present cannot be ignored, it also functions as a *promise*, as that which, in the future, in retrospect, yields a destination or effect, another thing. The thing is the precondition of the living and the human, their means of survival, and the consequence or product of life and its practical needs. The thing is the point of intersection of space and time, the locus of the temporal narrowing and spatial localization that constitutes specificity or singularity.

SPACE AND TIME

The thing is born in time as well as in space. It inscribes a specific duration and concrete boundaries within the broad outlines of temporal succession or flow and spatial mapping. It emerges out of and as substance. It is the coming-into-existence of a prior substance or thing, in a new time, producing beneath its processes of production a new space and a coherent entity. The thing and the space it inscribes and produces are inaugurated at the same moment that movement is arrested, frozen, or dissected to reveal its momentary aspects, the moment that the thing and the space that surrounds it are differentiated conceptually or perceptually. The moment that movement must be reflected upon or analyzed, it yields objects and their states — distinct, localized, mappable, repeatable in principle; objects and states that become the object of measurement and containment. The depositing of movement, its divisibility, and its capacity to be seen statically are the mutual conditions of the thing and of space. The thing is positioned or located in space only because time is implicated, only because the thing is the dramatic slowing down of the movements, the atomic and molecular vibrations, that frame, contextualize, and merge with and as the thing.

The thing is the transmutation, the conversion of two into one: the conversion of the previous thing, plus the energy invested in the process of its production as a different thing, a unity or a one. The making of the thing, the thing in the process of its production as a thing, is that immeasurable process that the thing must belie and disavow to be a thing. Both James and Bergson agree that, in a certain sense, although the world exists independent of us — although there is a real that remains even when the human disappears — things as such do not exist in the real. The thing is a certain carving out of the real, the (artificial or arbitrary) division of the real into entities, bounded and contained systems, that in fact only exist as open systems within the real. James provides one of the classical pragmatic descriptions of the thing:

> What shall we call a *thing* anyhow? It seems quite arbitrary, for we carve out everything, just as we carve out constellations, to suit our human purposes. . . . The permanently real things for you [James's live audience] are your individual persons. To an anatomist, again, those persons are but organisms, and the real things are the organs. Not the organs, so much as their constituent cells, say the histologists; not the cells, but their molecules, say in turn, the chemists. . . . We break the flux of sensible reality into things, then, at our will.[4 Ibid., 165.]

The thing is what we make of the world rather than simply what we find in it; the thing is the way we are able to manage and regulate the world according to our needs and purposes (even if not, as James suggests above, at will or consciously. We perceive the world in terms of objects. We do not do so as a matter of will). The thing is an outlined imposition we make on specific regions of the world so that these regions become comprehensible and facilitate our purposes and projects, even while limiting and localizing them. Things are our way of dealing with a world in which we are enmeshed rather than over which we have dominion. The thing is the compromise between the world as it is in its teeming and interminable multiplicity — a flux as James calls it, a continuum in Jacques Lacan's terms, or waves of interpenetrating vibrations in Bergson's understanding — and the world as we need it to be or would like it to be — open, amenable to intention and purpose, flexible, pliable, manipulable, passive — a compromise between mind and matter, the point of their crossing one into the other. The thing is our way of dealing with the plethora of sensations, vibrations, movements, and intensities that constitute both our world and ourselves, a practical exigency, indeed perhaps only one mode, not a necessary condition, of our acting in the world. James claims that we have the choice of seeing the world as objects: however, we do not. Just as Kant imposed space and time as a priori intuitions, which we have no choice but to invoke and utilize, so too must we regard objects, distinct from other objects and from a background, as necessary, if limited, conditions under which we act in the world. Space, time, and things are conceptually connected: space and time are understood to frame and contextualize the thing; they serve as its background:

> Cosmic space and cosmic time, so far from being the intuitions that Kant said they were, are constructions as patently artificial as any that science can show. The great majority of the human race never use these notions, but live in the plural times and spaces, interpenetrant and *ducheinander*.
>
> Permanent "things" again: the "same" thing and its various "appearances" and "alterations"; the different "kinds" of things; with the "kind" used finally as a "predicate" of which the thing remains the "subject" — what a straightening of the tangle of our experience's immediate flux and sensible variety does this list of terms suggest![5 Ibid., 118–19.]

Bergson elaborates on James's position: the world as it is in its swarming complexity cannot be an object of intelligence, for it is the function of intelligence to facilitate action and practice. The possibility of action requires that objects and their relations remain as simplified as possible, as coagulated, unified, and massive as they can be so that their contours or outlines, their surfaces, most readily promote indeterminate action. We cannot but reduce this multiplicity to the order of things and states if we are to act upon and with them, and if we are to live among things and use them for our purposes. Our intellectual and perceptual faculties function most ably when dealing with solids, with states, with things, though we find ourselves at home most readily, unconsciously or intuitively, with processes and movements:

Reality is mobile. There do not exist *things* made, but only *things* in the making, not *states* that remain fixed, but only states in process of change. Rest is never anything but apparent, or rather, relative. . . . *All reality is, therefore, tendency, if we agree to call tendency a nascent change of direction.*

Our mind, which seeks solid bases of operation, has as its principal function, in the ordinary course of life, to imagine *states* and *things*. Now and then it takes quasi-instantaneous views of the undivided mobility of the real. It thus obtains *sensations* and *ideas*. By that means it substitutes fixed points which mark a direction of change and tendency. This substitution is necessary to common sense, to language, to practical life, and even . . . to positive science. *Our intelligence, when it follows its natural inclination, proceeds by solid perceptions on the one hand, and by stable conceptions on the other.* 6 Henri Bergson, op. cit., 223.

We stabilize masses, particles large and small, out of vibrations, waves, intensities, so we can act upon and within them, rendering the mobile and the multiple provisionally unified and singular, framing the real through things as objects for us. We actively produce objects in the world, and in so doing, we make the world amenable to our actions but also render ourselves vulnerable to their reactions. This active making is part of our engagement in the world, the directive force of our perceptual and motor relations within the world. Our perception carves up the world and divides it into things. These things themselves are divisible, amenable to calculation and further subdivision; they are the result of a sort of subtraction: perception, intellect, cognition, and action reduce and refine the object, highlighting and isolating that which is of interest or potential relevance to our future action. To Bergson, the object is that cutting of the world that enables me to see how it meets my needs and interests: "The objects which surround my body reflect its possible action upon them." 7 Henri Bergson, *Matter and Memory*, trans. N.M. Paul and W.S. Palmer (New York: Zone Books, 1988), 21.

The separation between a thing and its environment cannot be absolutely definite and clear-cut; there is a passage by insensible gradations from the one to the other: the close solidarity which binds all the objects of the material universe, the perpetuality of their reciprocal actions and reactions, is sufficient to prove that they have not the precise limits which we attribute to them. Our perception outlines, so to speak, the form of their nucleus; it terminates them at the point where our possible action upon them ceases, where, consequently, they cease to interest our needs. Such is the primary and the most apparent operation of the perceiving mind: it marks out divisions in the continuity of the extended, simply following the suggestions of our requirements and the needs of practical life. 8 Ibid., 209–10.

This cutting of the world, this whittling down of the plethora of the world's interpenetrating qualities, those "pervading concrete extensity, *modifications, perturbations,* changes of *tension* or of *energy* and nothing else" 9 Ibid., 201. into objects amenable to our action is fundamentally a *constructive* process: we fabricate the world of objects as an activity we undertake by living with and assimilating objects. We make objects in order to live in the world. Or, in another, Nietzschean sense, we must live in the world artistically, not as *homo sapiens* but as *homo faber:*

Let us start, then, from action, and lay down that the intellect aims, first of all, at constructing. This fabrication is exercised exclusively on inert matter, in this sense, that even if it makes use of organized material, it treats it as inert, without troubling about the life which animated it. And of inert matter itself, fabrication deals only with the solid; the rest escapes by its very fluidity. If, therefore, the tendency of the intellect is to fabricate, we may expect to find that whatever is fluid in the real will escape it in part, and whatever is life in the living will escape it altogether. *Our intelligence, as it leaves the hands of nature, has for its chief object the unorganized solid.* 10 Henri Bergson, *Creative Evolution,* trans. Arthur Mitchell (New York: Random House, 1944), 153.

We cannot help but view the world in terms of solids, as things. But we leave behind something untapped of the fluidity of the world, the movements, vibrations, transformations that occur below the threshold of perception and calculation and outside the relevance of our practical concerns. Bergson suggests that we have other access to this rich profusion of vibrations that underlies the solidity of things.[11] Indeed, Bergson's discussion of William James's pragmatism in *The Creative Mind* (see "On the Pragmatism of William James") indicates that James's notion of truth is itself an acknowledgment of the limit of knowledge rather than its pervasiveness: "The definition that James gives to truth, therefore, is an integral part of his conception of reality. If reality is not that economic and systematic universe our logic likes to imagine, if it is not sustained by a framework of intellectuality, intellectual truth is a human invention whose effect is to utilize reality rather than to enable us to penetrate it. And if reality does not form a single whole, if it is multiple and mobile, made up of cross-currents, truth which arises from contact with one of these currents – truth felt before being conceived – is more capable of seizing and storing up reality than truth merely thought" (*The Creative Mind*, 259). Bergson describes these nonintellectual, or extra-intellectual, impulses as instincts and intuitions, and while they are no more able to perceive the plethora of vibrations and processes that constitutes the real, they are able to discern the interconnections, rather than the separations between things, to develop another perspective or interest in the division and production of the real. Intuition is our nonpragmatic, noneffective, nonexpedient relation to the world, the capacity we have to live in the world in excess of our needs, and in excess of the self-presentation or immanence of materiality, to collapse ourselves, as things, back into the world. Our "artisticness," as Nietzsche puts it, our creativity, in Bergsonian terms, consists in nothing else than the continuous experimentation with the world of things to produce new things from the fluidity or flux that eludes everyday need, or use-value.

TECHNOLOGY AND THE EXPERIMENTAL

Technology, as human invention, is clearly one of the realms of "things" produced by and as the result of the provocation of things-as-the-world. While things produce and are what is produced by the activities of life, things themselves are the object and project not only of the living but also of the technological. Technology is also a metaproduction: the production of things that produce things, a second-order production. Technology is in a sense the inevitable result of the encounter between life and matter, life and things, the consequence of the capacity of the living to utilize the nonliving (and the living) *prosthetically*. Technology has existed as long as the human has; the primates' capacity for the use of found objects prefigures both the human and the technological. From the moment the human appears as such, it appears alongside of both artifacts and technologies, *poesis* and *techné*, which are the human's modes of evolutionary fitness, the compensations for its relatively bodily vulnerability. According to Bergson, it is the propensity of instinct (in animals) and intelligence (in higher primates and man) to direct themselves to things, and thus to the making of things, and it is the status and nature of the instruments to which life is directed that distinguish the instincts from intelligence, yet connect them in a developmental continuum, with intelligence functioning as an elaboration of and deviation from instinct.[12] Bergson suggests that instinct finds a kind of technology ready at hand in the body and its organs, in found objects whose use is instinctively dictated, and in the differential dispersal of instinctual capacities in social animals that are highly stratified, as many insects are. Intelligence, on the other hand, invents, and makes technology, but it also diverts natural objects into technological products through their unexpected and innovative use: "Instinct perfected is a faculty of using and even of constructing organizing instruments; intelligence perfected is the faculty of making and using unorganized instruments." The advantages and drawbacks of these two modes of activity are obvious. Instinct finds the appropriate instrument at hand: this instrument, which makes and repairs itself, which presents, like all the works of nature, an infinite complexity of detail combined with a marvelous simplicity of function, does at once, when required, what it is called upon to do, without difficulty and with a perfection that is often wonderful. In return, it retains an almost invariable structure, since a modification of it involves a modification of the species. ...The instrument constructed intelligently, on the contrary, is an imperfect instrument. It costs an effort. It is generally troublesome to handle. But, as it is made of unorganized matter, it can take any form whatsoever, serve any purpose, free the living being from every new difficulty that arises and bestow on it an unlimited number of powers. Whilst it is inferior to the natural instrument for the satisfaction of immediate wants, its advantage over it is greater, the less urgent the need. Above all, it reacts on the nature of the being that constructs it; for in calling on him to exercise a new function, it confers on him, so to speak, a richer organization, being an artificial organ by which the natural organism is extended. For every need that it satisfies, it creates a new need; and so, instead of closing, like instinct, the round of action within which the animal tends to move automatically, it lays open to activity an unlimited field into which it is driven further and further, and made more and more free" (*Creative Evolution*, 140–41).

Animals invent. They have instruments, which include their own body parts, as well as external objects. Humans produce technologies, and especially instruments, that are detached and different from their own bodies, instruments that the body must learn to accommodate, instruments that transform both the thingness of things and the body itself:

> Invention becomes complete when it is materialized in a manufactured instrument. Towards that achievement the intelligence of animals tends as towards an ideal. . . . As regards human intelligence, it has not been sufficiently noted that mechanical invention has been from the first its essential feature, that even today our social life gravitates around the manufacture and use of artificial instruments, that the inventions which strew the road of progress have also traced its direction. . . . In short, *intelligence, considered in what seems to be its original feature, is the faculty of manufacturing artificial objects, especially tools to make tools, and of indefinitely varying the manufacture.* [13] Ibid., 138–39.

Technologies involve the invention of things that make things, of second-order things. It is not that technologies mediate between the human and the natural – for that is to construe technology as somehow outside either the natural or the human (which today is precisely its misrepresented place) instead of seeing it as the indefinite extension of both the human and the natural and their point of overlap, the point of the conversion of the one into the other, the tendency of nature to culture, and the cleaving of culture to the stuff of nature. Rather, the technological is the cultural construction of the thing that controls and regulates other things, the correlate of the natural thing. Pragmatism entails a recognition that the technological is and always has been the condition of human action, as necessary for us as things themselves, the cultural correlate of the thing, which is itself the human or living correlate of the world.

As Bergson acknowledges, while it is clumsy and cumbersome relative to the instrumentality our bodies provide us, technological invention does not succumb to a preexistent function. While technology is in a sense made by us and for our purposes, it also performs a transformation on us: it increasingly facilitates not so much better action but wider possibilities of acting, more action. Technology is the great aid to action, for it facilitates, requires, and generates intelligence, which in turn radically multiplies our possibilities of action, our instrumental and practical relation with the world: "The essential function of intelligence is . . . to see the way out of a difficulty in any circumstances whatever, to find what is most suitable, what answers best the question asked. Hence it bears essentially on the relations between a given situation and the means of utilizing it." [14] Ibid., 150–51.

In an extraordinary passage, Bergson claims that the intellect transforms matter into things, which renders them as prostheses, artificial organs, and, in a surprising reversal, simultaneously humanizes or *orders* nature, appends itself as a kind of prosthesis to inorganic matter itself, to function as its rational or conceptual supplement, its conscious rendering. Matter and life become reflections, through the ordering the intellect makes of the world. Things become the measure of life's action upon them, things become "standing reserve," life itself becomes extended through things:

All the elementary forces of the intellect tend to transform matter into an instrument of action, that is, in the etymological sense of the word, into an *organ*. Life, not content with producing organisms, would fain give them as an appendage inorganic matter itself, converted into an immense organ by the industry of the living being. Such is the initial task it assigns to intelligence. That is why the intellect always behaves as if it were fascinated by the contemplation of inert matter. It is life looking outward, adopting the ways of unorganized nature in principle, in order to direct them in fact. [15 Ibid., 161.]

Inorganic matter, transformed into an immense organ, a prosthesis, is perhaps the primordial or elementary definition of architecture itself, which in a sense is the first prosthesis, the first instrumental use of intelligence to meld the world into things, through a certain primitive technicity, to fit the needs of the living. The inorganic becomes the mirror for the possible action of the living, the armature and architecture necessary for the survival and evolution of the living. Making, acting, functioning in the world, making oneself as one makes things – all these processes rely on and produce things as the correlate of the intellect, and leave behind the real out of which they were drawn and simplified.

ARCHITECTURE AND MAKING

What is left out in this process of making/reflecting is all that it is in matter, all that is outside the thing and outside technology: the "flux of the real," [16 Ibid., 250.] duration, vibration, contractions, and dilations, the multiplicity of the real, all that is not contained by the thing or by intellectual categories. The uncontained, the outside of matter, of things, of that which is not pragmatically available for use, is the object of different actions than that of intelligence and the technological. This outside, though, is not noumenal, outside all possible experience, but phenomenal, contained within it. It is simply that which is beyond the calculable, the framed or contained. It is the outside that architecture requires but cannot contain. Bergson understands this outside in a number of ways: as the real in its totality, as mobility, as movement, flux, duration, the virtual, the continuity which places the human within and as the material. What is now in question is the making of things, and that from which things are made, rather than the things made. This is what the rigorous process of intuition draws us toward, not things themselves so much as the teaming, suffuse network within which things are formed and outlined, the flux of the real.

This teaming flux of the real – "that continuity of becoming which is reality itself," [17 Bergson, *Matter and Memory*, 139.] the integration and unification of the most minute relations of matter so that they exist only by touching and interpenetrating, the flow and mutual investment of material relations into each other – must be symbolized, reduced to states, things, and numeration in order to facilitate practical action. This is not an error that we commit, a fault to be unlearned, but a condition of our continuing survival in the world. We could not function within this teeming multiplicity without some ability to skeletalize it, to diagram or simplify it. Yet this reduction and division occur only at a cost, which is the failure or inability of our scientific, representational, and linguistic systems to acknowledge the in-between of things, the plural interconnections that cannot be utilized or contained within and by things but that makes them possible. Things are solids, more and more minute in their constitution, as physics itself elaborates more and more minute fundamental particles:

Our intelligence is the prolongation of our senses. Before we speculate we must live, and life demands that we make use of matter, either with our organs, which are natural tools, or with tools, properly so-called, which are artificial organs. Long before there was a philosophy and a science, the role of intelligence was already that of manufacturing instruments and guiding the actions of our body on surrounding bodies. Science has pushed this labor of intelligence much further, but has not changed its direction. It aims above all at making us masters of matter. [18 Bergson, *The Creative Mind*, 43.] While the intellect masters that which we need for our purposes, it is fundamentally incapable of understanding what in this world, in objects and in us, is fluid, innumerable, and outside calculation. [19 Bergson writes: "We shall never explain by means of particles, whatever these may be, the simple properties of matter. . . . This is precisely the object of chemistry. It studies *bodies* rather than *matter*; and so we understand why it stops at the atom, which is still endowed with the general properties of matter. But the materiality of the atom dissolves more and more under the eyes of the physicist. We have no reason, for instance, for representing the atom to ourselves as a solid, rather than as a liquid or gaseous, nor for picturing the reciprocal action of atoms as shocks rather than in any other way. Why do we think of a solid atom, and why do we think of shocks? Because solids, being the bodies on which we clearly have the most hold, are those which interest us most in our relations with the external world, and because contact is the only means which appears to be at our disposal in order to make our body act upon other bodies. But very simple experiments show that there is never true contact between two neighboring bodies, and besides, solidity is far from being an absolutely defined state of matter. Solidity and shock borrow, then, their apparent clearness from the habits and necessities of practical life – images of this kind throw no light on the inner nature of things" (*Matter and Memory*, 199).]

The limit of the intellect is the limit of the technical and the technological. The intellect functions to dissect, divide, atomize: contemporary binarization and digitalization are simply the current versions of this tendency to the clear-cut, the unambiguous, the oppositional or binary impulses of the intellect, which are bound by the impetus to (eventual or possible) actions. The technological, especially including contemporary digital technologies, carries within it both the intellectual impulse to divide relations into solids and entities, objects or things, ones and zeros, and the living impulse to render the world practically amenable. Digitization translates, retranscribes, and circumscribes the fluidity and flux by decomposing the analog or the continuous – currents – into elements, packages, or units, represented by the binary code, and then recomposing them through addition: analysis then synthesis. But these processes of recomposition lose something in the process, although they reproduce themselves perfectly. The sweep and spontaneity of the curve, represented only through the aid of smaller and smaller grids, or the musical performance represented only through the discrete elements of the score, represent a diminution of the fullness of the real; the analog continuum is broken down and simplified in digitization. [20 On the distinction between the analog and the digital, see an early piece by Anthony Wilden, "Analog and Digital Communication: On Negation, Signification, and Meaning," in his *System and Structure: Essays on Communication and Exchange* (London: Tavistock, 1972).] What is lost in the process of digitization, in the scientific push to analysis or decomposition, is precisely the continuity, the force, that binds together the real as complexity and entwinement:

> Suppose our eyes [were] made [so] that they cannot help seeing in the work of the master [painter] a mosaic effect. Or suppose our intellect [were] so made that it cannot explain the appearance of the figure on the canvas except as a work of mosaic. We should then be able to speak simply of a collection of little squares. . . . In neither case should we have got at the real process, for there are no squares brought together. It is the picture, i.e., the simple act, projected on the canvas, which, by the mere fact of entering our perception, is <u>de</u>composed before our eyes into thousands and thousands of little squares which present, as <u>re</u>composed, a wonderful arrangement. [21 Bergson, *Creative Evolution*, 90.]

This is a prescient image of digitization: the recomposition of the whole through its decomposition into pixel-like units, the one serving as the representation of the other. The curve, the continuous stroke, the single movement of an arm, is certainly able to be decomposed into as many stops or breaks as one chooses. As Bergson again notes, "A very small element of a curve is very near being a straight line. And the smaller it is, the nearer. In the limit, it may be termed a part of the curve or a part of the straight line, as you please, for in each of its points a curve coincides with its tangent." [22 Ibid., 32.] But something of the curve or movement is lost when it is recomposed of its linear elements or grids, when the parts are added together – the simplicity and unity, the nondecomposable quality, disappears, to be replaced by immense complexity. That is, the duration of the movement disappears into its reconfiguration as measurable and reconfigurable space, object, or movement.

The thing and the body are correlates: both are artificial or conventional, pragmatic conceptions, cuttings, disconnections, that create a unity, continuity, and cohesion out of the plethora of interconnections that constitutes the world. They mirror each other: the stability of one, the thing, is the guarantee of the stability and ongoing existence or viability of the other, the body. The thing is "made" for the body, made as manipulable for the body's needs. And the body is conceived on the model of the thing, equally knowable and manipulable by another body. This chain of connections is mutually confirming. The thing is the life of the body, and the body is that which unexpectedly occurs to things. Technology is that which ensures and continually refines the ongoing negotiations between bodies and things, the deepening investment of the one, the body, in the other, the thing.

Technology is not the supersession of the thing but its ever more entrenched functioning. The thing pervades technology, which is its extension, and also extends the human into the material. The task before us is not so much to make things, or to resolve relations into things, more and more minutely framed and microscopically understood; rather, it may be to liberate matter from the constraint, the practicality, the utility of the thing, to orient technology not so much to knowing and mediating as to experience and the rich indeterminacy of duration. Instead of merely understanding the thing and the technologies it induces through intellect, perhaps we can also develop an acquaintance with things through intuition, that Bergsonian internal and intimate apprehension of the unique particularity of things, their constitutive interconnections, and the time within which things exist. [23] Although it is commonly assumed that intuition is some vague feeling or sensibility, for Bergson it is a quite precise mode that refuses or precedes symbolization and representation: "We call intuition here the sympathy by which one is transported into the interior of an object in order to coincide with what there is unique and consequently inexpressible in it" (*The Creative Mind*, 190). Instead of a mere sympathy or identification, which is nothing but a psychologization or subjectivization of knowledge, Bergson wants to link intuition to an understanding of the absolute. What the intellect provides is a relative knowledge, a knowledge of things from a distance and thus from a perspective mediated by symbols, representations, and measurements, while intuition is what can provide an absolute analysis, which means one that is both internal and simple. This absolute is not understood in terms of an eternal or unchanging essence, but is rather, from the outside, a complex interplay of multiple forces and factors that, from the inside, resolves itself into a simple unity: "Seen from within, an absolute is then a simple thing; but considered from without, that is to say relative to something else, it becomes, with relation to those signs which express it, the piece of gold for which one can never make up the change" (ibid.).

The issue is not, of course, to abandon or even necessarily to criticize technologies, architecture, or the pragmatics of the thing, but rather, with Bergson, to understand both their limits and their residues with what they so far have been incapable of dealing. Perception, intellection, the thing, and the technologies they spawn proceed along the lines of practical action, and these require a certain primacy in day-to-day life. But they leave something out: the untapped, nonpractical, nonuseful, nonhuman, or extra-human continuity that is the object of intuition, of empirical attunement without means or ends.

One of the questions ahead of us now is this: What are the conditions of digitization and binarization? Can we produce technologies of other kinds? Is technology inherently simplification and reduction of the real? What in us is being extended and prosthetically rendered in technological development? Can other vectors be extended instead? What might a technology of processes, of intuition rather than things and practice, look like?

ANYTHING BUT HUBERT DAMISCH

In her introduction to *Anybody*, the sixth volume in the series of ten Any books, Cynthia Davidson notes, with programmatic thrust, that each "*any* word" has served to introduce nonarchitectural questions into architecture. How, then, does this intention apply to the word *anything*? Were we meant at this last meeting, Anything, to deal with anything that has to do with architecture, or with anything that architecture may have something to do with, be it architectural or not? Looking at the range of issues debated in the Any volumes, one would be tempted to claim that everything seems to be relevant for the architect. Since Alberti, the curriculum traditionally assigned to the architectural apprentice has amounted to the same range and diversity as the training required today for becoming a psychoanalyst: the architect has had to be versed in all matters, in mathematics as well as in the humanities, in history and mythology, as well as in economics and technology, and be able to design, to speculate, and even, occasionally, to philosophize. Time has passed without making things any easier for the architect. My reference to psychoanalysis is just a way of pointing to what Rem Koolhaas calls the "hazardous mixture of omnipotence and impotence" that architects are currently experiencing when they deal with problems that preclude, on their part, any form of conscious mastery. As Rem used to say, "The architect is entitled to the unconscious."

Let us start by playing, in a philosophical mode, with the word that was chosen to conclude the Any series. If architecture is "anything," or if anything *deserves*, or, more neutrally (for "deserving" introduces an idea of value, or evaluation), if anything *is* to be labeled as "architecture," then what is it? Architecture as (a) thing; the "architectural" thing; the thing "architecture": as has been the case in other Any conferences, we seem to be confronted with multidisciplinary approaches that tend to pull apart the object under scrutiny. In *Anybody*, Davidson refers to the body as being dismembered in the process, and if not being destroyed, then at least dissected. "Anything" sounds different, for the invocation of the "thing" points toward some sort of unity, regardless of the prefix *any*. As Heidegger put it, in everyday life we do not encounter the "thing" as such, only the individual things that surround us. In terms of architecture, things are buildings and/or images, projects, plans, models of buildings, anything that is commonly held to belong to the realm of architecture, whatever that means. This leaves us free to extract – or to "abstract" – from such a multiplicity a general idea of this art and its whereabouts. Of course, this involves operating from a totally different perspective than Heidegger, whose questioning in *Die Frage nach dem Ding* moves toward what he calls "thingness": toward what turns *one* thing into *a* thing, the condition of its being a thing ("Was das Ding zum Ding be-dingt"). Nevertheless, we may benefit from some of his remarks. First, *das Ding*, the thing – in French, *la chose*, from the Latin *causa* – commonly refers to an affair, a process, in the judiciary sense; a matter of debate, an issue that calls for the judicial faculty, a "case" to be studied and solved. And second, beyond the world of everyday experience, things belong to different varieties of truth, or to use Ludwig Wittgenstein's term, things present themselves under various aspects. To paraphrase Heidegger, the sun is not one and the same thing for the peasant and for the astrophysicist; the body is not one and the same thing for the dancer or the biologist. In the same way, a house is not one and the same thing for the contractor who builds it and for the client who inhabits it, not to mention the diverse components, the various aspects of the "case," that the architect who designed it may have been playing with. But being a thing means precisely this: that one and the same thing allows for diverse (and eventually mutually exclusive) varieties of truth.

At first glance, it seems that one way of addressing the issue of what architecture is, or is supposed to be, would be to explore what it is not, or is not supposed to be. Such a move would lead us back to the issue of specificity, which Rosalind Krauss raises in *Anymore*. Strangely, dealing with architecture as a "thing," the "architectural" thing, the thing "architecture," not only means differentiating between what it is and what it is not (architecture being defined as "anything but . . ."), it also, at a deeper level, implies reconsidering the very relationship between what architecture is, or is supposed to be, and what it is not, or is not supposed to be. If, as far as architecture is concerned, there seems to be no room for "anything but . . . ," then this is due not just to the range of issues that are of relevance for the architect, in terms of both practice and theory. Historically speaking, the "specificity" of architecture has always been challenged by the need for the art to confront demands that were by no means "artistic." But more fundamentally, one has to recognize in architecture's present willingness to cope with what seems to be most foreign to it – time, movement, instability, shapelessness, etc. – a characteristic of its condition at the end of the millennium. Hence "undecidability," a keyword of the Any series and a concept that may seem contrary to the idea of specificity.

I would briefly like to test this keyword of *undecidability* in terms of dimensions, both temporal and spatial. From Koolhaas, we learn to stop thinking of architecture as being part of some quasi-utopian "things to come," the way the modernists did. Rather, his exploration of the Pearl River Delta or flying over Lagos is revealed as a way of measuring what is actually going on and how far things may have gotten out of control, in the traditional and most problematic sense of the word. It would be too easy, and overtly repressive, to decide that such developments are anything but architectural. Nonetheless, they certainly challenge the commonplace view of architecture as planning or building for the future. The new modes of producing architecture force us to reconsider to what extent, and no matter to what purpose or lack of purpose, the notion of the stage of the "project" is inherent to architecture, whether built or not. (Similarly, new architectural mediums, new tools, and new machineries of conception force us to reconsider the related concept of "projection.")

"Paper architecture" has been an integral aspect of architecture since the period of *perspectiva artificialis* provided a valid model and tool for both the art of building and that of painting. Geometric projection was used in both arts not only to represent objects or buildings as they appeared or were to be seen, but also to conceive or, according to the terminology of the period, to invent or to compose them. This technique was used first to construct the scene (the grid, the checkerboard) on which the invention, the composition, and eventually the *istoria* that for Alberti represented the supreme goal of painting, was to take place, including its architectural setting. It took several centuries before the painter was no longer satisfied, metaphorically speaking, with throwing ideas against the wall, as an architect might do on paper, and began, nonmetaphorically, to project paint directly onto the canvas, the only intermediary being the gap between the hand and the surface. But to what extent does the word *projection* apply to Jackson Pollock's drip paintings? The question is relevant to architecture insofar as it suggests a radical transformation of the idea of projection, rather than the concomitant notion of the project as such. It implies that the interval between the project and its realization strictly corresponds to the distance induced by the mode of projection itself; allowing or not for the possibility of a critical distance, or distanciation, specific to architecture (at least to paper architecture), if not to painting.

The problem is that the corporate museum architecture of the 1950s – the "white cube," as Brian O'Doherty labeled it – provided the perfect setting for Pollock's drip paintings as well as for Barnett Newman's antithetic attempts toward the sublime, Jean Dubuffet's explorations into the *informe*, or formless, and, later, for Frank Stella's and Ellsworth Kelly's alternate geometries. It was as if its own form of strictly repetitive, quasi-mechanical abstraction would itself accommodate different types or modes of painterly abstraction, be they based on automatism, meditation, or calculus, or a combination of all three. This may seem to be a simple play on words, but what is at stake is the very idea of abstraction, the matter being one of comparison: in what terms, at what level, from what point of view, and playing in how many dimensions are we going to tackle the issue of abstraction in architecture or in painting? In stylistic terms, what would allow for an approach both formal and historical, in which abstraction would be considered a period style characteristic of the 20th century (given that the century is now over)? Or are we to deal with abstraction in generative terms: with abstraction as a process that is independent of any particular stylistic manifestation, a process that is intrinsic and, in different ways, foundational to any form of art, be it labeled representational or nonmimetical, figurative or constructive?

Fifteen years ago, Gillian Naylor tackled this issue in a particularly instructive article, the title of which is itself problematic, because it refers to a specific moment in the history of modernism — the foundation of the De Stijl movement after World War I — and to Theo van Doesburg's attempts to demonstrate architectonic ideas that were in accordance with the 20th-century artists' "grand vision of placing man *within* the painting instead of in front of it." [1] Gillian Naylor, "De Stijl: Abstraction or Architecture?" *Studio International*, vol. 190, no. 977 (September–October 1975), 98–102. In asking "Abstraction or architecture?" Naylor questions whether the harmonies and values of painting could be translated without compromise into three-dimensional form. The question may sound odd, for we spontaneously (and in many ways mistakenly) think of architecture as an abstract art in its very essence, just as we do of music. Nonetheless, the matter was of real consequence at a decisive moment in the rise of what was to be called "abstract art." The debate among the founding members of De Stijl resulted in a schism between the artists (painters and sculptors) on the one hand, and the architects on the other. Meanwhile, van Doesburg aimed desperately at realizing in material form what he believed the other arts had already achieved in an imaginary manner. Material form was understood as three-dimensional space, whereas modern painting was supposed to have reduced corporeality to flatness, that is, to the two dimensions of the plane or the surface. What matters here is the assumption that painting, at that time considered "the most advanced form of art," had by then paved the way for modern architecture. Conversely, a useful approach to the relevance or nonrelevance, the working (or nonworking) value of the idea of abstraction today, would be to consider how and in what ways abstraction operates in the field of architecture, at a time when painting has ceased to be the trailblazing medium it was in the first decades of the 20th century.

According to Naylor, it was easy for van Doesburg to demonstrate architectonic ideas that incorporated all of the qualities De Stijl artists attributed to painting, since most of his projects remained in model form, that is, on paper. But the 20th century did not usher in the ability to conceive the relationship between architecture and painting in transformative terms. Five centuries earlier, Alberti's approach to the problem of ornament was already entirely dependent upon the passage, or shift, from the two-dimensional space in which the painter operated, in terms of *composition*, to the three-dimensional one the architect dealt with, and in which *construction* was to take place. We know of Alberti's definition of the column as "the first ornament of architecture": a definition in line with Bertold Brecht's famous proclamation that the proletarians were entitled to the column and had the right to enjoy it in their dwellings.[2] "In tota re aedificatoria primarium certe ornamentum in columnis est," Leone-Battista Alberti, *De re aedificatoria*, livre VI, ch. XIII, trans. G. Orlandi (Milan: Edizioni Il Polifilo, 1966) II, 521. But how are we to understand Alberti's statement that he borrowed this ornament from the painter, together with architraves, bases, capitals, pediments, and other such things, as found in his treatise on painting, written some twenty years before his text on architecture?[3] "Prese l'architettto, se io non erro, pure dal pittore gli architravi, le base, i capitelli, le colonne, frontispici e simili tutte altre cose," Leone-Battista Alberti, *De pictura*, ed. Cecil Grayson (Bari, 1975), 48. How could painting serve as a reservoir of forms for architecture unless we think of these forms in terms of "ornament," that is, in bi-dimensional terms?

The word *composition* does not appear in Alberti's *De re aedificatoria*, but in his *De pictura*, it corresponds to the second part of painting, immediately following *circonscriptio*: once the painter has delineated the surfaces, and a figure is "composed," in projective terms, then it is time for him to assemble or "compose" these elements on the picture plane as in a puzzle or a work of marquetry. In the same way, according to Alberti, the process of writing supposes, first, the tracing of letters and, second, their combination into words on a sheet of paper. *Compositio* thus relates to projection, that is, to the two-dimensions of the projective plane. Significantly, when in *De re aedificatoria* Alberti begins to deal with the different orders of columns, he directly refers to the same paradigm of writing. Starting with the capital, which identifies it as part of the "order" to which it belongs, the column is described as a succession of profiles that assume the shape, when projected on the plane, of different letters: an L, followed by an S, an I, etc. The column as ornament is thus reduced, projectively speaking, to a succession of elements that are assembled on the plane in the same way as letters on a page. To put it in Derridean terms, ornament, considered in its linearity and bi-dimensionality, is supposed to be supplemental to architecture in the same way that writing is supposed to be supplemental to speech. It was as *ornament* that the architect borrowed architraves, capitals, bases, columns, and pediments from the painter, thereby adding value to his art.

As far as composition is concerned, architecture, therefore, had to operate in the two dimensions of the plane. One may find it astonishing that Alberti, of all people, made no room for perspective in *De re aedificatoria*, even though he offered the first systematic exposition, in *Della pittura*, of the method by which it became possible to represent building as it appears in three-dimensional space. According to Alberti, architecture first had to settle within the two dimensions of the plane and to "compose" with painting in order to develop its own distinctive mode of representation – one that excluded any illusion of depth or distortion of volume that could alter the sense of proportion. It is remarkable that in the 20th century, under pressure from painting then considered the dominant medium, modern architecture still faced the same challenge, yet with a radical reversal of the problematics of ornament. The same Adolf Loos who held that "ornament is crime" found no better way to eliminate or repress it than to systematically apply an abstract and planar facing or coating over the built structure; whereas the members of De Stijl were still dependent, in "composing," upon the interplay between vertical and horizontal planes, conceived, according to Bart van der Leck's definition, as "the delimitation of light and space."

Given that I have been considering the thing "architecture" retrospectively, one might ask: How does this relate to the present? And if architecture is something more than a productive agency (for example, a way of thought), then how are we to deal with the models it is actually working on? Pierre Rosenstiehl, a French mathematician and friend of mine who specializes in *taxiplanie* – that is, the study of the nature and properties of different varieties of planes – makes a very simple demonstration of the kinds of problems we are confronting today at the juncture of diverse disciplines, diverse ways of thought, and one that incidentally also points toward a new alliance between mathematics and the arts. Imagine a piece of paper. It presents itself as a two-dimensional sheet. If I crumple it, I get a kind of sphere or ball that is three-dimensional in volume. But if I then uncrumple it, I have something neither bi-dimensional nor tri-dimensional, but what we might call "planar." (I could simply fold it; the result would be the same.) Planes should not be seen or considered as mere surfaces, reducible to two dimensions. Unlike surfaces, planes have a kind of *thickness* in that they allow for different modes of wrinkling, crumpling, folding and unfolding, overlapping, interweaving, and interknitting. These are all operations that architects are currently involved in, so we have to rely on their practice – even if it is strictly "virtual"– in order to learn how to think in topological terms. This calls for taking into account new and other mediums and technologies, new and other abstract procedures and machinery, that present architecture, to paraphrase Greg Lynn, with yet another possibility to both rethink and retool itself, just as it did with the advent of perspective and with projective and stereometric geometry.[4] Greg Lynn, *Animate Form* (New York: Princeton Architectural Press, 1999), 41.

Space, time, architecture: the theoreticians of the Modern Movement were at pains to add a fourth dimension to the game of architecture. Suggesting that art be considered as a way of thought no longer operates exclusively in either the two dimensions of paper architecture or the three dimensions of the built environment, but in the in-between. At the same time it dismisses the opposition between vertical and horizontal, which directly relates to the idea of undecidability that was fundamental to Any's approach to architecture. But it also induces a new approach to the notion of construction, as well as to the ideas of form and formlessness, an issue that was debated at length in the *Anybody* volume. Can we still pretend that architecture is anything but formless, a mere matter of form, when it deliberately operates between form and formlessness and confronts the *informe* at the risk of shapelessness itself being turned into a *constructum*? A move is required that would correspond to the shift from architecture as setting the stage for history to architecture being practiced as a game that can be looked at under different conditions. (Consider, for example, Peter Eisenman's use of the grid, no longer seen as a checkerboard or a support for any kind of board game but as an integral part of the game itself, whose variations, deformations, and transformations allow for its constant restructuring and redefining.)

I want to end with a question around not the idea of "anything but. . .," but the idea of "anything like. . . ." Even if we were to follow Fredric Jameson in getting rid of the concept of the aesthetic and in accepting the idea of beauty as definitively outdated (something which I doubt – it may rather be a matter of displacement, or relocation), there would still be the incentive to see the distinction between, or simply the existence of, "good" and "bad" architecture. Or to put it more radically, there will still be the urge to decide whether anything exists that could be labeled "architecture" *tout court*. Where does architecture begin? And where does it end? Where, to what extent, and within what limits, is architecture at play? The thing "architecture," or the "case" of architecture, does not only call for study but also for critical evaluation and judgment, leaving room for debate (a debate concerning aesthetics, according to Wittgenstein), and for choices that correspond to specific moves. Undecidability was, indisputably, the right keyword for the project. What will come next is another story, maybe another thing.

THING
AS OTHER
KOJIN
KARATANI

At this conference, "thing" is being discussed in terms of six themes: thing as abstraction, thing as object, thing as material, thing as feeling, thing as idea, and thing as obsession. But among these six constructs, one thing is missing: thing as other. I have been assigned to thing as idea — something about which I have no idea what to say. But since I can talk here about anything, I would like to talk instead about thing as other.

What do I mean by thing as other? In many ways, it relates to what Kant called the "thing-in-itself." In the Kantian view, what we call an object is actually a phenomenon rather than a thing. Because the object is already constituted by subjective forms and categories, we cannot know it in itself. However, the thing-in-itself is not mystical (in this sense, it is not like what Jacques Lacan called the real). Rather, it is a plain and secular matter. When Kant developed this concept, he in effect was saying that things exist regardless of our subjectivity, yet we cannot fully grasp them. But in discussing this concept, he specifically addresses a particular thing: others. We recognize the other person through the body, gestures, and language. These, though, are nothing more than phenomena, not the thing-in-itself, which is the subjectivity or freedom of others. (Incidentally, freedom in this case does not mean a free society, but rather the autonomy of the will; being free from causality.) Others remain opaque to us. This is the otherness of others. What Kant calls thing-in-itself then is precisely such a free subject. He regards it, therefore, not as a theoretical construct but as a practical and moral issue.

These ideas can be related to Bertrand Russell's question of how we know the pain of others. Russell imagined that we perceive other people's pain through external appearance, gesture, and language. As a result, he fell into a kind of skepticism. Wittgenstein subsequently criticized this view with the observation that when someone gets burned, we rush to treat that person. In other words, the pain of others is first and foremost a moral and practical question. The theoretical question of whether or not we can actually know the pain of others is then irrelevant. Wittgenstein, in this way, implicitly inherited a Kantian problematic. Just like Kant, he was talking about the other as thing-in-itself.

In his first Critique, Kant regards the thing-in-itself as a thing or natural object, whereas in the second, it appears as freedom or personhood. Scholars of Kant have long tried in vain to unify this apparent discrepancy. Yet there is really no enigma here. Karl Popper criticizes Kant's subjectivity as monological and lacking other subjects, claiming that the scientific proposition should be rendered in the refutable form and that it is provisionally true so long as it is not refuted by others. Kant would not have objected to this argument. In fact, Kant does not preclude others from scientific judgment. He argues that universal natural law is not obtained from exhaustive examinations but by induction from limited cases or singular propositions — so a hypothesis can only be true when it is refutable rather than refuted. Things as objects never refute; it is others who refute with their data about things. This is to suggest that for a natural law to be true, it requires not only the agreement of others but also the agreement of the unpredictable others of the future. Thus when Kant wrote about thing-in-itself, he was, in fact, implying others. In other words, others are a thing-in-itself, so there is no contradiction, then, between the first and second Critiques.

My own criteria for otherness would be with those who do not share our language. We might, in this way, take foreigners and psychotics as examples of others. A more extreme example of others would be the dead and the unborn. While it is not entirely impossible to come to some kind of understanding with others who are alive, no matter how different their culture or how insane they may be, it is, however, impossible to do so with the dead and the unborn.

Let us apply this to environmental problems. If the capitalist market economy continues as it is, we will no doubt face an environmental crisis on a global scale. In such a situation, it will not be easy for advanced countries to reach an agreement on how to handle the situation. However, it will be even more difficult for advanced countries to forge an agreement with third world countries. Why should the people of the third world sacrifice themselves and cooperate with the people of advanced countries, whose quality of life caused the crisis, and moreover, forced them to pay for it? In spite of this difficulty, it is still not impossible to negotiate with such "others." Yet we cannot negotiate with the unborn, who will surely be the ultimate victims of environmental contamination. According to Kant's moral principle, the ultimate message of moral law lies in the imperative: "So act that you use humanity, whether in your own person or in the person of any other, always at the same time as an end, never merely as a means." If we sacrifice the others of the future in order to maintain our living standards, then we are treating them merely as means to our own ends. In Kantian thought, such an attitude is in no way ethical. In contrast, what Jürgen Habermas calls communicative reason or public consensus is confined to the West, or at best to more advanced countries. There is no place here for thing-in-itself as the other.

Thus, as a theoretical object, the thing-in-itself is unknowable. Yet certain philosophers argue that we can reach this thing-in-itself through aesthetics. For instance, Henri Bergson believed that one could transcend linguistic articulation and intuit the thing-in-itself as duration. For him, things are images. Heidegger offers another example, distinguishing between thing and object, in effect as another version of the Kantian distinction between thing-in-itself and phenomenon. But for Heidegger, there was no ethical moment in the thing-in-itself — rather, it disclosed itself in poetry or art. Arguing this point, he offers the example of a painting of a shoe, stating that the painting enables us to see the shoe in itself by bracketing our interest in its practical usage. But does this really take us to the thing-in-itself? There is really nothing new about this idea of bracketing — it was already presented by Kant in his third Critique, seeing art as a way of looking at things by bracketing our interests. But does the thing-in-itself emerge through the bracketing of such divergent interests as use and exchange value? It never does. Instead, what we find are phenomena; for example, the discovery of beauty or the sublime is a result of subjective imaginative activity. Therefore, it would be wrong to claim that art reveals the thing-in-itself.

What Bergson and Heidegger demand is for us to take an aesthetic stance toward the actual world. Ceding to this demand, over the last ten years there has been a tendency to go back from Jacques Derrida to Heidegger, and from Gilles Deleuze to Bergson. I have witnessed this over the course of the Any conferences. Perhaps one reason for it is that Derrida and Deleuze took a more clearly Marxist position after the collapse of the Soviet Union. Those who instead regress to Bergson or Heidegger are doomed from the outset. (It should be noted that when these ideas were realized in politics, the inevitable result was fascism — that is, the aesthetic sublimation of actual class conflicts.)

In art, to be sure, we view things by bracketing our interests. However, bracketing is not confined only to art. When we confront the world, we have at least three kinds of simultaneous judgment: cognitive judgment of truth or falsity; moral judgment of good or bad; and aesthetic judgment of pleasure or displeasure. In actuality, these judgments are interwoven and difficult to distinguish; aesthetic judgments, for example, bracket questions of both true and false and good and bad. In the same way, scientists observe things by bracketing moral and aesthetic judgments: only by this act can the objects of cognition come into existence. This, however, is not limited to the natural sciences. For example, political science since Machiavelli has focused on the effect of political action by bracketing it with moral aspects. Moreover, we can also say that works of fine art become economic objects when they are considered only in terms of price. The scientific, aesthetic, political, and economic stances all come about through bracketing. As a result, a thing appears in various aspects. Nonetheless, it is not a thing-in-itself but a phenomenon. This being the case, where does the thing-in-itself emerge? It emerges only in the ethical stance of bracketing all other dimensions because this is to see the other as a free subject.

It does not necessarily follow, however, that an ethical stance assumes priority over all other criteria. What counts here is not simply bracketing but also un-bracketing. For instance, through a scientific lens, others are so-called objects. In fact, during surgery physicians bracket their patient's personhood, as well as their own aesthetic or sexual interests. To do this requires professional training. Needless to say, after surgery they should remove the brackets. As another example, when we see films whose heroes are Mafia or Yakuza gangsters, it is ridiculous to criticize them for their immorality, just as it is absurd to object to science-fiction films on the basis that they are not scientific enough. Rather, we bracket other interests at the movie theater. Once you leave the theater, you have to un-bracket. The same is also true of the moral stance. If you adhere to moral principles in assessing the cinematic work at the movie theater, it does not make you ethical, just foolish. Therefore, we need to learn both bracketing and un-bracketing at the same time.

The same is true of architecture. Architecture, like film, exists on a number of different levels. From a historical viewpoint, architecture first and foremost aims to supply habitable places to shelter human beings from the natural environment. Second, architecture builds monuments to display religious and political power. Since the ancients, architecture has existed between these two extreme poles. With modernity, however, came the vision of architecture as art. This view could only become possible by bracketing other interests — namely, the practical and the political. This is not to criticize the discipline but to recognize that architecture has its original dimension and its own language. However, we should be able to undo this bracketing at any time. The history of architecture has essentially centered itself around religious and political monuments, but these aspects are bracketed in its articulation as the history of pure form. In this context, architecture can be the quotation of past texts or be deconstructive or virtual. However, this perspective overlooks two points. One is that architecture should supply habitable places to shelter human beings from the natural environment. The second is that in reality most architecture is dominated by practical, economic, and political interests. Plainly speaking, architecture is part of the capitalist construction industry. Architects cannot transcend this basic condition, no matter how artistic they may be.

In regard to these two points, I remember two incidents that took place at previous Any conferences. First was the Anywise conference held in Seoul after the major earthquake in Kobe, Japan. Aside from Arata Isozaki and myself, none of the participants mentioned this earthquake. I thought that the destruction that it caused raised issues far more fundamental to architecture than simply ideas of deconstruction; namely, that architecture as construction exists first and foremost as protection from the natural environment. Could we then say that the earthquake disclosed a thing-in-itself? Did the earthquake disclose the power of nature, or what Akira Asada called the *Mononoke*, or the Lacanian real? In this instance, the answer is an unequivocal no. In this instance, the thing-in-itself meant the death of 6,000 people. The dead never speak. Of course, most of the architects at the conference were not directly involved in the urban development of Kobe, and they do not bear any personal responsibility for the disaster. But for me, architects who fail to take this problem to heart will never have any relevance.

Second, I remember that at the Anyplace conference in Montreal there was a discussion on "architecture and politics." I left with the impression that what was being termed "politics" was too abstract, tending toward the linguistic games that architecture plays. The conference also took place immediately after the arrest of an executive at the Shimizu-Kensetsu Construction Company, the principal sponsor of the Anyone Corporation. However, I was the only one to touch upon this issue. In Japan, the construction industry is the very foundation of conservative politics, and it continues to maintain close, and somewhat byzantine, connections to the Yakuza. Even if they are only indirectly tied to this web of associations, Japanese architects, including Isozaki, cannot claim to be innocent bystanders. Japan, of course, is not the lone exception. As David Harvey reminds us in his recent book, *Spaces of Hope*, in the midst of so-called globalization, we must look at how the construction industries of advanced countries behave in the third world, and how their presence there is supporting and influencing the relations of production and power structures. The Any conferences, circling the world, have been too indifferent to these issues.

These conferences have long been considered a place of interaction between architects and philosophers. However, I do not really see myself as a philosopher, and I have no interest in discussing architecture theoretically. With a couple of exceptions, I have attended all of the Any meetings over the past ten years, but who then have I been at these conferences? In effect, I have been a thing-in-itself as other. That is to say, I have not shared the same language with most of the other participants, nor did I try to do so. I refused. As a consequence, I was rejected. At Any, I have been a thing-in-itself but not a phenomenon. Indeed, many people were even unaware of my presence. Perhaps the organizers hoped that I would fulfill just such a function. But for me, this is not a pleasant position to be in. And so, in many ways, it comes as a relief to me that this role is finally over.

Anyone, the first Any conference, was held in 1991, after the collapse of the Soviet Union. Also crumbling at this time were the formerly radical resonances contained in postmodernism. There was no longer any validity in the postmodernist stance of ironically praising the deconstructive force of capitalism. This has become increasingly clear over the past ten years. During this time, or more precisely, in the last few years, my own position has fundamentally changed. I have come to hold the view that we should take a positive stance, that we should positively counteract the movement of capital and states. Thanks to Any, I was able to publish *Architecture as Metaphor*. However, this book was the work of the 1970s and '80s, and does not reflect my thinking today. These more recent thoughts will manifest themselves in English with the publication of a new book, *Transcritique – Kant and Marx*. From its title, it is clearly not a book about architecture, but in a broad sense I believe that it suggests the future course that architecture should take. This book is also the product of my interactions with Any participants over the last decade, and for that I am thankful.

MAKING THE CUT

PETER EISENMAN

After three days of this conference, I feel like I have been placed in an isolation booth, screaming at its glass walls, wanting to interact but unable to interrupt the sequence of performing minstrels that have wandered through in front of me. When the Any conferences began ten years ago in Los Angeles, two separate sessions ran simultaneously to satisfy the need of those people who wanted to speak. Upon reflection, this format did not seem to work, so for the second meeting the speakers were sequestered in a small village in southern Japan while the audience remained in Tokyo, witness to the meeting only through modern telecommunications. This had the advantage of generating less performance and more content. Again, in Montreal, the participants were sometimes cloistered together while an audience watched from an auditorium close by. This had the great advantage of allowing debate and a confrontation of ideas. In this sense, I was pleased that Tony Vidler moved away from the accepted script of presenting his own work, to critique the work of somebody here. I only wish there had been a reply to Vidler and an exchange of ideas.

Be that as it may, I want to take up a point that Jeff Kipnis made in his presentation concerning the question of architectural expertise. Expertise might be one way of defining why certain people were invited to be here. Expertise is perhaps why there is no cross-disciplinary debate of the kind that Kojin Karatani talked about. It is difficult for a philosopher to talk about architecture (as I discovered when working with Jacques Derrida), and it is certainly difficult for an architect to philosophize or psychologize. If I have learned anything from these conferences over the last ten years, it is that whatever the definition of expertise, an expert can really only speak using that expertise with experts in their own field – in other words, that in most cases architects ought to stick to architecture. Even though architects can host interdisciplinary debates, it might be more productive in the future to host these kinds of discussions among ourselves, because it seems we have lost the critical facility to discuss the real issues that confront us as architects. For example, when Greg Lynn presented his work and said, "There are any number of combinations that are possible based on our design principles," I wanted to ask, "Greg, what are your design principles? Are they beaux-arts principles? Are they principles of baroque composition? Are they modernist composition? What are the principles that you spoke of?" We never heard a word about any of this.

Similarly, Rem Koolhaas showed us a diagram of his Prada research but he never showed us one of the buildings. What does the research have to do with the buildings? What did his research on libraries have to do with the form of his libraries in Paris or Seattle? Although their forms may be stunning, they deal with a critique of architecture, not with a critique of libraries. Equally, Greg Lynn's blob houses are a critique of architecture and not a critique of the suburban house. There is nothing about the form of a blob that is inconsistent with the nuclear family or with the kinds of familial hierarchies that exist today. Many issues are raised by a project called a house, which Lynn's work must address, not least of which is the instrumentality proposed by the forms of his houses. It would seem that the new instrumentalities of the computer might cause such a change to occur. The instrumentality of a pencil, pen, and piece of paper was more or less neutral, but a computer program has its own ideology and style. These programs interfere with architecture in a way that was never seen in the past. In his use of animation programs for architecture, Lynn is demonstrating an architectural expertise, but how are we to assess this expertise? Maybe the question is not, then, about Kipnis's invocation of the term *expertise*, but whether expertise is the critical context that allows us to understand the instrumentalities of the computer.

Yesterday, Rafael Moneo said that he felt like an exile at this conference. Perhaps this is because architects are distancing themselves from architecture and from investigations into architecture. So, I was not as pleased as some at this Any conference with the state of the architectural discourse. Unlike Rem, I do not think it is a question of being for or against the city; I live in the city. But I am an architect, and I am for architecture. What architecture does and has always done is not solve political, social, economic, and urban problems; rather, it problematizes them. It opens up the city to its own repressive qualities. This has nothing to do with the accepted meanings of professional or disciplinary expertise.

I want to argue that what brings everyone here together is not a notion of architectural expertise. For example, Robert Stern and James Polshek have architectural expertise, but they are not here. Norman Foster also has expertise, but he would not be interested in being here. The German historian Tilmann Buddensieg has said that Foster's Reichstag dome is one of the most powerful gestures proposed in architecture, but it is so powerful and, as it were, so perfect in its power, that it draws energy from its context inward, leaving a conceptual void; that is, the dome, in a sense, is too easy, too unproblematic. So too are Polshek's Rose Planetarium at the Museum of Natural History and Stern's apartment buildings. What characterizes the architects who have attended the Any conferences over the years is that their work problematizes the contexts in which it is presented.

What makes a problematic architecture, and how does one define it? Rosalind Krauss gave one possible answer when she said, "In order to preserve the singularity of objects we must cut them off from their previous modes of legitimation." When one substitutes *architectural objects* for the word *objects* in this definition, the idea of cutting does not mean that architecture will not function, will not have a structure or a meaning or an image. It means that the work will propose these conditions in a way that causes them to be brought into question. Architecture in the past has been legitimated by functional diagrams, by programs, by beauty, by meaning, by expression. These conditions are not going to disappear. Equally, it should not be assumed that these are given as legitimating factors. One indicator of an architectural problematic would be for it to challenge the very essence of its own conditions. For example, while it *is* valid to design Prada stores and do research on Lagos at the same time, to operate in the critical context that I am proposing, these projects must in essence question their existing modes of legitimation.

The issue, therefore, is not only one of cutting off from previous modes of legitimation but also how, in practice, this operates critically. How does one choose between one cutting and another? In other words, how does one allocate value in such a context? Giving lie to the value of the new, the original, and the zeitgeist as a historical agent, poststructuralism has suggested that nothing is new; it is always a recombination of the old. If in fact we are always products of some zeitgeist or another, then such a spirit is neither progressive nor regressive – it has no value per se. What is interesting about any form of zeitgeist is that it tends to legitimate that which is normal to it. Thus, most architectural production tends to resemble what are thought to be current styles.

Objects conform rather than offer difference. In this way, any idea of cutting would also mean to disconnect not only from the new and the original but also from what is thought to be normal.

What is normal in architecture is made up of what could be called its sedimented history. This history — because its forms always shelter, contain, and structure in one way or another — will always look like architecture. But is it this history that gives architectural production its value? Certainly the classicists and postmodernists would say yes. But there must be some alternative between history on the one hand, and the new on the other, both of which are legitimating conditions. I want to propose, briefly, one possible alternative, one that lies in the interiority of architecture, perhaps side-by-side with a sedimented history. Unlike this history, it has little value other than its existence. It is neither a static condition of rules and essences as put forward in the early architectural treatises, nor is it a propelling, progressive, and thus historicist force open to constant change in each new moment in time. Rather, it is something else — an autonomy. Thus the neutrality of architecture's interiority can be said to be contravened not, as Karatani was saying, by the autonomy of will, but by its necessary will to autonomy.

Architecture's autonomy is different from the autonomy of other discourses in that the architectural sign poses different conditions than other sign conventions. In this sense, architecture's sign is already singular because it is not an explicit sign system — its form and meaning are not conventional. But also, a column, or a window, is so complicit with its function that it cannot be recognized as a sign. A column is not only a column; it is the sign of holding something up. The average person does not know whether he is looking at a sign of structure or structure itself. But all columns are also either a form of abstraction or figuration. To be of some critical value these need to be articulated as processes of abstraction as opposed to mere abstraction, or processes of signing as opposed to mere columns. It is this need to make manifest these processes that can be called the will to autonomy. Autonomy can become active by opening it to an expression of itself. When autonomy becomes active, its processes become differentiated from the new, the original, and from personal expression.

In his observations on the nature and history of architecture in 1878, Conrad Fiedler suggested that "In certain fields of intellectual life, the conditions occasionally prevail in which one searches in vain for points of departure, for the possibility of further development, in which the new and the promising can only come from a deliberate opposition to that which already exists." The idea of autonomy in architecture may of necessity be oppositional, precisely because architecture's singularity must question its social functions in a way that no other discourse does. This is not to say that architecture, in its response to a greater social community, does not provide function, shelter, and all of the conditions that define the interiority of architecture. Rather, it is architecture's necessary opposition to — and maintenance of — these supposedly legitimating conditions that defines one aspect of its autonomy.

DISCUSSION 6

SANFORD KWINTER I believe I'm too old to be still doing this, but let's get it started. Peter, what about us? Personally, I feel compelled to applaud the force and clarity of your arguments, which are nothing less than the concluding arguments of ten years of sustained reflection on the problems and the state of architecture – to use the terms framed by the Any agenda. I especially applaud your attempts to remind us that architecture, at its loftiest, can and must aspire to be a form of thought. Yet I also feel that I need to remind everyone in the audience here today that what we have just heard was an unapologetic expression of stunning parochialism. For me, the problem of architecture (if architecture really does risk and dare what you say it ought to) is that it must confront and engage the particular historical problems that press upon it today. To seek to isolate architecture, to try and mobilize a kind of **rappel à l'ordre** so that the problems formulated within architectural practice cite and target problems that do not continue beyond the comfortable academic borders of an architecture defined four or five hundred years ago, seems to condemn us to a kind of aphasia.

PETER EISENMAN I said that we must cut ourselves off from previous modes of legitimation, i.e., parochialism. In order to survive, architecture must disengage itself from modes of legitimation that formerly guaranteed its existence.

JEFFREY KIPNIS But your critique of Greg Lynn and the others was that they cut themselves off from previous modes of legitimation.

EISENMAN I was supporting Greg.

KIPNIS No, you were arguing that . . .

EISENMAN I was saying that Greg has to tell us what the design principles are. He merely said, "my design principles." I wanted to hear what the design principles were that cut them off from previous modes of legitimation.

[**KIPNIS** and **KWINTER** approach the microphone together]

EISENMAN Go ahead, guys! Come on!

KIPNIS What do you call it when you go up to speak after someone has died and you say something good about them?

KWINTER It's an elegy. For you, Peter. A eulogy.

KIPNIS I want to ask a question that I think connects to everybody, and you can't do that very often. It starts with evolution and goes first to Kojin Karatani and then on to Tony Vidler before getting right into Peter's argument that theory has essentially ended the possibility of discussing anything new. Now, Tony actually laid out an argument for something new; Elizabeth Grosz also introduced the idea of evolution. I thought about evolution and how it used to be about new things. There was, for example, no Earth and then there was Earth. That was fairly new. There was no life on Earth and then there was life on Earth. Again, a new thing. And I'll tell you, Kojin Karatani, I'll tell you something new for me. I saw evolution occur. I sat with you on the very first Any panel in 1991. I couldn't understand a word you said, and for nine years I've never been able to understand a word you have said. But today you have finally

evolved, whether for better or worse, into somebody who speaks perfectly good English. That's new. So I would like to hear each of you reflect a little on what Peter said – that there's no possibility of the new; there's only the reinvention and recombination of the old.

ELIZABETH GROSZ I strongly agree with this idea of Peter's. It's a mistake for us to misunderstand the radical newness of every moment. Part of why we need notions like "history" and notions like "things" is to allow us to recognize the outline of what we already know and then to give it a context for that which we can't yet know. So I feel incredibly optimistic both about the state of architecture and about the state of philosophy. Maybe I'm the only person in the room who feels this way, because we are continually producing the new. Our problem is by what means can we recognize the new, given that recognition itself is always about conforming to patterns that we already know. It's that which slips out of the patterns we already know that is the new.

ANTHONY VIDLER It's a little like Greg's wasp and the orchid – the wasp thinks it knows what it's looking at and goes for it, but then finds it was wrong and goes for something else that it thinks it knows. What I'm interested in with Greg and other digital-morph architects is, when are they going to produce an architecture that, when I look at, I think I know what I'm looking at, and go for it?

RALPH LERNER Tony, you'll have to buy one of Greg's houses.

IGNASI DE SOLÀ-MORALES This discussion should be especially fruitful because finally it has turned to the issue of autonomy, presented by Peter as something that is continually overlooked. But for me there is also another issue. As Tony framed it, at what point are certain methods rich enough to arrive at a certain level of achievement? Because it seems to me that the experiences presented here today are more approaches to a certain legitimation — but it's a legitimation in which the object is absent. In some sense, it is a very deductive process of establishing general principles and trying to arrive at the so-called architectural facts. But this development is something that I don't see as working very well. Rather, I'm interested in architecture as shock, architecture as something that astonishes. I don't like to think about objects that for the moment don't exist.

KOJIN KARATANI I would like to thank Jeff Kipnis for offering me up as evidence of evolution. But you know, Jeff, you have changed too — you have lost weight compared to ten years ago. Anyway, I was thinking of something else while listening to Peter talking about the legitimation of architecture and architects. I don't have complete sympathy for architects or the situations they find themselves in because I'm not an architect and not a critic of architecture; rather, I have worked as a literary critic. To be a literary critic in Japan, however, is quite different from how you would function in America. You have to deal with everything from literature to politics to the fluctuating realities of the present day. In this country it's very easy to be a critic, you just study Shakespeare. Faced with the multitude of things you are expected to write about, last year I finally gave up being a literary critic in Japan, and came to America. So I have been doing the same things in literature as

Peter was saying about architecture — cutting off the legitimation. But the thing is, literature is dead in Japan. I know that. I have been working with literature for nearly thirty years, realizing all along that it was dead. Finally I stopped, fed up with the effort and fed up with my own self, and so I understand what Peter was talking about. This break with legitimation can apply to any field — every field has its own singularity.

HUBERT DAMISCH I agree with Peter about the necessity of cutting off from old modes of legitimation, but does this mean that we have to look for new modes of legitimation? I think that instead we should get rid of the very idea of legitimation. Cutting off from established modes of legitimation would then necessitate the eradication of legitimation itself. I'm not an architect, but considering this issue in terms of the discipline, I see it as a problem of whether there is any room left for architecture. And if there is room, how do we define it? These, I feel, are exactly the ideas that Rem is dealing with. (The fact that he can be so contradictory is part of the approach, because you cannot be anything but contradictory when dealing with these issues.) I also like Peter's way of dealing with this issue — that architecture doesn't have to solve uncertainties but simply problematize them; that is, to raise the real issues and then try to frame them, to formulate them in the most clear and radical way possible.

SASKIA SASSEN Peter, I think I agree with you, but I would like to ask a few questions that perhaps destabilize the architecture that you spoke about. A number of the Any discussions we have had over the years might have been more compelling and engaging

(even for nonarchitects like myself) if we had heard more architects speak the voice of their expertise. Because as Karatani just said, we who are experts in something appreciate expertise even when it's located in another field. But through Any, I have come to feel that architecture and architectural expertise are ever-changing events. When I think of the work of Greg, of Ben van Berkel and Caroline Bos, of Hani Rashid, and of Rem, I see it as blurring the edges of the discipline. So my question has two elements. First, even if we accept the category "architecture," then we have to understand that it has enormous diversity. Second, if there is such ambiguity in what architecture is, then it seems to me that the real stuff is happening at some ambiguous edge, some sort of frontier zone where the old rules of engagement no longer hold. This then poses a problem. How do you reach a disciplined engagement when there are no rules of engagement?

EISENMAN Saskia, what I was saying about the edge is that the architects who have participated in Any have never built buildings in this city — Bernard Tschumi is the one exception, but I'm talking about major works. I don't believe that in the 50 years since the Guggenheim Museum and Mies's Seagram Building there have been what I would call "critical" buildings built in this city. Where does all of this expertise and all of this edginess go? Why is there no more architecture? And we all know what architecture means. It's the buildings out there. How come there have been no more than two critical buildings in this city over the last 50 years? That's the question I am raising.

SASSEN You're right, but at the same time we need to make the distinction between what gets built and something that is an exploration, a project that cannot be confined to built form.

EISENMAN It's got to trickle down some time.

SASSEN But I think it does. All of you are building somewhere – okay, not in New York, but New York has imploded a bit anyway. I wouldn't overvalue New York. Too much of what happens in New York loops through two things: celebrity and the market. Maybe we should forget about being so obsessed with New York (I move between Chicago and London so you have to let me bitch a little).

EISENMAN I've been totally obsessed with this city and now you're telling me not to be.

SASSEN No, all I'm saying is that your response that nothing gets built here is not valid to the project that Any represents, which is an exploration of a different kind of architecture; a conceptual architecture, which eventually may have its own effects and affects.

EISENMAN I don't agree. I think of Any as something not formed in a vacuum, and that it may have had effects in the intellectual community, in the student community, in the academic community, but it's had very little effect in the cities that I occupy. I would love to see all of the architects of Any build in this city. In each of the cities that Any has taken place in, except for New York, there has been a representative of the city government, or a manifestation of the city's concern at the meeting. The City of New York couldn't care less about this meeting. Oh, I'm sorry, I just saw a representative of the City of New York coming to the microphone.

HERBERT MUSCHAMP [architecture critic for the **New York Times**] This is the first Any conference that I've attended, and my perception of it has changed a lot over the course of the past two days. Partly because of the fact that it's always been out of town and partly because I couldn't get in, I felt that Any was rather introverted in its ambitions, and that therefore its practical applications were going to be limited. The thing that Any has generated, though, is some kind of vocabulary that could be absorbed by the public and used to gain some kind of understanding of what has been going on here in New York. Peter, you and I had a discussion about this a couple of nights ago, and I think we agreed that postmodernism was a catastrophe for the city and for architecture in general. But the postmodernists did put a few words out there that the public could hold on to; words like **tradition**, **preservation**, and **heritage**. I've noticed that many of the speakers here at Any use Freudian and Marxian constructs – terms that my readers seem to be familiar with but that are obviously not part of the conventional architectural vocabulary. So I think there is a need for some kind of theory, some kind of mediating language or virus, that can allow the public to expect more and to demand more from its environment.

AUDIENCE I'm surprised at the lack of complete radicality here today. I left the U.S. four years ago, in which time so much has changed. But the discussions we are having today are almost as dead as they were four years ago – not necessarily at this particular conference but certainly in academia. I agree with Peter that there is little discussion of how things work within the profession (if one could call it a

profession), and that by ignoring these things, we also ignore the things that we deal with everyday; we never talk about them. I feel that the political and the social have been completely removed from the discussion about architecture in favor of the purely formal. Greg Lynn is interesting if you like those kinds of forms; but then Hani Rashid is using them as Web site navigation. What the hell is that? So I would like to get back to Peter's question. Why is it that so many smart, creative people are not producing critical work within their own domain, and why is there this repetitive escapism to other domains to try to justify what we do?

GROSZ What do you mean by radical?

AUDIENCE That when you look at something you understand that it questions what's there, that it takes pieces of the context and reassembles them so that you don't look at it in the same way.

GROSZ But isn't that partly a problem of how you look at it rather than how it's articulated?

AUDIENCE Me personally, as an individual?

GROSZ Not you as an individual but all of us as individuals. In a way, this is partly a repetition of the debate of the author function and the reader, and the question is, why aren't there any dramatic new takes? Well there are. You just have to have the right readers.

KIPNIS Let me offer an analogy to help you see a certain radicality that you may have missed. It is a mistake to think that Hani and Greg have anything to do with each other, just because their forms happen to look alike. Greg is saying something like this: singularity (the ambition that was discussed here) is not an adequate replacement for originality. And the expressive gesture, which at one time was the way architecture established singularity and resisted prototypicality, can in fact be made a prototype and can inhabit professional practices in exactly the same way as political arguments for modular housing in Levittown and other places were made. So 1,054 selectable, designable, prototypical houses that every practice can now produce and manufacture is a radical argument here. It's an argument about politics and an argument about practice. It's not about the voluptuous character of the form — that's an artifact that has nothing to do with the argument.

EISENMAN Jeff, how do we know they're radical?

KIPNIS Because it's a radical practice.

AUDIENCE No, I don't think so.

KIPNIS You may not think so, but it is.

AUDIENCE No, no, no. If the pretense was prefabricated modern housing, okay, but that's not what he's looking at. It is a **formal** preoccupation.

KIPNIS When you go to Levittown or any similar kind of development, you get a catalogue with a prototype house and 1,054 variations on it that can be built at the exact same cost. This is exactly what Greg has produced. He couldn't care less that it happens to look like a Cape Cod.

AUDIENCE [To Greg Lynn] Do you not care what it looks like?

EISENMAN Oh, he does care.

KIPNIS The radical point is not that it looks weird, but that it can be made into a prototype.

AUDIENCE I don't believe that for a second. That's not what he's doing.

GREG LYNN It's actually very important that it looks weird. And it's also very important that it inhabits all of the production and cultural logic of the modern house. But the thing that I think you're taking for granted is that when you see modern architecture, you don't think it looks like anything. You think it's the result of manufacturing processes. For me, the most interesting thing about design today is that the automobile industry is doing it much more efficiently than architecture; it is addressing these questions of appearance in a nonnostalgic and radically new way compared to modern architectural processes.

AUDIENCE It works only with the car, but . . .

LYNN But these studies work as housing.

KIPNIS Let's go back to the single most interesting slide of the day — as much as I hate to refer to it yet again, it was in Rem's talk. However, I don't think he knows it was the most interesting slide, because when he showed the image of the brain, it looked just like Greg's architecture, like Hani's, Ben and Caroline's, and Jesse Reiser's — like everybody who is looking at the way material reacts to information. But we don't look at the brain and think, wow, that's voluptuous. We like the brain because it's a weird looking thing and because of the

effects it produces. Those foldings and convolutions of the material that come from the impression of a single substrate with information produces radical new effects. So the radicality is clear. The problem is that you don't know how to interpret the radicality. All you interpret is the resemblance of radical issues to a former expressionism.

AUDIENCE Don't you feel, though, that what is interesting about the brain is the power of abstraction?

KIPNIS No, I don't think that that is what's interesting. What I think is interesting about the brain is that it's a bunch of wet matter that folds and shapes when it gets impressed by information and then starts to process differently. Just as I said to Ignasi — there are no abstract ideas in the brain.

KWINTER For the sake of argument and duty, I must take exception to everything I have heard in the last few minutes. For starters, the brain was neither the most interesting slide nor was it the most radical thing. The most interesting thing I saw today was tomatoes. The organization of tomatoes in Lagos was so entirely — yes, radically — different. I have never seen anyone actually execute an architectural drawing in situ with tomatoes, but now that I have seen it, I know I don't get out enough. Listening to this debate, I also remembered that Marshall McLuhan said all of the things that we're saying today about information technology, only he said it about the airplane. He argued that with the advent of fast and cheap transportation, the entire world had started to press upon us, and that controlling information would be the big problem.

Just ten years ago I was considered a young Turk, while today I find myself slipping into an establishment figure in some weird way, I realize that ten years ago we used to laugh derisively at what we called the "constitutional argument" in architecture ("What is architecture?"). Well, what **isn't** architecture? We used to laugh at these narrow-minded old guys worrying about these kinds of questions because we understood that it was a big damn world and that this world was our playground, not architecture alone as some kind of clerically defined discipline. When I saw those tomatoes today, I realized that a lot of what I heard in Peter's presentation (and in this little skirmish that just took place) is the terrible inability to evolve that results from never having incorporated the airplane into architecture. The rest of history has gone beyond the airplane. So everybody is still arguing about this form and that form, but of course what everybody is really thinking right now is, "What the hell is Rem doing and how does he get off doing it?" It seems to me that on some level one has to accept the idea of the airplane and everything that ensues from it as an open challenge. I'm just not convinced that as the constitutional argument raises its fearful little head yet again at the end of these Any conferences – at the end of the ten years – that the real challenges are being faced.

PHYLLIS LAMBERT Sanford, I think that's pretty idiotic. You know, architecture is a long, slow process and we just haven't gotten there yet. But we're going somewhere, so for God's sake just sit down a bit and wait.

KWINTER That was lovely, Phyllis. But ten years! There's some impressive patience in waiting ten years! The proper worry is that in ten more years I'll be listening to Peter telling us we should be studying stained glass windows.

BERNARD TSCHUMI Let me quickly try to answer Sanford. I think that some of the real issues were alluded to by Peter in discussing how to get things built in this city. The problem we are facing is that it is typically lawyers advising their clients or developers who determine what a building looks like. Politicians don't even get involved – they have no interest in architecture. In France it is different – Jean Nouvel has built a number of major works thanks to politicians who thought that they would gain an extra two percent at the next election if his building looked good. Our Mayor Giuliani never thinks of that. I believe that it's a question of culture, and that events like the Any conferences are about trying to get that culture out. You always have to assume contradictions in architecture and you have to engage them project by project. Revealing those contradictions, like Peter said, is perhaps what architecture can do best. It has legitimized the base historically, but today it has to act as something that reveals those contradictions.

JOAN OCKMAN The surprising thing for me at this conference is to hear so much essentialist rhetoric again and again – talk of irreducible essences, of specificity, of the interiority of architecture, of what architecture is and what it's not. But I was quite interested in what Kojin Karatani had to say about bracketing and un-bracketing, and also in the questions about expertise. Are we limited to just one kind of expertise? Are we all consigned to be computer wizards? And who are we? White men mostly. Why shouldn't some of us, Saskia, become experts in sociology and economics or politics, or several of the above, if we so choose? Manfredo Tafuri developed a notion of methodological eclecticism in trying to explain his own veering between different modes of analysis, given the range of work that architecture encounters. How is it possible that any one methodology, discourse, or set of principles can possibly cover the field, and why would that be a good thing? I don't believe that anything goes. But do the kinds of identity crises that we have seen today surface with the same kind of regularity in other fields, in the conclaves of philosophers, biologists, physicists, or even artists? Are they constantly going back to the basics every time – What is art? What is philosophy? What is biology? This seems to be a trauma that is very specific to architecture.

VIDLER Not at all. It's in every single discipline. Otherwise there would be no disciplines.

GROSZ I think that this self-questioning is architecture's greatest strength. I agree with you to a certain extent that law isn't questioning what's legal; medicine is not going around debating what's medical. But this is the strength of architecture rather than its weakness. As a philosopher, I've never been to a philosophy conference to which an architect has been invited, and that's to our loss, not our gain. So it seems to me that it's precisely this identity crisis that architecture is going through that makes it open to its outside in a way that no other professional discipline is.

MARK TAYLOR Peter, there was so much in your remarks that I found profoundly disappointing. I just want to mention one thing partly because it runs so counter to what I have really appreciated over the past ten years of Any. Some of your rhetoric I found surprising – the invocation of the category of autonomy, the metaphors of cutting that ran throughout your talk – but that rhetoric then manifested itself in your conclusion that after ten years of Any it is time for architects to start talking to themselves again. As I understood this, it cuts off precisely the kind of dialogue between people of different areas that I, for one, have found profoundly educational. Also lost would be the moments in which the remixing of the old allows for the unexpected emergence of the new. I hope that these avenues of communication and exchange continue to stay open the way Any has helped them to be.

EISENMAN Mark, I was at a conference two weeks ago where I was the token architect. The discussion was about philosophic, sociological, economic, and political issues, and I sat there for three days and thought, what can I possibly say at this conference? Whatever I may think, I do not possess the capacity to talk to Homi Bhabha or Ian Buruma or Susan Sontag or God knows who else was there. I felt, though, that with these Any conferences, architecture could be host to other disciplines, as well as promote conversations within architecture itself. But I find that we are not communicating. We talk across each other. If we were to honestly say how many of the presentations we actually found relevant to what we are talking about as architects, I think there would be very few. In this profession we don't talk to one another anymore. I don't talk to Rem Koolhaas like I used to; I don't talk to Rafael Moneo; I don't talk to my colleagues in any meaningful forum. The most important architectural debate that I ever remember taking place in this country was the meeting in Charlottesville, where we

only had architects, and it was just dynamite; an open, viable thing where it was no holds barred because everybody understood the ground rules. [See **The Charlottesville Tapes** (New York Rizzoli, 1985).] All I was saying was that I miss the fact that I don't talk to Rem anymore, or to Jacques Herzog, or to Greg, because there's no opportunity to do so. This isn't to say that I don't want to talk to you or to other people from disciplines outside of architecture. I've learned a lot from Kojin; I've read Liz Grosz's books. But that doesn't mean I can take that information and use it in ways that are necessary to my own particular practice. I think theory in architecture **is** practice. When Greg presents his work, I want to know what the design principles are that operate in his work so that we can have a critical debate. That's all I'm saying. We don't do that here.

LYNN I'm resistant to talking here because I think that Peter is throwing down a gauntlet that's either some kind of red herring that I don't understand, or is just about putting an artificial cap on the Any project.

EISENMAN No, I'm just asking you a question. I've asked it in private; I asked it in public. How do you choose the one out of 169; how do you know when you've gotten there, and what makes it more than just an illustration of architecture? What kind of interiority of the discourse does it have? Just because it shelters does that make it architecture?

LYNN No.

EISENMAN And I've asked you on many occasions to tell me how I would know that what you do could be better or worse.

LYNN First of all, the embryological houses were essentially an R&D project addressed to an audience outside the field of architecture. But I agree, we need to have internal discussions precisely to talk about these kinds of issues that make for judgment and evaluation. I also think we need to keep thinking about the address of the work, presenting it not to some abstract public or to some sense of a common architectural good, but to other fields that are going to give us information about the way we're working. I actually like to spend as much time as I can with other disciplines – sitting in a room full of physicists or biologists – as much as I like to sit in a room full of architects. But in terms of evaluating and picking which one is best, the whole point is that I don't want to have to do that. I mean, all 1,054 are good, obviously. Some are better than others, but . . .

EISENMAN That's exactly the issue. How are some better than others?

LYNN The whole point is that there is no perfect one. There's no ideal villa against which you can evaluate the others, there is an endless series. So I won't answer that question because I don't think it's interesting. It's what I'm trying to avoid.

VIDLER In your defense, Greg, I think it would be tragic if Peter in any way understood the kind of subjectivity that you're implying in your work. Never in a thousand years could he understand it. I don't think I will be able to either, but at least I know that I won't be able to.

EISENMAN Tony, that makes you quite enlightened.

BEN VAN BERKEL I would like to return to Peter's point of how architecture can problematize culture, because how do you know when that happens?

EISENMAN When 97 percent of the people vote against your project you know it's problematic.

VAN BERKEL But who are the people who are voting?

EISENMAN Our clients.

VAN BERKEL I don't think this is who we make architecture for. I mean, do you make it for the general public? Or do you do it for yourself? Isn't it a question about the way the production of architecture is related to a public you have imagined? Do you always have in the back of your mind a question of how you could problematize architecture?

EISENMAN The question that I pose to myself is, how do I know when one of my projects has what I call a critical edge? How do I know when it does and when it doesn't? How do I know when yours do or don't? That's a problem that disturbs me enormously. Otherwise, why don't I do Bob Stern's work? I could be rich, successful, and a dean. But I don't believe that Bob Stern's work has a critical edge. And this criticality is the only thing that keeps me going. But then I have to ask myself, how do I know that my work does? And what are the criteria for evaluating it? These, I think, are legitimate questions – how does anyone know when they have reached that cdgc point?

MUSCHAMP But when it turns out that your Holocaust memorial is the most heavily visited tourist attraction

in Berlin, will you draw a different conclusion accordingly?

EISENMAN That is a serious question.

HENRY COBB Peter, the question, How do you know? is a good one, but your answer completely trivializes the question. Nothing could be less meaningful as an answer than the fact that 97 percent of the people in Berlin voted against your proposal. That has absolutely nothing to do with the issue of whether your project successfully problematizes the culture, and never will have.

EISENMAN Then how do I know?

COBB You have to find the answer yourself, and I'm sure you do find the answer yourself. But what I don't appreciate is the posture – the posture of casting the answer to it as some kind of popularity contest – because I think it really does trivialize a very important question.

EISENMAN Harry, I didn't mean to suggest that. All I was saying is that one indication that a project has succeeded is the degree to which the sui generis population cannot understand or accept it. I don't think that's a trivial thought.

AUDIENCE I hesitate to talk, but I will talk if you don't record it in the publication.

EISENMAN Isn't that censorship?

AUDIENCE Are you still talking?

EISENMAN No. But we all spoke on the record. I just think it's strange that you don't want to.

AUDIENCE I just want to make a call for listening – the lost art of listening.

You ask why the young architects are not responding, but I think they're listening. And it matters if what I say gets recorded because in the publication of this meeting what survives is a record always of talk. In architecture we talk and talk and talk and talk. What I feel is so valuable about these Any events is that they provide an opportunity to listen to astonishing research by characters who are so interesting precisely because you can't make connections between them. But if you listen you can understand this research, and even understand a little more of your own research, without necessarily being able to communicate to somebody else what that change might be. I think it also has a lot to do with this question of legitimation, because of course what legitimation means is making the bastard legitimate. And you are no less a bastard except for the decree, the public decree, which is a form of speech that legitimatizes the bastard. You bring people together from different disciplines and different practices and different generations not so that they breed and produce a new animal that you then legitimate as the future new transaction or collaboration, but somehow to actually understand that it's a bastard, and just leave it there. The majority of the people in this room, and in architecture, are really ready to listen, and I think this is something I would call for, but I'm calling for it quietly so that it doesn't get mentioned.

DAMISCH I think that the questions that Any has articulated can typically be approached from two sides. Why do architects want to talk with people from other fields, and why do people from other fields want to talk with architects? What do we have to learn from each other? This is exactly what

Peter means by problematizing architecture. And it is this problematization that is of great interest to us. This morning Rem pointed out that the architectural has become more and more efficient, but you know, it has always been efficient from the very beginning – from Plato to Descartes to Kepler. Today, though, it is efficient in a different way, and for me, this is what I am trying to understand. What is the relevance of the architectural model now not only for architecture but for thought in general?

SOLÀ-MORALES If these ten years have been a training for articulating certain discourses on architecture, then I think they have been a great success. Typically architects don't articulate explanations of their own work. So to fill this void left by the architects' own resistances to talking, we communicate with other disciplines like science, literature, poetry, rhetoric, etc. I think it's sad that we expect after ten years to have the solution or to have developed the alternative. In many ways we are successful because these ten years have been a great failure – but it's a great failure of discussion and cross-interferences between many sides.

VIDLER At the first Any conference, Anyone (which was obviously appropriately titled), there was particularly close attention paid to individuals and to objects. In the last two conferences, however, for all the banal definitions and repetitions of words and phrases like **globalization** and **digitalization**, I think there has developed a strong sense of measuring – a major sea change in the way in which architecture measures itself in the world and the world measures architecture. In this way, I feel that the last three days in fact measure our incomprehension,

or map the incomprehension of what's happened in architecture, and I think that that's very positive. If there are other gatherings, they will never again be like Any, and that's the significance of Any.

AUDIENCE I just want to add another character to the cast of characters in this conference – the architect, trained as an architect, practiced as an architect, who makes a decision to return to school and learn more about architecture, and to speak about the history and theory of architecture, so as not only to have authority over the plan and section but also to have some semblance of authority over Heidegger, Derrida, Kant, Foucault, you name it. How then do we grapple with the bastard in that sense? The anxieties and the confusions are numerous, but what are the limits and the boundaries for someone like that?

GROSZ The beauty of limits and boundaries is that one never knows what they are until one undertakes the activity. In a certain way, it's always a political gesture to preempt in advance what those limits might be. What I see as one of the wonderful things about "the thing" is that the thing never exists except in the process of being made. Choice never exists except in the processes of being made, so you can never know what the limits are, and in a way, I suspect this is our political frustration. Many people have argued over how we can answer these political, social, economic issues. We can't. We can't answer them. We can't force them. We have to learn to live with them, which means learning to find limits rather than see them in advance. This in a way is the joyous productivity of the unintentioned, of the random, of trying something, of risking being wrong, of taking a chance.

ANY LETTERS

DEAR CYNTHIA,

In contrast to the letters that I have written to Any in the past, this one is not only a testimonial to, and reflection upon, the last conference in New York back in June, but also an overall examination of the whole ten years of the project; a project that has now drawn to an end.

The Anything conference had something of a retrospective quality about it – a kind of reunion for those of us who had contributed most assiduously to the debates over the years, and a cordial and festive celebration of having managed to see through to the end what initially seemed to be no more than a rather undefined desire. So, in the Guggenheim in New York, we saw that ten years is a significant period of time, and that the more mature among us at the start are now even more so, while those who were then young greenhorns have now gained in consistency and in the definition of their priorities. At the same time, this New York finale revealed how important it was that Any had not only a beginning but also an end, and that like all things, the formula that had produced such interesting results was clearly starting to show certain signs of exhaustion.

I am convinced that Any has produced – not only through the conferences but also via the subsequent annually published volumes – a permanent X ray of the hot spots of contemporary debate, and a difficult but worthwhile exercise in maintaining a discourse on the current state of architecture at the start of the new millennium.

I really must thank you, dear Cynthia, most especially, for the decisive contribution that you have made. I feel confident in saying that a very important part of the results that we have achieved are directly due to your intelligence and tenacity: intelligence in your understanding of the relationships, the possibilities, the right names for each occasion, carefully quantifying the aims of each conference, assembling the necessary materials, and presenting them in a lively, flexible, and appealing way. But also tenacity: tenacity in maintaining a permanent organization, in taking advantage of the possibilities that arose on each occasion, in fighting for the project and the funding, in your sensitive attention to all of us who have taken part in the conferences. No doubt there are other people who have also made significant contributions to the successful unfolding of the project, but your dedication and enthusiasm have been crucial to the attainment of all that has been achieved.

Attempting a swift appraisal of what has been, in my view, the most positive aspect of the ten conferences, I see Any as reflecting the currents of architectural discourse. Making architecture is inevitably a limitless proliferation in space and time. But to think it out, to explain it, to problematize it, is now no longer such a diffuse phenomenon. Any

allowed for this by establishing an internal discourse with architecture itself, and through the multidisciplinary input of a multitude of contributions – critical, anthropological, philosophical, political, linguistic, aesthetic, etc. – Any initiated an assault on contemporary architectural phenomena with the aim of dismantling them, criticizing them, confronting them.

In my academic work, and from Europe, where Any has not been extensively disseminated, I can see that as time passes the texts of Any and **ANY** magazine are increasingly constituting a central referent for the issues currently under debate. In the beginning, though, we were coming from a time in which the autonomy of architectural discourse was virtually a dogma. With all the necessary confrontations and tensions, this autonomy has now been revised to embrace the diversity of other discourses – not only the discourses of the human sciences but also those that globalization called for. For me, one of the most important things about Any has been its concern to include reflections on architecture from other cultures: from Asia, from Latin America, and a little (a very little) from the Islamic world. The idea of doing away with the old center/periphery model and moving on to a horizontal, nonhierarchical, networked debate, constitutes one of the project's key achievements.

It is the case, however, that not all our good intentions have been blessed with success. Even the intermeshing of a global debate between north and south, east and west, seems to me to have demonstrated how hard it still is to bring this about, and how far, perhaps fortunately, we still are from a single discourse. In taking stock of the problems that Any leaves on the table, this seems to me one of the most important. Today the intercultural dialogue and the common language that seem to be apparent in the forms of constructing are a fiction without any firm bases. Either current architecture is superficially consumed in the most banal way all over the world, or its response to the state of our cities and nations is alarming in its coarseness and lack of sensibility.

Another dissatisfaction that I am left with in the aftermath of this experience is the lack of centrality accorded to the urban in the architecture/culture discourse. I am convinced that the many values – political, social, cultural – of architecture evolve out of its urban condition, and that an architecture of objects or icons only arrives at wider meanings when it comes to construct the city – that space of interaction that is mutating ever more rapidly all over the world yet still continues to be the privileged stage for relations between people. Any has not proved particularly acute in this area, and the theoretical debates on architecture have been figurative or generative without devoting very much attention to conceptions of architecture as not so much a formal diagram but as a shaper of collective metropolitan activities.

It also seems to me that Any has failed to attract and involve many of those producers of architecture who do not themselves elaborate a verbal discourse on their work but create extremely potent artifacts loaded with new meanings. Personally, I think that those of us who are interested in the theoretical discourse run the risk of too readily dismissing the most genuine architectural discourse, the one that is articulated precisely in the designing of architectures. I believe that Any has lacked those mechanisms for listening, understanding, and deconstructing the discourse of the purely creative – of actual projects, of those works that, as old Marx said of the masses, "do not know, but do."

Perhaps these self-critical reproaches and the other examinations of conscience that might well be undertaken can help us avoid the triumphalism of thinking that nothing better could have been achieved. They may also be useful in reminding us that the challenge of understanding, reflecting upon, criticizing, and listening to multiple points of view is still open. The millennial change and the ten compound **any** words were a pretext, a predetermined convention that made it possible to sketch out a plan, to carry through exchanges, and to try and put diversity and contradiction on the table.

Peter Eisenman likes to make gentle fun of a good-bye expression that, in a tone somewhere between worried and wondering, is often used by Rafael Moneo: "Many things, Peter, many things." (His literal translation of **tante cose**.) Let me, in place of the nihilistic and skeptical "any" of our last decade, reintroduce the excessive and marveling "many" of our good friend: "Many things, Cynthia, many things."

IGNASI DE SOLÀ-MORALES
BARCELONA

DEAR CYNTHIA,

I am now on my flight back to Australia and have taken up your suggestion that I use this long return journey to write to you about Anything.

Fingering through my notes from the conference, I find that its very first line is from your opening address: "Where anything goes there are also multiple new beginnings." I am taken back now to that opening moment, as we all sat on the edge of what was about to become: I imagined a licentious terrain of abandon, spontaneous irruptions, unrestrained effusion, and bursts of magnificent monstrosity. This imagined scene was somewhat at odds with the finely groomed and poised auditorium of people around me. I nevertheless held out hope that something sticky would emerge out of this cabinet of clean composure. My hope was not without reason – recently my writing has been toying with what appears as an implacable pressure to abandon the fragile disciplinary containments of architectural practice; to burst the clean, reflective bubble of critical thought and space. My hopes were not dashed.

Abandon. To my delight there was plenty of it, most explicitly perhaps with Rem Koolhaas crying "YES!" (Flashing up the ¥, €, and $ signs.) YES, he cried, in his unconditional love for the city (but not for architecture); YES to a new organicism, to junkspace, to corporate values; YES to the meltdown of rational programs: YES!! This abandon is oh-so-close to the requisite yielding to late capitalism; producing yield through yielding to the pressure; the wild abandon of the spaced-out corporate junkie to pressures of producing yield.

Abandon had many more moments: Saskia Sassen calling for a giving up of the old categories; Bernard Tschumi's leaps into air travel in maintaining the saving distance of abstraction; Bruce Mau's collapses into stress; Jeffrey Kipnis's project for architecture as one relinquishing criticality for mood-changing affect; UN Studio's open embrace of fashion, entertainment, "lifestyles," and all things stylish (albeit under a somewhat disjunctive rubric of the "critical package"); Zaha Hadid's formal fingering of open systems and explosive moments of creative destruction ("giving new forms of functionality a chance"); Giuliana Bruno's motions toward emotion; Elizabeth Diller's twisting of the visual from the spectacular to the auracular; Anthony Vidler's caress of Greg Lynn's voluptuously tectonic abstract-bodies-of-the-skin; and finally, Peter Eisenman's calling architecture back from its own exile, his plea to rejuvenate the abandoned carcass of architecture's autonomy while cutting off and leaving behind old forms of legitimation.

All these cries and calls and claims built up to their own version of that terrain of abandon imagined earlier. As we agreed when you and I spoke, the tempo of the conference had risen over the course of the three days. Now in flight, remembering the gesture of your hand mapping out the action of the build-up, that memory image is remapped onto the airplane takeoff and the place in which I have "landed": suspended 11,000 meters or so above sea level. Here, where the air is thin, the lines unseen (immersed in the line of flight), and time uncertain, this condition is one of a peculiar levity and suspense. It seems perhaps that this is akin to the state in which architecture finds itself (or loses the self); a condition marked out by the tenth and final Any conference: on air, on edge, in flight, and outstretched. In the sense of abandon.

This is the kind of suspense one experiences at the end of a chapter of a brilliant novel: something has happened, although whatever sparks the air with affect is not entirely explicit, and whatever is about to happen has its tongue twisted about this unspeakable static. Crisp incalculability. The crunch is in the simultaneity of the end and now the beginning — a gasp and an exhalation over the same blank page. Stillness (infinitely small movements); static; abandon. Sparked in the flesh by the friction of simultaneity between the deserted and its immanent recasting and reappearance.

That spark seems to further this affinity between contemporary conditions and the tenterhooks of air flight. I often become emotional in airport lounges and weep in the dark cinema of in-flight movies. So much is in suspense, so much is left behind and going elsewhere, so much is abandoned that holes open up and containments leak like the very porosity of architecture itself. Emotional abandon — leaky, weepy suspense (a version of Koolhaas's junkspace, perhaps). There is a poignant paradox in being so touched through the act of forging distance. Within this, I will hastily suggest, may well be the turning out of critical distance into another form of saving distance; the recasting of disciplinary models of criticality through a kind of intimate distance. New beginnings. If the "new," as Elizabeth Grosz said (as always, so beautifully), is that which "slips out of the pattern of the known," then perhaps we need to strain toward that potential abandon, that unspeakable static. The end of Anything, as the end of all Any conferences, was a touching moment. As a moment of abandon it twisted the line of flight into that straining suspense.

So, as promised, here is my letter – about to be folded up, stamped, and posted before I can depart this particular journey. As Anything went, and **ANY** is over, I look forward to witnessing the continuing movements of multiple new beginnings.
KIND REGARDS,
PIA EDNIE-BROWN
MELBOURNE

DEAR ANY,
Most modern architectural sagas, however intense, have been brief. The CIAMs extended over three decades but their most memorable moments lasted only a couple of years, at their beginning in 1928 and around the time of the 1953 Aix-en-Provence meeting. This is always the case with our most incisive movements and conspiracies. Yet the waves from some of these short-lived tempests are not yet gone.

What has made the Any decade unique in the endless sedimentation of movements, magazines, congresses, meetings, conspiracies and plots through which modernism has risen and fallen, is neither, therefore, its length, nor its geographic extension — the bureaucrats of the Union of International Architects have logged many more miles since 1945. It is the ongoing dialogic dimension of Any's moveable conferences that have shaped a unique space of interaction. Of course, in shifting from city to city each year, the fluctuating geometries of Any have relied on inclusion and exclusion. Some speakers were always invited throughout the decade, while others appeared episodically or topically (for political reasons particular to each venue). But even if the cast had permanent members and replaceable guests, what is left from the collective odyssey is a dense and contradictory discursive product.

In contrast to those developments in architecture that have seen the image invading all aspects of professional culture, the Any conferences have stuck to the seemingly lost art of conversation. Of course, some of the talks given from Seoul to New York, from Buenos Aires to Barcelona, can be interpreted as fragments from an endless monologue, but the rule is rather one of difference than repetition.

The original idea behind these meetings was that architecture could only gain through a confrontation with other discourses. In this respect, the various disciplines invited to participate has been wide-ranging, as well as reflecting the shifting intellectual currents of architectural culture, from philosophy (a constant, if sometimes estranged presence) to economics, from mathematics to art, and from sociology to history. Architecture, therefore, has constantly been put into question, with the very object of its practice being redefined in many ways. In this sense, the Any meetings have recorded both an expansion of the field and defined the core concepts for a critical practice. Yet these issues have not been questioned within the perspective of a new, universal, homogeneous framework, as the CIAMs attempted to do in their first quarter century, nor have they been reduced to local specificity. What has emerged through these meetings is a new, more subtle perception of local conditions, in which wider patterns of culture and theory can be articulated.

In a way, Any represents a sort of cargo cult, with its planeloads of "critical" architects and theorists landing among "natives" avidly expecting salvation from their expertise. But the clever, and opportunistic, intermeshing of the founding members with aggregating outer groups and many other participants has solidified into a new collective intellectual. Ten years of conversations have also encouraged the emergence of new discourses; exchanges that have undoubtedly inspired new patterns of face-to-face encounters between individuals, still the very basis of civility in a troubled architectural community.
JEAN-LOUIS COHEN
PARIS

DEAR ANY,

As an architecture student at Anahuac University in Mexico City, I had the opportunity to attend the Anything conference in New York. I thought the experience was amazing.

I believe that architecture cannot be taught or learned, but that we can only approach its understanding by feeling, observing, and exploring it. Architecture as a whole cannot be limited to one theory or one process, for it takes place at the junction of time, place, society, economy, culture, belief, and all those things that define the now; a sensibility that is constantly changing and aging as much as evolving. If we were to restrict architecture to a definition, we would only be limiting its evolution.

Today there are many things that oppose and put architecture in line: the search for the "soul" of things; the attraction, always, of the visual; the inevitable recycling of the past with a utopian sense of the future; and all those forces that stand between the architect and the public. When architecture is forced to oscillate between these two extremes its true essence is always lost. When we start making only objects rather than true things – with no resonance beyond their own form, with no link to the people that pass through them – we stop being architects.

In countering this reductiveness, the Any conference was so enjoyable. As Cynthia Davidson said in response to the comment that Any had reached its end without any conclusion, this was not the end, it was the beginning; the beginning of the chance to question, to think, to explore, to evolve, to believe, to imagine. Architecture in effect exists largely as a collection of ideas. Any provided an inspiring forum for us to listen and to interact with those ideas.

I just wanted to write to thank you, to get some of my thoughts down on paper – thoughts that are the direct consequence of the conference. I cannot thank you enough for the chance you have given me to dream of new architectures, to think, to understand a little more.

BEST REGARDS,
JOSE A. GONZALEZ-CID
MEXICO CITY

DEAR ANY,

The beginning of June, when the Any conferences are typically held, falls right in the middle of the semester in the Japanese school system. Each year then, as June came, I would always be rushing off to a foreign country, and then rushing back home to Japan. It was almost as if I were only participating for the purpose of wearing myself out. At the last Any conference, however, I was living in New York, and so was able to commute from home to the Guggenheim Museum for the three days of the conference. Over the last ten years this had never happened. Even when the Anywhere conference was held in Japan at Yufuin, the place was about as far from Tokyo as Seoul. Although I am a foreigner in New York, this time, for the first time, I had the sense of being at home.

Thinking back over the last ten years, I remember it was in a Japanese restaurant in New York, in the fall of 1990, that I was first introduced by Arata Isozaki to Peter Eisenman. For awhile Peter talked to me under the mistaken impression that I was also an architect. But when he found out that I was not, I remember him saying, "That's why you look so smart." For my part, I thought he looked like Charlie Chaplin. At the time, I would never have dreamed that over the next decade I would be associating with architects through Any. It had only been two years since I had first met Isozaki, and until then I had had nothing to do with architecture, even though I had just finished my book **Architecture as Metaphor**. Since then, it is not as though I have taken up the study of architecture. Having no interest at all in such a pursuit, once a year, in June, I just thought about architecture right before the conference, and did this every year. At the conferences I was an outsider, and I made no effort to escape from that position (something that I do feel a little badly about now).

But ten years, it would seem, is a sufficiently long stretch of time. The world changed, and so did I. By the last conference, even someone as resistant as myself began to take a concrete interest in the issue of architecture. I am sure that this must have had something to do with the fact that in my work in recent years I have been moving away from negative dissolution and deconstruction and toward more positive "construction." And this, maybe, is also part of the reason why I felt at home at the last conference in New York.

MANY THANKS,
KOJIN KARATANI
TOKYO

DEAR CYNTHIA,

This last Any conference, estranged by an all too familiar urban context, was certainly redeemed by Frank Lloyd Wright's superb underground auditorium, as chill as the tomb, about which the chief question remained whether the Master meant to punish his audience, leaning and sliding in their seats along the sloping orchestra floor, by making them seasick. But the end of the ten years itself did not seem to sadden unduly, rather, the principle of closure struck most people as a splendid formal precaution (like the end of the hour in psychoanalysis), designed to ripen and mature all the questions without prolonging them unduly and draining them of their urgency. Whether the participants understood how to bring this off, and to break the decade off with style, remains, however, a different matter.

My sense of the ten years was that conflicts that had in the beginning looked generational – the Greg Lynn group versus Peter Eisenman, for example – now proved to have had real content. Computer-generated forms and so-called digitalization – which to a layman certainly seemed to live up to the rather ill-advised concluding slogan "anything goes" – ultimately also generated various conservative and traditional stances on the other side, most notably the position – eloquently expressed by Rafael Moneo – that it is architecture's own history which, by lending it its internal constraints, makes architecture's development and innovations possible in the first place. Eisenman then inflected this position in a different way by suggesting that it was only within architecture's intrinsic historical realm that genuine critique and subversion, genuine breaks and deconstruction, were made possible.

As I want to show in a moment, I think both these positions – the new and the traditional – are deplorable, but first I want to say that I think even this opposition does not capture the deeper meaning of the conference. That meaning, of course, could only take the form of a question, and not of answers. But the question was not a question about architecture (or not only), it was a question about history. Better still, it was **the** question about history today, namely, whether what we are witnessing is a fundamental and absolute break with the past – all pasts, and not only that of architecture's – or whether the changes are only relative, a matter of fashion or of pendulum swings, a matter of degree and not of kind. This, I think, is what the crystallization of the theme of digitalization really meant, the deeper question behind Moneo's attack on Ben van Berkel, and Eisenman's paradoxical return to "the tradition"; it constitutes the political content of the seemingly more academic or scholarly problem of historical periodization. Are we in a new period altogether? Do computers mean the definitive end of even the most recent architectural past? Does anything really "go"? Is everything now finally (so many years after the death of God) permitted? (Or, in my own language, is postmodernity a whole new mode of production – or just a new stage of the older one?) One might also throw in Jacques Lacan's remark, that if God is dead nothing is permitted.

I believe that the pertinence of Moneo's remarks was generally missed; various interventions attributed to him the recommendation of something that sounded like socialist realism – shouldering the social and political responsibilities of architecture or some such thing, as though that were a clear-cut personal option, achieved simply by abandoning the computer as a dangerous invitation to empty formalism. I understood Moneo as saying that the computer-generated forms had insufficient critical distance from their context. He might just as well have observed that nobody knows what critical distance is anymore. I myself would have been tempted to offer the word **replication**. The problem with the new forms is not that they are new, and also not that they are formal; it is that they replicate the system itself, very much including its excitement. The new forms are certainly exciting, and not the least of that excitement is the thrill of the computer itself, of its unbound energies, and the postmaterial freedom of its projections (note the ominous return of Bergsonian spiritualism in these celebrations). But I would argue that that seemingly technological euphoria is itself borrowed from the brand-new excitement of the market and particularly of finance capitalism. It is this that is really new, and it is in the name of a revolutionary digitalization that finance capital pronounces architecture's "end of history," along with that of everything else. This is not a moralizing or puritanical judgment on my part; the new is always exciting, and excitement is the "moment of truth" in all history. The authenticity of art – including that of these splendid younger architects – lies in capturing it and indeed in "replicating" it. The larger ideological consequences are the fault of the critics and ideologues and of the public itself, the people who brought you finance capitalism in the first place.

So Moneo was right, in my opinion, but also wrong. A nonarchitect is poorly placed to criticize any call for the return to history in a given art (presumably it would include the proviso to do that history in a new way); but the word **tradition** (which he may or may not have used) necessarily sends a chill through the audience. Even worse, in my view, was Eisenman's evocation of "autonomy." The autonomy of art! Shades of the New Critics, if not of generations of academic aestheticians: I suddenly felt myself teleported into the midst of the dreariest attacks on "cultural studies" by the defenders of literature and the canon – who said these arguments and self-doubts were only happening in architecture? But the rhetoric of "artistic autonomy" has its own internal logic, and fatally leads into the other kind of outburst Eisenman found himself committing, namely, the attack on theory. Like Mao Zedong "bombarding the headquarters," Eisenman ended by trashing the whole conference series, deciding it had been a bad idea to invite the nonarchitects in the first place, and concluding that henceforth architects ought to stick to their task and talk only among themselves. None of us took this very seriously, I think, coming as it did from the biggest theorist and theory-addict of us all; but it is always a mistake to give ammunition to the enemy, that is to say, to the traditionalists and antitheoreticians.

Thus two of the conference heavyweights were scarcely at their best in this one (Arata Isozaki remained serenely equal to himself). Meanwhile, Rem Koolhaas, while he avoided this particular debate, divided his limited time between his two favorite preoccupations, the current projects of his office and his own research on third world cities, doing justice to neither. He did throw down another theoretical gauntlet, namely, declaring his preference for the city over individual building. Eisenman was then willing enough to pick up this particular challenge, but it was too late in the decade for a new topic to emerge.

So Koolhaas didn't show us many pictures, and Eisenman didn't show us any (or ''any'' if you prefer). Here, I have to confess my shameful bias: it is to prefer, to any of the theoretical statements, the images of the projects, which I always think are more fun than any movie or novel. Any has been the place I get to see these slide shows (a true genre or form in its own right), and how I keep posted on the latest developments. Where am I going to see them now that Any is all over?

BEST,
FREDRIC JAMESON
DURHAM, NORTH CAROLINA

DEAR FRED,
I am taking the liberty of addressing my last letter to Any personally to you, because more than any of the other social thinkers, you have consistently tried to open up our discourse to some kind of mutual understanding. Therefore, I was quite surprised at the vehemence of your reaction in your letter to certain things that were said at the Anything conference.

Ten years ago, if you remember, I was too intimidated to approach you and ask you to participate in the first conference. Rosalind Krauss had to act as my surrogate. I suppose this letter is a testament to my overcoming of philosophy envy, since I now have the temerity to confront you in print.

What I admire about you is that you are always a contrarian. In your letter, however, you confuse Rafael Moneo's conservative view of architecture's discourse with my view of autonomy, criticality, and singularity. It is not possible in the space of this letter to address all of your concerns, so I want to damp down the antitheory furnace that you assume I was fueling.

My view of autonomy begins with the inherent problem of the architectural sign. Architectural signs will always be either abstract or figural. Abstraction and figuration are

not as complicit in the form and meaning of a linguistic sign as they are in architecture. The linguistic sign is most often conventional and self-evident. In architecture, it is not. Abstraction and figuration in and of themselves are neither critical nor compliant; rather, it is when their relationship to the architectural sign is articulated, questioned, i.e., caused to become an issue in the physical fact, that the sign becomes critical. In this sense it is not the abstract or the figural per se but the manifestation of their processes that becomes critical.

Thus, it is the need to make self-evident the difference between, say, an abstract sign and the sign of the processes of abstraction that defines architecture's difference from other discourses. It is this singular need that I call architecture's ''will to autonomy.'' Architecture can only be critical when it displays the internal struggle between the processes of abstraction and figuration and the requirements of the sign. Architecture's autonomy always strives to overcome the sign's resistance to this struggle. Here, autonomy is seen in a new light, as enacting the survival of the discipline itself. This, Fred, is what I meant by my invocation of the term.

My own doubts about the validity of the interaction between philosophy and architecture should not be interpreted as an abandonment of my concern for theory, for I see my work as the practice of theory. What I have abandoned is the concern to shed any light on the dualisms of theory and practice, mind and matter; these issues are outside my expertise.

I trust we can continue our discussion even without Any cover.

BEST REGARDS,
PETER EISENMAN
NEW YORK CITY

DEAR CYNTHIA,
Well that's a decade over. Anything was my second conference and I enjoyed it enormously. The image of New York has always suspended itself in my imagination as some kind of exotic fruit, but one typically too concealed to reach out for; I did love the opportunity to take a bite of it during Anything. The taste of New York, as well as the experience of this last, concluding conference, didn't remind me of anything even remotely familiar. The city, the conference, and the visit to see Philip Johnson in New Canaan remain with me now as events from another space and time.

Sitting in the basement auditorium at the Guggenheim, I became aware that in New York the full extent of Any's delimited zone was clearly visible. In a sense, I became conscious of the general mood and message of the participants as one either opposed or indifferent to human history. Certainly the disconnection between the concerns of most of the speakers and the rest of human experience and activity was felt. The conference seemed to reflect the mood of New York, which also regards itself and its activities as relevant and influential only to itself.

To me the Any conferences are unique because they provide a cocooned space/time in which minds leave the realms of the known and step into the unknown. This is heretical space/time, the place for unorthodox thought formation. It is precious. It does not need reminders issued by the orthodox telling us that every galaxy in the architectural universe has to be viewed through the lens of the human condition.

It was really marvelous for me to take part in a conference within both a city and country that remain so self-referential and yet are able to exude such dynamic energy. I could not help but reflect upon my own situation, so concerned with the human condition, with interdependencies, and with the contexuality and passage of human history. The outer limits of abstraction that were so wonderfully represented in Greg Lynn's presentation seemed to me to have merits and relevance that went beyond any horizons and were wholly without any foreground. That such an architectural activity can be the product of its own craft and conception and yet remain truly beautiful fills me with wonder. Wonder, because it is able to tug itself free from the rootedness of known architectural concerns and float free in another galaxy with who knows what prospects for life. Some of the other presentations are now located in the outer recesses of my memory and are too hazy to recall, but Hani Rashid's virtual stock exchange is still clear in my mind. And Rem's design and gallantry as manifested in the interiors of Prada's retail showrooms was also heroic; the unusual and exceptional images, and the effort to connect them to the realities of the world passing by, were, of course, part of his valiant effort to hammer it all into the mainstream (or mAnystream) of architectural debate. But his defenses were unnecessary. There was no need to claim "innocence" or to dismiss radicalism as a fiction. Some steps that one takes into the unknown land on terra firma but others sink into sticky substances, and Rem had obviously encountered a lot of these less stable surfaces, which he might as well concede as no-go areas.

But Peter Eisenman's chastisement that "architects ought to build" was a warning from the pulpit of orthodoxy. His concern that architects have somehow strayed away from the real issues of the discipline and forgotten how to talk about buildings struck at the very heart of the heretical space/time of Any. Since Peter has been so deeply involved in the venture, one could not help wondering whether his overview had concluded that heretical ideas need to be con-

tinually bounced off brick walls. Is it possible that these debates had become so self-referential that they had assumed the characteristics of their own orthodoxy? Was he saying, at the end of the decade, that most of the steps into the unknown had drowned in their own amorphousness?

I understand that you may now be involved with alternative publishing ventures now that the Any decade has concluded. I look forward to the new space/time that these will open up. I am sure the heretics will crowd around you soon.
REGARDS,
ROMI KHOSLA
NEW DELHI

DEAR ANY,
Thank you. Your project has fallen within a key and necessary movement of cultural history, when advanced thinkers meet in sustained discourse over a significant period of time. The exchanges of Any's core group of architects with each other and with participants in Los Angeles, Yufuin, Barcelona, Montreal, Seoul, Buenos Aires, Rotterdam, Ankara, Paris, and New York for three intense days every year seeded new perspectives, friendships, on-going discussions, and above all created a community of architects, artists, critics, and philosophers. This architecturally oriented avant-garde had the aura of those of the Renaissance and the 1920s in affirming architectural culture at the razor's edge, eliciting change, heightening the very nature of thought and practice, and percolating societal cognition. The Any books, which have recorded each of the conference papers and ensuing discussions, manifest an immense intellectual achievement, making available a dense compendium of the importance, growth, and shifts of meaning in architectural culture in late-20th-century thought. I write to praise Any, not to bury it. With passage from the optimism attending the centennial and millennial change to the dour face of repressive regimes worldwide, a continuation of the Any spirit is urgently needed.
PHYLLIS LAMBERT
MONTREAL

DEAR ANY,
If one were not careful, one could easily imagine, when recalling the details of this year's Anything conference, that something important had changed. But this would be a mistake. Of course it is too early (and too necrophilic) to inquire as to whether Any managed to make a difference (in a world where almost nothing any longer makes a difference) or whether it

merely served as a heroic bridge thrown into the future (and this is no small thing), preserving for one more decade at least the possibility that real ideas will still be able to walk from an organically engaged past into the more cynical, philistine, and uncertain future. What the "worthwhile ideas" and styles of engagement from the past are, and what the cynical and philistine elements of what is coming are, has not, in these Any conferences, or anywhere else, been a source of consensus, nor even the clear subject of debate. And yet, in the end, that is what the ten-year Any debate was about.

Any did not produce great conferences, great papers, great movements, or even discernible clarities. But it brought the increasingly shapeless and disaggregated structure of contemporary mental life to the fore in a way that very few enterprises could have. Ten years, nine countries, and four continents were brought into the melée and asked to speak. Yet for the most part, their voices were obscured, sometimes trampled on, by an overly self-assured mandarin group less interested in finding out what marvelous and unexpected things were out there in the world, than in providing a paternalistic example for their hosts to follow. Provincialism, and a stubborn inability to perceive its own staleness, in time became Any's greatest liability. Any was a bona fide globalist project avant la lettre, but it did not at first know that this is what it was; in the end, obsessed with teaching rather than discovering, it did not find the flexibility to learn, to listen, to acquire, and to self-transform.

Yet Any bravely occupied a critical and very difficult decade, a decade whose deeply transitional and indeterminate nature no enterprise could have escaped. If Any had not preserved the (even formal) position and habit of critical-intellectual organization we would certainly feel even more desperately cut off from ourselves than we do today. Yet most important for me in these last years was the discovery of how little we had to "teach" our friends, and how necessary it was to thwart that universalist expectation that we had inculcated in them. Globalization is a process of bringing local knowledge and local genius into creative play with non-local forces. The brilliant admixtures that are everywhere resulting from this new cultural-economic theater are dividends that the Any project has, in the short term, renounced.

If I had attended only one Any conference I'd have wanted it to have been the second one, in Yufuin, Japan. We were expected there to think about the Asian spatial concept Feng-shui; yet upon arrival I was both titillated and shocked to learn that few of our Asian counterparts could offer a clue as to what it was. They came prepared rather to talk about Descartes, Kant, and Gide. I had a paper on theoretical biology in tow, but also a week of appointments with priests at the Buddhist monasteries of Kyoto. Over the next 15 days I discovered "teaism," Bushido metallurgy, the gardens, the insane kimono textile shops, the remarkable tradition of contrapuntal composition derived from the philosophy of nature, and even Basho's fireflies, and my thinking about everything was changed (it took six months at least to assimilate the experiences). I had discovered the hydraulic world lying below the metrical and discrete one (as if the prodigious baths at Yufuin alone were not enough), and more importantly, a coherent culture through and in which this universe was expressed. Japan's own complicated history, and the traumas and contradictions that this forces its designers and intellectuals to endure and struggle with today, are an unbroken litany of encounters between the local and the traditional with the global (external) and the modern. I saw there more clearly than ever before the brilliant forces of history and form and ideas, and the unstable, creative chaos it may produce through miscegenation. This, in a phrase, is what the Any enterprise could have been, but wasn't.

In thinking back then to the most recent Any meeting in New York, I am, like many who were there, struck by the final day of presentations and discussion. Neither the reader nor the spectator should be fooled into thinking that Peter Eisenman's final plaidoyer for autonomy was much more than the momentary howl of an old wolf blinded by moonlight and temporarily distanced from the pack. More troubling and limiting were, on the one hand, the positions inadvertently expressed by other participants (Saskia Sassen on the virtues of bounded "expertise," Tony Vidler on the mysticism of "computer subjectivity" the dead world of "disciplines," etc.) and, on the other, the general, mounting, but unspoken horror and anger that followed the presentation of Rem Koolhaas. Why were the architects, critics, professors, and philosophers unable to give voice to the disgust and disorientation they felt that day? Perhaps because what was pushed in their faces was the very reality that the whole Any project was designed to protect itself from in the first place?

Perhaps too there was a great deal more aggression taking place that day than anyone actually was able to bring themselves to acknowledge. Koolhaas, who once risked to fuck context, had perhaps decided to fuck the pieties and principles of his colleagues right there in front of them. (His lecture did not, for example, affect the tone of humility or gentle encouragement. Nor was it messianic. It was just, well, "fuck [architects'] docility ") There is no possible defense for what Koolhaas presented. Nor should there be. But it was pathetic that so much reactive affect should have been stirred up among so many talented people and still no one could muster a coherent peep of response. Except for Eisenman's brave, reflexive, and retrograde acknowledgment, of course.

There were, to my mind, three elements that clearly stuck in the architects' craw that day: (1) the tendency to view the entire world as a now **local** phenomenon that directly addresses all of us all of the time – the Lagos research project (2) the focus on research and development and the designer's necessary new role – and responsibility – as a producer of knowledge – the AMO office (3) the need to engage openly and without prejudice the emerging forces and domains of markets, mindshare and postcorporate, postcultural enterprises – the Prada relationship. Many found impossibly vulgar especially the way Koolhaas's presentation seemed to juxtapose the "misery" of Lagos with the complacency and decadence of Prada. Few, however, seemed to catch the fact that Lagos was **not** sentimentalized with any such "family of man" humanism but rather was presented as an irreducibly human work of mysterious and opaque "genius" that merited not only study but also direct experience. Prada may wish to see itself as a brave new world of retail audacity, but in fact it is but an extraordinary symptom of our time: the mutating large-scale economic enterprise that is seeking to enmesh itself with a whole host of concrete and cultural realities in extension from building. (Is there to be no delayed wave of nausea vis-à-vis the '60s master architects who dedicated their talents to designing banking monoliths for the very institutions that funded the Vietnam War, the manipulation of third world financial infrastructure, apartheid, and the bogus and sometimes deadly "aid" programs?) A more generous, "doubt-suspending" judgment of Koolhaas's current enterprise as he presented it, I would suggest, is to see his concept of architectural practice as rather a way of transforming the world into a vast, shall I say, **Multiversity**, into a place where one can learn anything and learn it infinitely. If Any had been able to do this itself we could today applaud ourselves. Any, however, didn't do it, though perhaps – no, assuredly – it helped some of us to find this new path ourselves.

SANFORD KWINTER
NEW YORK CITY

DEAR ANY,
Looking back at the list of cities from the ten Any conferences, one location, for me, seems to be missing – we were never able to realize a conference in China. There were four meetings in North and South America, four in Europe (including Ankara), and two in Asia. The balance is clearly off. Living in Asia, and looking to help the Any project, I tried to make it happen, but it never worked out. I approached Chinese colleagues to see if it would be possible to host a conference in Shanghai or Beijing, but despite public organizations that work toward realizing large-scale events in China, there are no private, enlightened groups that would help realize something smaller, like Any.

Large cities in China are changing their skylines and boundaries at an incredibly rapid pace. The scale of the development is unprecedented. Even Rem Koolhaas's report on the development of the Zuhei Delta fails to grasp the incredible transformation that has occurred since the early 1990s, as it was just a reconfirmation of past conditions. There is a huge amount of construction taking place, but there are few architects who work independently and freely, so, for the time being, there is no margin to host Any. The depression that hit the countries in Asia in the late 1990s has dealt an additional blow to fostering architectural discourse in China. The capital flow that once supported the prosperity was absorbed into Wall Street, and the economy came to be dominated by the colonialism of the International Monetary Fund under the guise of globalization. Although China exists beyond the direct focus of this globalization, it was affected, indirectly. But now, the gate that was closed to diverse cultural projects has finally begun to open. In the fall of 2000, the first Shanghai Biennale was held; an art exhibition based upon international critical standards. Of course, a number of Chinese artists are already appreciated abroad (in Venice, for instance), but this was the first occasion that they could return home.

The Japanese economy is essentially in the same state as that of other Asian countries. In 1995, Japan lost all of the socio-cultural strides it had made during the 50 years after the war (a regression physically symbolized by the Hanshin Awaji earthquake, and socially by the Aum Shinrikyo's subway attack). Since then, the country has been floating, as it were. There has been no place for it to anchor. Consequently, the economic basis to support artistic culture has collapsed, the result being that support for Any and the subsequent Japanese publications has been stopped for now. But even with the three-year delay in translating the Any books, we are still struggling to continue, thanks to the incredible efforts of a group of people.

My impression of the last New York conference is this: simply said, it represented a bankruptcy of Any's original intent: a project that looked for a way to synthesize the dichotomies of the 20th century – architecture/city, culture/finance, local/global. It seemed to confirm how every one of us has been pulled back, grounded again in one or another of the dichotomies that we first sought to escape. This was due, I believe, to the fact that the last two conferences took place in capitals of past centuries: Paris, the capital of the 19th century, and New York, capital of the 20th century. The dichotomies were themselves the products of these two cities during the last two hundred years.

Here, China intervenes as the third term. As I see it, China will present the problematic of the whole world of the 21st century, and is why I wanted to conclude the conference series in China. In the near future, however, there will be a new architectural society, and a totally new discursive constellation will be born. What is certain is that there will be no Any then. I would, then, like to organize a non-Any conference as soon as possible.

ARATA ISOZAKI

TOKYO

DEAR ANY,

My most vivid impression of Anything is a snapshot fixed in my mind's eye of an event that occurred after the conference ended. On the following day, Sunday, some of the participants travelled to New Canaan, Connecticut, to visit Philip Johnson's remarkable estate. While I have written about the Glass House, I had never seen it; nor had I ever met Philip. As our group strolled down the hillside enjoying the lush green of late spring, we approached the Glass House to discover its architect sitting near the corner of the lawn. We formed a line not merely to greet but to pay homage to Philip. To see many of today's leading architects and writers paying their respects to this remarkable man whose life is a compendium of 20th-century architecture was a memorable moment. When I returned home, I looked again at the image of the Glass House that I included in my book **Disfiguring**. I was startled by what I found: there was Philip sitting in the same kind of chair at the exact spot where we had greeted him the day before. It was as if the photograph in my book had been taken yesterday. As Philip grew tired, he walked slowly – very slowly – to his car and disappeared up the hill. Though we all had the sense of an ending, nothing was said.

What impressed me about this moment was its stark contrast with the events of the days preceding it. As I listened to the presentations, I was struck by how completely the terms of the discourse have changed in the ten years we have been meeting. In Los Angeles, Jacques Derrida was the primary player. His impact on architecture had, of course, been developing for several years, and was beginning to become as significant as it had been in other fields. We have yet to understand the cultural phenomenon of Derrida. What made a thinker, whose demanding work grows out of a tradition so alien to America, such a cultural force in this country for so long? This question is not merely academic but involves broader social, cultural, political, and, perhaps most importantly, economic forces, which could yet surpass the limited world of the academy. However these currents are eventually understood, it is clear that the tide has turned. In New York, Derrida and his work were conspicuous by their absence. Indeed, I do not remember a single trace of Derrida or deconstruction.

In place of deconstruction, now there is the digital. Far from a new development, the preoccupation with the digital has been growing throughout the last decade. The question of the digital includes problems of globalization, information, capitalism, and the role of technology. The presentations at Anything, however, made it perfectly clear that digital technologies not only call for more adequate theorization but also are transforming architectural practices in ways that never could have been anticipated a decade ago. If there seems to be less interest in theory among many younger architects, it might be because of the poverty of current theoretical resources for understanding the digital and the network culture it is creating. During the 1980s, it often seemed that architects looked to philosophers and critics for creative inspiration. The situation has now changed dramatically. The world in 2000 is not the world that Derrida, Foucault, and Deleuze helped us to understand. Many architects, it seems, have a much keener appreciation for the significance of the changes that digital technologies are bringing than academic critics. If theorists are not to become irrelevant, then they must turn their critical gaze toward the practices that are emerging in our new sociocultural condition.

Looking back over the decade of Any, it becomes apparent that what is distinctive about our era is the increasing acceleration of the rate of change. Speed, of course, has always been an obsession of modernism. In network culture this obsession becomes overwhelming until speed becomes an end in itself. Though speed has been the subject of much discussion in recent years, it is rarely noted that as speed increases, memory decreases. Speed, in other words, is directly related to forgetting. As the rate of change continues to accelerate, society approaches cultural oblivion.

The trip to Philip's garden was so memorable because of its contrast to the pace of the conference. Two rhythms, which represent two very different styles and forms of life: slowness and memory versus speed and oblivion. This tension is not new but as old as time itself. And yet, as developments approach warp speed, tensions seem close to a breaking point. Speed and the oblivion it brings mark the unavoidable transience of life. While this process cannot be stopped, it might be slowed down. Perhaps there is more wisdom in the feeble steps of an old man than in tomorrow's new, new thing.

MARK C. TAYLOR

WILLIAMSTOWN, MASSACHUSETTS

AFTER-

In the swirl of discussions that the Anything confer-ence generated on June 1, 2, 3, 2000, in New York City, it was sometimes difficult to sort out the various currents of thought and emotion that animated the three days. There was Rafael Moneo's almost monas-tic devotion to the context and scale of "real" archi-tecture, and then Ben van Berkel and Caroline Bos's play with phenomena and the nonscalar; Rem Kool-haas's conflation of the technological abattoirs of Lagos with the global mapping of Prada stores; Eliza-beth Diller's amorphous Blur Building "constructed" with man-made fog versus Jacques Herzog's homily to the palpable qualities of a naked wood floor; Peter Eisenman's continuing argument for architecture's autonomy and Zaha Hadid's defense of radicalism and the strange, and so on. After sorting it all out in the months' long process of preparing this book, it seems that undecidability has unwittingly become "anything goes" in architecture today.

This book is called Anything, but for the conference that it documents Anything Goes seemed a more apt title; one that described not only the exit of Any from a decade on the architectural stage, but also one that commented upon the state of things – not just any things, but architectural things. When the virtual trading floor of Hani Rashid and the war-torn territo-ries where Romi Khosla works each elicits the term architecture; when Arata Isozaki's metaphorical voids bump up against Jean Nouvel's literal transparency, there is no one truth about architecture anymore, not even that it shelters. These diffusions have developed over time, in part as the didactic social ideology of modernism waned, but more importantly because the postmodern historicism was less about truth and more about commodified corporate banality. When the series of Any conferences was conceived in 1990, it attempted to reestablish a didactic moment that could also define this diffusion, and proposed undecidability as a theme. This followed immediately on the heels of the philosophy of deconstruction and the 1988 "Deconstructivist Architecture" exhibition at the Museum of Modern Art in New York. For many archi-tects, deconstruction questioned the very direction and intention of contemporary architecture. Hence Any's deliberately misaligned lens of undecidability, a tool designed not so much to focus on a singular

discipline as to blur architecture's relationships with contemporary cultural discourse. This amorphous theoretical construct was intended to stay in place for ten years and then to dissolve – to let the "any" thing go, so to speak, in the anticipation that something other would emerge and develop. The idea of undecid-ability that came out of deconstruction, and that provided the keyword to the whole Any project, opened up the complexities of an increasingly global culture, demanding new strategies of thinking from the practice of architecture. Yet it was not until the last conference, at Anything, that the art historian Hubert Damisch offered a new reading of this idea in a relocated context, which suggested that undecidabil-ity had another value altogether, and one that could not be "formally" put to rest with the end of Any.

On the last afternoon of the conference, Damisch gave a rapid overview of five hundred years of art and architectural history in order to situate architecture today. Suddenly he seized a piece of paper and crum-pled it into a ball. When he flattened it out again, he held up the now wrinkled sheet as an example of an idea of thickness; a thickness that is neither two- nor three-dimensional, but what he termed planar. The planar is similar to Gilles Deleuze's idea of the fold in that it brings together ideas about surface, skin, and topology that predominate in issues of experimen-tal (or avant-garde) form-making and aesthetics in architecture today. In reopening a discussion of the fold from the topological, the thickness of the planar reunites the conceptual dimension of architecture with the contemporary mathematics of computation. This has not occurred since the Renaissance. In using the computer, the mode of architectural conception has been radically altered because the plane of its composition has changed. The "thickness" of the planar, or virtual plane, shifts the idea of composition from the purely perspectival, which has dominated architectural production for five hundred years, to virtual topographies, and from projective geometry to topological geometry. This change in what could be called architecture's picture plane also changes the conception of architecture's mode of representation and how it is received by the subject.

The phenomenal expansion of the use of the com-puter in making architecture has introduced forms far more outrageous than Frank Gehry's Guggenheim Museum Bilbao; forms like Lars Spuybroek's crouching Water Pavilion in Holland and Greg Lynn's proposed series of Embryological Houses. Each has its similarities in history, whether in the biological or the architectural; but the mode of their composition today is distinct from previous models, and therefore we must understand them differently. In fact, we already see them differently, because they no longer represent anything other than the fact of their own making. In this sense they fall into Eisenman's idea of autonomy, of forms "cut off from previous modes of legitimation." Lynn's Embryological Houses, for example, have no relationship to the typology of the house other than that which Lynn names in presenting them. They do not represent dwelling; they represent their mode of composition. That is, they represent the process of their production in the computer. Here Fredric Jameson's return to allegory is worth revisiting, when he observes that certain buildings no longer represent the city but have been internalized in such a way that they have become the city.

Though such forms emerged from the intellectual milieu of the poststructural, this change in modes of representation in architecture poses a challenge to the poststructural critique of the new, which has argued that there is no possibility of the new, only the reinvention and recombination of the old. Ideas of the new and newness have overrun concepts of what was thought to be modern or contemporary since the Enlightenment, which invested in architecture a hope for a better future. And in a culture constantly seeking the new, insofar as it can be distinguished from the novel, or novelty, it is not a desire that will go away. Damisch suggests that "a move is required that would correspond to the shift from architecture as setting the stage for history to architecture as a game practiced under different conditions." One such shift can be seen in the use of the Cartesian grid. For example, where the artist Daniel Buren still sees the grid as a stabilizer, the architect Wolf Prix would transform the grid to an energy field – a chessboard turned fuzzy, like the buzzing screen of a television with no picture reception. Another shift is the change from the flatness of the plane to the thickness of the planar. For example, the surface of the computer screen has a different property than the surface of a sheet of paper. Even the stylus used to "write" on screens does not affect the surface; rather, it changes the medium behind the surface; the depth – no matter how thin – of the digital planar.

These shifts do not mean that history, or the future, has to be abandoned. Just as Damisch uses history to locate the planar, the philosopher Elizabeth Grosz finds value in history as a means for identifying the new. "Part of why we need notions like 'history' and notions like 'things,'" she argued during the conference's final discussion, "is to allow us to recognize the outline of what we already know and then to give it a context for that which we can't yet know. Our problem is by what means can we recognize the new, given that recognition itself is always about conforming to patterns that we already know." Here the new is equated with reconceptualizing as opposed to recombining what is already known. Rather than being "the prisoners of older categories" that Saskia Sassen refers to, learning to see differently allows one to recognize the previously unseen, or the new. For Sassen, this would potentially allow the pursuit of what she calls "new conceptual architectures in order to capture the new topographies of digital space."

The framework of undecidability did not specifically set out to cultivate the new. In its ability to recognize and then question the already known, Any generated layers of thought and discussion, each coded with a critical suffix: one, where, way, time, etc. The thing called Any, or as Damisch might term it, the case of Any, in retrospect discovered and opened up many thicknesses in architecture and between architecture and other disciplines. Just as the planar slips out of the history of the plane, the thicknesses of Any let slip out beginnings that we may now start to recognize as new patterns of understanding. For architecture this may mean a shift, as Ignasi de Solà-Morales writes in his final letter to Any, from thinking about any things to many things. And from those many things, which come from so many discourses, will slip potential architectural things: the issues for architecture as a history and as a contemporary practice to consider for the next ten years. As the new planar of the computer has already shown, new things, that is, any things, are not necessarily architectural things.

WORD

Cynthia C. Davidson

Anyone Corporation and its decade-long program of Any books and conferences was made possible by continuing support from Shimizu Corporation.

Based in Japan, Shimizu Corporation is an international design, engineering, and construction firm that takes pride in supporting leading-edge research and development to better the human environment.